Cisco® Networking For Dummies, 2nd Edition

OSI Reference Model Layers

Layer	Name
7	Application
6	Presentation
5	Session
4	Transport
3	Network
2	Data Link
1	Physical

Protocols by OSI Layer

OSI Layer	Protocols, coding, conversions
Application	Telnet, FTP, SMTP
Presentation	ASCII, EBCDIC, JPEG, GIF, encryption
Session	RPC, ZIP, SCP, SQL, NFS
Transport	TCP, NBP, UDP
Network	IP, ICMP, BGP, OSPF, RIP
Data Link	MAC, LLC, Frame Relay, LAPB, PPP
Physical	Ethernet, Token Ring, HSSI, 802.3

Five steps of data encapsulation

1 User information is converted into data
2 Data is converted into segments
3 Segments are converted into packets (or datagrams)
4 Packets (or datagrams) are converted into frames
5 Frames are converted into bits

IP Address Classes

Class	Range	Default Subnet Mask
A	0 – 127	255.0.0.0
B	128 – 191	255.255.0.0
C	192 – 223	255.255.255.0

Novell IPX Frame Types

Novell	Cisco
Ethernet_802.2	sap
Ethernet_802.3	novell-ether (default)
Ethernet_snap	snap
Ethernet_II	arpa

Switching Types

- **Cut-through:** Reads only destination address before forwarding frame
- **Store and forward:** Reads entire frame before forwarding it on

ISDN Terminal Equipment Types

Terminal equipment type	Description
TE1	ISDN standard terminal equipment
TE2	before ISDN standards, requires terminal adapter (TA)

ISDN Reference Points

Reference point	Used between
R	Non-ISDN ports and TA (terminal adapter)
S	User terminals and NT2 devices
T	NT1 and NT2 devices
U	NT1 devices and terminators

ISDN Lines

ISDN BRI: 2 B (bearer) channels at 64Kbps each and 1 D (data) channel at 16Kbps (144Kbps Total bandwidth)

ISDN PRI: 23 Bbps channels at 64Kbps each and 1 D channel at 64Kbps (1.54 Mbps)

Common Well-Known Port Assignments

Port Number	Assignment
20	FTP data transfer
25	SMTP (Simple Mail Transfer Protocol)
53	DNS (Domain Name System)
80	HTTP (Hypertext Transfer Protocol)
110	POP3 (Post Office Protocol)
161	SNMP (Simple Network Management Protocol)

For Dummies: Bestselling Book Series for Beginners

Cisco® Networking For Dummies,® 2nd Edition

Cheat Sheet

Common Router Commands

Command	Action
ipx routing	Turns on IPX routing
ipx network 1000 encapsulation novell-ether	Configures ipx network with ASN and frame type
conf t	Configure terminal
line vty 0 4	Configure virtual terminal lines beginning with 0 and ending with 4
enable password	Assign password
banner motd #	Create message of the day banner which shows during login
hostname Dummies	Assigns name to router
CTRL+A	Beginning of line

Command	Action
CTRL+P	Previous line
show history	Display console command history
startup-config	Configuration files stored in NVRAM
running-config	Configuration files stored in RAM
copy tftp run	Copies from TFTP server to RAM
router rip	Turns on RIP routing
access-list 15 permit 168.123.23.0 0..0.0.255	Permits actions from all hosts on this network
int e0	Ethernet interface 0
int s0.2	Subinterface 2 on serial interface 0

LAN Switching Basics

LAN Segmentation breaks up collision domains by creating more segments with fewer workstations in each segment. A LAN can be segmented with a bridge, switch, or router.

Bridges operate at the Data Link layer (Layer 2) and examine the MAC (Media Access Control) address of a frame and then forwards the frame if it is not a local address. Bridges forward multicast messages.

Routers operate at the Network layer (Layer 3) and examine the network address of a packet and forwards the packet using the best available route. Multiple active paths can exist to a destination.

VLAN (Virtual LAN) is a switch port that has been assigned to be of a different subnetwork.

Access List Numbers

Type	Range
IP Standard	1 – 99
IP Extended	100 – 199
IPX Standard	800 – 899
IPX Extended	900 – 999
IPX SAP	1000 – 1099

Subnetting Formulas

Maximum number of subnets available on a network:

$$2^{(masked\ bits)} - 2*$$

Maximum number of hosts available on a subnet:

$$2^{(unmasked\ bits)} - 2*$$

* Two is subtracted to remove the all 1s and all 0s addresses.

Routing Protocols

Interior routing:

Distance Vector: Uses metrics (such as the number of hops) to determine the best route to a destination and knows the direction and distance to any network connection.

- **RIP** uses a 15 hop count maximum
- **IGRP** uses a 255 hop count maximum

Link State: Creates a topographical view of the network by exchanging LSP ("Hello") packets with other routers. Uses SPF (Shortest Path First) algorithm to determine route.

- **OSPF** makes routing decisions on route costs

Exterior routing:

EGP (Exterior Gateway Protocol)

BGP (Border Gateway Protocol)

™

References for the Rest of Us! ®

BESTSELLING BOOK SERIES

Are you intimidated and confused by computers? Do you find that traditional manuals are overloaded with technical details you'll never use? Do your friends and family always call you to fix simple problems on their PCs? Then the For Dummies® computer book series from Wiley Publishing, Inc. is for you.

For Dummies books are written for those frustrated computer users who know they aren't really dumb but find that PC hardware, software, and indeed the unique vocabulary of computing make them feel helpless. For Dummies books use a lighthearted approach, a down-to-earth style, and even cartoons and humorous icons to dispel computer novices' fears and build their confidence. Lighthearted but not lightweight, these books are a perfect survival guide for anyone forced to use a computer.

> **"I like my copy so much I told friends; now they bought copies."**
> — *Irene C., Orwell, Ohio*

> **"Quick, concise, nontechnical, and humorous."**
> — *Jay A., Elburn, Illinois*

> **"Thanks, I needed this book. Now I can sleep at night."**
> — *Robin F., British Columbia, Canada*

Already, millions of satisfied readers agree. They have made For Dummies books the #1 introductory level computer book series and have written asking for more. So, if you're looking for the most fun and easy way to learn about computers, look to For Dummies books to give you a helping hand.

Wiley Publishing, Inc.

5/09

Cisco® Networking
FOR
DUMMIES®
2ND EDITION

by Ron Gilster

Wiley Publishing, Inc.

Best-Selling Books • Digital Downloads • e-Books • Answer Networks • e-Newsletters • Branded Web Sites • e-Learning

Cisco® Networking For Dummies,® 2nd Edition

Published by
Wiley Publishing, Inc.
909 Third Avenue
New York, NY 10022

www.wiley.com

Copyright © 2002 by Wiley Publishing, Inc., Indianapolis, Indiana

Published by Wiley Publishing, Inc., Indianapolis, Indiana

Published simultaneously in Canada

For general information on our other products and services or to obtain technical support, please contact our Customer Care Department within the U.S. at 800-762-2974, outside the U.S. at 317-572-3993, or fax 317-572-4002.

Wiley also publishes its books in a variety of electronic formats. Some content that appears in print may not be available in electronic books.

Library of Congress Cataloging-in-Publication Data:

Library of Congress Control No.: 2002106048

ISBN: 0-7645-1668-X

Manufactured in the United States of America

10 9 8 7 6 5 4 3 2 1

O2/QY/QX/QS/IN

Ⓦ Wiley Publishing, Inc. is a trademark of Wiley Publishing, Inc.

About the Author

Ron Gilster (CCNA, A+, Network+, i-Net+, MBA, and AAGG) has been involved with networking and internetworking as a trainer, teacher, developer, merchant, and end-user. He has over 35 years of total computing experience, including over 13 years involved with the networking of computers. He is the bestselling author of a number of career certification books, including *A+ Certification For Dummies, Network+ Certification For Dummies, i-Net+ Certification For Dummies, Server+ Certification For Dummies,* and *CCNA For Dummies,* plus several books on networking, the Internet, computer and information literacy, and programming.

Dedication

To my sister Lynda, whose love and support makes this all possible. Thanks!

Author's Acknowledgments

I would like to thank the wonderful folks at Wiley Publishing who helped get this book published, especially Melody Layne, Christine Berman, Diana Conover, Rebecca Huehls, and the virtual cast of tens who work behind the scenes to shield me from the cold, cruel, technical part of the editorial and printing processes.

And to Brenda Cox and the Technical Support crew for their continued support to my valued readers.

A very special thanks to Dan DiNicolo for the excellent and thorough technical editing job.

Publisher's Acknowledgments

We're proud of this book; please send us your comments through our online registration form located at www.dummies.com/register/.

Some of the people who helped bring this book to market include the following:

Acquisitions, Editorial, and Media Development

Associate Project Editor: Christine Berman

Acquisitions Editor: Melody Layne

Copy Editors: Diana Conover, Rebecca Huehls

Technical Editor: Dan DiNicolo

Editorial Manager: Leah Cameron

Media Development Manager: Laura VanWinkle

Media Development Supervisor: Richard Graves

Editorial Assistant: Amanda Foxworth

Production

Project Coordinator: Jennifer Bingham

Layout and Graphics: Jackie Nicholas, Jacque Schneider, Betty Schulte, Jeremey Unger, Mary J. Virgin

Proofreaders: Dave Faust, Susan Moritz, Angel Perez, Carl Pierce, TECHBOOKS Production Services

Indexer: TECHBOOKS Production Services

General and Administrative

Wiley Technology Publishing Group: Richard Swadley, Vice President and Executive Group Publisher; Bob Ipsen, Vice President and Group Publisher; Joseph Wikert, Vice President and Publisher; Barry Pruett, Vice President and Publisher; Mary Bednarek, Editorial Director; Mary C. Corder, Editorial Director; Andy Cummings, Editorial Director

Wiley Manufacturing: Ivor Parker, Vice President, Manufacturing

Wiley Marketing: John Helmus, Assistant Vice President, Director of Marketing

Wiley Composition Services for Branded Press: Debbie Stailey, Composition Services Director

Wiley Sales: Michael Violano, Vice President, International Sales and Sub Rights

Contents at a Glance

Cartoons at a Glance

By Rich Tennant

"Please Dori- do we have to hear the story of Snow White's OSI model and its 7 layers again?"

page 85

"If it works, it works. I've just never seen network cabling connected with Chinese handcuffs before."

page 7

page 155

"I guess you could say this is the hub of our network"

page 293

"It's okay. One of the routers must have gone down and we had a brief broadcast storm."

page 389

"A centralized security management system sounds fine, but then what would we do with the dogs?"

page 347

Cartoon Information:
Fax: 978-546-7747
E-Mail: richtennant@the5thwave.com
World Wide Web: www.the5thwave.com

Table of Contents

Introduction

If you have purchased or are considering the purchase of this book, you most likely fit one of the following categories:

- ✔ You are an experienced network administrator who wants to find out more about Cisco Systems networking and internetworking because this information is valuable to your career and advancement.
- ✔ You're wondering just what Cisco networking is all about.
- ✔ You think that reading this book may be a fun, entertaining way to find out about networking and internetworking with Cisco Systems, Inc., routers and switches.
- ✔ You love all *For Dummies* books and wait impatiently for each new one to come out.
- ✔ You're a big fan of anything Cisco and just can't get enough of it.
- ✔ You're a big fan of mine and eagerly anticipate my next book.

If you fit into one or more of these descriptions, (except the last one for which I am not qualified in the appropriate medical areas to help you), then this is the book for you!

Why Use This Book

So, if your goal is to discover more about Cisco Systems' networking devices, then you are in the right place! This book is intended to provide you with a basic review of Cisco networking fundamentals and principles, as well as a brief overview of how Cisco networks are designed, installed, configured, and operated.

Cisco Systems, Inc., is the largest manufacturer of networking systems in the world. It dominates the router and switch market to the extent that Cisco routers and switches are considered by many networking professionals to set the standard for all other companies.

The reasons behind this success are the same reasons why Cisco equipment is chosen by most network administrators for their networks, big or small: reliability, scalability, flexibility, and interoperability. Yes, this does sound like a lot of abilities, but Cisco routers, switches, and other equipment keep running without problems, are readily upgraded, are easily adapted to new network configurations, and are compatible with virtually every transport or access method.

Foolish Assumptions

In developing this book, I made two groups of assumptions:

- ✔ You have an entry-level knowledge of networking, routers, bridges, switches, and other networking components, as well as a fundamental knowledge of electronics, computers, software, protocols, and troubleshooting procedures.

- ✔ You have some experience with Cisco hardware and its integration into networking environments but are looking for a general overall guide to Cisco networking.

How to Use This Book

As with all other *For Dummies* books, this book is a no-nonsense reference and study guide. It focuses on the areas that you are likely to need as you begin working with Cisco networking equipment. I also include some background and foundation information to help you understand both the basic and the more-complex concepts and technologies.

This book presents the facts, concepts, processes, and applications that a Cisco network administrator needs to know about in step-by-step lists, tables, figures, and text, without long explanations. The focus is on providing you with information on the hows and whys of choosing a Cisco network and not on impressing you with my obviously extensive and impressive knowledge of networking and its related technologies (nor my modesty, I might add).

And although it is not a primary objective of *Cisco Networking For Dummies,* 2nd Edition, this should be an excellent study aid for preparing for the CCNA (Cisco Certified Networking Associate) or the CCDA (Cisco Certified Design Associate) exams, although, you may find *CCNA For Dummies* by Ron Gilster, Jeff Bienvenu, and Kevin Ulstad and *CCDA For Dummies* by Ron Gilster and David Dalan (both published by Wiley) to be more-specific study guides.

How This Book Is Organized

This book is organized so you can find out more about Cisco networking in the sequence you prefer, or you can read about specific networking areas without the need to wade through stuff you already know. Each chapter gives you a list of the topics covered in it that you can use as a guide to what's in the chapter.

You'll also find that some topics may be covered in more that one place in the book, with one location providing more information than the other. I did this for emphasis or to put a topic into the context of a network concept or practice. When this happens, I provide you with a cross-reference to where the topic is covered in detail.

The following sections tell you what I included between the covers of this book.

Part I: Cisco Networking Basics

Parts I and II of the book are intended for readers new to networking in general, not just Cisco networking. I have included an overview of networking terminology, concepts, and fundamentals to help you work with the other parts of this book. If you have a good working knowledge of networking in general, you can most likely skip this part of the book (but it won't hurt you to look it over anyway).

Part II: Cisco and the Internetwork

This part of the book delves a bit deeper into networking principles and how they are supported by or impact Cisco networking devices. In this part, I review the logical and virtual hardware, and software elements used to transmit or carry data over the network. A very important part of this review deals with network addressing and the essential principles of the often-misunderstood subnetting.

Part III: Routing and Switching: Inside and Out

In this part, I finally get to the good stuff. This is the first of the book's parts to relate specifically to Cisco networking and Cisco routers, switches, and other internetworking devices and the roles they play in a LAN or WAN. The point of this part of the book is to help you understand how routers work, how they fit into a LAN (inside) or WAN (outside) network, and how a router can best serve your needs, which is exactly the point, isn't it?

Part IV: The Softer Side of Cisco

Cisco Systems often claims that it is not a hardware company — it's a software company. Which means that, like any networking software, the Cisco IOS (Internetwork Operating System) must be managed, including the tasks of administration, configuration, monitoring, and (in most situations) cursing, stomping, muttering incantations, and praying. So, this part gives you an overview of how the network administrator works with a Cisco router's IOS, including the command line interface, the ways to get help (and everyone needs help from time to time), and the configuration process. However, I leave the cursing, stomping, and incantation overview to other more-highly-qualified references.

Part V: Privacy, Security, and Other Secrets

As its name implies, this part of the book covers the devices, features, and technologies that can be applied to provide privacy, security, and protection to your network resources. This part includes such things as the definition of an access list on the router, the installation and use of a firewall or proxy, and the installation and operation of a virtual private network (VPN).

Part VI: The Part of Tens

This part provides at least ten pieces of very valuable information. The lists in the Part of Tens are the following: ten network design tips that can help you create a better network; ten tips for a safe and trouble-free installation; and ten things you should pay attention to when configuring a Cisco router.

This book has an appendix that serves as a reference of common IOS commands and their options and parameters.

Icons Used in This Book

The Technical Stuff icon highlights a technical discussion on how a concept works or is applied.

Remember icons point out general information and subjects that you should remember for application on your network.

Tip icons flag information that can come in extra-handy during the testing process. You may want to take notes on these tidbits!

The Warning icon alerts you to some potentially dangerous or treacherous material. Heads up!

Feedback

I'd like to hear from you. If any aspect or topic of Cisco networking isn't covered as well as it should be, or if I've provided more coverage than you think is warranted about a particular topic, please let me know. Or if I have made an error or misstated a fact (it could happen!), I'd appreciate hearing about it. Your feedback is solicited and welcome. You can send e-mail to me at this e-mail address: rgilster1@attbi.netcom.

Part I
Cisco Networking
Basics

The 5th Wave   By Rich Tennant

"If it works, it works. I've just never seen network cabling connected with Chinese handcuffs before."

In this part . . .

If you're new to networking in general, not just Cisco networking, Part I is meant for you. I include an overview of the key networking terminology, concepts, and fundamentals you need to apply to other parts of this book. If you have a good understanding of networking principles and basics, you can most likely just browse through this part of the book.

If you're completely new to networking, you may want to read *Networking For Dummies,* by Doug Lowe, or my book *Network+ Certification For Dummies* prior to reading this book.

As a Cisco networker, you need an understanding of network structures, the OSI model, networking hardware, software, cabling media, and the role each of these components plays in building a network.

Chapter 1

The Cisco Networking World

*1*n the universe of networking, you can find the very small local area network (LAN), the medium-sized campus area network (CAN), and the globally sized enterprise wide area network (WAN). This is the network world in which Cisco and other networking device manufacturers exist.

Layering a Cisco Network

In designing a network that can grow with a company or organization (or, in other words, a network that is scalable on an upward migration), one must consider the various roles to be played by the internetworking devices. To this end, Cisco has developed a three-layer network design model.

The three layers of the Cisco Network Design Model are as follows:

✔ **Core layer:** The networking devices located on the core layer are those that only perform routing and switching functions. Unless unavoidable, these devices do not perform access checking, encryption, address translation, or any other activity that would impede routing and switching at the fastest speed possible. In a larger network, routers between network segments are on the core layer.

✔ **Distribution layer:** This layer of the design model is where policy-based routing occurs. *Policy-based routing* uses established criteria for the handling of specific network traffic types, including routing information updates (see Chapter 12) and VLAN switching (see Chapter 10).

✔ **Access layer:** This layer of the design model includes devices that feed network traffic into a network and perform network entry. In a smaller network, the access layer is perhaps the only level of routing and switching applied. On this layer, security functions, such as access control lists (see Chapter 18) and firewall activities (see Chapter 19), are applied.

The way this plays out is that in a larger network, one like that shown in Figure 1-1, the network could have networking devices on all three layers. The core layer devices, like the switches used to segment portions of the network, are only concerned with forwarding packets as fast as possible. The distribution layer router provides forwarding to get traffic to the appropriate core layer device. The access layer router and firewall provide a secured "front-door" for both inbound and outbound traffic.

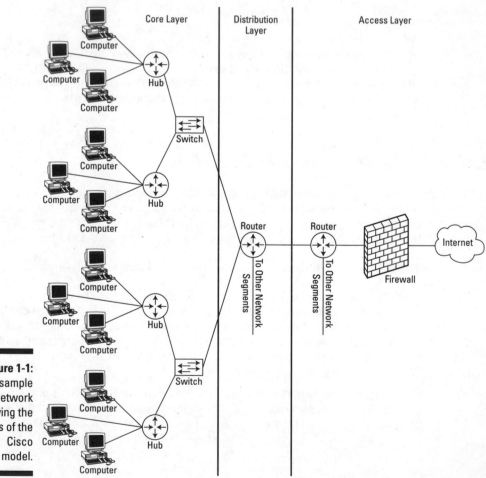

Figure 1-1:
A sample network showing the layers of the Cisco model.

When you use the layered approach to network design, you are sure to understand the function of each networking device and configure them appropriately to the tasks of their layer. This design approach ensures that devices are matched to the requirements of each layer.

Bear in mind that the Cisco model applies more to larger networks. However, should your network grow, you will very likely need to begin adding the lower layers as required.

Taking Stock of Cisco Products

If you visit the Cisco Systems, Inc., Web site (www.cisco.com), you will find, under its Products link, a list of the various product types it manufactures. This list includes the following (the products I have not included in the list are either very low- or very high-end devices that have very specific applications not typically found on most networks):

- **Access servers:** This family of products provides access control services for small offices to large enterprise networks and network service providers.

- **Cisco IOS software:** It is not unusual for a Cisco representative to tell you that Cisco is not just a hardware company, but also a very successful software provider as well. That Cisco is also a software house is very evident in their Internetwork Operating System (IOS). The Cisco IOS is a very robust and feature rich networking system that supports the switching, routing, and security functions of virtually any network.

- **Content networking devices:** The various device configurations available in this product family offer a wide range of functions, including optimizing bandwidth utilization, supporting e-business applications, distributing content to regional routers, and concentrating data, video (including television), and voice traffic onto a single transmission medium.

- **Hubs and concentrators:** These product lines include Ethernet hubs for use in 10 and 100 Mbps networks and, on the high end, IP traffic concentrators for use in service provider or metropolitan area network (MAN) environments.

- **Interfaces and modules:** Cisco manufactures a wide variety of interface ports and multiport and multifunction add-in modules that allow its networking devices to be configured for virtually any requirements.

- **Network management:** In its software provider role, Cisco provides a number of management and monitoring tools to support and facilitate design, configuration, monitoring, and administration of networks, large and small.

- **Routers:** In the face of the fact that this book is mostly about the functions, features, configuration, and application of Cisco routers, and the fact that you probably already know that Cisco provides routers, it is important to note that you may be amazed at the *range* of routing products that Cisco actually manufacturers. Cisco has a router for virtually every networking situation, ranging from a one-person desktop to global networking environments.

- **Security components:** Cisco has a product for just about any network security situation, including firewalls, intrusion detectors, VPN controllers, and access control servers.

- **Switches:** That Cisco makes switches should be no surprise; but like its router products, the range of switching products available may surprise you. No matter how big or small, the type of traffic (data, voice, or video), or the transmission service in use, Cisco has a product to provide fast and efficient throughput and resource utilization.

- **Telephony:** In addition to its routing, switching, and concentrator products, Cisco also has a full line of telephony products to support voice telephone services in analog, digital, or IP applications.

- **Video:** Cisco provides a variety of devices to support video transmission, including products for streaming video, video teleconferencing, and *multimedia convergence* (the combined support of data, voice, and video over the same network medium).

- **VPN:** The devices under this product category include adaptations and specifically designed products for the management, control, and operation of a virtual private network (VPN). Chapter 20 has more information on VPNs.

- **Wireless:** Cisco manufactures wireless networking products to implement a wireless LAN or to provide for mobile wireless networking.

Building a Cisco Network

As illustrated earlier in Figure 1-1, a Cisco network typically contains several layers of networking devices, each playing its own part in the overall networking configuration. From the lowest-level device up through the highest-level device, the overall goal of Cisco hardware and software is to provide the most efficient, scalable, and cost-effective network environment to any given networking situation.

Starting at the desktop

Because the lowest-level device in most networking situations, other than the network cable and its connectors, is a desktop computer (or a printer or another type of peripheral device), I start there. In order to connect to the network, a network interface card (NIC) or a network adapter must be installed in (or at least attached to) each personal computer (PC). Cisco isn't in the NIC business, but you can find an abundance of quality manufacturers from which to choose. You can purchase a NIC at virtually all computer or electronics stores. If you are brave (or crazy like me) enough to shop online, enter the words "network adapter" or "network interface card" in Google or another search engine and you'll find a plethora of sources.

Hubbing it all together

You could run a cable directly between each PC and the network's server, but clustering network devices together for a number of reasons (most of which are discussed *ad nauseum* in this book) makes much more sense. In the typical Ethernet network, which is the most common type of network, PCs and other networked devices are clustered by using a hub. A *hub* provides a clustered interconnection to the network backbone, either directly or indirectly, for the devices attached to it. A group of hubs can also be clustered into another hub, if needed. A hub allows its attached devices to share the bandwidth available equally, which can be good or bad, depending on the situation. This type of sharing is good if the volume of traffic is low or bad if one or more of the nodes require more bandwidth than the others.

The downside of a standard hub is that it doesn't include processing capability to limit traffic, especially broadcast traffic, to only its attached devices. This means that any traffic it receives is also passed to the network at large.

Smart hubs, hubs that also perform some form of switching, are available. However, some debate exists on whether they are hubs or actually low-function switches.

Switching the network

When sharing bandwidth on a hub isn't working, you may find it necessary to install a LAN switch. Doing so will, in most situations, improve the overall throughput of the nodes attached to the switch. A switch, through its operating system (such as the Cisco IOS), has the intelligence to send network traffic only to where it belongs, which increases the bandwidth available on the remainder of the network.

Switches are core layer devices that focus only on forwarding network traffic the fastest way possible. Cisco switches also can include higher-level functions, such as packet filtering and support for virtual LANs (see Chapter 10). However, the primary function of a switch is to determine on which interfaces a destination address exists and to forward any traffic addressed to it only to its segment.

Connecting to the outside world

Connecting a network to a WAN (the Internet is the BIG WAN) requires the use of a router. Requests from users to download Web pages or files from across the internetwork must be routed to the host devices servicing the network on which the requested content resides. The content could be on a company's WAN, or it could be on a network clear across the world. Regardless, the services of at least one router, and likely more, are required to get the request to its destination and back again.

Routing by layer

Routers can be applied on the distribution layer within a large LAN. As shown earlier in Figure 1-1, intermediate routers may be necessary to divide a network into smaller segments for management and bandwidth utilization purposes. But the most common use of a router in LAN situations is as an access layer device.

On the access layer, a router provides access both in and out of a LAN or WAN. Access layer routers may also be configured to limit incoming and outgoing traffic by using access control lists (ACLs — see Chapter 18), packet filtering, and firewall functions.

Controlling access with a firewall

Another access layer device is a firewall. Cisco's Secure PIX (Private Internet eXchange) firewalls provide an added layer of protection to keep evildoers from accessing your network for unauthorized purposes.

If you want to allow external users, such as remote employees, suppliers, or customers, to access shared files or place or update orders, you may want to install a VPN or set up an intranet or extranet (see Chapter 20).

Working in the wide wide world

Service providers and very large enterprises must look to Cisco's higher-end products for solutions to their access, bandwidth, media, and efficiency issues. In many of these situations, a need for convergence, Voice over Internet Protocol (VoIP), telephony, call center support, and other enterprise-level applications exists.

To this end, Cisco provides a variety of products (see "Taking Stock of Cisco Products," earlier in the chapter) both on the distribution and access layers to facilitate any or all of these applications.

Before You Go On . . .

This book is intended to provide you with an introduction to the world of Cisco networking. The higher-end applications discussed in the preceding sections are not discussed in much detail with the focus being on the elements, components, configurations, and requirements of Cisco in a local networking environment.

If you want to find more information on any Cisco product and its application, you can find all of the information you need on the Cisco Web site (www.cisco.com).

Chapter 2

The OSI and Other
Network Models

In This Chapter

▶ Understanding why a layered approached is used for networking

▶ Defining the OSI Reference Model

▶ Describing the functions and protocols defined by the layers of the OSI Model

▶ Explaining the TCP/IP protocol suite and how it relates to the OSI Model

The underlying foundation of all Cisco networking is the Open Systems Interconnection Reference Model. In fact, the OSI model is the foundation of all network communications — Cisco networks as well as all others. To succeed on the job, you really must know the OSI model and each of its layers, including each layer's scope of operations and its relationship to the other layers.

By understanding the OSI model and its layers, you have a good general knowledge of networking. One goes with the other. A thorough understanding of the OSI model is critical to success as a Cisco network administrator. Simply knowing the names of the seven layers is not enough. You need to know what each one does and understand why the communications industry uses layered network models. This chapter gives you an overview of the OSI model and all seven of its layers, with an emphasis on the four layers on which Cisco networks operate.

In addition to the OSI model, a few other networking models exist, most of which are either subsets of or complementary to the OSI model. For example, in this chapter, I also discuss what is known as the Internet model and a layered network structure model that Cisco uses to define how internetworking equipment, primarily routers, interact and support one another.

Layering It On

A network model that defines all of its functions, features, protocols, and formats as a single entity or layer creates two problems: The first problem is that you would have a model that is so complex that it would likely be unintelligible; the second problem is that the model would have functions so interdependent that they could not be easily separated for modification or improvement, which is why working with a layered network model is a better approach.

Good reasons to layer up

The networking industry uses layered interconnection models for five primary reasons. There are probably dozens of valid reasons why a layered network model works the best, but I think that these five are probably the most important:

- ✔ **Standardization:** Probably the most important reason for using a layered model is that it establishes a prescribed guideline for interoperability between the various vendors developing products that perform different data communications tasks. Remember, though, that layered models, including the OSI model, provide only a guideline and framework, not a rigid standard that manufacturers can use when creating their products.

- ✔ **Change:** When changes are made to one layer, the impact on the other layers is minimized. If the model consisted of only a single all-encompassing layer, any change would affect the entire model.

- ✔ **Design:** A layered model defines each layer separately. As long as the interconnections between layers remain constant, protocol designers can specialize in one area (layer) without worrying about how any new implementations will impact other layers.

- ✔ **Learning:** The layered approach reduces a very complex set of topics, activities, and actions into several smaller interrelated groupings. This approach makes learning and understanding the actions of each layer and the model on the whole much easier.

- ✔ **Troubleshooting:** The protocols, actions, and data contained in each layer of the model relate only to the purpose of that layer. This isolation allows troubleshooting efforts to be pinpointed on the layer that carries out the suspected cause of the problem.

A model of efficiency

A layered model takes a task, such as data communications, and breaks it into a *series* of tasks, activities, or components. Several layered models are in use. The Department of Defense (DoD) defines a five-layer model, called the DDN (Department of Defense Network) model, on which the four-layer Internet model is based. Figure 2-1 contrasts the Internet model to the OSI Reference model (which I discuss in the next section).

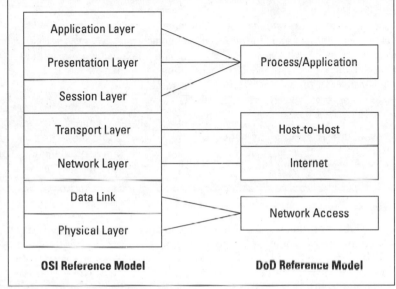

Figure 2-1:
The seven-layer OSI model contrasts to the four-layer Internet model.

OSI: The Networking Supermodel

In 1984, the International Standards Organization (ISO) spruced up its specifications for connecting network devices and released the "Open System Interconnection Reference Model," which goes by the nickname of "Open System Interconnect" or OSI model. The ISO OSI (easy to remember, huh?) model is the internationally accepted standard for networking. It provides the networking world with a common and standard blueprint for designing, implementing, and operating networking hardware and software. It also provides the basic operating and interconnection rules for all network operating systems, network messaging, and communications connectivity devices.

Why bother with the OSI model? Probably the most important reason is that nearly everything Cisco (and virtually every other network equipment manufacturer) does is defined, documented, and described in terms of the OSI model layer on which it operates. This translates to the fact that you really need to learn the OSI model, its layers, what each does, and with whom it does it if you expect to understand networking, especially internetworking.

The difference between networking and internetworking (for those who are really interested)

Throughout this book, if you haven't noticed already, I use the terms *networking* and *internetworking,* along with *network* and *internetwork,* as if they are interchangeable. Well, on a Cisco network that includes a Cisco router or high-end Layer 2 (see "And Now for the Soft Stuff . . .," later in this chapter) switch, your network is an internetwork. Huh? Well, bear with me.

A network without a router is just a network. (See Chapter 1 for a good description of a network.) However, adding a router usually makes

a network into an internetwork. This isn't automatic, of course. You could add the router just to control internal network traffic and not connect to the outside world, but a router is used primarily to connect your internal network to an external network.

So, if your router connects your network to other networks, your network is an *internetwork.* In fact, "the big I" internetwork — the Internet — is the granddaddy internetwork, which is where it got its name.

The OSI model is not a standard in the sense that it can be implemented like an Ethernet or token ring network standard. And it is not a suite of protocols, although it defines the guidelines used by many protocols. Just what the OSI model is or isn't can become confusing because of the way it is referenced. You will read, here and in other books, that a certain activity is implemented on a particular OSI level. All this means is that the guidelines that govern that certain activity are included in the standards of that particular level on which a specific protocol or software application was based.

If you work with internetworking long enough, you will eventually think of the OSI as a working model, but only in the sense that devices begin taking on an OSI identity. For example, you may think of routers as Layer 3 functions, switching as a Layer 2 activity, and cabling as Layer 1 media. The router, switch, and cable are not OSI devices; they just perform functions defined in its standards.

The *OSI model* is more of a blueprint or framework for the ways in which networking devices and services should interact with one another in handling the activities involved with carrying data from one network node to another.

Betting on the lucky seven

The OSI model consists of seven layers. However, much to your sweet tooth's dismay, the OSI model is more like an onion than a cake, with each layer encompassing the preceding layer. Figure 2-2 illustrates the seven layers of the OSI model.

```
┌─────────────────────────────────────┐
│   ┌─────────────────────────────┐    │
│   │    7. Application layer      │    │
│   ├─────────────────────────────┤    │
│   │    6. Presentation layer     │    │
│   ├─────────────────────────────┤    │
│   │    5. Session layer          │    │
│   ├─────────────────────────────┤    │
│   │    4. Transport layer        │    │
│   ├─────────────────────────────┤    │
│   │    3. Network layer          │    │
│   ├─────────────────────────────┤    │
│   │    2. Data Link layer        │    │
│   ├─────────────────────────────┤    │
│   │    1. Physical layer         │    │
│   └─────────────────────────────┘    │
└─────────────────────────────────────┘
```

Figure 2-2:
The seven
layers of the
OSI model.

Here is a brief overview of each OSI layer:

- **Physical layer:** This is the bottom layer for the OSI model, and (as its name suggests) it is concerned with the physical nature of a network, which includes cabling, connectors, network interface cards, and the processes that convert bits into signals for sending and signals into bits when receiving. See "Getting physical on Layer 1," later in this chapter.

- **Data Link layer:** This layer is concerned with providing context to the Physical layer's bits by formatting them into frames, providing for error-checking and correction, and avoiding transmission conflicts on the network. "Connecting to Layer 2 hardware," later in this chapter, provides the details for this layer.

- **Network layer:** This layer handles addressing of data for delivery and converting network addresses into physical addresses. Routing messages on the network and internetwork also happens at this layer. See Chapters 5 and 6 for more information on what happens on the Network layer.

- **Transport layer:** This layer of the OSI model deals with network computers communicating with each other and matching the message to the capabilities and restrictions of the network medium. At this layer, network messages are chopped into smaller pieces for transmission and reassembled at their destination, preferably in the correct order. See Chapter 6 for more information on the activities of the Transport layer.

- **Session layer:** The Session layer manages communication "sessions," including handshaking, security, and the mechanics of an ongoing connection. *Handshaking* is the very technical term for the actions two communicating devices perform to build a connection over which a session is conducted.

✔ **Presentation layer:** This layer, the sixth of the OSI model, is where raw data messages are packaged in generic form so they can withstand the rigors of being transmitted over a network. On this layer, incoming messages are broken down and formatted appropriate to the receiving application, too.

✔ **Application layer:** This is the seventh and top layer of the OSI model. As its name suggests, it interfaces with applications wishing to gain network access. Do not confuse the Application layer with Microsoft Office, WordPerfect, Corel Draw, or end-user application software. Such applications as Windows NT Server or NetWare operate at this layer.

The top three layers (Session, Presentation, and Application) are used primarily to support applications. I don't mean the applications on your desktop, such as Microsoft Word, Lotus 1-2-3, or Oracle. These layers include such functions as FTP (File Transfer Protocol), HTTP (HyperText Transfer Protocol), and data conversion, compression, and encryption, which interface with your desktop applications to get data ready for transport by the bottom four layers or (after transport) to prepare the data being received for use by your desktop applications.

The bottom four layers (Physical, Data Link, Network, and Transport) are used for moving data from one network device to another and are referred to collectively as *the lower layers* of the OSI model. The Session, Presentation, and Application layers (Layers 4, 5, and 6 respectively) are collectively referred to as the upper layers.

Cool ways to remember the layers of the OSI model

Should you wish to impress your friends or relatives by reciting the seven layers of the OSI model in sequence, either top to bottom or bottom to top, here are a number of different sayings that you can use to remember the layers of the OSI model:

"Please Do Not Throw Salami (or Sausage, if you prefer) Pizza Away" — This works for bottom to top. And it's my personal favorite: the saying and the pizza.

"APS Transport Network Data Physically" — APS refers to Application, Presentation, and Session (the upper layers).

"All People Seem To Need Data Processing" — Another top to bottom reminder.

"Please Do Not Tell Secret Passwords Anytime" — Okay, I know; enough already — it's getting lame!

Down one side and up the other

Remember that the OSI model is never actually implemented, but the network hardware, protocols, and other software used to build a network act in a layering and unlayering fashion that is defined by the guidelines of the OSI model. As illustrated in Figure 2-3, a packet is passed down through the OSI layers from the Application layer to the Physical layer, where it is physically transmitted to the Physical layer of the destination network. At the receiving end, it is passed back up through the layers, from Physical layer to the Application layer.

As the data passes down through the OSI layers, each layer uses the services of the layers above or below it. From the upper layers, data is broken into smaller pieces and encapsulated into data units that are sent down to lower layers. This process continues down to the Physical layer, by which time the original data is converted into binary form that is transmitted across the network's physical media. At the receiving end, the process is reversed and the data is passed back up until it reaches the Application layer, converted back into application data.

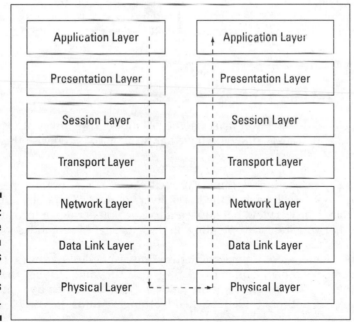

Figure 2-3:
The route that data takes through the OSI model's layers.

The official OSI name for the data passed around on networks is PDU. There are several versions of what PDU stands for, including the original "protocol data unit," the easily remembered "packet data unit," and the heavyweight "payload data unit." A *PDU* is a unit of data that is packaged for movement from one OSI layer to another as it winds its way from its source to its destination. PDUs are also called *data frames,* or *frames* for short, when the Data Link layer passes them to the Physical layer. As a PDU passes down through the OSI layers, it takes on a variety of formats and its name changes to segment to packet or datagram, to frame to bits as it is passed along.

As shown in Figure 2-3, the PDU is passed down through the sending side layers, and each layer performs its own brand of magic: formatting it, breaking it into smaller pieces, adding error-checking tools, and more. Some of the layers also add their own headers (or trailers) to the PDU as it passes down through the layers. When transmitted across the Physical layer, the original message has picked up four headers and perhaps a trailer.

The headers added by some of the layers provide instructions to the counterpart layers at the other end of the transmission. For example, the Transport layer breaks up the message into segments. The header added by the Transport layer on the sending side contains instructions for sequencing and reassembly of the segments for the receiving side Transport layer. As the packet passes up through the receiving side layers, the headers are stripped away at the appropriate layers until the original message is delivered to the destination application.

First the Hard Stuff . . .

Essentially, only the lower layers of the OSI model (the Physical, Data Link, Network, and Transport layers) have hardware associated with them. So, I focus on these layers.

In the next few sections, I provide you with an overview of the types of hardware that operate at each of the lower layers of the OSI model. I don't get too detailed in this overview, but I do want to give you enough information to ensure that you and I are operating on the same set of semantics in this book.

If you need an in-depth review of networking principles, hardware (beyond routers and switches), and network protocols (beyond TCP/IP), then I recommend that you look into one of the following books, written by some of my most favorite authors (and published by Hungry Minds, Inc.):

- *Networking For Dummies,* 5th Edition, by Doug Lowe
- *Network+ Certification For Dummies,* 2nd Edition, by Ron Gilster
- *Server+ Certification For Dummies,* by Ron Gilster and Mike Glencross
- *CCNA For Dummies,* by Ron Gilster, Jeff Bienvenu, and Kevin Ulstad

Medium and media: Do you really mean wire?

A cable's medium is the metal, glass, plastic, or radio waves that make up its core material. This core material is what is used to carry the electrical signals into which a message has been coded for the purpose of being transmitted. In a twisted-pair cable, the medium is copper. In a fiber-optic cable, the medium is either glass or plastic. In a wireless transmission, the medium is radio waves.

When I use the term *media,* I am not referring to newspaper or TV reporters. I am referring to more than one medium. *Medium* is singular, and *media* is plural. This is one of those gifts from the Romans that just keeps on giving.

Yes, beyond being a shameless plug, many of these books are for one certification exam or another, but they are also excellent sources of detailed information regarding network hardware, software, and functions.

Getting physical on Layer 1

The Physical layer (Layer 1 of the OSI model) defines, well, the physical parts of the network. This layer is concerned with moving bits on the physical media. Therefore, it deals only with the hardware affecting the physical movement of data from point A to point B, which includes such things as

- Electrical issues and standards that have been developed by various contributing organizations, such as the EIA/TIA (the Electrical Industry Association/Telecommunications Industry Association), the IEEE – (pronounced "eye triple-E" and meaning the Institute of Electrical and Electronics Engineers), and UL (Underwriters Laboratories)

- Networking hardware, including network interface cards (NICs), network media (copper wire, glass fiber, or even wireless signals), repeaters, hubs, and other devices that move the electrical impulses of binary data across the network

- The distance limitations of network media and how these limitations apply in wiring closets through horizontal and intermediate cross-connects

- Some basic network topologies and other physical properties of a network

Physical layer hardware

All of the physical hardware used to transport bits around the network is on the Physical layer. This hardware includes network adapters, cabling, wall plugs, cross-connects, hubs, repeaters, and connectors. Even wireless network media is on the Physical layer.

The equipment you are most likely to encounter when working with a wired network are hubs, but you could also encounter repeaters, although they are much less common today than they were a few years back.

However, before I get into hubs and repeaters, I need to mention a condition that can happen when data is transmitted over a physical medium, especially copper wire. This condition, which is called *attenuation,* is the point in a transmission when a signal begins to lose its strength due to friction and distance and must be re-energized in order to avoid being lost or garbled. Most cable types have recommended maximum cable segment distance limits that take into account the attenuation point of the cable's core medium. Chapter 4 provides all the detail on cable segment distances you should need.

Hubs and repeaters have different basic functions, but a hub can also provide the same service as a repeater. The primary purpose of a hub is to provide access to the network cabling for a group of network nodes. A repeater merely re-energizes transmitted signals on long cable runs that must exceed the attenuation point of a particular medium.

Just a hub of activity

A network hub is very much like the old railroad roundhouse in its basic concept. However, unlike the railroad roundhouse, which let an incoming train leave on a different track, a hub repeats an incoming message back out through all of its ports (something like the secrets I would tell my younger sister when we were children).

Network hubs are either active or passive. A *passive hub* merely repeats any signals that it receives from one of its ports to all the other ports without re-energizing (repeating) the signal. Passive hubs do not help the attenuation distance of their network segment.

On the other hand, an active hub includes a repeater-type (see "Could you repeat that?" later in this section) feature that re-energizes the signal before sending it on to its ports. There are also smart hubs that can intelligently direct a signal to only the single port on which its destination exists. Smart hubs work on the lines of a bridge or switch (see "Connecting to Layer 2 hardware," later in this chapter).

In an Ethernet network, which is by far the most common type, a hub is used in a star topology to provide multiport connectivity to a network. Many workstations and peripherals can be clustered on a hub, which is then connected to another hub, a switch, a router, or directly into a cross-connect.

Could you repeat that?

A *repeater* is a device that is added to a network to solve attenuation problems in cable wire. A repeater cleans up the signal, gives it a little boost, and sends it on its way. Although a repeater may sound a little like your mom, it's actually a small device that usually has only one input connector and one output connector that can be inserted into the network anywhere the signal needs a boost. A common use for a repeater is to extend the effective range of the cabling by overcoming the distance limitations of the cable, such as extending the 100-meter segment distance limitation of CAT 5 cabling.

Connecting to Layer 2 hardware

The hardware that operates on the Data Link layer (Layer 2) is concerned with addressing packets on the physical network and making sure that a packet is properly addressed to get to its destination. The physical network is not limited to the local physical space and can, and does, include many WAN activities (see Chapter 14). The primary devices on the Data Link layer are bridges, switches, and multilayer brouters (pronounced "*brow*-ters").

The MAC bridge

No, McDonald's is not in the networking business, at least not yet anyway. Bridges are commonly referred to as MAC layer bridges because they operate on the MAC sublayer of Layer 2. Each network device has a unique MAC address assigned to it during manufacturing. A bridge recognizes and tracks the MAC addresses on the segments connected to it to perform its tasks, which include

- Monitoring network traffic
- Identifying the destination and source addresses of a message
- Creating a bridging table, or forwarding table, that identifies MAC addresses to the network segment on which they are located
- Sending messages to only the network segment on which its destination MAC address is located

A bridge builds up its bridging table by cataloging the network nodes that send out messages. A bridge examines the MAC address of a message's source or sending node. If this address is new to the bridge, the bridge adds the address to the bridging table along with the network segment from which it originated. The bridge's bridging table is stored in its RAM, and just like a PC's RAM, it is dynamic — when the power goes off, it goes away. When the power is restored, the bridge will rebuild the table. Because most network nodes send and received packets continuously, the complete rebuild of the bridging table doesn't take long.

A bridge is used to connect two or more network segments to form a larger individual network. Another way to look at this definition is to think that a bridge is used to divide a larger network into smaller segments. A bridge records the physical addresses of network nodes and on which of its ports an address is located. The physical address of a node is represented by the Media Access Control (MAC) address of the NIC (network interface card) of the node. By recording the MAC addresses located on its segment, a bridge can determine whether a packet should cross the bridge to reach its destination.

Switching around the network

A *switch,* also called a *multiport bridge,* is a smart bridge. It uses MAC addresses to determine the port on which a message should be sent and sends it only to that port. Some of the higher-end devices that are still called switches actually contain some Layer 3 (Network layer) functions, including routing. Understand that switching is synonymous with forwarding and is one of the functions involved in routing a packet across the network (see "Routing on Layer 3 hardware," later in the chapter). Chapter 10 provides more detail on switches and network switching.

It's a bridge; it's a router; no, it's a brouter!

A *brouter* is a cross between the Layer 2 bridge and the Layer 3 router. (See the next section, "Routing on Layer 3 hardware.") A brouter is able to perform services as required to bridge two dissimilar networks (for example, TCP/IP to IPX/SPX) or to route packets to another network segment or to the Internet, depending on what is needed by the network at any particular instance.

You won't find a lot of brouters these days. In fact, if you search the Internet for the name *brouter,* you will primarily find links to definitions and explanations in many different languages.

The Cisco Catalyst switch series and the Cisco Internetwork Operating System (IOS) have been expanded to the point that the level of bridging and switching, and in some cases rudimentary routing, required for any given situation can be handled by one Catalyst model or another.

Routing on Layer 3 hardware

Hardware devices that operate on Layer 3 (the Network layer) of the OSI model are concerned with logical network addressing on larger networks that are physically made up from many separate networks or network segments. Network layer devices use addressing information to logically merge networks into an internetwork.

The primary device that operates at this layer is a router, which has more intelligence than a bridge or a switch, and can determine the best and most efficient route for a network packet to reach its destination.

Is this a physical or a logical relationship?

Let me briefly explain the distinction between physical and logical addressing.

Essentially, two types of addresses are used on a network: physical and logical. *Physical addresses* are uniquely and permanently associated with a network device, such as a network interface card (NIC). In fact, a device's physical address is burned into the device during manufacturing. The best example of a physical address is the MAC address that is associated with almost every network-capable device.

On the other hand, logical addresses are assigned, well, logically. Logical addresses, such as IP (Internet Protocol) addresses, bear a logical relationship to other addresses on the network. Have I said *logical* enough so that you see how logical this all is?

So, in summary, bridges and switches use physical addresses, and Layer 3 devices (such as routers) use logical addresses. Got it?

Routers are the keystone devices in Cisco networking. Although you can have a network without a router, a LAN requires a router, which can be either hardware or software, to connect to the outside world, especially the Internet. In fact, it is downright nearly impossible to connect to the Internet without a router. You can find all the information you need about routers and routing in Part III of this book.

Transporting on Layer 4 hardware

You won't find a large selection of hardware defined on the Transport layer of the OSI model. Essentially, Layer 4 is a software or protocol layer, but some devices are known as "Layer 4 switches," although this term is mostly a marketing term. A Layer 4 switch extends the Layer 2 switching to include the TCP (Transmission Control Protocol)/UDP (User Datagram Protocol) port numbers in making its forwarding decisions. See Chapter 10 for more information on switching, including Layer 4 switching.

One device that is definitely associated with the Transport layer is a gateway. A *gateway* can be either hardware or software or both. The main purpose of a gateway is to join two dissimilar systems that have similar functions but cannot otherwise communicate, such as interconnecting a LAN to a WAN or a mainframe computer.

In many cases, a gateway is an adaptation of a network device from another layer, but mostly those operating at Layer 3. Often a router that provides the connection between a LAN and the Internet is called the gateway (or even the default gateway). In this situation, the router has additional capabilities added (such as the capability to forward or filter protocols from Layers 4 and up) directly to specific network devices, such as a Web server or an e-mail server.

Although a gateway operates at the Transport layer, it can also operate at any of the top four layers of the OSI model. (See "Betting on the lucky seven," earlier in this chapter, for the list of layers.)

And in summary . . .

Table 2-1 summarizes the layers of the OSI model and the hardware that operates on each layer.

Table 2-1	The Hardware Operating at Each OSI Model Layer
OSI Layer	*Device(s)*
Physical	NIC, cable and transmission media, repeater, hub
Data Link	Bridge, switch, NIC, brouter, smart hub
Network	Router, brouter
Transport	Gateway, switch
Upper Layers	Gateway

And Now for the Soft Stuff . . .

In addition to hardware, communications activities are provided by software and protocols defined by the OSI model. Just as different types of hardware operate on each of several OSI layers, standards and protocols are also defined on just about every layer of the OSI model. From the Data Link layer (Layer 2) up to the Application layer (Layer 7), each layer defines one or more addressing, connecting, formatting, or conversion standard or procedure. (See "Betting on the lucky seven," earlier in the chapter, for a description of each OSI layer.)

There is one exception to this statement — the Physical layer. The Physical layer defines the physical parts of the network and how they connect and can be laid out, but it doesn't include any software or protocols. (See "Getting physical on Layer 1," earlier in this chapter.)

Although I am discussing the software and protocols of the OSI model in this section, remember that I am doing so on a conceptual level. I can't tell you often enough that the OSI model is only a guideline and not a piece of software. Throughout this chapter and the rest of the book, I describe items as being on or at a certain OSI layer. This means only that an item is defined by the standards that exist for that layer. However, eventually, you, too, will probably begin to picture in your mind the OSI model as a conceptual working model, real or not.

The softer side of Layer 2

Layer 2 (the Data Link layer) is the shipping and receiving dock of the OSI model. This layer is where data is packaged for transmission on the Physical layer as well as where data from the Physical layer is unpackaged to be passed to the Network layer (Layer 3) and above. The Data Link layer encapsulates the packets passed to it from the upper layers into frames for transmission on the Physical layer. At the receiving end of the transmission, the Data Link layer reassembles incoming messages for processing on the higher layers.

To a certain extent, all OSI layers wrap and unwrap data before sending and after receiving it from the layers above and below it. However, the Data Link layer is the point of entry where the data transported over the physical network media enters and leaves your network.

Looking into the IEEE 802 standards

The functions and activities of the Data Link layer of the OSI model, at least in terms of Ethernet and token ring networks, is defined in the 802 standards of the Institute for Electrical and Electronics Engineers (IEEE). The 802 standards were written to establish a standard and guideline to help ensure interoperability between network hardware and software from different developers. (See the sidebar, "Stacking up the IEEE 802 standards," for more information.) Table 2-2 lists the major IEEE 802 standards incorporated into the Cisco networking world.

Table 2-2		The IEEE 802 Standards
Standard	**Name**	**Description**
802.1	Internetworking	Defines routing, bridging, and internetwork communications
802.2	Logical Link Control (LLC)	Enables Network layer protocols to link to Physical layer and MAC sublayer protocols
802.3	Ethernet	Ethernet standard; defines CSMA/CD
802.4	Physical bus	Defines physical token bus topology, media, and interfaces
802.5	Token ring	Defines logical ring topology, media, and interfaces
802.11	Wireless LANs	Defines physical media and interfaces for applying wireless technology to networking
802.12	Demand priority	Defines 100 Mbps VG-AnyLAN technologies networks
802.15	Wireless Personal Area Networks	Defines the use of wireless technologies to create a limited range personal area network

Getting down to sublayers

The Data Link layer is divided into two sublayers by the IEEE 802 standards:

- **Logical Link Control (LLC) sublayer:** The LLC sublayer is defined in IEEE 802.1 and 802.2, although some of 802.1 extends into the MAC sublayer as well.
- **Media Access Control (MAC) sublayer:** The MAC sublayer is defined in the 802.1, 802.3, 802.4, 802.5, and 802.12 standards.

The logical link control (LLC) sublayer

The LLC sublayer is defined in the 802.2 standard to be topology (Ethernet, token ring, and the like — see Chapter 3) independent. Regardless of the type of network or media in use, the LLC sublayer allows the Network layer to interact with the Data Link layer and its sublayers. Among other things the LLC sublayer does is provide an interface for the MAC sublayer and manage frames, which involves controlling, sequencing, and acknowledging frames being passed on to either the Physical or Network layers. The LLC sublayer also performs some error-control tasks at the same time.

The media access control (MAC) sublayer

The MAC sublayer of the Data Link layer identifies the devices attached to the network, defines the topology used on the network (but not the media), and controls network activity. On a network, where multiple computers compete for use of the media, the MAC sublayer controls access to the network by deciding who can access the media, when, and for how long. Put your hand down, User #3, you just went!

Another of the Data Link layer's important jobs is addressing. The MAC sublayer carries the physical device address of each device on the network. Commonly called a device's MAC address, this 48-bit address is encoded on each device by its manufacturer. The address system works on the same principle as the individually numbered homes in your neighborhood — each domicile on your street has a unique address assigned to it by the postal service. The MAC address is used by the Physical and Data Link layers to deliver data to nodes of the network. Figure 2-4 shows the MAC address (shown as the Adapter Address) of a PC's network interface card (NIC).

In a workstation, the MAC address is usually burned into the NIC. On a router, each port has its own MAC physical address. The idea is that no two devices should ever have the same MAC address. However, I have heard of instances in which this has occurred in a network with very unpleasant circumstances resulting.

Virtually all NICs have their MAC addresses burned into their circuitry during manufacturing. However, some older legacy cards that require you to use jumpers or DIP switches to manually configure the physical address on the device are still around.

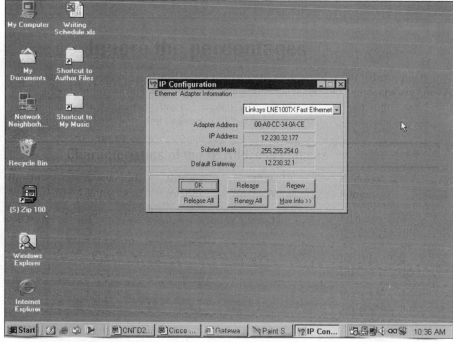

Figure 2-4:
The
Windows 98
WINIPCFG
command
displays the
MAC
address
(Adapter
Address)
of a
computer's
NIC.

Communicating on the MAC sublayer

The MAC address works on the same principle that each house or apartment on your street has a unique street address or apartment number assigned to it. On the Data Link layer, the MAC address is used to provide the unique address that allows data to move between nodes on a network. Just like you need to know a friend's address to find his or her house, computers must know each other's address to communicate. However, not all network operating systems (NOS) use the physical address to reference network nodes, which can create a conflict between the network (logical) address and the MAC (physical) address.

Network operating systems assign a logical network name to each networked device, such as ACCTG_SERVER, NT1, or FRED, to make it easy for its human administrators and users to reference its resources. On the other hand, Layer 2 activities use physical addresses to reference devices on the network. When you request services from the file server FRED, the Data Link layer translates the name assigned to your computer by the network administrator and that of FRED into their MAC addresses. *Resolving* (the techie term for translating the addresses) these addresses involves a process called, ta-da, *address resolution*. Address resolution associates a logical network address with its physical MAC address and vice versa.

Stacking up the IEEE 802 standards

Immediately after someone invented networking — by connecting two computers together to share files and pass secret messages — it was immediately apparent that this was a good thing. As local area networks (LANs) began to spread, it became obvious that, in order for networks to grow large or to communicate with each other, some rules had to be developed.

Never shy about making rules, those fun-loving, madcap guys at the Institute for Electrical and Electronics Engineers (IEEE) began a project to define Data Link layer standards in February 1980. This date is significant because, for want of a better name, IEEE named the project the 802 Project (as in 80 for 1980 and 2 for February). The 802 Project is actually the name of the committee assigned to develop the networking standards. Each of its subcommittees, assigned to

develop standards for a specific networking area, has a subcommittee number, such as 802.1, 802.3, 802.10, and so forth. For example, the 802.3 standard is assigned to the 802.3 subcommittee. This logic is unparalleled in its simplicity.

Probably the most important of the 802 Project's subcommittees, in terms of Cisco networking, is IEEE 802.3. This subcommittee came up with the standard (802.3) that defines Ethernet, by far the networking standard of choice. The 802.3 standard defines the bus topology, network media (10BaseX), and functions of an Ethernet network. It also defines the functions of the MAC (Media Access Control) sublayer and, of particular interest to the Ethernet world, the CSMA/CD access method.

Resolving the issue with ARP

A special protocol, called *ARP (Address Resolution Protocol* — what else would it be called?), is used for this service. ARP maintains a small database, the *ARP cache,* that cross-references a network's physical and logical addresses. The ARP cache provides each computer with a local network address book. When a device wants to communicate with another local device, it checks its ARP cache to determine if it has that device's MAC address. If the ARP cache doesn't have the MAC address, it sends out an ARP broadcast request, as illustrated in Figure 2-5, to all devices on the local network. Each device examines the message; if the request is intended for that device, it responds with its MAC address. The sending device stores the address in its ARP cache.

In the example shown in Figure 2-5, USER1 wants to communicate with FRED, a file server. However, USER1 doesn't have a MAC address in its ARP cache for FRED, so it sends out a broadcast message that asks FRED to respond with its MAC address, which FRED does.

When a workstation or server needs to communicate with a device remote to the local network, essentially the same ARP process takes place. However, instead of requesting the address of the remote device, the MAC address of its network router is actually requested. This allows the data to be transmitted to reach the remote device's network. If the MAC address of the remote device is needed to reach it, the processing takes place within the remote network.

Controlling access to the network

The primary tool defined in IEEE 802.3 for use on the Data Link layer is the CSMA/CD (Carrier Sense Multiple Access/Collision Detection) access method. *CSMA/CD* is the method used in Ethernet networks for controlling access to the physical media by network nodes. As you may infer from its name, CSMA/CD (quick, say it ten times fast) tries to keep network devices from interfering with each other's communications by detecting access attempts by multiple devices. When sneaky devices avoid detection, and they sometimes do, CSMA/CD detects and deals with the data collisions that will undoubtedly occur.

Avoiding collisions

To avoid collisions when two or more workstations are transmitting to the network at one time, CSMA/CD devices "listen" or sense signals on the network backbone before sending a message over the network. If the network is quiet, meaning that it is not in use, the device can send a message. Otherwise, the device should wait until the network is not in use. However, if another device sends a message between the time that the first device has decided the network is available and the time it actually transmits its message, the two messages may collide on the network. When this happens, the device that detected the collision sends out an alert to all network devices that a collision has occurred. All devices quit transmitting for a random amount of time to clear the line.

What's up with you, MAC?

A MAC (media access control) address is actually an identification number assigned to a networkable device during manufacturing. A MAC number is made up of two parts: the manufacturer's ID number and a unique serialized number assigned to the device by the manufacturer. The 48-bits (6 bytes) of the MAC address are divided evenly between these two numbers. The first three bytes of the MAC address contain a hexadecimal manufacturer code that has been assigned by the IEEE. For example, Cisco's IEEE MAC ID is 00 00 0C (each byte holds two half-byte hexadecimal values), and Intel's is 00 55 00. The remaining three bytes of the MAC address contain a unique hexadecimal serial number that is assigned by the manufacturer to each individual device.

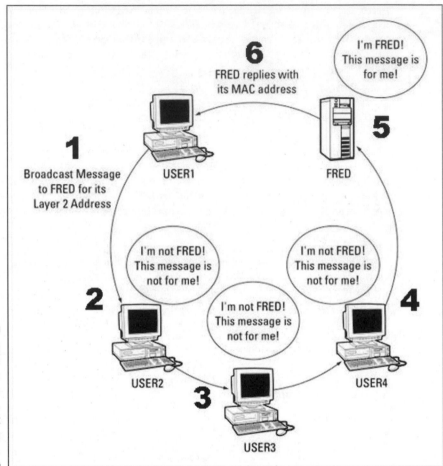

Figure 2-5:
To resolve
an unknown
address on
the network,
a broadcast
request is
sent.

The CSMA/CD process can be described as follows:

1. Listen to see if the wire is being used.

2. If the wire is busy, wait.

3. If the wire is quiet, send.

4. If a collision occurs while sending, stop. Wait a random amount of time and send again.

When a sending device detects a collision, it sends out a jamming signal that is of sufficient enough duration for all nodes to recognize it and stop broadcasting. Then each device waits a random amount of time to begin the CSMA/CD process again. This random amount of time is determined through a back-off algorithm that calculates the amount of time the device should wait before resuming its attempts to transmit.

Working on a busy intersection

A *collision domain* is a network segment in which all devices share the same bandwidth. The more devices you have on a segment, the more likely it is that collisions will occur. Too many devices on a segment means that network performance is considerably less than optimal. Increasing bandwidth is one way to deal with the problem, but a better way to deal with this problem is to use the available bandwidth more efficiently.

Spanning the network

Because a Data Link frame can effectively live forever, a packet addressed to an unknown or nonexistent MAC address could bounce around the network indefinitely. This condition is solved by allowing only a single path to be active between two segments at any time through the spanning tree protocol.

The *spanning tree protocol* designates each interface on a bridge to be either in Forwarding or Blocking state. When an interface is in Blocking state, only special packets reporting the status of other bridges on the network are allowed through. All other packets are blocked. As you can probably guess, an interface in Forwarding state allows all packets to be received and forwarded. The state of a bridge's interfaces are affected whenever a path on the network goes down, and the bridges negotiate a new path, changing interface states from Blocking to Forwarding as needed.

The normal operating mode for a bridge is called *store and forward*. Bridges receive (store) and examine a whole frame before forwarding it on to the appropriate interface. The time that it takes to examine each frame increases the latency (delay) in the network. *Latency* is the amount of time that it takes a packet to travel from source to destination.

Going with the flow control

Flow control is used to meter the flow of data between network devices that may not be running at the same speeds. For situations in which one communicating device is sending information at either a faster or a slower rate than the other device, some form of control is necessary to meter the flow of data between the devices to avoid a loss of data. Flow control prevents the slower device from being swamped and, more important, prevents data from being lost or garbled. Flow control works by pausing the faster device to allow the slower device to catch up.

Two types of flow control are implemented in data communications:

- **Software flow control,** common to networking, involves *a process called XON/XOFF,* which roughly stands for *transmission on/transmission off.* In this process, the sending device continues to send data until the receiving device sends a control character telling it to stop transmitting until the receiving device can catch up. When the receiving device is ready to go, it sends another control signal that tells the sending device that it can begin transmitting again.

✔ **Hardware flow control,** also called *RTS/CTS (Ready To Send/Clear To Send),* uses two wires in a cable, one wire for RTS and the other wire for CTS. The sending device uses the RTS signal to indicate when it is ready to send. The receiving device uses the CTS to indicate that the receiving device is ready to receive. When either device is turned off, the flow is interrupted.

Detecting errors in the flow

Error detection is the process of determining if any errors may have occurred during a transmission of bits. A calculated value, called the *CRC (Cyclical Redundancy Check),* is added to the message frame before it is sent to the Physical layer. The receiving computer recalculates the CRC and compares it to the one sent with the data. If the two values are equal, it is assumed that the data arrived without errors. Otherwise, the message frame may need to be retransmitted. Although the Data Link layer implements error detection, it does not include functions to perform error recovery. This task is left for the upper layers to deal with, primarily on the Transport layer.

Following the Protocol Rules

A *protocol* is a set of rules and requirements that two communicating devices must follow in order to conduct an effective communications session. Hundreds of protocols are used in today's networked environment. Some are generally supported, and some are more proprietary and specific to a particular operating system, hardware type, or manufacturer.

In general, networking protocols follow the OSI model and its layers. Network servers have suites of protocols that perform the actions and activities of each layer as a packet passes down or up the OSI model.

Ain't it suite?

A *protocol suite* is an interrelated group of protocols that have been grouped to help carry out a single activity. For example, the TCP/IP protocol suite is made up of a number of protocols that allow you to interact with the Internet. Most protocol suites, and especially the TCP/IP suite, have different protocols for each layer for the OSI model.

Three general types of protocols exist: Network protocols, Transport protocols, and Application protocols. Figure 2-6 illustrates the general relationship of the three protocol types to the OSI model's layers. Most network administrators spend most of their time working with Transport and Network protocols.

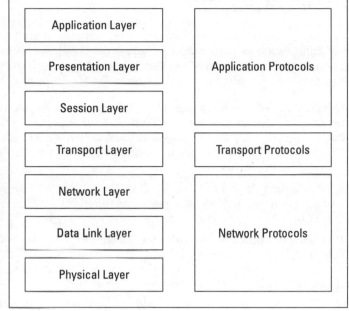

Figure 2-6:
How the three main types of protocols match up to the OSI model layers.

Network protocols

Network protocols provide for packet addressing and routing information, error-checking and correction, and enforcing the rules for communicating within a specific network environment. Network protocols provide what are called *link services* to other protocols operating at other layers. Following are the common Network protocols:

- ✔ **DLC (Data Link Control):** DLC is used for network-connected mainframes and Hewlett Packard printers.

- ✔ **IP (Internet Protocol):** This is the IP of the famous TCP/IP duo. IP provides addressing and routing information.

- ✔ **IPX (Internetwork Package Exchange) and NWLink (NetWare Link):** Novell's NetWare protocol and Microsoft's IPX clone are used for packet routing and forwarding.

- ✔ **NetBEUI (NetBIOS Extended User Interface):** This provides transport services for NetBIOS. NetBEUI is also listed as a Transport layer protocol (see "Transport protocols") because it actually spans both layers.

Transport protocols

Transport protocols actually do more than just move things around as the name may imply. Some (such as TCP) transport data across the network very reliably by using end-to-end control, and others (such as UDP) just send the packets as fast as they can in a best-effort manner. Common Transport protocols are

- ✔ **NetBIOS/NetBEUI (Network Basic Input/Output System)/(NetBIOS Extended User Interface):** Although NetBIOS manages communications between computers, NetBEUI provides the data transport services. NetBEUI also performs Network layer functions (see the preceding section "Network protocols").

- ✔ **SPX (Sequenced Packet Exchange):** On a Novell NetWare network, SPX functions much like TCP and IPX performs functions similar to IP. Like TCP, SPX is used to guarantee data delivery.

- ✔ **TCP (Transmission Control Protocol):** This is the other half of the TCP/IP duo. TCP is commonly misnamed Transport Control Protocol, which is understandable. TCP/IP is responsible for guaranteeing the transport and delivery of packets across networks.

- ✔ **UDP (User Datagram Protocol):** This protocol is used in situations where control and reliability are not needed. For example, UDP is used to transmit real-time audio and video, where speed is important and lost packets can simply be ignored because there is no time to retransmit them. Any reliability or error-checking must be done in the source application itself.

Application protocols

Application protocols provide application-to-application services at the upper layers of the OSI model. Some common Application protocols are

- ✔ **SMTP (Simple Mail Transfer Protocol):** This member of the TCP/IP gang is responsible for transferring electronic mail.

- ✔ **FTP (File Transfer Protocol):** FTP, another protocol wearing the TCP/IP colors, is used to transport files from one computer to another.

- ✔ **SNMP (Simple Network Management Protocol):** This is YATP (yet another TCP/IP protocol) that is used to monitor network devices.

- ✔ **NCP (NetWare Core Protocol):** This is *not* a TCP/IP protocol! This protocol cluster contains the NetWare clients and redirectors.

How TCP/IP stacks up

The most commonly used protocol suite is TCP/IP, also known as the Internet Protocol Suite (not to be confused with IP, the Internet Protocol). Well, that's why it is commonly called just TCP/IP to represent all the protocols in the suite. Although TCP/IP has been around about ten years longer than the OSI model, it matches up nicely with the layers of the OSI model. Funny how that works out, huh?

Table 2-3 contains an OSI layer-by-layer breakdown of the TCP/IP suite.

Table 2-3	TCP/IP and the OSI Model
OSI Model Layer	*TCP/IP Protocol(s)*
Physical	Physical hardware device connectivity
Data Link	NIC driver, ODI/NDIS
Network	IP, ICMP, ARP, OSPF, RIP
Transport	TCP, UDP
Upper layers	DNS, Telnet, FTP, SMTP

The TCP/IP suite protocols included in Table 2-3 are explained here:

- **ODI/NDIS (Open Data-Link Interface/Network Driver-Interface Specification):** This Data Link layer interface enables NIC drivers to connect to dissimilar networks and have them appear as one.

- **IP (Internet Protocol):** This Network layer protocol provides source and destination addressing and routing.

- **ICMP (Internet Control Message Protocol):** This Network layer protocol carries control messages, such as error or confirmation messages.

- **ARP (Address Resolution Protocol):** This Network layer protocol converts IP addresses to MAC physical addresses. (See "Resolving the issue with ARP," earlier in this chapter.)

- **OSPF (Open Shortest Path First):** This protocol is used by TCP/IP routers to determine the best path through a network.

- **RIP (Routing Information Protocol):** This protocol helps TCP/IP routers to use the most efficient routes to nodes on the network.

- **TCP (Transmission Control Protocol):** This primary TCP/IP transport protocol accepts messages from the upper OSI layers and provides reliable delivery to its TCP peer on a remote network.

- **DNS (Domain Name System):** This Application layer Internet-name-to-address-resolution service allows users to use human-friendly names.

- **UDP (User Datagram Protocol):** This is another Transport layer protocol that can be used in place of TCP to transport simple single-packet messages.

✔ **Telnet:** This is the protocol used to remotely log into a server, work-station, or router.

✔ **FTP (File Transfer Protocol):** This is the TCP/IP protocol that is used to transfer files from a server to a host without analyzing the contents.

✔ **SMTP (Simple Mail Transport Protocol):** This is the TCP/IP protocol used to move electronic mail from its origination point to the server hosting its destination address.

Chapter 3

Taking It from the Topology

In This Chapter

▶ Reviewing network types and terminology

▶ Describing standard network topologies and their characteristics

▶ Explaining network topology advantages and disadvantages

Before you can start building a Cisco network, you should first know and understand the concepts that are the basic building blocks of networking. As in all walks of computing life, the devil is definitely in the details. If you understand the basic concepts of networking, the common network topologies, and their usage, you can avoid the network devil and the pitfalls that await the uninformed, the foolish, and the hasty.

All Cisco networkers are expected to speak a certain language. The vocabulary of a true Cisco networker includes such basic terminology as *network, topology, peer-based, server-based, LAN, WAN, MAN,* and *fault-tolerance,* not to mention all of the really technical terms and concepts that I cover in later chapters. In addition to your ability to amaze and impress your friends with your steel-trap grasp of networkspeak, you will be able to understand documentation, new product announcements, and upgrade bulletins, and be able to determine if new products are appropriate for your network.

If you are new to networking, spend the time building a strong and wide foundation of basic networking terminology and concepts. You may not become a topology expert, but you'll certainly be ready to work on a Cisco network, and isn't that why you're here?

Hardware, Software, and the Magic

I can talk forever about network topologies and technologies, but eventually it all boils down to the stuff — the hardware and software — that makes up the network and the magic applied by the network administrator to make it all function as a network. Networks are mostly things, as in hardware, software, and administrative processes, and these things are used to build, configure, and manage a network.

The most basic elements of any network are the cabling, servers, workstations, and other network nodes used to connect them:

- **Cable:** The physical medium over which information is transmitted between nodes in a network. The five main types of cable used in networking are coaxial, shielded twisted-pair (also referred to as just *twisted-pair*), unshielded twisted-pair, and fiber-optic. See Chapter 4 for more information on network cabling types.

- **Server:** A network computer from which workstations (clients) access and share files, printers, communications, and other services. A server can be dedicated to a single service — for examples, file servers, print servers, application servers, Web servers, and so on.

- **Node:** Any addressable network point, including workstations, peripherals, or other network devices. *Node* is commonly used interchangeably with *workstation*.

- **Workstation:** A personal computer, connected to a network by a cable, that is used to perform tasks using application or utility software or using data stored locally or provided by a network server. A workstation is also known as a *client*.

Stringing along with the cable

Chapter 4 lists more than 30 different types and uses for cable and wire in a networked environment, but in general, nearly all networks being created today use cables from a very short list of cable types. Probably the most common type of cable used on networks is UTP (Unshielded Twisted-Pair) copper wire cabling. Coaxial cables are still frequently used, with fiber-optic cables gaining fast; and, although not always thought of as a network media type, wireless networking is gaining popularity.

Workstations and nodes

A *workstation* is a computer attached to the network, and a *node* is an addressable workstation, peripheral, or other device attached to the network. Although in general usage, *node* is commonly used to refer to a workstation, when *node* is used, you should consider all things that could possibly be a network node.

I'll put this another way: Only those computers on which you can actually perform work that uses network resources is a workstation. It gets its name from the fact that you can perform work at this network station. A *node,* on the other hand, is any networkable computer, printer, scanner, fax machine, or other piece of hardware that can be attached to the network. And before you start with the "a printer can do work" business, the focus here is on *you* and where *you* can get work done.

Now that I've explained in it nauseating detail, you'll find that often the terms *workstation* and *node* are used interchangeably. But, there really is a difference.

Starting at the Beginning

I am going to start you off with the most basic of network basics:

- ✔ A *network* is two or more computers connected by a transmission medium for the purpose of sharing resources.

- ✔ Any two computers that are directly connected by some medium, such as a wire, a cable, or a wireless connection, for the purpose of sharing files, programs, or even *peripherals,* such as printers, scanners, CD towers, and so on, form a *network,* like the one shown in Figure 3-1. The underlying truth of networking is something that you must absolutely understand: One computer cannot be a network!

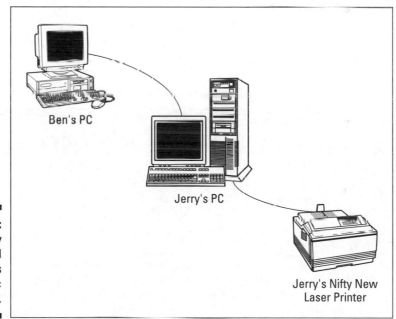

Figure 3-1: Two directly connected computers form a basic network.

Ben's PC

Jerry's PC

Jerry's Nifty New Laser Printer

Figure 3-1 illustrates a network of the kind I'm describing. Ben's computer has been connected to Jerry's so that Ben can share Jerry's nifty new laser printer. In this configuration, Ben and Jerry can also share data on each other's hard disk as well, should they wish to give each other permission to do so. Regardless of its simplicity, as illustrated in Figure 3-1, Ben and Jerry's computers form a network!

Sharing resources (yes, data is a resource) is what networks are all about. Networks have advanced to the point that most network users now take the network for granted — which should be the objective anyway when you really think about it. Users want immediate access to the resources they need to carry out a task on their computers. Whether a user needs software, data, or access to a particular piece of hardware, such as Jerry's printer, the user wants the network to make every available resource seem as if it is directly connected to his or her personal computer, with the network itself transparent.

Building Networks at Home and Away

Regardless of how a network is constructed internally, it is also classified by the proximity of its nodes and its intended function. Networks can be classified primarily in two standard ways:

- **Local area network (LAN):** A LAN interconnects its nodes in a relatively small geographical area, usually a single office, workgroup, department, or building.

- **Wide area network (WAN):** A WAN interconnects LANs that are dispersed over large geographical areas, such as states, countries, or even globally, by using dedicated long-distance, typically high-speed communication services. In fact, the Internet is considered to be the Big WAN.

Cisco's organizational hierarchies

As you discover throughout this book, Cisco Systems has its own view of how an organization should be structured, along with a number of very strong opinions on how its products should be used for your maximum enjoyment and their maximum profit. Seems like a fair trade-off!

In a Cisco org chart for a networked organization, the lowest level is the *user workstation* or the *network node,* meaning any stand-alone device that can be connected to the network, including printers, servers, and the like.

The next level up is the workgroup. Essentially, a *workgroup* is a LAN or LAN segments that are

interconnected to share a common set of resources, such as a database or an application software package.

Workgroups are combined to form *departments,* as in a very large Accounting, Manufacturing, or Sales department, a division, or some other entity. Departments represent an organizational component that is less than an entire *enterprise,* which is the next and highest level of the organization.

So, nodes make up workgroups that make up departments that make up enterprises.

Keeping it local

The most common type of network is the *local area network* or *LAN*. As its name implies, a LAN exists to service the resource needs of a group of local workstations, usually in one geographical location. A LAN can be in one room, one building, one campus, or one city. As long as the network does not include servers or hosts from outside the family, organization, or company, and the purpose of the network remains focused on sharing local resources, the network is a LAN.

At one time, the general rule was that a local area network existed on media that was totally owned by the network operators — for example, a single company or agency. In some ways, this rule still holds true, but as LANs grow larger and the line between a LAN and a *WAN (wide area network)* becomes less distinct, a local network may include telecommunications services from an outside provider.

Taking it wide

A *wide area network (WAN)* connects nodes and interconnects LANs located over geographically large areas, such as states or countries, and even globally, by using long-distance, high-speed lines (in most cases high-speed transmission services are used, but a WAN can also be created using a dial-up modem, which can be fairly slow). A WAN is probably more commonplace than you may think. The largest and most well-known WAN around is the Internet. A WAN combines local area networks over some form of public communications service. If a company's LAN in Los Angeles is connected to its LAN in Louisiana (in other words, the LAN in L.A. is connected to the LAN in LA over the public telephone system), it forms a WAN. In order for you to connect to the Internet from your workplace computer (strictly for business purposes, of course), your LAN must connect to the Internet WAN and must actually become a part of it. The *Internet* qualifies as a WAN in that the Internet is merely a network of networks, all of which are connected over a variety of public communications lines.

Please Accept My Topologies

The layout or shape of a network generally must conform to a couple of major constraints, not counting the cost of the network. One primary consideration is the physical layout of the space into which the network is to be integrated. Another is the networking technology most desired by the network administrator. Generally, the space into which the network must go does not dictate the technology that must be used. However, size and layout considerations within each of the major networking technologies can make one network layout more functional than another.

If you could look at a network from a bird's-eye view, you would get a sense of a general shape to the network. This shape and the pattern used to connect the workstations to the network, is its *topology,* or its physical layout.

Four basic topologies are commonly used in laying out networks:

- ✔ **Bus topology:** The network's nodes are connected to a central cable, called a *backbone,* which runs the length of the network. The bus topology is most commonly associated with Ethernet networks, the most commonly installed form of the bus topology, although most Ethernet networks consist of star clusters attached to the bus backbone (see "Working with an Ethernet network," later in this chapter). Figure 3-2 illustrates the bus topology.

- ✔ **Ring topology:** The primary network cable (backbone) is installed as a loop, or ring, and the nodes are attached to the primary cable at points on the ring. The ring topology is the basis for the token ring network structure, the most common implementation of the ring topology (see "Won't you wear my ring around your net?" later in this chapter). Figure 3-3 shows an illustration of the ring topology.

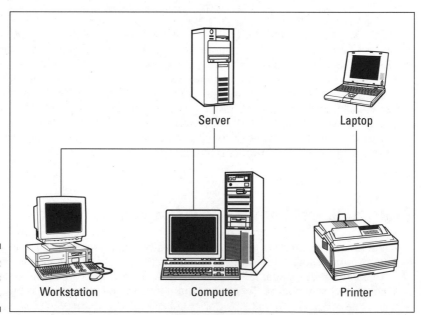

Figure 3-2:
The bus
topology.

Server   Laptop

Workstation   Computer   Printer

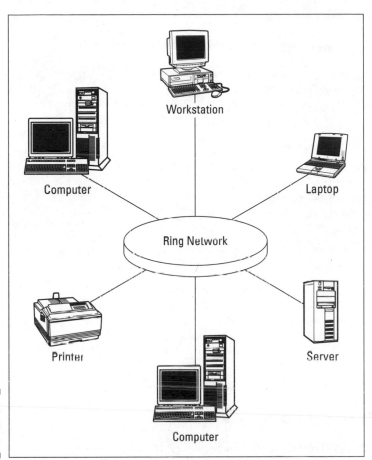

Figure 3-3:
The ring
topology.

- **Star topology:** On networks using the purest form of the star topology, each workstation is connected directly to the central server with its own cable, creating a starburstlike pattern. This topology, which became common with the now largely defunct ARCNet network, is now more commonly used with Ethernet and token ring networks to cluster workstations, which are then attached to the primary network cable. Figure 3-4 shows a common use of the star topology with a bus topology network.

- **Mesh:** In a mesh topology, each node is directly connected to every other node on the network. As it may sound, this topology attempts to create a mess, er, mesh of network connections. This topology is not very common but is used in situations where a high degree of network redundancy is required. I haven't included an illustration of a mesh topology because it would look more like a mess topology. Just as it sounds, every node on the network is connected to every other node on the network. Draw six small circles on a piece of paper in no particular pattern. Now connect each circle to every other circle. *Voilá,* you have a mesh topology diagram.

Let's get conceptually physical

A *conceptual layout* of a network is one that exists in the perfect world. In a conceptual rendering of the network, the bus topology is shown as a straight line, the ring topology is round, the star topology looks just like a daisy, and the mesh topology is almost neat.

The conceptual network layout is intended to show the network as near to how the network will see itself. It identifies each of the nodes, assigns them an identity, and relates them to the other elements of the network.

On the other hand, the *physical layout* attempts to depict the network as it will actually and physically be installed. In the physical layout, the bus meanders, the ring is lopsided, the star looks like the work of a gorilla with a pencil, and the mesh is very messy. The physical layout identifies cable lengths, connection points, interconnection devices (hubs, switches, bridges, routers, and the like), and any other element, part, component, or device that must be physically installed for the network to function as designed.

Another term used to describe a network is *infrastructure*. This refers to all of a network's components, including its hardware, software, cabling, conceptual layout, and physical layout (see the sidebar "Let's get conceptually physical"). This term is commonly used to describe the operating elements of a network to contrast from the data carried over the network. In fact, it is accurate to say that the network infrastructure carries the network's data.

Riding the bus

In a network built on the bus topology, the nodes are connected to a *backbone cable,* the primary network cable that runs the length of the network. The backbone extends to a length long enough to connect every node in the network (refer to Figure 3-2). Bus topologies are defined by three unique characteristics: their signal transmission, their use of cable termination, and the way that they maintain continuity.

Signal transmission

To avoid problems, which I discuss in Chapters 2 and 4, only one computer can transmit a signal at a time on a bus network backbone. There are specifications around (such as the IEEE 802.4 standard) that define technologies that can be used to allow multiple signals over a bus network, but in general, bus networks are limited to a single message.

Politely, when one node is "talking," the other nodes are "listening." As the signal travels down the cable, each node examines the signal to see if the signal was sent to that node. If not, the signal moves on down the cable to the next workstation, which repeats the examination. Because a bus network node only listens for messages sent to it and does not actually pass signals along by regenerating the signal, the bus topology is considered a *passive* network structure.

Cable termination

Unless some mechanism stops a signal from bouncing back and forth on the network backbone, a signal would bounce off the ends of the cable indefinitely. With the signal (obviously lost and without a destination on the network) occupying the backbone, all other nodes would be prevented from sending out any other signals. Remember that, by definition, only one signal can be on the backbone at a time. To prevent clogging the system, the backbone cable must be terminated at each end. The *terminator,* far from the movie type, is a single resistor placed at each end of the backbone cable to absorb any signals to keep them from "bouncing" back onto the network, which has the effect of clearing the cable.

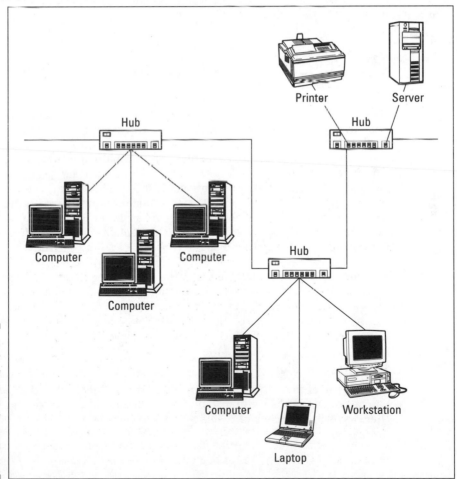

Figure 3-4:
The star topology used with the bus topology (called a star-bus topology).

A network cable can also be terminated by a connection to another network cable with a bridge, a router, or another connectivity device. Each network cable in this situation is known as a network *segment*. Two computers on the same cable are on the same segment. Two computers on two different cables may be on the same network, but are on separate network segments.

Continuity

As long as a bus network's cable is terminated at each end, the network continues to function. If one of the nodes on the network fails, the network cable is operable as long as its cable connections are intact. This statement *doesn't* mean that any problems caused by the failed node will magically disappear; it only means that the network cable is still okay.

For this reason, among others, the star-bus topology is used to connect nodes to the backbone through a clustering device, such as a hub or multi-station access unit (MAU). Should the attached cluster fail, there is little or no effect on the remainder of the network.

Won't you wear my ring around your net?

Token ring networks, although not as popular as the bus or star-bus topologies, are quite common and supported by Cisco Internetworking devices. IBM has developed and popularized the token ring technology that is used for virtually all ring topology networks. Other Ring structures, such as Apple Computer's TokenTalk, are available, but the vast majority of them are token ring. The ring topology looks like a, well, like a ring (refer to Figure 3-3). What can you say? The primary network cable forms a loop that, in effect, has no beginning or end. This eliminates any termination problems on the network. Signals placed on the network cable travel around the ring from node to node until they reach the correct destination. In reality, a ring structure rarely is installed in a perfectly round shape (but then, I'll bet that you knew that).

In contrast to the bus topology, the ring topology is an *active* topology. Each node on the ring network receives the signal, examines it, and then regenerates it onto the network (if the signal was not meant for that node). As a result, when a computer on the network is unable to regenerate the signal, the entire network is affected and continuity is lost.

Passing the token

Have you ever been to a meeting in which some object is used to control who can talk? For example, suppose that at a meeting, all the participants arrange themselves in a circle and pass a pine bough around the circle. Whoever is holding the pine bough is allowed to share his or her thoughts on how to solve the group's dilemma or share his or her opinions on a particular topic. If everyone follows the basic sharing rules, that only the person holding the sappy stick can speak, order is maintained, and everyone gets a turn. Well, as lame as it may sound for holding a group discussion, this concept works very nicely for the ring topology. However, instead of a pine bough, the object passed around is called a *token,* which is much like an electronic hall pass. Only the node possessing the token can transmit on the network. Believe it or not, this process is called *token passing.*

As on a bus network, only one network node — the node holding the token — can send data at a time. A node proves that it has the token by embedding it in the message it sends over the ring network. None of the other nodes can send messages to the network because they don't have the token and cannot access it. The destination node, the node to which the original message was addressed, must include the token in its response to the sending node. When it has completed its session, the sender releases the token to the network, and the next node wishing to send a message over the network picks it up.

Continuity

Any breakdown on the ring network impacts its continuity. This impact is one reason why genuine ring networks are rarely implemented. More often than not, a ring network uses some form of mixed topology, such as a star-ring. (See the next two sections for more information on mixed topologies.)

I want to see stars!

Once upon a time, terminals were directly connected to mainframes, each with its own piece of wire resulting in a configuration that had the wires emanating from the central unit like a starburst. Ah, the good old days! This same configuration is the basis for the *star topology* in which network nodes are directly connected to the central server.

The star topology is a case of good news and bad news. The good news is that if one node goes down, the rest of the network won't even know about it. The bad news is that if the server goes down, the entire network goes down, which is one of the big reasons that this topology is rarely, if ever, used as the foundation topology for an entire network.

However, the star topology is used to improve the configuration and performance of both the bus and ring topologies, creating the star-bus and the star-ring topologies. (See the next section for more information on these mixed topologies.)

Mixed topologies

The star topology is more commonly used today to cluster workstations on bus or ring networks. This clustering creates hybrid or mixed topologies, such as the star-bus and the star-ring:

- **Star-bus:** A hub is used as a clustering device that is attached to the network backbone (refer to Figure 3-4). This is the most common topology of Ethernet networks.

- **Star-ring:** This is also called the *ringed-star* (not to be confused with a Ringo Starr). A multistation access unit (MAU) is used to group workstations into a cluster. The MAU is interconnected to the next MAU in line to complete the ring. The star-ring topology is the most common form used for ring (token ring) networks.

Applying LAN Technologies

Each of the most commonly used network topologies — bus, star, and ring (see "Please Accept My Topologies," earlier in this chapter) — is the basis for the standard LAN technologies used to define and implement local area networks. The three common LAN technologies are

- Ethernet
- Token ring
- Fiber Distributed Data Interface (FDDI)

Working with an Ethernet network

An Ethernet network, the most popular networking technology in use, is by definition built on a bus topology operating on baseband rates of 10 Mbps, 100 Mbps, or 1,000 Mbps (1 Gbps). However, in actual use, Ethernet networks are usually implemented on a star-bus topology with either 10 Mbps or 100 Mbps of bandwidth.

The advantages of Ethernets

The main advantage of building an Ethernet network is that the components needed are readily available and relatively inexpensive. This situation is the result of Ethernet's popularity. It may be a case of the chicken and the egg as to which came first: that Ethernet is popular because it is cheap and easy, or that Ethernet is cheap and easy because it's so popular. There's no doubt that Ethernet is popular. I believe that its popularity is a result of these facts: It is easily implemented and administered; virtually all operating systems and network devices support it; and it's vendor and platform-independent.

Broadband versus baseband

Here's a brief definition of broadband and baseband signaling:

✔ **Baseband networks** use only one channel to support digital transmissions. Most LANs are baseband networks.

✔ **Broadband networks** use analog signaling over a wide range of frequencies. This type

of network is unusual, but many cable companies are now offering high-speed Internet network access over broadband systems. Broadband services include such things as LMDS (Local Multipoint Distribution Services) and DSL (Digital Subscriber Lines).

Another advantage of Ethernet is that the technology has few limitations beyond those imposed by the network cable itself (see Chapter 4). Also, Ethernet's relatively simple installation, maintenance, and expansion make it a good choice.

When an Ethernet network is installed by using the bus-star topology, losing one hub-based cluster has no direct effect on the rest of the network, beyond the fact that any node attached to the missing hub is now not addressable.

The disadvantages of Ethernets

Ethernets can be tricky to troubleshoot, especially if the network has not been built with troubleshooting in mind. Networks installed on UTP (unshielded twisted-pair) cable are limited to cable lengths of around 100 meters and are limited to the number of repeater segments that can be effectively supported on a network. A *repeater segment* is a portion of the network that is beyond a repeater placed on a network cable to extend its signal length. These distance limitations can also be solved with Cisco switches and routers, which also include repeater functions. Media distance limitations can become troublesome when growing or updating a *legacy network* (an existing network that uses pre-existing technology).

In its simplest form, an Ethernet network is installed in a daisy-chain form (see Figure 3-5) with each node connected to the next to create the backbone. In this arrangement, common to thin coaxial cable installations, when one node goes down, any nodes beyond the down node can't be reached. On a bus topology, nodes connect to the backbone by tapping into the backbone along its path (see Figure 3-6). In this arrangement, should a node fail, the other nodes are unaffected. This arrangement is one very good reason why the pure bus topology, as opposed to the daisy-chain form, is used on Ethernet networks. However, you'll find that few networks implement the bus topology in its purest form. Most Ethernet networks, like the one shown in Figure 3-6, are implemented using a star-bus hybrid approach. The star is formed to an intermediary device, like the hub in Figure 3-6, but the overall topology is very much a bus structure.

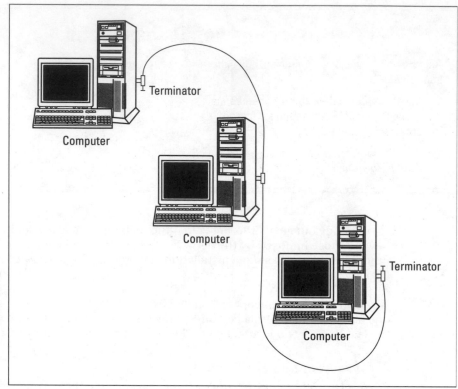

Figure 3-5:
An Ethernet
network
created in a
daisy-chain
pattern.

When Ethernet networks get really busy, the network can become congested by colliding messages, despite the best attempts of CSMA/CD (see "Policing the Ethernet" in this section) to prevent it from happening. So an Ethernet network will surge and recede in waves of activity followed by periods of nodes waiting to send, and on and on. The Ethernet network administrator's life is spent figuring out ways to prevent this from happening.

Policing the Ethernet

The mechanism used on a network technology to control access to the network media and to prevent message collisions is called an *access method*. The access method used by Ethernet networks is *CSMA/CD (Carrier Sense Multiple Access/Collision Detection)*. Under CSMA/CD, when a station wishes to send information over the network, it listens to see whether other stations are broadcasting. If the network is not in use, the station sends its message. On occasion, two stations may broadcast at the same time, and a collision occurs. When this happens, each station retransmits its message by using a back-off algorithm that specifies a period of time that each workstation should wait before retransmitting. Each network node examines all network traffic, looking for messages addressed to that node. If the message is addressed to a particular node, the node processes it accordingly; otherwise, the message is ignored.

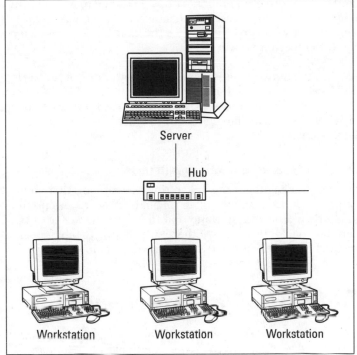

Ring around the token ring network

Typically, token ring networks operate at either 4 Mbps or 16 Mbps, but 100 Mbps token ring is available (and 1000 Mbps token ring is being tested). Logically, token ring networks are laid out in a loop that starts and ends at the same node, forming a ring — hence its name.

In contrast to the processes used on an Ethernet network, a token ring node receives messages only from its *nearest active upstream neighbor (NAUN)* and sends signals to its *nearest active downstream neighbor (NADN)*. Like Ethernets, though, token ring networks are implemented in a mixed star-ring topology in which each station is connected to an MAU, and MAUs are connected together to actually form the ring.

The access method used for a token ring network is token passing. In this method, only the workstation possessing the token is allowed to transmit on the network. As the workstation completes its tasks, it places the token on the network for another node to use.

The advantages of a token ring network

The largest single advantage of a token ring network, especially when created with nodes clustered on MAUs, is that when a node fails, the network is still alive and well. Another commonly cited advantage to a token ring structure is the reduced chance for message collision. The token passing access method used on ring networks greatly reduces the chances for message collisions as compared to Ethernet networks.

To speed up the network, most new implementations of token ring now support 16 Mbps (as compared to the older standard of 4 Mbps). Some now support two tokens alive on the network at the same time, to really speed things up. However, the tokens must circle the network in the same direction to avoid collisions.

The disadvantages of a token ring network

Some of the disadvantages of a token ring network are that equipment for token ring networks, because token ring networks are less popular, tends to be just a little more expensive and that their top-end speed is 16 Mbps. Compared to 100 Mbps for Fast Ethernet, and now Gigabit-speed Ethernet, the speed of the token ring network is downright slow.

FDDI is a double-ring ceremony

FDDI (Fiber Distributed Data Interface) is an *ANSI (American National Standards Institute)* standard that defines a dual-ring technology that operates at 100 Mbps over fiber-optic cabling. FDDI is not nearly as popular as Ethernet or token ring, but it is a particular favorite of Cisco and is included in its literature and white papers quite often.

FDDI is better suited for networks that operate over large geographic areas in electronically hostile environments (or for networks that have large bandwidth demands) because it is implemented on fiber-optic media and uses high data-transmission rates. FDDI employs two attached and interconnected rings that operate independently, which give FDDI systems a built-in media redundancy (which means they have built-in backup cabling) that can be applied when one or more ring segments fail. FDDI, and its newer cousin CDDI (Copper Distributed Data Interface), are used primarily to interconnect departmental or building LANs on a corporate or collegiate campus.

Chapter 4

Stringing It All Together

• •

• •

In spite of the fact that our world is fast becoming mostly a wireless one, most networks continue to be on cable and wired infrastructures. The security and reliability of a good, solid piece of copper over which to send your data almost can't be beat. I still feel this way, even after being totally indoctrinated to the virtues and wonders of wireless media during my stint with a wireless communications company.

The wireless technologies available for local area networks are maturing. But then, so are fiber-optic and copper wire technologies. I suggest that until wireless becomes cost and functionally competitive with physical media, which shouldn't be too awfully far in the future, the hard stuff will remain king.

Perhaps more important than a network's operating system or topology, the physical medium sets the maximum data transmission speed, the network's overall distance, the number and type of connectivity devices required, and the number of devices the network can support. For this reason, any network administrator worth his or her weight in RJ-45 connectors must be familiar with network media. You don't need to be an expert, but you should know the construction and best use of the most common cable and media types and be able to identify them by sight. No sweat, you say! Well, you also should know their characteristics, limitations, advantages and disadvantages, and the conditions under which each type of cable is an appropriate choice for a network. Piece of cake!

The Fascinating World of Cables

Three materials are primarily used to produce the cables used in local area networks: copper, glass, and plastic. Yes, I mean the same stuff used to make pennies, windows, and soda pop bottles. All three are relatively inexpensive and abundant, but more important, they are also excellent conductors. Copper is an excellent conductor of electricity, and glass and plastic are excellent conduits for light. This situation works out very well, because electricity and electricity converted into light are why you need cables in the first place.

Network cables or radio waves over which data is transmitted are referred to as the *network media,* which is a plural term. When referring to a single type of cable installed in a single network (for example copper cabling), the cable is called the *network's medium* or, more formally, the *transmission medium.* Just didn't want these terms to throw you.

For one computer to communicate with another computer, a transmission medium must be available over which the electrical impulses that represent commands and data can be transmitted. In a networked environment, the computers and peripherals must be interconnected through some form of media so that data can be exchanged and resources can be shared. Cabling and wiring have laid (pun intended) the foundation on which networks have grown — literally.

The big four of cabling

Four network media types are available today: coaxial cable, twisted-pair cable, fiber-optic cable, and wireless networking (see "Working Without a Wire," later in this chapter). Tracing back in history, other media types (such as smoke, mirror flashes, drums, sneakers, and others) have been used for networking, but these have largely proven ineffective for modern networks. For purposes of our discussions here, I focus on only the three physical media types, leaving the wireless discussion to later:

- **Coaxial (coax) cable:** This cable type is a little like the cable used to connect your television set to the cable outlet. Coax cable for networks comes in two varieties: thick coaxial cable and thin coaxial cable. Both are explained later in the chapter.

- **Twisted-pair:** (And no, I don't mean the upstairs neighbors.) Twisted-pair cable comes in two flavors, unshielded twisted-pair (UTP) and shielded twisted-pair (STP) cables. UTP is very similar to the wiring used to connect your telephone. These are also explained later in the chapter.

- **Fiber-optic:** Glass or plastic fibers carry modulated pulses of light to represent digital data signals. Several different types of fiber-optic cables exist, but they are generally referred to as a group called fiber-optic cable.

The technical stuff about cables

All network cabling has a set of general characteristics to guide you in selecting the right cable for a given situation. These cable media characteristics are important:

- **Bandwidth (speed):** Bandwidth is the amount of data that a cable can carry in a certain period. It is often expressed as the number of bits (either Kilobits or Megabits) that can be transmitted in a second. For example, UTP cable is nominally rated at 10 Mbps, or 10 million bits per second.

- **Cost:** Cost is always a major consideration when choosing a cable type. Look at this relative cost comparison for the major cable media:

    - **Twisted-pair cable** is the least expensive, but it has limitations that require other hardware to be installed.

    - **Coaxial cable** is a little more expensive than twisted-pair cable, but it doesn't require additional equipment, and it's inexpensive to maintain.

    - **Fiber-optic cabling** is the most expensive, requires skilled installation labor, and is expensive to install and maintain.

- **Maximum segment length:** Every cable is subject to a condition called *attenuation,* which means the signal weakens and can no longer be recognized. Every type of cable has a different distance at which attenuation occurs. This distance (measured in meters) is a cable medium's *maximum segment length,* or the distance at which signals on the cable must be regenerated.

- **Maximum number of nodes per segment:** Each time a device is added to a network, the effect is like putting hole in the cable. Like leaks from pinholes in a balloon, too many devices attached to a network cable reduce the distance at which attenuation begins. So each type of cable must limit the number of nodes that can be attached to a cable segment.

- **Interference resistance:** Different cable media have varying vulnerability to electromagnetic interference (EMI) or radio frequency interference (RFI) caused by electric motors, florescent light fixtures, your magnet collection, the radio station on the next floor, and so on. As the construction of the cable and its cladding (coverings) varies, so does its resistance to EMI and RFI signals.

Table 4-1 shows the standard characteristics of the most commonly used network cable types.

Table 4-1	Cable Types and Their Characteristics			
Cable Type	*Bandwidth*	*Max. Segment Length*	*Max. Nodes per Segment*	*Interference Resistance*
Thin coaxial	10 Mbps	185 meters	30	Good
Thick coaxial	10 Mbps	500 meters	100	Better
UTP	10–1000 Mbps	100 meters	1024	Poor
STP	10–1000 Mbps	100 meters	1024	Fair to Good
Fiber-optic	100–10000 Mbps	80 kilometers	No limit	Best

Coaxial Cables through Thick and Thin

Although recently deposed as the ruling network cable type, coaxial cable is still a popular choice for networks. It is inexpensive, easy to work with, reliable, and moderately resistant to interference, which makes it a good choice in many situations, such as in environments with a lot of electrical equipment or instances where longer segment runs are needed.

Coaxial cable is constructed with a single solid copper wire core, which is surrounded by an insulator made of plastic or Teflon material. A braided metal shielding layer (and, in some cables, another metal foil layer) covers the insulator, and a plastic sheath wrapper covers the cable. The metal shielding layers act to increase the cable's resistance to EMI and RFI signals. Figure 4-1 illustrates the construction of a coaxial cable.

The Institute of Electrical and Electronics Engineers (IEEE) 802 Project defines coaxial cable as either thick or thin. Coaxial cable is used primarily in Ethernet networking environments, where it is also referred to as *Thicknet* and *Thinnet.* Other aliases coaxial cable goes by are the generic "coax," *10Base5, thickwire,* and *yellow wire* (all nicknames for thick coaxial cable), and *10Base2, thinwire,* and *cheapnet* (aliases for thin coaxial cable).

What's this 10Base stuff?

In the Ethernet world, as defined by the IEEE 802 standards, the designation of cable is also descriptive of its characteristics. Thick coax cable is designated as 10Base5; thin coaxial cable is designated as 10Base2; and UTP and STP are generally designated as 10BaseT.

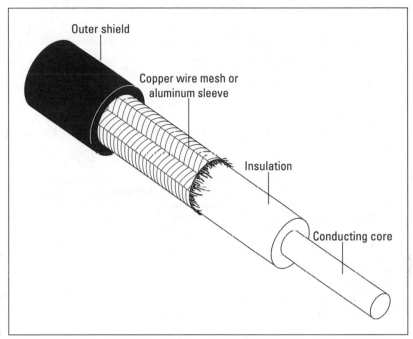

Outer shield

Copper wire mesh or
aluminum sleeve

Insulation

Conducting core

Figure 4-1:
The layers
of a coaxial
cable.

The *10Base* part indicates that these cables carry 10 Mbps bandwidths and use baseband, as opposed to broadband, signals. (See Chapter 1 for an explanation of baseband and broadband.) For a coax cable, the 5 and the 2 mean 500 meters and 200 meters, respectively. These distances are the approximate maximum segment length of the cable. Actually, the maximum segment length of thin coax is 185 meters, but 200 works better in this case (and besides, it's easier to remember than 10Base1.85). The T in 10BaseT refers to "twisted-pair" cable. See "The Ethernet Cable Standards," later in this chapter, for more information.

The coaxial couple has one additional designation: Thick coax is also designated as RG-11 or RG-8 and thin coax as RG-58. (The coax used for television service is RG-59, by the way.) The RG stands for Radio/Government and is the rating of the cable based upon the type and thickness of its core wire.

Does this cable make me look fat?

Thick coax is the more rigid of the coaxial twins (fraternal, no doubt). Thick coax is about 1 centimeter (about .4 inches) in diameter and is commonly covered in a bright yellow Teflon covering (the origin of its "yellow wire" nickname). Its thicker hide makes it more resistant to interference and attenuation, resulting in a longer segment length and the ability to support a greater number of nodes on a segment compared to its thinner sibling.

Connecting thick coaxial cable to workstations is a fairly complicated, simple process. What I mean is that it really is simple, but it is complicated to explain. An external transceiver attached to a piercing connector (appropriately called a "vampire" tap) is clamped onto the thickwire, making a connection that pierces to the central core wire. Then a transceiver cable (called a *drop cable*) is used to connect a computer's network adapter with an AUI (attached unit interface) connector, which is a XX-pin connector used to connect external transceivers to a network adapter in a computer. Figure 4-2 illustrates how simple this really is, despite our convoluted description. Table 4-2 lists the characteristics of thick coaxial cable.

Table 4-2	Thick Coaxial Cable Characteristics
Characteristic	*Value*
Maximum segment length	500 meters (about 1,640 feet)
Bandwidth (speed)	10 Mbps
Number of nodes per segment	100
Connector type	AUI (attached unit interface)
Resistance to Interference	Good

The thinner side of coax

In contrast to its thicker relative, thin coaxial cable is lightweight and flexible. It is about .2 inches in diameter and is easily installed. After UTP, this is the second most popular type of network cabling. Thinnet, its more popular nickname, is used to "daisy chain" computers together by using BNC-T connectors, a sample of which is shown in Figure 4-3. As is shown in Figure 4-4, thin coax cable runs between each network node, connecting one workstation to the next. The characteristics of thin coaxial cable are summarized in Table 4-3.

Table 4-3	Thin Coaxial Cable Characteristics
Characteristic	*Value*
Maximum segment length	185 meters (a little over 600 feet)
Bandwidth (speed)	10 Mbps
Number of nodes per segment	30
Connector type	BNC
Resistance to Interference	Good

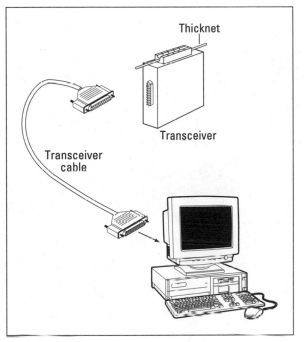

Figure 4-2:
Thick coax
cable is
connected
to an
external
transceiver
which is
then
connected
with a patch
cable to the
computer.

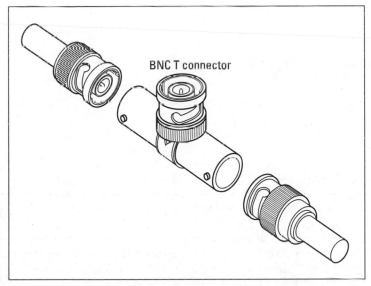

Figure 4-3:
A BNC-T
connector.

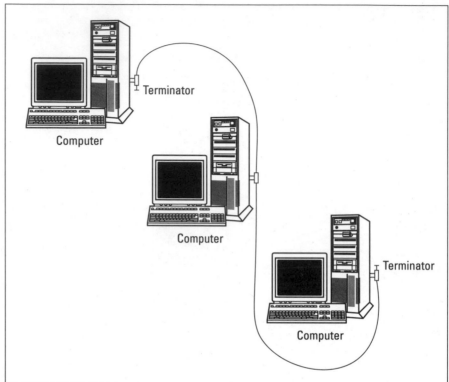

Figure 4-4:
An Ethernet
using
Thinnet
cable.

The Twisted Pair

Although it sounds like the bad title of an even worse movie, the most popular cabling in use for local area networks is twisted-pair copper wire. This media type has all of the attributes to be truly popular: It is the lightest, most flexible, least expensive, and easiest to install of any of the popular network media. The bad news is that it is also vulnerable to interference and has attenuation problems as well. *Interference* is the electrical noise that copper cabling picks up from other wires or electrical devices near it. (A good example is what happens to the TV sometimes when the vacuum cleaner is running.) A signal running through a copper wire begins to lose its strength after a certain distance. This situation is caused by the resistance in the wire (friction, bouncing molecules, and so on). This condition is called *attenuation*. But, given the right network design and implementation, problems like interference and attenuation are easily overcome.

Two types of twisted-pair wire are used in networks: unshielded (UTP) and shielded (STP), as shown in Figure 4-5. Of the two, UTP is the most commonly used and is very popular on Ethernets. STP wire is common on token ring networks and in environments where its shielding is required to protect the cable from electrical noise and other interference.

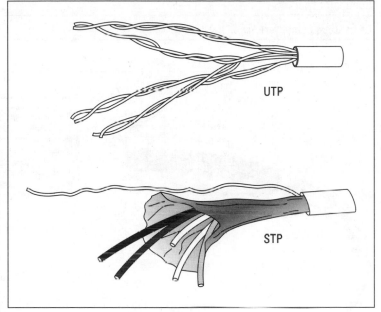

Figure 4-5:
Unshielded
(top) and
shielded
twisted-pair
(bottom)
cables.

Unshielded is not unheralded

Unshielded twisted-pair wire is just about what its name implies — two unshielded wires twisted together. UTP, commonly referred to as *10BaseT,* is the most common type of cabling used in networks. For all of the reasons discussed in the previous section, it provides the most installation flexibility and ease of maintenance of the big three cabling media types. UTP uses an RJ-45 connector (as shown in Figure 4-6), which looks very much like the little clip connector on your telephone, only a little bigger. (RJ stands for Registered Jack.) Table 4-4 summarizes the characteristics of UTP cable.

Table 4-4	Unshielded Twisted-Pair Cable Characteristics
Characteristic	*Value*
Maximum segment length	100 meters (not much over 320 feet)
Bandwidth (speed)	10-100 Mbps
Number of nodes per segment	1,024

(continued)

Table 4-4 *(continued)*

Characteristic	Value
Connector type	RJ-45
Resistance to Interference	Poor

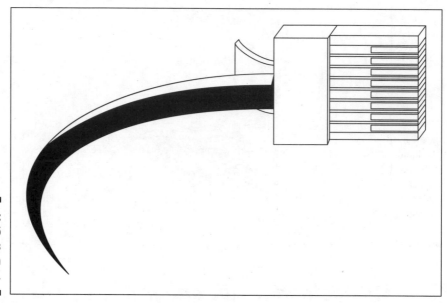

Figure 4-6:
An RJ-45
connector is
used with
UTP cable.

IEEE 802 groups UTP cable into five categories, or "Cats" as the real techies
call them (as in Cat 3, Cat 4, Cat 5, and so on):

- ✔ **Category 1 and 2** — not used in networking. (These aren't here and you
  didn't see them, but if I left them out, you'd be wondering where they
  were, right?)

- ✔ **Category 3** — a four-pair cable supporting bandwidths up to 10 Mbps
  and the minimum standard for 10BaseT networks.

- ✔ **Category 4** — a four-pair cable commonly used in 16 Mbps token ring
  networks.

- ✔ **Category 5** — a four-pair cable with bandwidths up to 1000 Mbps, used
  for 10BaseT, 100BaseTX, 1000BaseTX, CDDI (Copper Distributed Data
  Interchange), and ATM (asynchronous transfer mode) networking.

- ✔ **Category 6** — a new cable specification and connector proposal for a
  four-pair unshielded twisted-pair cable that supports bandwidths as
  high as gigabit speeds, although no specific standards or applications
  have been defined yet.

✔ **Category 7** — a new cable specification and connector proposal being developed for a fully shielded (which means each pair is shielded as well as the entire cable) four-pair twisted-pair cable. At the time I wrote this, no specific applications were defined for Cat 7, but I didn't want to leave it out for fear that it may become very important later.

Several developers are working feverishly to perfect the transceivers, NIC, and connectivity devices that will allow 10 Gbps Ethernet to run over copper twisted-pair cabling. This may be where Cat 6 or Cat 7 cable may fit into the overall scheme of things, but I'm sure that 10GbE (Gigabit Ethernet) over Cat 5 wire can't be too far off.

Leading a shielded life

The other half of the twisted-pair twins is shielded twisted-pair (STP). The best way to tell UTP from STP is that STP is the one with each of its wire pairs wrapped in a grounded copper or foil wrapper. This interference protection helps shield the internal copper wires from interference and helps STP support higher transmission speeds over longer distances, but it also makes STP more expensive than UTP.

The cable categories (Cat 3, Cat 5, and the like) listed earlier (see "Unshielded is not unheralded," earlier in the chapter) are not limited just to unshielded cable. You can also find and purchase STP versions of Cat 3 and Cat 5 cable, and Cat 7 cable is only a shielded cable specification.

STP is most commonly used in token ring networks. In fact, IBM has its own standards for twisted-pair cable for ring networks. The IBM cable standard includes nine categories that range from a two-pair shielded cable (Type 1) to a UTP cable (Type 3), a fiber-optic cable (Type 5), and a fire-safe cable (Type 9).

You Need Your Fiber

Data is carried over fiber-optic cables in the form of modulated pulses of light. To demonstrate how the data is represented as modulated light pulses, you need a dark room, a friend, and a flashlight. Stand in a dark room facing your friend. Now switch the flashlight on and off at the rate of a million times in a second. Although the fiber-optic cable actually uses a faster rate than this, this rate is adequate to demonstrate the technology in use. The friend? I'm told that outside in the real world, even network administrators have friends. At least, I've been lead to believe that.

Fiber in general

The core of fiber-optic cable consists of two or more extremely thin strands of glass or plastic. An opaque glass or plastic cladding covers each strand, helping to keep the light traveling through the strand and in the strand. The strands are capable of carrying signals in both directions, but as you may have guessed, in only one direction at a time. The glass or plastic core (cladding and strands) is then covered by a plastic outer jacket. Figure 4-7 shows the construction of a fiber-optic cable.

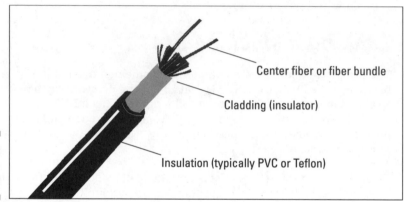

Center fiber or fiber bundle

Cladding (insulator)

Insulation (typically PVC or Teflon)

Figure 4-7:
Fiber-optic
cable.

Because fiber-optic uses light and not electrical signals, fiber-optic cable is not susceptible to electromagnetic (EMI) or radio frequency (RFI) interference. This (and also the very high purity of the glass or plastic) gives fiber-optic cables incredibly long attenuation and maximum segment lengths. Fiber-optic cable is commonly used for network backbones. Table 4-5 lists the most important characteristics of fiber-optic cable.

Table 4-5	Fiber-Optic Cable Characteristics
Characteristic	*Value*
Maximum segment length	up to 80 kilometers (a little less than 50 miles) using single mode cable
Bandwidth (speed)	10 Mbps to 40 Gbps, depending on the fiber type.
Resistance to Interference	Excellent

Single mode and MultiMode fiber

Fiber optic cable can either be single mode or multimode. The mode type indicates the transmission method used to transmit those tiny bursts of light through the cable. Here's a brief description of each:

- ✔ **Single mode fiber optic cable (SMF):** This type of fiber optic cable is also known as monomode fiber. SMF cable has very thin strands of glass or plastic at its core, which do not allow light bursts to spread out (disperse). This translates to faster speeds and longer distances.

- ✔ **MultiMode fiber optic cable (MMF):** MMF cable has a thicker core strand that allows the light bursts to disperse to the outer edges of the core (and even into the cladding covering the cable), which can cause some parts of the data stream to arrive at the far end of the cable at different times. The longer the cable, the more this can happen, which is why MMF cable is normally best used for shorter distances, such as a LAN or FDDI application.

The Ethernet Cable Standards

Ethernet cable is referred to by a descriptive name, for example 10BaseT, which includes its bandwidth/speed, transmission mode, and a number or letter representing its segment length (coaxial cable) or cable type. Table 4-6 breaks down the meaning of the most common Ethernet cable designations. The "10Base" part of each standard indicates that it supports a 10 Mbps transmission speed and uses a baseband transmission mode.

Table 4-6	Basic Ethernet Cable Standards	
Cable	*Maximum Distance*	*Cable Material*
10Base2	185 meters (the 2 is for approximately 200)	Thinnet coaxial
10Base5	500 meters (the 5 is for 500 meters)	Thicknet coaxial
10BaseF	2 kilometers	MMF fiber-optic
10BaseT	100 meters	UTP

In addition to the standards listed in Table 4-6, the 10BaseF and 10BaseT standards have a few variations, these being the most commonly used standards:

- ✔ **100BaseT:** A four-wire 100 Mbps technology usually installed on Cat 5 wiring. This and 100BaseX are the generic terms for four-wire Fast Ethernet.

- **100BaseT4:** A specification for four-wire Fast Ethernet that is very similar to 100BaseT, but uses a different interface circuitry.

- **100BaseFX:** Fast Ethernet using two-strand fiber-optic cable.

- **100BaseVG (voice grade):** A 100 Mbps standard over Category 3 cable.

- **100BaseVG-AnyLAN:** Hewlett Packard's proprietary version of 100BaseVG.

- **1000BaseTx:** Gigabit Ethernet (GbE) over twisted-pair cable.

- **1000BaseFX and 10GbE:** GbE and 10GbE over fiber-optic cable.

I mention the 100VG and AnyLAN specifications only so you will know what they are should you encounter them in your research. In the Cisco world, the 100VG modules are now EOS (end of service/support) or EOL (end of product life), which means they are no longer supported, have limited support, or no longer sold.

Working without a Wire

Wireless LANs provide all of the same benefits of a wired LAN, plus a few extras. On a wireless LAN, users (especially roaming users) can access shared information without looking for a place to plug in, and the network administrator can set up or augment networks without the need to install or move wires, connectors, or furniture. Often, when a facility simply cannot support the installation of network cabling, wireless network technology is the best way to go.

The primary thing you should know about wireless networking is that it uses radio frequency (RF) or infrared light to transmit data between two points on a network. Beyond that, a wireless network functions essentially the same as a wired network. The data packets are formatted, and the layers of the OSI

Baseband versus broadband

Here's a brief definition of baseband and broadband signaling:

- **Baseband networks** use only one channel to support digital transmissions. Most LANs are baseband networks.

- **Broadband networks** use analog signaling over a wide range of frequencies. This type

of network is unusual, but many cable companies are now offering high-speed Internet network access over broadband systems. Broadband services include such things as LMDS (Local Multipoint Distribution Services) and DSL (Digital Subscriber Lines).

model and the standard protocols are still in use. One important difference though is that wireless data is formatted using the 802.11 standard, which is different from the 802.3 standard used on wired networks.

According to the folks who produce wireless LAN systems, a wireless LAN offers a number of productivity, convenience, and cost advantages over a traditional wired network:

- ✔ **Mobility:** LAN users can access information from anywhere in the organization without the need to plug in to a network connector.

- ✔ **Installation ease:** You don't have to pull cable through the floor, walls, or ceiling to a new network station.

- ✔ **Flexibility:** The network can go where the wire can't.

- ✔ **Cost:** This is where some debate exists, but the wireless folks say that, although the initial investment may be higher for a wireless LAN than for a wired network, the overall installation and operating expenses can be much lower than those of a wired network. The reasoning is that the expenses involved with moving, adding, and changing workstation locations are virtually eliminated.

- ✔ **Scalability:** Changing the topology or configuration of a wireless LAN is easily done. A wireless LAN can be configured anywhere from a peer-to-peer network for a small number of users to a full infrastructure network with thousands of users.

The technical stuff about wireless networks

A range of technologies, each with its own set of advantages and limitations, is used with wireless LANs. The most common of the wireless network technologies are spread-spectrum, narrowband, and infrared.

Spreading out the spectrum

Most wireless LANs use the *spread-spectrum technology (SST),* which is a wideband radio frequency (RF) technique. Spread-spectrum was originally developed by the military as a reliable and secure communications system. It trades off bandwidth efficiency for reliability and security, which means that more bandwidth is needed to transmit data than is needed for a narrowband type of network. However, SST results in a signal that is easier to detect, provided that the system is properly tuned.

Spread-spectrum technologies come in two varieties:

- **Frequency-hopping spread-spectrum technology (FHSST):** This type of SST changes frequency in a pattern recognized by both transmitter and receiver that, when the sending and receiving devices are properly synchronized, results in a single logical channel. To receivers that don't know the pattern, the transmission looks like background noise.

- **Direct-sequence spread-spectrum technology (DSSST):** This wideband form of SST uses a redundant bit pattern, called a *chipping code,* for each bit that is transmitted. Statistical techniques in the RF equipment, which are able to determine the data, reduce the need for retransmission of damaged data. To a narrowband radio, DSSST signals appear to be low-power wideband noise and are ignored.

The straight and narrowband

Narrowband radios transmit and receive data by using a specific radio frequency, keeping the radio frequency as narrow as possible. *Crosstalk* (where one channel picks up noise from another channel) between communications channels is avoided by coordinating different users on different channel frequencies.

A radio frequency is very much like a private telephone line. When you are talking on your phone, your neighbors cannot usually listen to your conversation (unless, of course, they are very snoopy and have special equipment). Using a different frequency for each user on a network accomplishes this same privacy and noninterference. The radio receiver filters out all radio signals except the ones on its designated frequency.

Lighting up infrared technology

Infrared (IR) systems use very high frequencies that are just below visible light in the electromagnetic spectrum to carry data. Unlike RF signals, but like light, IR signals cannot penetrate solid objects and must use a *line-of-sight (LoS)*. Line-of-sight is also called *diffuse,* or *reflective,* technology. Most inexpensive systems are LoS, offer a very limited range (between 3 to 30 feet), and mostly are used for what are called Personal Area Networks (PANs). (See "Wiring up a personal area network," later in the chapter.) A PAN can be created around a single computer to connect peripheral devices (such as a keyboard, mouse, and printer) via IR technology. Higher performance IR systems are used primarily to implement fixed wireless subnetworks. A diffuse IR LAN does not require line-of-sight to the radio units (called *cells*), but its range is generally limited to an individual room. In fact, wireless technologies, like infrared (IR) and radio frequency (RF) technologies, are referred to as *cable replacement technologies.*

Installing a wireless LAN

Wireless technology can be applied at two levels in a LAN: to create one or more segments on the network or to create a personal area network at a user's workstation. Cisco has incorporated Wireless LANs (WLAN) into its networking world.

Another Ethernet standard

To recognize and standardize the emergence of wireless technologies, the IEEE developed the 802.11 standard to cover the use of wireless devices to install all or part of an Ethernet network. The 802.11 standard has two primary parts:

- **IEEE 802.11a:** This standard covers wireless networks that use the Unlicensed National Information Infrastructure (U-NII — pronounced as "you-nee") band at 5Ghz as its Physical layer medium. The 802.11a technology, because of its longer range, is more typically used to interconnect distant buildings of a LAN, with LoS of course, or to provide a high bandwidth WAN service.

- **IEEE 802.11b:** This standard covers wireless networks that transmit over the *Industrial, Scientific, and Medical (ISM) band* at 2.4Ghz. This is the most commonly used band for most wireless applications, including wireless Internet access, WLANs, and even some two-way radios. However, this band is also used for many consumer devices, such as portable telephones and baby monitors.

Wireless LAN technology is used more often to add to an existing network rather than replace a wired network. However, WLAN technology is being used more and more to install new networks where it makes the most sense. Wireless technology is still a bit more expensive than (and not quite as fast as) its wired relative, so its use must be considered carefully and justified.

Wireless LAN configurations

In its most basic form, a wireless LAN is two computers with wireless network adapter cards communicating whenever they are within range of one another, as illustrated in Figure 4-8. To be a part of a wireless network, a workstation requires a wireless network adapter, which can be installed in the same ways you would add a modem to a computer: as an expansion card, as an external peripheral device, or in a PC Card slot. Figure 4-9 shows a PC Card wireless network adapter, the kind that would be used with a notebook or other portable computer.

Figure 4-8:
A wireless
network can
be as simple
as two
portable
devices
equipped
with
wireless
network
adapters.

Figure 4-8:
A wireless
network can
be as simple
as two
portable
devices
equipped
with
wireless
network
adapters.

Portable PC   Portable PC

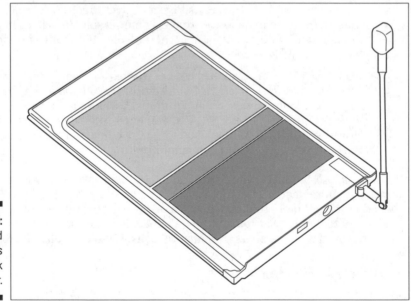

Figure 4-9:
A PC Card
wireless
network
adapter.

If you are going to employ wireless network technology, you are likely to do so on a bit larger scale than just two portable PCs. You may want the portable PCs to have access to the network server; you may want to add a new workstation to the network in an area where pulling cable would be impossible; or you may want both. The beauty of wireless networking is that both are possible.

As illustrated in Figure 4-10, adding a wireless network access point to the existing wired network can extend the range of the network for both portable and desktop devices. Because the access point is connected to the wired network, any wireless nodes connecting through it are able to access the same network resources as the wired nodes. A wireless network access point, such as the Cisco Aironet access point models, can accommodate from 1 to as many as 50 clients, depending on the traffic and nature of the transmissions involved.

Access points typically have a range of around 500 feet inside a building and about 1000 feet outside. Bear in mind, though, that the range of the wireless adapters installed in PCs is often less than 100 feet and rarely more than 300 feet. So, you have to arrange the network to provide access to the nodes, even when they are roaming around. Typically, this arrangement requires multiple access points, installed much like hubs, that must be positioned so that they provide overlapping coverage and no dead spots.

A wireless LAN is implemented as either an extension to or an alternative for a wired LAN within a single building or campus. Using electromagnetic RF or IR waves, a wireless LAN transmits and receives data through the air, eliminating or minimizing the need for wired connections. The electromagnetic waves are called *carriers* because they deliver data in the form of energy to a remote receiver. Multiple carriers can exist in the same space at the same time without interfering with each other, provided the radio waves are transmitted on different radio frequencies.

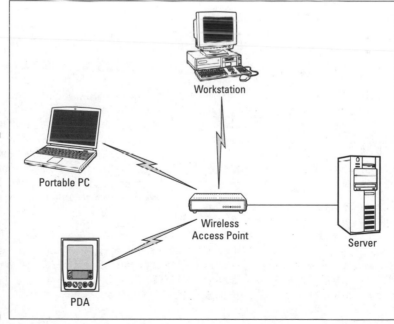

Figure 4-10:
A wireless network access point can support a fairly large number of clients, as long as they are in range.

Workstation

Portable PC

Wireless Access Point

Server

PDA

Wiring up a personal area network

The wireless technologies used to create what is called a *wireless personal area network* (WPAN) are essentially cable replacement technologies that have very limited range, which is what makes them excellent for creating a network within a personal workspace. As in wireless LANs, the primary transmission technologies are radio frequency (RF) and infrared (IR).

IR technology, as explained earlier (see "Lighting up infrared technology"), requires a line-of-sight connection and is limited to not more than 30 feet typically. The two most prominent radio wave-based networking technologies used for creating a PAN are HomeRF and Bluetooth.

Working at home

HomeRF is an acronym for an open-standard wireless personal area network technology for a radio frequency standard for short-range transmissions of digital voice and data between portable or fixed devices. HomeRF uses the 2.4Ghz band and can interconnect up to 127 devices within a range of 150 feet with a bandwidth of up to 2 Mbps. This technology is commonly used with wireless home networking kits and in many of the "intelligent" house demonstrations that enable all the home's lighting, appliances, heating, and air conditioning to be centrally controlled from your PC. (If only it would also pay for the house, it would be truly complete.)

The wireless watchdogs

Besides the IEEE, the 802.11b standard has a number of trade organizations that develop, review, and recommend new standards for wireless communications, especially in manufacturing and interoperability. The more prominent of these organizations are the following:

✔ **Wireless LAN Association (WLANA) (www.wlana.org)**: This nonprofit trade association serves as a clearinghouse for information and education on wireless LAN and personal area network technologies. Its members are most of the usual suspects, including Cisco Systems, who manufacture wireless hardware and software products for use in these applications.

✔ **Wireless Ethernet Compatibility Alliance (WECA) (www.wifi.org)**: This trade organization publishes a standard and a certification program under the name Wireless Fidelity or Wi-FI. Wireless Ethernet (802.11b) devices meeting the testing and performance criteria of the Wi-FI program can carry a certification logo, sort of a wireless electronics version of the Good Housekeeping seal.

And there is even an organization, called the Wireless Internet Service Providers Association (WISPA — www.wispa.org), for those who provide wireless Internet services.

Do you have a Bluetooth?

Bluetooth technology is a proprietary network standard managed by the Bluetooth Special Interest Group (SIG) that was originally developed by Ericsson (the Swedish cell phone company). Bluetooth is also an RF standard that supports short-range transmissions of digital voice and data between portable and fixed devices. If that sounds very much like the definition of HomeRF, it should. Bluetooth and HomeRF are variations on a theme. However, where Bluetooth differs is in its discovery and management protocols that allow devices to search and find other devices to provide it services and form ad hoc networks, which are called *piconets* in Bluetoothspeak, on the fly.

Bluetooth can support virtually an unlimited number of devices within a range of 10 meters (around 30 feet), but can be extended to 100 meters (300 feet) with a power booster. Bluetooth also uses the 2.4Ghz band and provides up to 720 Kbps in bandwidth.

So, why is it called Bluetooth? The name comes from a Danish king from the tenth century, King Blatant (Bluetooth), who Christianized the Scandinavian countries.

Getting Some Backbone (And Segments)

The Layer 1 facilities and cable that provide the entire length, or diameter, of a network that is used to interconnect all of the computers, printers, servers, access points, and other devices of the network, are called the *backbone*. Visualize the skeleton of a fish: It is the backbone to which all of the other little-catch-in-your-throat bones attach. A network backbone serves the same purpose of connecting and interconnecting all of a network's resources, only without the smell. The backbone serves as the trunk line for the entire network. Remember that the backbone is actually the conglomeration of hubs, cable, switches, patch cords, routers, bridges, and so on, that makes up the primary pathway of the network to its servers, gateways, and other points east.

In the Cisco networking world, you find two main types of backbones:

- FDDI
- Ethernet

In the context of a local area network, a *segment* is a group of workstations, servers, or devices that have been isolated on one side of a bridge or router as a part of its logical design or to improve the overall network's performance or security. However, in the context of cabling, a *segment* is a single run of cable terminated at each end.

In the fish skeleton analogy, each of the bones that emanate from the backbone would be segments, just like the cables that attach hubs, workstations, and other nodes to the backbone are cable segments. A very common technology used for network backbones is Fiber Distributed Data Interface (FDDI). FDDI is pronounced "F – D – D – I," but some people insist on pronouncing it "fiddy." Is nothing sacred? FDDI is a 100 Mbps fiber-optic network technology that uses token passing as its media access method. FDDI is usually used to form a portion of a network's trunk and is applied to move traffic around a network's trunk.

FDDI implements networks as two parallel and interconnected rings. By definition, the two rings run side-by-side around the network in parallel paths; but in reality, they may be strung together or have completely separate paths, coming together only at the points where they are connected. Workstations can be attached to one or both rings of the backbone. The two rings serve as redundant network trunks; and if one ring breaks or fails, the other ring takes over, routing around the trouble spot. If both rings are broken, the remaining pieces bond together to form a new ring. Although this feature sounds like lizard tails or space aliens, FDDI's ability to regenerate the network backbone is what makes it popular.

Ethernet is the technology most commonly used for network backbones. Because network administrators can use the same network technology throughout the network, it is safe to say that most Cisco networks use Ethernet as the overall network implementation.

Layer 1 electrical standards

Another part of creating a network's backbone is how the cable is connected together. This includes such things as wiring closets and wiring practices. All networking technicians worthy of the title spend a goodly portion of their time in a wiring closet, if for no other reason than to just marvel at the wire colors and the pretty patterns they make.

If you have never been in a wiring closet, equipment room, phone closet, or whatever it may be called in your location, where the network cabling interconnects, you should try to do so. This is where the electrical and connection standards defined on the Physical layer are applied to their fullest.

Wiring standards

The EIA/TIA standards 568A and 568B are the most widely used wiring standards for network media. These two standards detail six elements of LAN cabling:

- Telecommunications closets
- Equipment rooms

- Entrance facilities
- Work areas
- Backbone cabling
- Horizontal cabling

The portion of the 568 standards (568A and 568B) that directly impacts most networking situations is horizontal cabling. This part of the standard deals with the network media (wire, connectors, and the like) that run horizontally from the wiring closet to the workstation. Here is a summary of these standards:

- **Cable segment distances:** A maximum distance for Cat 5 UTP (unshielded twisted-pair) cable in a horizontal cabling run (segment) is 90 meters. Remember that this is not the maximum distance for Cat 5, which is 100 meters. This distance is the EIA/TIA standard for horizontal cabling runs using Cat 5 UTP.

- **Network connections:** A minimum of two telecommunications outlets in each work area.

- **Patch cords:** Shorter cables used to interconnect two devices in close proximity at the horizontal *cross-connect* (the connection that bridges the gap between the workstation cabling and the network cabling) are not to exceed 6 meters, and patch cords from the wall to the workstation should not exceed 3 meters.

- **Wiring closets:** Each floor of a building should have its own separate wiring closet. In cases where the square footage of the floor is more than 1000 square meters or the horizontal cabling is longer than 90 meters, another wiring closet should be added on the floor.

Hiding in the wiring closet

In all networks, the horizontal cabling from any network workstation must connect to the network backbone (the main network cable). Typically, this connection is made in a wiring closet and involves a cross-connect to make the connection of the workstation's cable to the network cable.

Okay, not every network requires a wiring closet. A small LAN located in a single room or in a relatively small office area can be interconnected to the network server fairly simply with a single hub or switch. However, in instances where an organization's network extends to include workstations, servers, and connectivity devices on multiple floors of a building or in multiple buildings of a campus, wiring closets become very important.

A wiring closet doesn't really need to be in a closet. In fact, all too often, what amounts to the wiring closet is actually a cluster of equipment in a corner of a room, behind a desk, or even on the administrator's desk. Having a little room in which the wiring connections can be secured behind a locked door has advantages, but this is not a prerequisite for a good cross-connect.

Connecting into a patch panel

The *cross-connect* is the connection that bridges the gap between the work-station cabling and the network cabling. A common method of creating network cross-connects is through a patch panel. A *patch panel* is like a static switchboard for the network with a number of ports that are used to connect two wires together. Figure 4-11 shows a patch panel from the front side. Each port on a patch panel has two sides: an RJ-45 (the standard twisted-pair connector) port and a punch-down block, a connector that connects each wire separately to the port. Figure 4-12 shows the two sides of a patch panel port.

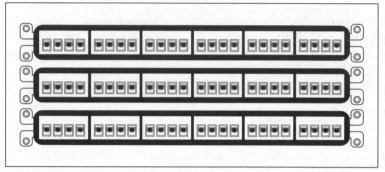

Figure 4-11: A patch panel is used to inter-connect a network's cabling.

A patch panel provides an interconnection point between incoming and outgoing lines. In a typical installation, it is used to provide an intermediary connection point for the wiring of individual workstations and a hub, switch, or other network device. A patch panel (see Figure 4-11) can have 4, 8, 16, 24, 48, or 96 jacks that have an RJ-45 jack on one side and what is called a punch-down connector on its other side (see Figure 4-12). There is no rule that requires either side of the jack to be used for any specific run of cable, which allows a patch panel and its jacks to be used at the network technician's discretion. Typically, workstation cabling is connected to the punch-down side and a short cable, called a *patch cord,* connects the patch panel jack's RJ-45 connector to the cabling that runs to the next upstream device, such as a server, LAN switch, or router. The true benefit of a patch panel in a network's wiring plant is the flexibility it provides for reconfiguration of the network on the cabling level.

Showing some backbone

As illustrated in Figure 4-13, the cabling that interconnects the various levels of cross-connects and the cross-connects themselves create what is, in effect, the network's backbone. By definition, a *network backbone* consists of a single cable that runs the entire length of the network; but in reality, this is impractical. In most larger network implementations, the network backbone consists of all cross-connect levels and the cables that interconnect them. While most networkers think of cross-connects as patch panels, they can also be hubs, switches, or even routers.

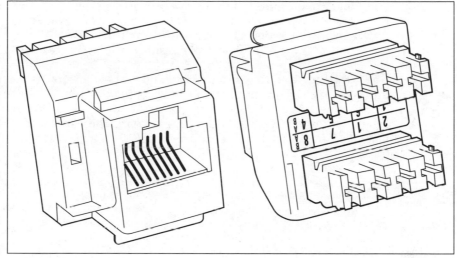

Figure 4-12:
A patch panel jack has two sides: an RJ-45 port (left) and a punch-down block (right).

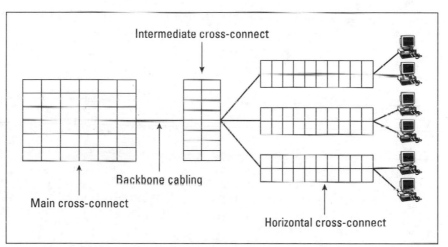

Figure 4-13:
A network's cross-connections and inter-connecting cabling can form the network's backbone.

Intermediate cross-connect

Main cross-connect

Backbone cabling

Horizontal cross-connect

The three primary cross-connect levels are illustrated in Figure 4-13. They are (listed lowest to highest):

✔ **Horizontal cross-connect:** The cross-connect level closest to the end-user's workstation. A simple passive hub can provide this level of cross-connection.

✔ **Intermediate cross-connect:** An intermediate cross-connect consolidates horizontal cross-connects. No workstations are attached to an intermediate cross-connect.

✔ **Main cross-connect:** As you have probably surmised, a main cross-connect (typically, you find only one, or at least very few, of these on a network) interconnects intermediate cross-connects. The main cross-connect is the highest level of consolidation for a network's media.

One last thing about the Physical layer and cross-connects. As you read through the Cisco documentation and white papers, you will see the various cross-connection points, especially the intermediate and main cross-connects, called *distribution facilities*. In any large network, there is at least one intermediate distribution facility (IDF) and most definitely a main distribution facility (MDF).

Part II
Cisco and the Internetwork

The 5th Wave   By Rich Tennant

"Please Dad—do we have to hear the story of Snow White's OSI model and its 7 layers again?"

In this part . . .

Many hardware components come together to make a network (see Part I), but even more logical elements give a network its life. Like Part I, this part of the book provides background information on Cisco networks, but then that's why you're here, isn't it?

Data traveling over a network must be packaged according to generally accepted and implemented standards. It also must be addressed in a way that leaves no doubt about its destination.

This part of the book looks at the more technical elements of a Cisco network, including the relationship of the OSI model to the various networking hardware, the wonders of logical addressing, and subnetting. Oh joy!

Chapter 5

Cisco and the OSI Layers

. . . .

. . . .

The OSI model (see Chapter 2) has been likened to a seven-layer cake. Each layer is separate and distinct, yet all layers are bonded to at least one other layer by the frosting. The layers of the OSI model have a similar relationship. However, instead of being stuck together with custard or chocolate icing, they are cooperatively related by formatted data bundles being passed up or down through the devices, protocols, and services defined on each layer.

An essential part of Cisco network design and administration is an understanding of which Cisco hardware performs on which OSI layer and which of the functions defined on each layer a device performs. This knowledge can save you time and money by allowing you to apply the appropriate Cisco devices to any networking situation. It would be a huge waste of time and money to use a router as a bridge or to try to use a switch to connect to the Internet. Not to mention the huge headache you'll have from trying to figure out just what went wrong — it all seemed so logical, right?

So, on a mission of mercy, I've included this chapter to help you avoid using the wrong equipment in the right situation and suffering the angst that is sure to follow if you do.

Connecting on the Physical Layer

The commonly used Physical layer (Layer 1) devices in a LAN are network interface cards (also called *network adapters*), repeaters, and hubs. What separates Layer 1 devices from those devices operating on higher layers is that Physical layer devices operate only on the bitstream level, make no choices or decisions, and merely forward what they receive.

Repeating what it hears

A repeater does just what its name implies: It repeats whatever it receives. However, the primary purpose of a repeater is to re-energize the transmitted signal strength before passing the signal along. Repeaters are used to overcome the distance limitations inherent in network cabling (see Chapter 4).

Cisco doesn't make a repeater, per se. Instead, Cisco FastHub and Catalyst switch products also perform repeater functions. Cisco FastHub products combine the functions of a repeater with those of a hub for Ethernet networks. Catalyst switch products, such as the Catalyst 2820, can be configured to perform repeater functions on its Ethernet ports.

Getting to the hub

A network hub is a clustering device that serves as a means for multiple workstations to connect to the network media. Hubs can either be passive or active. A passive hub merely passes along signals it receives from any port to all of its other ports. An active hub at least knows the port a signal came in on and doesn't resend it back on that port. Active hubs typically have repeater capability as well.

Cisco's FastHub products are active hubs and are available as either fixed 10 Mbps Ethernet hubs or as autosensing 10/100 Mbps Ethernet hubs. An *autosensing hub* is able to detect the bandwidth of a port and make the necessary speed adjustments before forwarding its traffic to other ports.

Bridging, Switching, and Cisco

A network bridge is appropriately named. Like a bridge in a road, a network bridge connects two LANs. (Get it? Lands? Oh, never mind!) The LANs or segments connected to a bridge can be either two networks using the same networking technology or, in its originally intended use, dissimilar networks. What this means is that one network can be Ethernet and the other token ring, for example.

Bridges are Layer 2 (Data Link layer) devices. Cisco does make a few bridges, but they are more specialized than your average, plain, network bridge. Cisco's bridges are used in wireless LAN situations to interconnect two buildings on Ethernet networks, either as a workgroup bridge, used to connect remote or portable computer users, on a wireless network or as a unity bridge on a voice network in support of unified messaging (integrated e-mail and voicemail messaging).

A bridge can be used to segment a network and should reduce network-wide traffic by forwarding messages to the segments on which their destination addresses reside. Bridges aren't overly intelligent devices (in comparison to switches or routers, for example), but they have enough smarts to keep track of where a physical address (typically a MAC address — see Chapter 8) resides and to use this information to forward network messages to only the segment on which that physical address can be reached.

Because bridging and switching applications are inherently similar, Cisco recommends the use of one of its Catalyst switches in most bridging situations. Because a Cisco Catalyst switch has the ability to make forwarding decisions at a slightly higher level than your normal network bridge, for about the same cost, it's a much better value.

Bridges and switches both use the same bridging methods, keeping what they learn from incoming messages in a bridging (or switching) table for later use. However, when you boil it all down, a switch is actually just a multiport bridge with some smarts added in that allows it to switch at what is called *wire-speed* (which is very fast). One advantage a bridge may have over a switch is that a bridge typically adds just a bit less delay (latency) to message delivery time. Many lower-end switches can add latency to the delivery time of a packet because of their software overhead.

Because a Cisco Catalyst switch runs the Cisco IOS (Internetwork Operating System), it can provide many additional features, not the least of which is improved bandwidth utilization. In fact, many Cisco switches could be called *srouters* (I made this up) because they incorporate functions also found on routers.

See Chapter 10 for more information on switching and Layer 2 operations.

Finding a Route through Layer 3

Layer 3 is the Network layer of the OSI model. It is on Layer 3 that many networking professionals believe networking in general really happens, at least as far as the internetwork is concerned. The primary device on Layer 3 is the router, which is the device that has provided the interconnecting links that made the Internet possible. It is very safe to say that without routers, there would be no Internet, at least not as we know and love it today.

Cisco is best known for (and really shows its moxie on) Layer 3. Cisco Systems, Inc., (its friends just call it Cisco) is generally associated with routers; and as I've stated, routers are the primary Layer 3 device. Layer 3 has other devices, such as the *brouter,* that schizophrenic device that operates on both Layers 2 and 3; but when you hear Layer 3, you should immediately think router. (I discuss the brouter later in the chapter — see the section "It's not heavy; it's my brouter.")

Routing with a router

Chapters 11 and 12 deal specifically with routers and their functions, but I want to briefly detail the activities defined on Layer 3 and the ways that Cisco equipment implements them.

Monitoring changes on the network

At any given moment, the available paths through an internetwork can change, and they change more often than you may think. These changes are the result of equipment failures, failed cables, administrator errors, power failures, environmental conditions, or the boss stumbling around in the IT area and kicking out the cord. (How did HE get in here?) Not all path changes are the result of something bad. Path changes can also be the result of physical or logical changes made to a network layout or configuration — made in an attempt to improve its performance.

Regardless of the reason, the route from one network (meaning its router) to another network (meaning its router) can and does change. The result is that the routers on any internetwork must track the changes that it detects and determine the feasibility of each path that could be used to reach each of the networks to which it is connected. Of course, you must configure a router to do this, it won't just do it by default.

Routing versus routed

Throughout this book, or any other book about Layer 3 functions, you will be accosted with the terms *routing* and *routed*. Where these terms come into play is in defining the protocols used on a router. In essence, routing defines an action and routed defines the acted upon, but they also have fairly unrelated meanings, at least in the context of a router. Here is a brief definition of routing and routed:

- ✔ **Routing:** The *routing elements* of a router are those that maintain the information needed by the router to log changes made to the network and its *topology* (meaning its physical and logical condition). Routing information allows the router to have the best available information to use in determining the path to reach any remote network. Routing and routing protocols are discussed in Chapter 12.

- ✔ **Routed:** This term, although not always used with proper grammatical application, applies to the protocols that can be forwarded to an internetwork. Data from a network protocol (excuse the semantics — I'll clear it up in a bit) may or may not be able to be routed. The distinction between a *network* protocol (such as TCP/IP, IPX/SPX, or NetBEUI) and a *networking* protocol (such as IP) is a fine line, but you will see these terms often in your reading, so be sure that you know which is being discussed. Not all network protocols, for example NetBEUI, can be routed; and this factor can make a big difference when you attempt to connect one of these networks to an internetwork, like the Internet. Chapter 12 discusses routed or routable protocols in some detail.

Keeping routing information up-to-date

Routers use routing protocols, such as the Routing Information Protocol (RIP) and others (see Chapter 12), to send and receive information to and from its neighboring routers about changes to its network's topology. Without the services of a routing protocol, a router would have no idea of which of its interface ports to use to reach any given remote network or network segment. If a router has no idea that a neighboring router has failed or that the link connecting one of its interface ports to a remote network is congested, it would merrily continue to forward traffic in that direction with less than favorable results. Of course, you could manually enter and maintain this information; but if your router is a part of a very large internetwork, this could prove to be more than a 24/7 task.

The value of the routing protocols is that they automatically keep the routing information up-to-date and provide the router with the best available information for use in determining the route to use to reach any given destination network.

Determining the path

Routers use various algorithms (and no, this isn't a term describing Al Gore's dancing ability) to determine which of their available routes to the internetwork or their *internal networks* (the local networks or segments for which the router works) provides the better option at any given moment. Drawing on the statistical routing information provided by its routing protocol, a router calculates the better path to use to forward a packet of transmitted data.

Notice that I use the term *better* and not the term *best* to describe the path chosen. The best path may not always be available, and at any given instant, a better path may be available. Chapter 12 discusses the statistics (actually they are officially called *metrics*) used and how a router maintains and uses its metrics in determining a route.

Routing with Cisco routers

Cisco routers, like virtually all devices called routers, perform the routing and routed functions defined on Layer 3. Where Cisco may be slightly ahead of the other manufacturers in the networking arena is in its differentiated and highly scalable product line.

Cisco has a wide range of router options, one of which is suitable and appropriate for virtually any given networking situation. Whether your application is a single small office network connecting to the Internet or a global enterprise creating a Wide Area Network (WAN) on either private lines or through the Internet, there is a Cisco router designed to fit your requirements. I don't mean this to sound like a commercial, but, after all, this book *is* about Cisco networking.

Cisco routers can also be configured to perform some tasks beyond just plain old routing. Many Cisco routers can also be configured to provide security, telephony, and other network services. I mention this only to dispel any notion I may have given you that a router is merely a router. In fact, a router, in certain situations, can be used to provide configuration, control, and management of nearly all of a network's interconnections to the outside world.

It's not heavy; it's my brouter

Not every networking device operates strictly on just one of the OSI layers. A case in point, and there are others, is the *brouter* (pronounced as "brow-ter"). A brouter gets its name from the functions it is designed to support. The *b* is from bridge and the *router* — well, it should be obvious. This name is certainly better than any of the other choices that could have been used. Somehow, *bridouter* or *bridgeter* just don't have the same elegance.

A *brouter,* as you may surmise, is a hybrid device that combines the functions of both bridging (see "Bridging, Switching, and Cisco," earlier in this chapter) with routing (see "Routing with a router," earlier in the chapter). A brouter is able to determine when bridging or routing actions are appropriate to forward a message packet to its destination.

Where a brouter makes sense in a network is in situations where two dissimilar networks are joined, and both bridging and routing capabilities are needed. For example, if an IPX/SPX network is joined to a TCP/IP network, a brouter can act as a bridge between the IPX/SPX and TCP/IP networks and as a router for both networks. Of course, an even better solution is to run the same protocol suite (typically TCP/IP) on the main portion of the network and install a software gateway to handle those segments that absolutely must use a different protocol suite.

Cisco doesn't actually manufacture a brouter, recommending a switch with some routing capabilities added *(srouter?)*. For example, the Catalyst 8400 and 8500 series switches support both Layer 2 and Layer 3 switching through its Integrated Routing and Bridging (IRB) module, and optional add-on feature.

Cisco Catalyst switch/routers are typically used as campus switch/routers (CSRs) or multiservice switch/routers (MSRs). The Catalyst switch models that have this capability have either CSR or MSR as a part of their model number, for example, Catalyst 8510 CSR or 8540 CSR.

Transporting over Layer 4

A Transport layer (Layer 4) packet carries a port number to identify the Application layer or network server function that should be used to process its payload. The port number, which should actually be called a *function or application identity,* is unique to a particular application function. For example, if a packet carries a destination port number of 80, it is a HyperText Transfer Protocol (HTTP) packet and should be passed to the HTTP application on the receiving end (which is typically a Web browser). See Chapter 6 for more information on port numbers and their assignments.

On Layer 4, packets are forwarded based on information they contain. This process is called *Layer 4 switching* or *content switching.* In specific situations, Layer 4 switches are also referred to as Web switches or e-commerce switches, but in every case, the switching decision is based on the Layer 4 information included in each packet.

Balancing the load

Perhaps the most common usage of content switching is load balancing. *Load balancing* is commonly used by large Web site hosting services, very busy e-commerce sites, and some enterprise networks to direct inbound request traffic to specific servers for processing.

On a Web site that sees a very high *hit* (request) rate, using multiple servers connected to a Layer 4 switch makes sense. The Layer 4 switch promotes a faster response time by distributing the incoming requests to the servers so that no one server is overloaded.

The enterprise application may have a single router that performs Layer 4 switching to distribute incoming messages to various servers that process a variety of corporate applications. A Web site hosting service may have incoming multiple router links that feed a server farm that holds the Web sites of its customers. In an e-commerce situation, the priority is to support server-to-server transactions over reliable connections that provide fast and efficient processing. In any of these cases, the ability to route incoming traffic to the best network service for processing, which is the exact same goal of Layer 4 switching, is essential.

Layer 4 switching and Cisco

Perhaps the most rudimentary way to implement content-switching on a Cisco router or switch is through an access control list (ACL) (see Chapter 18 for more information on ACLs). An ACL can examine incoming traffic based on the destination port number, permit access, and forward it to the interface port attached to the appropriate service for processing.

Cisco does provide a specific Layer 4 switching product for its Catalyst 6500 and 7600 models. This product, the Content-Switching Module (CSM), includes the capability to balance incoming traffic to server farms, firewalls, or VPN gateways.

Switching and the Upper Layers

Layers 5 through 7 (the Session, Presentation, and Application layers) are typically referred to as *the upper layers* of the OSI model. The Session layer is concerned with establishing and managing the communications link between two points on a network. The Presentation layer deals with the format and characteristics of the data, including data conversion, encryption, and compression. The Application layer, not to be confused with the applications running on a desktop, provides an interface for desktop applications to network protocols.

Switching on Layer 5

To this point, switching has not advanced to include Layers 6 and 7. Support for the Presentation and Application layers is actually handled by Layer 4 switching anyway. For example, an incoming packet that requires special encryption handling would be forwarded using its Layer 4 information to the application that performs that service. Likewise, port 80 traffic is forwarded to the HTTP application.

However, Layer 5 switching is being touted as the next best thing (NBT). Layer 5 switching adds the dimension of forwarding a packet based on its uniform resource locator (URL). High volume hosting services or e-commerce operations can direct requests to different Web servers based on the path included in the requested URL, even though the incoming requests may all have the same destination address and port number.

Layer 5 switching and Cisco

The Cisco product that best incorporates the switching requirements of Layers 4 through 7 is the Cisco Secure Content Accelerator (SCA) 11000. This product is sold as a self-contained network appliance solution that is designed to handle Secure Sockets Layer (SSL) traffic in e-commerce environments. Combining the SCA 11000 with one of the Cisco products that provide load-balancing, such as Cisco's Content Switching Module (CSM), provides a secure and robust service for the handling of SSL traffic.

Chapter 6

Transporting Data over the Internetwork

● ●

In This Chapter

▶ Identifying and detailing TCP/IP Transport layer protocol functions

▶ Explaining the functions of ICMP

▶ Defining data encapsulation

● ●

This chapter should be subtitled TCFOA (The Chapter Full Of Acronyms). What with UDP, TCP, TCP/IP, FTP, HLEN, IP, SMTP, DNS, SNMP, ICMP, ARP, RARP, and PING, if this chapter has nothing else, it has TLAs (three-letter acronyms) and FLAs (four-letter acronyms) galore. I certainly understand why you may be PTO (Plain Tuckered Out) at the end of this chapter.

A large part of the secret language spoken by Cisco network administrators comes from the TLAs and FLAs of the TCP/IP protocols and services covered in this chapter. Don't be discouraged if you can't remember them all — in spite of what you may hear, nobody can. But, a reward awaits those who learn the secret language of TCP/IP: fame, fortune, clear skin, white teeth, lots of dates, and a better, more fulfilling job. Well, maybe I can't really promise you all that (forget the part about the dates). However, being able to read Cisco white papers and articles about WAN networking and understand them is its own reward.

How Suite It Is

The Transmission Control Protocol/Internet Protocol (TCP/IP) suite, also known as just the Internet Protocol suite, has quickly become the standard for network communications on both the global (WAN) and local (LAN) levels. A number of factors account for the rapid and widespread growth of TCP/IP:

✔ **Portability:** TCP/IP is platform-independent and is interoperable with virtually every communications system, hardware, or software. There are some legacy systems that don't support TCP/IP, but just about all modern systems include support for and are interoperable with TCP/IP.

✔ **Universal support:** TCP/IP protocols run equally well on virtually every general or network operating system, including UNIX, Linux, Windows (9*x*, Me, NT, 2000, or XP), Novell, and so on.

✔ **Adaptability:** The TCP/IP suite contains at least one protocol that is designed for or can be adapted to just about any process or function of virtually any networking application.

✔ **Open structure:** Nobody owns TCP/IP. Although many software publishers — including Microsoft, Novell, and others — have their own versions of it, TCP/IP is a public-domain freely distributed set of protocol standards that are available to anyone wishing to use them.

TCP/IP is actually a suite of protocols that interconnect and work together to provide for reliable and efficient data communications across an internetwork. The TCP/IP protocol suite includes these major protocols:

✔ Transmission Control Protocol (TCP)

✔ User Datagram Protocol (UDP)

✔ Domain Name System (DNS)

✔ Internet Protocol (IP)

✔ Address Resolution Protocol (ARP)

✔ File Transfer Protocol (FTP)

✔ Simple Mail Transfer Protocol (SMTP)

✔ Post Office Protocol (POP3)

✔ Internet Message Access Protocol (IMAP)

✔ Internet Control Message Protocol (ICMP)

✔ Routing Information Protocol (RIP)

✔ Open Shortest Path First (OSPF)

✔ HyperText Transfer Protocol (HTTP)

✔ TCP/IP utilities (PING, Telnet, IPCONFIG, ARP, and more)

Knowing the functions of the primary TCP/IP protocols (TCP, IP, UDP, and ICMP) is far more important than memorizing the protocols in the suite. You really don't need to know all the protocols in the TCP/IP suite. Knowing how certain protocols behave will be helpful when you configure your Cisco router, but you don't need to waste time memorizing all the protocols. I haven't listed them all here anyway. Look over the preceding list and make mental notes of them.

Stacking up the TCP/IP protocols

The TCP/IP protocol suite can also be arranged into a *protocol stack*. This means that the TCP/IP protocol suite can be broken up into groups of smaller suites that can be stacked or layered on each other to cooperatively complete a task or activity.

The best way to see the makeup of the TCP/IP protocol stack is to view it in contrast to the OSI model (see Chapter 2). The TCP/IP stack contains one or more protocols that function on each OSI layer. Table 6-1 shows how the TCP/IP protocol stack maps to the OSI model. Notice that each layer (or group of layers) has at least two protocols that operate on that layer.

Table 6-1	The TCP/IP Protocol Stack
OSI Layers	*TCP/IP Protocols*
Application	Telnet, FTP, SMTP, SNMP, DNS, HTTP*
Transport	TCP, UDP
Network	IP, ICMP, ARP, RARP
Data Link, Physical	Ethernet, Token Ring, FDDI**

* These protocols or services are not exactly TCP/IP protocols. Some are, and some aren't, but they are listed as protocols that can be combined into a TCP/IP protocol stack.

** These are networking technologies that function at the Data Link and Physical layers. They aren't actually TCP/IP protocols and aren't included as a part of the TCP/IP protocol stack. They're included in Table 6-1 only to show the technologies that function on that level of the model.

The following sections give you a brief overview on the TCP/IP protocols that operate on each layer (or group of layers) of the OSI model.

Applying the application protocols

The TCP/IP Application layer (not to be confused with the OSI Application Layer) protocols that you will most likely encounter on your Cisco network are listed in Table 6-1. The TCP/IP Application layer corresponds to the upper layers (Session, Presentation, and Application layers) of the OSI model. TCP/IP Application layer protocols are not actually applications in the sense of Microsoft Word, Lotus 1-2-3, or Unreal Tournament. Application layer protocols interface with user-level applications to facilitate the services provided by the other layers of the OSI model and the TCP/IP protocol stack. Application layer protocols commonly used by a Cisco network administrator are FTP, TFTP, SNMP, and Telnet.

Transferring files, trivial or not

The File Transfer Protocol (FTP) is a reliable, connection-oriented tool (see "Connecting ways," later in this chapter) that is used to copy files from one computer to another over a TCP/IP network, such as the Internet or an intranet. You are likely familiar with this TCP/IP Application layer protocol. It is the workhorse of Web site maintenance and file downloads and uploads. FTP includes functions that allow it to log on to a remote network, navigate its directory structure, list the contents of its directories, and copy files by downloading them to the local computer or uploading them to a remote computer.

Another flavor of FTP is the *Trivial File Transfer Protocol (TFTP),* which is an *unreliable* (meaning delivery is not guaranteed) file transfer protocol. This TCP/IP protocol is used by Cisco routers to *transfer* (store and retrieve) configuration files from a computer supporting a TFTP server. The *trivial* part of the name refers to the supposition that you would only use this protocol to move files that you don't care much about (trivial data). If you really cared enough to transfer the very best, you would use FTP. However, for small files over a LAN, TFTP works quite well, regardless of how you really feel about the data.

TFTP is actually a very good tool when the data being transferred does not enter or travel on the public network. This tool works very well for transferring configuration and boot files from a local network host to a router or switch. Because of TFTP's lower overhead (it doesn't require packets to be acknowledged), it is much faster and more efficient than FTP for transferring router files. (See Chapter 11 for more information on TFTP.)

Connecting with Telnet

Telnet is a terminal emulation protocol used on TCP/IP-based networks to remotely log on to a remote device (a computer or router, most likely) to run a program or manipulate data. Telnet was originally developed for ARPAnet (the Department of Defense's early precursor to the Internet) and is now an inherent and highly used part of the TCP/IP communications protocol suite. In the Cisco world, Telnet is used to access and configure routers from remote locations. This is the tool that is used to connect and log on to virtual terminal interface ports. Remember, you heard it here first.

Running into other protocols

There are a few other protocols you should encounter as a network administrator. On the Application layer, you can count on running into the HyperText Transfer Protocol (HTTP), Simple Network Management Protocol (SNMP), Domain Name System (DNS), and Simple Mail Transfer Protocol (SMTP). SNMP is likely to be the protocol of this list that you'll use as a part of your job because it's used to monitor and manage network and network node configurations.

If your network operating system is or will be Novell NetWare, you should know that IPX/SPX networks (see Chapter 3), which naturally use the IPX/SPX protocol stack, have two protocols that perform many of the same functions as the TCP/IP Application layer protocols — SAP (Service Advertising Protocol) and NCP (NetWare Core Protocol). However, not all Novell NetWare networks run the IPX/SPX protocol stack. NetWare 5 has made TCP/IP its default protocol suite, instead of IPX/SPX, which is still available.

Moving Packets and Datagrams

The two primary TCP/IP protocols that function on the OSI model's Transport layer are the *Transmission Control Protocol (TCP)* and the *User Datagram Protocol (UDP)*. These two protocols have a number of things in common, but as I describe in the following sections, they have one major difference — how reliably they transport data over the internetwork.

Controlling the transmission

TCP is a connection-oriented (see "Connecting ways" later in this chapter), reliable, delivery protocol that includes processes to ensure that packets arrive at their destination error-free. TCP provides reliable, point-to-point communications that two devices on a TCP/IP network can use to communicate with each other. To communicate, each device must create a connection to the other by binding a socket (see "Socketing it to me" later in the chapter) to the end of the connection that it controls. The devices read from and write to the application represented by the socket bound to the connection.

Using TCP is similar to sending a registered letter. When you send the letter, you know for sure that it will get to its destination and that you'll be notified that it arrived in good condition. Of course, like registered mail, you pay a higher price to use TCP. Luckily, the higher price doesn't involve money, but rather the amount of bandwidth and time used to complete the transmission, with all that checking and rechecking going on.

This is what's cool about TCP:

- It's connection-oriented.
- It offers reliable transfer.
- It performs error-checking.
- It has full-duplex transmission.
- It performs flow control.
- It even does multiplexing!

Socketing it to me

FTP, Telnet, SMTP, and HTTP are a few of the Application layer protocols that take advantage of the transport services included in TCP. These protocols use TCP to open a socket between two computers. A *socket* directs incoming data traffic to the appropriate application process on a TCP/IP network. A socket is made up of the combination of the IP address of a network node and a port number. I deal with ports a little later in this chapter (see "Getting noticed in all the well-known ports"), but for now, just say that a *port* is a number assigned to a certain type of application, such as FTP, HTTP, Telnet, and so on.

Actually, two types of sockets can be used:

- ✔ **Stream sockets:** These sockets work with connection-oriented (see "Connecting ways" later in this chapter) protocols, such as TCP, to transfer data between two computers.

- ✔ **Datagram sockets:** These sockets work with UDP.

Application layer protocols use TCP to open a socket by recording the TCP/IP protocol in use, the destination IP address, and the port number of the application (see "Getting noticed in all the well-known ports," later in this chapter) to be used on the destination device to process the information being transferred.

Connecting ways

Network protocols are either connection-oriented or connectionless. This doesn't mean that some protocols make connections and others don't. What it refers to is the nature of the connection made between two communicating devices while using a specific protocol. This section explains each type:

- ✔ **Connection-oriented protocols** require that a direct connection be established between two devices before data can begin to transfer between the devices. Packets are transferred by using a prescribed sequence of actions that includes an acknowledgment to signal when a packet arrives and possibly to resend the packet if errors are detected. As a result of this method's reliability and the overhead involved, connection-oriented protocols are much slower than connectionless protocols. TCP is a connection-oriented protocol.

- ✔ **Connectionless protocols** are largely based on your faith in the technology. Packets are sent over the network without regard to whether they actually arrive at their destinations. You get no acknowledgments or guarantees, but you can send a *datagram* (as connectionless protocol packets are called) to many different destinations at the same time. Connectionless protocols are fast because no time is used in establishing and tearing down connections. A fair analogy is mailing a first-class letter at the post office: You trust the post office to deliver the letter, but you're not guaranteed that the letter will, indeed, be delivered. UDP is a connectionless protocol.

Connectionless protocols are also referred to as *best-effort* protocols. This type of delivery system is common to protocols that do not include some form of acknowledgment system to guarantee the delivery of information.

Knowing whether a protocol is connection-oriented or not isn't important, but when setting up a network and looking at the elements included in the network's protocol stack, you will understand more of its inherent behavior if you do know this difference. Table 6-2 identifies common protocols by their connection type.

Table 6-2   Connection-Oriented and Connectionless Protocols

Connection-Oriented	Connectionless
FTP	IP
TCP	IPX
SPX	UDP

Making a three-way handshake

Establishing a connection-oriented connection involves setting up sequencing and acknowledgment fields and agreeing upon the port numbers to be used. This is accomplished by a three-step handshake process that works like this:

1. Handshake one: Host 1 sends a synchronization message to Host 2.

2. Handshake two: Host 2 acknowledges Host 1's synchronization message and sends back its own synchronization message.

3. Handshake three: Host 1 acknowledges Host 2's synchronization message.

At this point, the connection is sufficiently synchronized and successfully established, and the applications can begin transferring data. Throughout the communications session, TCP manages the transfer of data packets, ensuring that they reach their destination. If errors occur, TCP supervises the retransmission of the packet.

Checking for errors and closing the window

If TCP ever has a retirement dinner, when they give it the gold socket, they'll say, "You could always rely on good old TCP!" TCP data transfers are reliable. This isn't an opinion; it's a technical characteristic that was designed into TCP. TCP uses two mechanisms to provide its high level of reliability: error-checking and received-segment acknowledgments.

Error checking is accomplished through the use of two numbers stored in the packet header: a checksum and the number of bits in the packet payload. The checksum is calculated through an algorithm, and the bit count is a straight tally. These two values are stored in the packet header and sent along as a part of the packet. The receiving end recalculates, recounts, and checks its numbers against those in the packet header. If they are not equal, a request is sent to the sending station to resend the packet.

The acknowledgment of segment receipts is accomplished through a process called *windowing,* which is a form of flow control. In windowing, a window, which is represented as a number of packets, sets the interval before an acknowledgment must be sent back to the sending station by the receiving stations. Windowing gets its name from the fact that windows can be opened and closed to allow more or less airflow. (Of course, you realize that I'm speaking of the windows in the walls of your home and not those of the software type.)

Windowing works like this:

1. Host 1 tells Host 2 that it has a certain window size and sends the appropriate number of segments.

2. If Host 2 receives all the segments, it sends back an acknowledgment indicating that the next segment should be sent and the size of the window that Host 2 can accept.

   This tells the sending station that Host 2 is ready for more, and because packets were sent without problems, maybe this time Host 1 should try more if it would like to do so. As the transmission proceeds, the receiving station slowly increases the window size as long as segments are received without errors.

3. If Host 2 fails to receive a segment, Host 2 resends an acknowledgment for the preceding segment, which means that Host 1 should send that preceding segment again.

   For example, if errors are detected in segment 3, Host 2 sends an acknowledgment for segment 2, indicating to Host 1 that segment 3 needs to be sent again.

Because Host 1 can't be trusted to send the first experimental number of packets without a failure, Host 2 resets the window to the minimum window size, and the trust relationship is rebuilt.

However, if the correct number of segments is received, which is normally the case, the two hosts will continue to optimize the window size to a size both can support — at least until the next error occurs.

This example uses what is called a *sliding window,* which is so called because the window can be adjusted on the fly to meet the needs of either the sending or receiving device.

Staying connected

After the connection is open, it remains open, providing a virtual circuit. TCP supports *full-duplex transmission,* which means that both the sender and receiver can transfer data simultaneously over the same connection. To accommodate this, the devices at each end of the connection must maintain two windows — one for sending and one for receiving.

TCP allows for *multiplexing,* which is the ability for more than one application to use an open transport connection. Multiplexing is possible for two reasons:

- ✔ Each TCP segment is self-contained, with its data and addresses encapsulated in the segment packet.
- ✔ Segments are sent on a first-come, first-served basis, without regard to what came before or comes after each segment.

Getting noticed in all the well-known ports

A *port* is a logical connection device that allows the system to assign the incoming data to a particular application for processing. Each port is assigned a *port number,* which is a way to identify the specific process to which the message is to be passed.

For example, if you request a file from a remote FTP server, TCP sets the port number to 21 (the standard FTP port number) in order to communicate the nature of the request to the remote server. The remote server sees the request for port number 21 and forwards your request to its FTP program. Both TCP and UDP use port numbers to move information along to the Application layer.

Because someone has to do it, the registering body, *ICANN (Internet Corporation for Assigned Names and Numbers)*, divides port numbers into three groups:

- **Well-known ports** are the most commonly used TCP/IP ports. These ports are in the range of 0 through 1023. These ports can be used only by system processes or privileged programs. Well-known ports are TCP ports, but they are usually registered to UDP services as well.

- **Registered ports** are in the range of 1024 through 49151. Registered ports are used on most systems by user programs to create and control logical connections between proprietary programs.

- **Dynamic (private) ports** are in the range of 49152 through 65535. These ports are unregistered and can be used dynamically for private connections.

You should know this additional information about port numbers:

- Port numbers below 256 are assigned to public applications (such as FTP, HTTP, and so on).

- Port numbers 256 – 1023 are assigned to companies for saleable applications.

- Port numbers above 1023 are dynamically assigned in the host application.

- Source and destination port numbers don't have to be the same.

Table 6-3 lists the port numbers and corresponding applications for some of the more common application types. This information is also very useful when doing access lists on a Cisco router (see Chapter 15).

Table 6-3	Well-Known Ports
Port Number	*Application*
21	FTP
23	Telnet
25	SMTP
53	DNS
69	TFTP
80	HTTP
110	POP3
161	SNMP

Formatting the TCP segment

On the Transport layer, data packets are referred to as *segments*. Table 6-4 lists the fields that form the TCP segment. Compare this table to the UDP segment table presented in the next section.

Table 6-4	TCP Segment Lengths	
Field	*Size in Bits*	*Purpose*
Source port	16	The number of the calling port
Destination port	16	The number of the called port
Sequence number	32	Ensures correct sequencing of data
Acknowledgment number	32	Sequence number of the next expected TCP octet
HLEN	4	Header length (as number of 32-bit words)
Reserved	6	Set to zero
Code bits	6	Functions that set up and terminate the session
Window	16	Size of window that the sender can accept
Checksum	16	Error-correction feature, sum of header and data fields
Urgent pointer	16	End of the urgent data
Option	0 or 32 bits per option	0 bits in length if there are no options included, or 32 bits for each option included Maximum TCP segment size is the most common option
Data	—	Data from upper layers

Flying Fast with UDP

User Datagram Protocol (UDP) is the other major Transport layer protocol in the TCP/IP protocol suite. In contrast to TCP and its reliability, UDP is unreliable, which means that it doesn't monitor the transmission of its segments (which, as you probably guessed, are called *datagrams*), and it doesn't require confirmation of datagram delivery. UDP is a best-effort, connection-less protocol best known for its speed.

UDP is fast because it doesn't take the time to check for datagram delivery, acknowledgments, or even error-checking functions like windowing. The UDP header frame, the fields that come before the data in the UDP segment (see Table 6-4), is only 8 bytes long compared to the 24 bytes (1 option included) of the TCP header frame. (In theory, a TCP header could be up to 60 bytes long if enough options are included.) The primary protocols using UDP are SNMP, NFS (Network File System), TFTP, and DNS.

If you compare the UDP datagram's format (shown in Table 6-5) to that of the TCP packet (detailed in Table 6-4), you should notice now how much less overhead, in the form of extra fields, a UDP segment contains.

Table 6-5	UDP Datagram Lengths	
Field	*Size in Bits*	*Purpose*
Source port	16	The number of the calling port
Destination port	16	The number of the called port
Length	16	The length of the datagram
Checksum	16	Error-detection feature, sum of header and data
Data	Variable	Data from upper layers

Transmitting on the Network Layer

A number of TCP/IP protocols operate on the Network layer of the OSI Model, including Internet Protocol (IP), Address Resolution Protocol (ARP), Reverse ARP (RARP), and the Internet Control Message Protocol (ICMP). The OSI Network layer (see Chapter 2) is concerned with routing messages across the internetwork.

Letting you see some IP

Although TCP is connection-oriented, IP is connectionless. IP provides for the best-effort delivery of the packets (or datagrams) that it creates from the segments it receives from the Transport layer protocols. IP also provides for *logical addressing* (IP addressing) on the Network layer.

Converting Transport layer segments

The size of IP packets is based on the *maximum transmission unit (MTU)*, which is the largest number of bytes that can be transmitted over a certain network protocol. IP selects an appropriate packet size and then proceeds to fragment larger packets. This process, known as *fragmentation,* usually occurs on a router between the source and destination and results in a fragment that's sized just right to fit into a single frame for shipment over the network. The fragments are then reassembled at the final destination.

IP also provides for *logical addressing,* which is the hierarchical addressing scheme used on the Network layer. Where Layer 2's hardware addressing only defines a particular network node, logical addressing also defines the node's network and other location information. IP determines the action to take on a packet based on the information in a routing table. On a router, this means that the decision of which of a router's hardware ports should receive the packet to move it along its way is based on the information contained in its routing table. (See Chapter 12 for more information on routers and routing.)

Looking inside an IP packet

The IP packet (or *datagram*) is variable in length. Table 6-6 lists the fields that comprise its format.

Table 6-6	IP Packet Lengths	
Field	*Size in Bits*	*Purpose*
IP version number	4	Identifies the packet as IPv4 or IPv6
HLEN	4	Header length
Type of service	8	How the packet should be processed
Length	16	The total length of the packet, including the header and data
ID	16	Used for reassembly of fragmented packets
Flags	3	Used for reassembly of fragmented packets
Flag offset	13	Used for reassembly of fragmented packets
TTL	8	Time-to-live value (see Chapter 12)
Protocol	8	Identifies the Transport layer protocol that passed this packet to IP

(continued)

Table 6-6 *(continued)*

Field	Size in Bits	Purpose
Checksum	16	Error-correction feature, sum of header and data
Source IP	32	IP address of sending node
Destination IP	32	IP address of destination node
IP Options	Variable	Optional use for testing and debugging
Padding	0 or 8	Used to pad the packet size to allow for the calculation of the checksum
Data	Variable	Data being transmitted

It's okay for the packet to be smaller than the MTU. The checksum of an IP packet is calculated by using the number of 16-bit words that make up the packet. If the number of bytes in the packet is an odd number, the padding is used to bring the number of bytes to an even number. The sole purpose of the padding field is to enable the checksum calculation, and it is not actually transmitted with the packet.

Here's some cool stuff to know about IP and its packets:

- ✔ IP is primarily concerned with routing.
- ✔ IP is a connectionless, unreliable, best-effort delivery service.
- ✔ IP, which operates on the Network layer, manages the fragmentation and reassembly of segments being sent by or passed to the upper layers (Session, Presentation, and Application).

Sending notes with ICMP

The Internet Control Message Protocol (ICMP) is another Network layer protocol. ICMP is used primarily for control and messaging services. It carries messages between systems regarding status, passes control codes, and delivers error codes and messages. ICMP is also the underlying protocol for many TCP/IP utilities, such as PING and traceroute (see Chapter 2).

ICMP has a set of standard messages that it carries. ICMP uses these common messages:

- ✔ **Echo request** — tests connectivity
- ✔ **Echo reply** — replies to echo messages

- ✔ **Buffer full** — indicates that a router's memory is full
- ✔ **Destination unreachable** — indicates that a destination IP is unreachable
- ✔ **Source quench** — a flow control message
- ✔ **Redirect** — tells the sender to use a better route for a message
- ✔ **Time exceeded** — TTL (time-to-live) field time has been exceeded

Unraveling the Mysterious World of Encapsulation

As data flows from the top of the OSI model to the bottom, the protocols that operate at each level repackage the message into each protocol's own version of a segment, packet, datagram, or frame. Each protocol may add a message header, possibly a message trailer, or divide the original message's data up into smaller chunks to eventually transmit the data over the network or internetwork. As the data passes from one layer (protocol) to the next, its form may change subtly or even radically.

Each protocol (layer) transforms the header, trailer, and message data into a single entity, called a *protocol data unit (PDU)*. This process is called *encapsulation,* and a PDU is the unit passed by one protocol to the next and eventually sent out on the network. Each layer in the TCP/IP protocol stack gives its version of a PDU a different name, as listed in Table 6-7.

Table 6-7	Data Encapsulation Levels
OSI Layer	*Data Encapsulation Level*
Application	Data
Transport	Segments for TCP; datagrams for UDP
Network	Packets (datagrams)
Data Link	Frames
Physical	Bits

I call the process that moves data up and down the OSI and TCP/IP layers the *Five Steps of Data Encapsulation.* Ooh, sounds so mysterious, like some old monster movie, doesn't it? Actually, all this amounts to is the addition of data headers to a PDU on the way out and the removal of these headers on the way in as the PDU passes through the OSI layers. Table 6-7 lists the OSI layer and the name given to the encapsulated data on that layer. Figure 6-1 shows the five data encapsulation levels. This is good to know so that you won't embarrass yourself around network administrators who are really picky about this stuff.

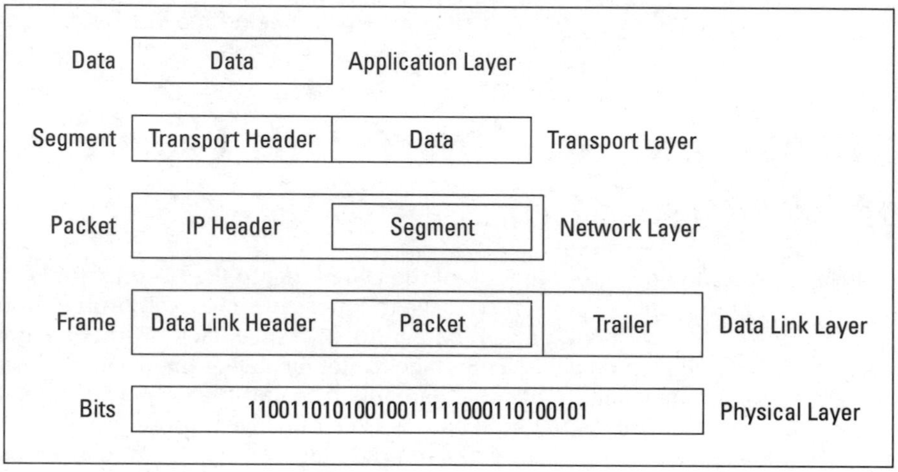

Data	Data	Application Layer

Segment	Transport Header	Data	Transport Layer

Packet	IP Header	Segment	Network Layer

Figure 6-1:
Five steps of data encapsulation.

Frame	Data Link Header	Packet	Trailer	Data Link Layer

Bits	11001101010010011111000110100101	Physical Layer

Chapter 7

Working with Those Weird Numbers

As a Cisco network administrator, you encounter addresses, parameters, table entries, and more uses of binary, hexadecimal, and decimal numbers. Binary numbers are the basis for subnetting and routing; hexadecimal numbers are used for such things as interfaces, operating system interrupt IDs, and port addresses; and decimal numbers are rampant. To a certain extent, your ability to read and understand binary, hexadecimal, and decimal values determines how successful and efficient your network operates.

Assuming that you are up to speed on decimal numbers, we'd like to focus on binary and hexadecimal numbers in this chapter to give you a solid foundation in these numbering systems.

A Word About Why You Need to Know This Stuff . . .

The world of networking, and not just the Cisco networking world, is one of numbers. On occasion, you get to use the good old decimal numbers that you have been using since you discovered your fingers and toes, but you are very likely to be using the binary or the hexadecimal number systems as well.

This chapter is provided to help you to understand the relationships and conversions between decimal, binary, and hexadecimal. If you do not know and understand binary, please do not attempt Chapter 8 without reading this chapter first.

Network subnetting (the topic of Chapter 8) is neck-deep in binary numbers, Boolean algebra, decimal to binary conversion, and sometimes back again. If you wish to succeed in the world of Cisco routers, switches, and other connectivity devices, you really must know this number stuff. Knowing this math stuff is not really that hard. It isn't at all like taking math — trust me. (We'll talk about the swampland sale later.)

Feeling Ambivalent about Binary Numbers

Love 'em or hate 'em, binary numbers are integrated into the very fabric of computers and computing. And taking it one step further, binary numbers are an underlying foundation of networking as well. In fact, the binary number system is the basis of the logic, arithmetic, and addressing functions of all computers, routers, or other networking devices. For no other reason than that, you should be familiar with the binary number system.

In its most complex form, the *binary number system* consists of only two digital values: 1 and 0. Because a transistor is a semiconductor device that is capable of storing only one of two toggled values, the binary number scheme, with its two digital values, and the electronics of the PC are made for one another.

Assigning power to the places

To understand the basics of binary numbers, you should begin with a brief review of decimal numbers. "What!" you say. You know decimal numbers and don't need a review? Trust me: You need this review.

When doesn't 101 equal 101?

When you encounter the number 101, I assume you think of one hundred and one. Sure, anyone would. But what if you were asked to prove why 101 was equal to one hundred and one? "Just because" doesn't explain how you know that these three numbers represent that value. Chances are that you have become so familiar with the decimal number system that you've forgotten what you learned in primary school about number systems.

The number 101 actually represents 1 unit of 10^2 plus no units of 10^1 plus 1 unit of 1^0, or 100 plus 0 plus 1, or one hundred and one (101).

However, if the number system being expressed were to change from decimal to binary, octal, or hexadecimal, the value represented by the numbers 1, 0, and 1 would change dramatically. Table 7-1 shows the effect of changing the number system on the value represented by the digits 101.

Table 7-1	Values in Different Number Systems	
Number System	**Base**	**Decimal Equivalent of Value Represented by 101**
Binary	2	5
Decimal	10	101
Hexadecimal	16	257
Octal	8	65

What the entries in Table 7-1 show is that, although the digits 101 are somewhat universal, the value represented by these digits is quite different under different number systems.

The base of a number system indicates how many characters can be used to represent values. For example, a number system with a base of 2 *(binary)* represents all values by using only two numbers, which in this case are 1 and 0. In the *decimal* system, all values are represented by the numbers 0, 1, 2, 3, 4, 5, 6, 7, 8, and 9. (That's a total of 10 numbers, by the way.) The *hexadecimal* (which means six and ten) system, as you might imagine, uses 16 characters, and the *octal* system uses 8 characters.

Keeping the columnar score

When you write a number in any number system, what you are really writing is how many of each successive columnar value is included in generating the value being represented. Here's an example, using the old trusty 101 again. (Remember that any number raised to the zero power produces 1.)

In decimal, the columnar values represent the powers of ten:

$$10^7 \quad 10^6 \quad 10^5 \quad 10^4 \quad 10^3 \quad 10^2 \quad 10^1 \quad 10^0$$

To represent the value one hundred one, tallies are placed in the appropriate columns to represent that value:

$$10^7 \quad 10^6 \quad 10^5 \quad 10^4 \quad 10^3 \quad 10^2 \quad 10^1 \quad 10^0$$
$$0 \quad\quad 0 \quad\quad 0 \quad\quad 0 \quad\quad 0 \quad\quad 1 \quad\quad 0 \quad\quad 1$$

This is also proof that the digits 101 equal one hundred one in the decimal system.

Turning numbers on and off to create value

Binary values are the result of combining the number 2 being raised to different exponential powers in the same way as decimal numbers. The difference between decimal and binary is that in decimal, although we avoided using them, you can represent columnar values with the numbers 0 through 9. The number placed in the column represents how many of that column's values are used in the number being represented. However, in binary, although the same function is in use, the numbers that can be used to represent how many of a column value are in use are limited to either a 0 or a 1. It is easier to think of binary columns as having an on-and-off switch. If a 1 is used in a column, that column's value is included; if the column has a 0, then that column is off, and no value is represented.

Binary numbers all in a row

The majority of what you need to know about binary numbers for use in networking is the value for each of the 8 bits in a byte. Each of the 8 bits represents a different power of two, in exactly the same pattern used for decimal numbers.

The decimal values for each position of the 8 bits of a byte are:

2^7	2^6	2^5	2^4	2^3	2^2	2^1	2^0
128	64	32	16	8	4	2	1

Using these values, you can determine that the binary number 10101101 represents $128 + 32 + 8 + 4 + 1$ or 173 in decimal values. Those positions with a one are included; those positions with a zero are not — it's really just that simple.

As a network administrator, you (unfortunately) need to know enough about the binary number system to express decimal numbers as binary numbers and which binary positions are used to yield a specific decimal value. You don't need to know binary arithmetic, you know, addition, multiplication, and so on. That should be a relief.

Working with binary numbers is a required skill in developing and applying subnet masks to IP addressing (see Chapter 8). The commonly used IP address (IP Version 4 addressing) consists of four 8-bit binary octets that are typically, and thankfully, expressed as decimal numbers. See Chapter 8 for the details on why this is important to know.

Proving the value of another 101

The key to binary numbers is to remember that each bit in the 8-bit byte represents a power of 2, starting with 0 on the right end up through 7 at the left end. For example, the binary number 00000101 contains the following values:

$1 \times 2^0 = 1$ (any number to the zero power is 1)

$0 \times 2^1 = 0$ (any number to the one power is the number)

$1 \times 2^2 = 4$ (two times two)

$0 \times 2^3 = 0$ (two times two times two)

$0 \times 2^4 = 0$ (two times two times two times two)

$0 \times 2^5 = 0$ (two times two times two times two . . .)

$0 \times 2^6 = 0$

$0 \times 2^7 = 0$

Totaling 5

So 00000101 in binary is the same as 5 in decimal. The largest value that can be stored in 8 bits is 255. This is the decimal value of the binary number 11111111, which is the same as saying $128 + 64 + 32 + 16 + 8 + 4 + 2 + 1 = 255$.

Practice makes perfect conversions

As I say earlier in this section, you should know how to convert decimal values to binary and, especially, binary values into decimal. Use these steps to convert a decimal number into a binary number:

1. **Determine the largest power of two that can be subtracted from the number.**

   For the number 248, the largest binary value that can be represented in 8 bits is 128, or 2^7. The easiest way to determine this is to find the highest value that is less than the number you are converting. Because you know for sure that 128 is less than 248, you can place a 1 in the left-most position of the 8-bit set. So far, your binary number is 10000000.

2. **Subtract the bit value from the original number.**

   The difference of $248 - 128$ is 120. Repeating the process used in Step 1, the next highest value that can be subtracted from the number is 64, or 2^6. Your binary number is now 11000000.

3. **Until the remaining value of the original decimal value reaches zero, repeat Step 1.**

   The final binary number for 248 is 11111000.

Now try these steps for any number between 11 (no reason to make it too easy) and 255.

You can also convert a decimal number to binary in a less-complicated way. You simply divide the number by 2 and save the remainder. (It will be either 1 or 0.) Continue dividing the *quotient* (the answer in a division problem) by 2 and saving the remainder until all you have is remainder. For example, in our original problem of converting the decimal 248, you would:

1. Divide 248 by 2 to get 124, with a remainder of 0.

2. Next divide 124 by 2 to get 62, with a remainder of 0.

3. Divide 62 by 2 to get 31, with a remainder of 0.

4. Divide 31 by 2 to get 15, with a remainder of 1.

5. Divide 15 by 2 to get 7, with a remainder of 1.

6. Divide 7 by 2 to get 3, with a remainder of 1.

7. Divide 3 by 2 to get 1, with a remainder of 1.

8. Divide 1 by 2 to get 0, with a remainder of 1.

Now write down the remainders, last to first, 11111000, and you have the binary number for the decimal 248. When converting a number like 25, you would end up with the binary number 11001, but all 8 bits must be accounted for, so zeroes must be added to represent the leading positions: 00011001. Try converting a few decimal numbers yourself, perhaps a smaller number like 17. Remember that all 8 bits must be accounted for.

Of course, an even simpler way is to use a scientific calculator or the Windows Calculator (in Scientific view) to convert these numbers, but you won't always have one with you, so being able to convert decimal numbers to binary is a good skill for a network administrator to have.

Hexing the Numbers

The word *hexadecimal* means six and ten, and that's just what this number system is about. Where binary includes only 0 and 1, *hex,* as it's known to its friends, includes the decimal numerals 0 to 9 (the 10) and replaces the decimal values of 10 to 15 with the symbols A, B, C, D, E, and F (the 6).

In networking, the principal use of hexadecimal numbers is to provide a shorthand way of recording and displaying long binary numbers. Hexadecimal is commonly used to display the long binary addresses of memory, ports, and interfaces, which would be too prone to error not to mention tedious to work with, if their addresses or information were entered or displayed in binary. Computer technicians use hex numbers to identify IRQs, LPT, or COM ports. For example, the hex number 2F8 is the default address of IRQ3 and COM2.

In most cases, you rarely need to know the decimal equivalent of a hexadecimal number. However, the ability to convert hexadecimal numbers is a good basic skill for anyone working with personal computers and networking hardware, because you often need to convert a range of hex addresses to decimal to determine the size of a block of memory or storage or an address range.

One more bit of good news is that you never, repeat *never,* should need to convert a decimal number to a hexadecimal number, although you should probably know how, just in case.

Hexing decimal numbers

The *number base* (technically, the *radix*) for decimal is 10, for binary it's 2, and for hexadecimal it's 16. While you roll that around in your head for a while (not too long — it causes headaches), remember that you have nothing to fear. What we have is just another way to represent exponential powers of a base in columns.

Hexadecimal numbers are expressed as powers of 16 in exactly the same way that I've shown earlier in this chapter for decimal and binary:

16^5	16^4	16^3	16^2	16^1	16^0
1,048,576	65,536	4,096	256	16	1

As you can see from the preceding, hexadecimal numbers can represent very large numbers with only a few characters. Although you will rarely need to think of it, the hexadecimal number 101 is equivalent to decimal 257. This is $256 + 0 + 1 = 257$.

Bear in mind that, like decimal with its 10 numeric values that can be used in each column of the number, hexadecimal has 16 values that are used to represent how many of a power of 16 are included in the number being represented. For example, the hexadecimal number 3A7F9 has the decimal equivalent of 239,609.

Converting hexadecimal numbers

To convert any nondecimal number system into decimal is a matter of knowing two things: the base value of the number system and the numeric value of each position. In binary numbers, each position represents a different power of two; the same holds true in any number system, including hexadecimal. The difference with hexadecimal is that each position represents a different power of 16.

The base value of a number is the value represented by the expression "10." The base of decimal is 10, the base of binary is 2, and the base of hexadecimal is 16. Therefore, 10 in decimal is 10; 10 in binary is 2; 10 in octal (base 8) is 8; and 10 in hexadecimal is 16.

Use the following steps to find the decimal equivalent for the hex number A012F:

1. **Figure the value of the first character.**

   Because each position represents a power of 16, the A in A012F represents the positional value of 16^4. The A has the decimal equivalent of 10. So this position is worth 10×16^4, or 655,360.

2. **Repeat Step 1 until you have figured the values for the rest of the characters.**

   The next position of value is a 1 in the position of 16^2, which is worth 256.

   The next position has a value of 2×16^0, or 32.

   The last position has the value of F (15) $\times 16^0$, or 15. Any number to the zero power is worth 1, so this is the same as 15×1.

3. **Add up the values for the final value.**

   Add 655,360 + 256 + 32 + 15, and you get the sum of 655,663, which is the decimal equivalent of A012F hexadecimal.

Just a nybble more on hexadecimal

If you understand how hexadecimal works and how it is used to represent decimal numbers (see the preceding two sections), you are ready to deal with how hexadecimal is used to display binary numbers.

Each 8-bit byte can be divided into two 4-bit halves, each of which is called a *nybble*. Seriously, that is what it's called. A nybble is perfect for holding one hexadecimal number, because four binary bits are capable of storing the decimal values 0 to 15.

If you were to convert the binary number 11111111 (decimal 255) to hexadecimal, the resulting hex number is FF. Converting the decimal address 2587469 to binary yields 1001110111101101001101, but this same value in hexadecimal is 277B4D. Hexadecimal takes the bytes holding the binary number, splits them into nybbles, and then converts each nybble to a hex number.

Table 7-2 shows how this works for the numbers in the preceding paragraph.

Table 7-2	Converting Binary to Hexadecimal
Nybble Contents	*Hexadecimal Number*
0010	2
0100	4
0111	7

Nybble Contents	Hexadecimal Number
1001	9
1011	B
1101	D
1111	F

As Table 7-2 shows, long binary numbers are easily represented as hexadecimal numbers for entry and display. If you ever really want to know the value of an address (and there may or may not come a time that you do), simply convert it to binary and then to decimal.

Hexadecimal numbers are usually written with a small *h* following them. For example, the number used in the preceding steps is commonly written as A012Fh. You will also see hexadecimal numbers represented as 0xA012F, where the *0x* is another way to designate a hexadecimal number. However, as you will see in later chapters, some Cisco router commands expect hexadecimal parameters without any designation characters.

Using the tool available

Probably the best, because it is the most readily available, tool you have for converting decimal, binary, or hexadecimal numbers is the Windows Calculator. This handy tool is found on the Windows Start⇨Programs⇨Accessories menus of just about any Windows version, including 98, NT, and 2000. To select the Scientific version of the calculator, choose Scientific from the View menu option.

Using a calculator is by far the easiest way to convert number systems, but knowing how to convert them can come in handy, especially when working with debugging and troubleshooting tools, configuring a router, or subnetting a network.

Chapter 8

The Curse of the Subnet Mask and Other Boolean Tales

. . . .

In This Chapter

▶ Explaining network addressing

▶ Describing the IPv4 addressing scheme

▶ Discussing network subnetting

▶ Reviewing the IPv6 addressing scheme

. . . .

*N*etworking is like delivering pizza — without the right address, it doesn't matter how good the pizza is or how fast the delivery service. Your product is wasted if it can't reach its destination. On the network, a message, like the pizza, must have a valid address if it ever hopes to reach its destination. Knowledge and understanding of network addressing schemes, especially the IPv4 (IP addressing, version 4), are essential to your success as a network administrator. This is true whether or not your network connects to the Internet. In this chapter, I look at all aspects of network addressing. Well, at least, as it relates to Cisco networking, that is.

How May I Address You?

Just as the post office and the pizza dude expect you to have an address that uniquely finds you and your home, each node on a network must also be uniquely identified. If you wish to log onto a network, use a network's resources, download information from a Web site, or receive e-mail, the workstation you are working on must be able to be found on the network. Without some unique identification for your node, the network won't know where to send any information, e-mail, or files intended for you.

As a person, you also have many ways to be identified, including your social security number, your phone number, your Wal-Mart frequent shopper card number, and others. On a network, a computer also has several ways to be identified. It can be addressed by its MAC address (see "Getting physical with

MAC addressing," later in this chapter), an IP address, perhaps an IPX address, and perhaps even a URL.

Two forms of addressing can be used to locate a node on a network:

- ✔ **Network address:** A network address, which is also called a *logical address,* relates to all other addresses on the network in the sense that the address is assigned as a part of a logical grouping, such as with an IP address, and uniquely identifies both the network node and the network on which it is found.
- ✔ **Physical address:** A *physical address* bears no relationship to any other physical address on the network because it is assigned by a manufacturer of network adapters and, therefore, can be used to identify only a single network interface in a single workstation or node.

Dissecting the network address

A network address has two parts: a host ID, which identifies an individual node or workstation, and a network ID, which designates the network or network segment on which the host ID can be found. Various network addressing schemes are in use, but the IPv4 addressing scheme is the one most commonly used on Cisco networks.

Look at this example of an IPv4 network address:

204.106.100.131

In this example, 204.106.100 represents the network ID of this Class C address, and the .131 portion is the host ID.

Getting physical with MAC addressing

The most common physical addressing scheme used on Cisco networks, and all other networks as well, is the *media access control (MAC)* address. The MAC address is a Data Link layer (Layer 2 of the OSI Model) address and is generally the address of a network interface card (NIC). The MAC address is also referred to as the *Ethernet address, physical address,* or the *burned-in* (as opposed to burned-out) *address.* See Chapter 2 for information on the OSI Model and its layers and Chapter 3 for information on the Ethernet standards.

MAC addresses are flat addresses, which means they identify only the node to which they are attached and have no relation to the rest of the network. In a network address, the hosts on a single network segment all have the same network ID, but MAC addresses are issued individually to network adapters and other networking devices when they are manufactured. The only thing MAC addresses may have in common is the manufacturer's ID in the number assigned to its products.

In case you didn't know it, the equipment on your network doesn't all have to be from the same manufacturer, no matter what Cisco or the kid at the computer store tell you. Therefore, the chance of having even two MAC addresses in sequence on one network is extremely slim. Think of a MAC address like the number on your credit card — that number is assigned to you and can be used to identify you, but it doesn't link to much beyond your name.

A *MAC address* is a 48-bit (6-byte) number that is represented on Cisco equipment as six two-digit hexadecimal numbers separated by dots (periods). Figure 8-1 shows the display generated by the Windows utility WINIPCFG that includes an Adapter Address box that displays the MAC address of this computer's network interface card.

In the MAC address shown in Figure 8-1, the first three bytes (24 bits) contain a code assigned to the manufacturer of the card by the IEEE (in this case 44-45-53, which is LinkSys), and the last three bytes (24 bits) contain a unique serialized number assigned to this particular network interface card by the manufacturer when it was manufactured (54-00-00).

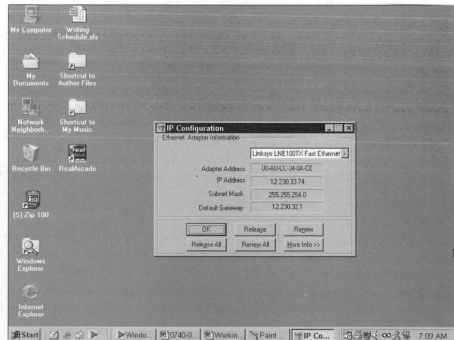

Figure 8-1:
The WINIPCFG display includes the MAC address of a computer's network adapter.

Just so you know, Cisco has many MAC address manufacturer codes assigned to it, including 00 00 0C, 00 06 7C, 00 06 C1, 00 10 07, and others. For a complete list of MAC manufacturer codes, the IEEE has the complete list at standards.ieee.org/regauth/oui/index.shtml.

Networking devices, such as routers, often use a couple of protocols — ARP and RARP — to learn about addresses on their network. *ARP (Address Resolution Protocol)* is used to find a MAC address from a known IP address. *RARP (Reverse Address Resolution Protocol)* is used to translate a MAC address into an associated IP address.

Working with MAC addresses

What you should know at this point is that a MAC address is the unique identifier of the adapter, usually a NIC, used to connect a device to the network. This is all well and good as long as the only addresses ever used on a network are MAC addresses. What happens when somebody from outside your network wants to address one of your network's nodes with something other than the MAC address, such as an IP address? What then?

If your network is using a network protocol that allows for addressing other than the MAC address, it will have a mechanism for translating these other addresses to the MAC address of each node. For example, if your network is using TCP/IP (a wise choice, I might add), then each of your network nodes also has an IP address. This is great for communicating over a WAN, but on the LAN, it is the MAC address that is king.

TCP/IP includes two protocols that are used to resolve (which is the really cool network way of saying "translate") the MAC and IP addresses of a node, ARP and RARP:

- **ARP (Address Resolution Protocol):** This sends out a broadcast message to learn the MAC address of a specific IP address. The node with the broadcasted IP address responds with its MAC address, completing the set. There are no discounts to older networks by this protocol — that's AARP.

- **Reverse ARP (RARP):** Broadcasts messages to learn the IP address corresponding to a specific MAC address. This requires the presence of a RARP (pronounced "rarp," what else?) server on the network.

The associated pairs of addresses, the MAC and IP addresses, for a network node are stored in memory in a table referred to as the *ARP cache.*

What a Novell idea!

Some network addresses incorporate a MAC address. A primary example of this is Novell's IPX protocols. IPX addresses are not classified into address classes as are IP addresses. The IPX address is ten bytes (80 bits) long. Of these ten bytes, four bytes (32 bits) represent the network ID, and six bytes (48 bits) are used for the hexadecimal node ID, which is normally the MAC address of the node. The ten-byte length of the network ID is often misleading because any leading zeroes, something quite common, are not usually shown in the number.

For example, look at the following IPX address:

```
4b2c.0000.06d2.ef67
```

In this example, the network ID is 4b2c (actually it is 00004b2c, but the leading 0s are suppressed), and the node ID is 0000.06d2.ef67.(Notice that leading 0s are shown in the node ID.)

The Wondrous World of IP Addressing

The most commonly used addressing scheme on Cisco networks is the IP (Internet Protocol) addressing scheme. In fact, the IP addressing scheme is the scheme of choice on the Internet as well. As a network administrator of a Cisco network, IP addressing will become second nature, as well as a second language, for you.

Keep these IP address basics in mind:

- ✔ IP addresses are assigned by Internet Corporation for Assigned Numbers and Names (ICANN) and one of its subagencies, the American Registry for Internet Numbers (ARIN), the agencies responsible for assigning and tracking the network IDs used on the Internet.

- ✔ IP addresses are made up of four 8-bit decimal numbers connected by periods (dots). For example, the IP address for www.hungryminds.com is 168.215.86.100.

- ✔ IP addresses are 32 bits in length, with each of the four numbers using 8 bits.

- ✔ Each of the 8-bit numbers is called an *octet*.

- ✔ What each separate octet means depends on the *class* of the IP address.

- ✔ The octets in an IP address, depending on the address class, are a part of either the network identity or the host (node) identity.

- ✔ IP addresses are divided into five address classes: Classes A, B, C, D, and E.

The four octets are usually written as what is called dotted-decimal notation. The four octet number format is also commonly known as IP version 4. The four does not have anything to do with the four octets. In fact, the rapid expansion of the Internet is causing a shortage of IPv4 addresses, which is why the 128-bit IP version 6 address is now available. An IPv6 address has 16 octets.

Bringing on the binary

The binary system is a numbering system that uses only two values (0 and 1) to represent numbers. Computers, unlike most humans, flourish in binary. In order for a computer to process an address, the address must be expressed in terms that the computer can understand. This situation is the reason for the binary values. Fortunately for us humans, binary numbers can be expressed as decimal numbers by converting the binary value into a decimal value — a talent that you need to acquire as a network administrator.

I'm not going into too much detail here on the binary number system. If you aren't too familiar with binary numbers, you really should review Chapter 7 before you continue with this chapter. IP addressing and subnet masks require that you have at least a basic understanding of the binary number system and how it represents values.

You must absolutely know two fundamental and essential principles of binary to work with network addresses: the largest decimal number that can be expressed in an 8-bit binary number is 255, and the lowest value that can be expressed in 8-bits is 00000000. So, if an 8-bit binary number is all 1s (11111111), it represents 255, and if it is all 0s, it is 0. Actually, you do need to understand why. If you don't, check out Chapter 7.

As discussed earlier in this chapter, an IP address consists of four 8-bit binary numbers, called *octets*. In binary, an IP address may look something like this, at least to routers and computers:

11111111.11111111.11111111.11111111

But because binary values are difficult for humans to deal with, IP addresses are typically displayed (at least among the humans) as decimal numbers, for example

255.255.255.255

This may seem pretty straightforward, but as I discuss later, the binary value in the octet (and not the decimal value it represents) is what is important.

Separating the IP Classes

Before reading this section, you may want to review the IP addressing rules in "The Wondrous World of IP Addressing," earlier in the chapter, to refresh your understanding of how an IP address is constructed.

Ignore the percentages

Yes, I know that the percentages in the IP address classes do not add up to 100 percent. Don't worry about why. In fact, don't worry about these percentages at all. I included them to give you a sense of scale. But now that you've asked, the remaining addresses are special IP addresses or unassigned addresses.

Characteristics of the IP Address Classes

Class	Bits in Network ID	Number of Networks	Bits in Host ID	Number of Hosts/ Network	Address Range
A	8	128	24	16,777,214	1.0.0.0 to 126.255.255.255
B	16	16,386	16	65,534	128.0.0.0 to 191.255.255.255
C	24	2,097,154	8	254	192.0.0.0 to 223.255.255.255
D	0	0	32	268,400,000	224.0.0.0.0 to 239.255.255.255
E	Class E addresses are reserved for future use				

IP addressing is divided into five address classes that are designated as A through E. As you read about the different IP address classes, bear in mind that the inventors of this class system thought the Internet would remain a fairly small and exclusive club. The original meaning has eroded a bit, but by and large, the address classes represent a hierarchy of IP address assignments in which Class A addresses are intended to be assigned to larger, complex networks, Class B addresses to less-complex and somewhat smaller networks, and Class C addresses to local networks and ISPs (Internet service providers).

Class A IP addresses

Class A IP addresses are awarded to large networks. Class A addresses use only the first octet (8 bits) for the network ID. The other three octets contain the host address. These addresses range from 1.*hhh.hhh.hhh* to 127.*hhh.hhh.hhh*, where all of the *hhh*s identify a host computer's address, and the numbers indicate the address ranges assigned to this address class. More than 50 percent of the available IP addresses are Class A addresses.

There are 128 network (0 to 127) values available, but the network addresses with all 0s or 1s and the network addresses in the 127 group are reserved as special network addresses (see "Using Special Network Addresses," later in this chapter). So, the net effect (no pun intended) is that the available group of Class A networks is essentially 1 through 126.

Calculating the number of hosts on a network

Each Class A network can address 16,777,214 network nodes. To compute the number of hosts or nodes that can be addressed on a Class A network (or Class B or C network, for that matter), use this formula:

$$(2^n - 2) = \text{\# of available hosts}$$

In this formula, n represents the number of bits in the host ID portion of the address.

In a Class A address, 8 bits are used for the network ID, and 24 bits are used for the host ID. So, by applying the formula, you can verify the number of hosts available on a Class A network as

$$(2^{24} - 2) = (16,777,216 - 2) = 16,777,214$$

For the Class A address, the number of host ID bits is 24. Two to the 24th power is 16,777,216 (my lucky number!), and this number minus two is 16,777,214. So the number of hosts that can be addressed on a Class A network is 16,777,214. Why subtract two addresses? Two are subtracted because IDs (addresses) with all 1s and all 0s have special purposes (see "Using Special Network Addresses," later in this chapter).

The number of bits in the network ID plus the number of bits in the host ID will always equal 32. Another way to think of this is that the number of bits in the host ID is 32 minus the number of bits in the network ID, which you know from the address class. How do you know the address class? By the number in the first octet.

Class B IP addresses

Class B addresses are assigned to medium-sized networks. Around 25 percent of all available IP addresses are Class B addresses. Class B addresses use 14 bits to identify the network (2 bits are reserved to indicate that the address is a Class B address), which limits Class B to a total of 16,382 network addresses that can be used. Class B networks are in the range of 128.0.*hhh.hhh* (*hhh* represents the host address) to 191.255.*hhh.hhh*. This means that each Class B network can address more than 65,534 hosts.

Class C IP addresses

Class C networks are assigned to relatively small networks. Class C addresses account for 12.5 percent of all available IP addresses. Class C addresses use 21 bits to identify the network (three bits are used to indicate that the address is a Class C address), which allows for more than 2 million networks to be identified in the range of 192.0.0.*hhh* to 223.255.255.*hhh*. This leaves 8 bits to identify the host computers, and as is the case with all IP addressing, the host addresses with all 0s or 1s are special function addresses (see "Using Special Network Addresses," later in this chapter).

Each Class C network can address a maximum of 254 host addresses ($2^8 - 2 = 254$). If you understand your binary, you're probably wondering why — if there are 8 bits available to identify the hosts — only 254 hosts are possible. In case I haven't mentioned it before, the hosts with all 1s and all 0s are reserved for special address functions.

Class D and Class E IP addresses

Class D is set aside especially for *IP multicasting* and does not have network and host ID parts. IP multicasting sends datagrams to a group of hosts, which may be located on many separate networks. Class D addresses are in the range of 224.*hhh.hhh.hhh* to 239.*hhh.hhh.hhh*. Address 224.0.0.0 is reserved and cannot be used, and address 224.0.0.1 is reserved for addressing all hosts participating in an IP multicast.

Class E addresses, which are in the range from 240.0.0.0 to 254.255.255.255 are reserved for future use and are not presently available for use. But before you ask about 255.255.255.255, think about it for a minute.

Using Special Network Addresses

Network addresses that contain all binary 0s and 1s and network addresses beginning with 127 are special network addresses. Table 8-1 lists the special network addresses.

Table 8-1		Special Network Addresses	
Network Part	*Host Part*	*Example*	*Description*
All 0s	All 0s	0.0.0.0	This host
All 0s	A host ID	0.0.0.34	A host on this network

(continued)

Table 8-1 *(continued)*

Network Part	Host Part	Example	Description
All 1s	All 1s	255.255.255.255	Broadcast to local network
A network ID	All 1s	197.21.12.255	Broadcast to all logically networked hosts of given range
127	All 1s or 0s	127.0.0.1	Loopback testing

Additional ranges of numbers are set aside for use by network managers for intranets and internal networks that do not connect to the Internet. These addresses are in three ranges:

> 10.0.0.0 through 10.255.255.255
>
> 172.16.0.0 through 172.31.255.255
>
> 192.168.0.0 through 192.168.255.255

Subnetting a Network

Okay, I put it off as long as I could, but I can't avoid it any longer, I have to use the "S" word — subnetting. I'm sorry to be so blunt and just blurt it out like that, but I've found that the best way is to just jump on in and either sink or swim.

Subnetting is the process of logically dividing the network IP address into a group of segments, called subnetworks. The subnet mask is the 32-bit binary number used by the router to *extract,* or *mask out,* the subnet address.

Subnetting a network can solve many networking problems, including reducing traffic, increasing throughput, improving performance, curing dandruff, getting dates, and others. But, the best reason for subnetting is simplified management of the network. Oh, and by the way, I was just kidding about the dandruff. The two main reasons to subnet are

✔ **An unlimited number of IP addresses is not available.** Unless you upgrade to IPv6, you have to do more with the addresses you have. (See "Expanding the IP Horizon," later in this chapter.)

✔ **A router needs a way to identify the network portion of an IP address.** All classes of addresses (A, B, and C) have a definite number of bits that are required for their network address, as shown in Table 8-2.

Table 8-2	IP Address Class Breakdowns	
Class	**Network Bits**	**Host Bits**
A	8	24
B	16	16
C	24	8

You should be able to easily spot the pattern in Table 8-2. Take your time; I'll wait for you. That's right! As the Class level decreases, from A to C, more bits are used for the network ID, and fewer are used for the host ID.

The other part of subnetting is the *subnet mask*. Table 8-3 lists the default subnet masks used as the basis for developing your own subnet mask. Don't worry about the default masks right now, but remember where you saw them for later reference.

Table 8-3	Default Subnet Masks
IP Address Class	**Subnet Mask**
Class A	255.0.0.0
Class B	255.255.0.0
Class C	255.255.255.0

For many people, subnet masks and subnetting are the most difficult parts of the network administrator's job to master. But, the need to memorize the details of subnetting is lessened every day. As the tools get more sophisticated, the network administrator can rely on them more and on his or her memory less. One such tool is a subnet calculator that you can use to help plan out your network, but even with this tool, you should try to gain as much ability as you can in doing those subnetting calculations.

May I borrow a couple of bits until Tuesday?

What is involved with subnetting is borrowing bits from the host ID portion of the IP address to allow for more networks (actually subnetworks). Remember that the number of networks in an IP address class is determined by the number of bits used to identify the network ID. By adding more bits to the network ID, you can naturally identify more networks. Of course, this ability comes with a price. IP addresses still have only 32 bits, so if you use more for the network ID, then fewer are available for the host ID portion. This setup is okay, because the goal is to have more addressable networks with fewer hosts on each subnetwork.

The trick is to borrow just enough bits from the host ID so that you can address the subnets you need and still be able to address all the host IDs you need as well. The 32-bit IP address is a fixed-length entity; you don't have more bits to use. Also remember that you, as the network administrator, control only the host ID portion of the address, so you can borrow bits only from that part of the address.

Most subnetting in real life, as opposed to the fantasy world of this book, typically involves only Class B and C addresses, because those are the addresses that are really available to smaller local area networks. If you will be working with a Class A network involving millions of nodes, just remember that the applications are the same, but the scale is much grander. But chances are good that you will work with Class C addressing on an internal private network address scheme, just like I do.

The best way to learn subnetting is to do it. Our explanations cannot possibly be so good that anyone can safely begin subnetting a network without some practice. Yes, subnet calculators are available and they are a helpful tool when accuracy is important, like on your network. It can't hurt for you to do some paper-and-pencil practice to help you lock in the concepts and fundamentals of subnetting and subnet masks.

Subnetting a Class A network

The Class A IP address includes only 8 bits for the network ID, leaving 24 bits for the host. If you wish to subnet a Class A network, you need to borrow a sufficient number of bits from the host ID portion of the mask to allow for the number of subnets you plan to create, now and in the future.

For example, if you wish to create two subnets with over 4 million hosts per subnet, you can borrow 2 bits from the second octet and use 10 masked (positions in the mask with a 1 value) bits for the subnet mask (11111111 11000000) or 255.192 in decimal. This results in a new subnet mask of 255.192.0.0

Keep in mind that the 8-bit octets have binary place values, as shown in Table 8-4. When you borrow bits from the host ID portion of the standard mask, you don't change the value of the bits; you only change how they are used and the decimal value that results from adding them.

Table 8-4	IP Address Octet Binary Values	
Bit Number	**Power of 2**	**Decimal Value**
8	2^7	128
7	2^6	64
6	2^5	32
5	2^4	16
4	2^3	8
3	2^2	4
2	2^1	2
1	2^0	1

For a Class A network that needs a maximum of 254 subnets with 65,534 hosts on each subnet, you must borrow 8 bits from the host ID, creating a subnet mask with 16 masked bits, 255.255.0.0.

Table 8-5 includes a sampling of subnet mask options available for Class A addresses.

Table 8-5	Class A Subnet Masks		
Subnet Mask	**Number of One Bits in Mask**	**Number of Subnets**	**Number of Hosts per Subnet**
255.0.0.0	8	0	16,777,214
255.192.0.0	10	2	4,194,302
255.240.0.0	12	14	1,048,574
255.255.0.0	16	254	65,534
255.255.128.0	17	510	32,766
255.255.240.0	20	4,094	4,094
255.255.255.128	25	131,070	126
255.255.255.240	28	1,048,574	14
255.255.255.252	30	4,194,302	2

The third entry in Table 8-5 lists a subnet mask of 255.240.0.0 that uses 12 bits to indicate the network ID. You know that 8 bits of the network ID are used for the Class A network ID, so 4 bits are used for the subnet portion of the address. Applying the number of networks formula ($2^4 - 2 = 14$), you know that you can address 14 subnets. The number of hosts formula ($2^{20} - 2 = 1,048,574$) indicates that more than a million hosts are available on each subnet.

How would you know that 12 bits were used in the network portion of the mask if Table 8-5 wasn't available? Well, if you convert the subnet mask to its binary equivalent, you get this:

> 11111111.11110000.00000000.00000000

You know that 11111111 is the binary equivalent for the decimal value 255, which is the first value in the mask. The next portion indicates that the binary values (refer to Table 8-4) of positions 8 (2^7), 7 (2^6), 6 (2^5), and 5 (2^4) are to be added. These are $128 + 64 + 32 + 16$, which equals 240, the value in the second position.

The number of 1s in a subnet mask cannot be more than 30 bits in length. (The subnet mask is always 32 bits long.) Also remember that the addresses with all 1s and all 0s cannot be used because they have special meanings (see "Using Special Network Addresses," earlier in this chapter).

You should see a pattern (a bit pattern actually) in Table 8-5. As more bits are taken from the host ID and used in the subnet mask to identify subnets, more subnets are possible but with fewer hosts per subnet.

Subnetting a Class B network

For a Class B network, 14 bits are available to be borrowed from the host ID (8 from the third octet and 6 from the fourth octet). The subnet masks available for a Class B network are listed in Table 8-6.

Table 8-6	Class B Subnet Mask Values		
Bits Used	*Binary Value*	*Decimal Value*	*Subnet Mask*
14	11111111 11111100	255.252	255.255.255.252
13	11111111 11111000	255.248	255.255.255.248
12	11111111 11110000	255.240	255.255.255.240
11	11111111 11100000	255.224	255.255.255.224
10	11111111 11000000	255.192	255.255.255.192

Bits Used	Binary Value	Decimal Value	Subnet Mask
9	11111111 10000000	255.128	255.255.255.128
8	11111111 00000000	255.0	255.255.255.0
7	11111110 00000000	254.0	255.255.254.0
6	11111100 00000000	252.0	255.255.252.0
5	11111000 00000000	248.0	255.255.248.0
4	11110000 00000000	240.0	255.255.240.0
3	11100000 00000000	224.0	255.255.224.0
2	11000000 00000000	192.0	255.255.192.0

For a Class B network with an IP address of 172.16.31.0 and a subnet mask of 255.255.255.252, how many subnets and hosts are available per subnet?

Do this one the hard way:

The decimal value in the fourth octet is 252, which has the binary equivalent of 11111100; I used the handy Windows Calculator to convert this number (see Figure 8-2). You could do it the really hard way, but why?

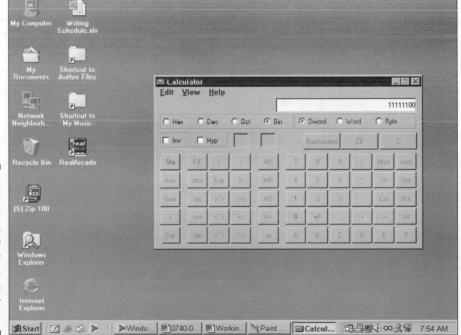

Figure 8-2:
The Windows Calculator is a handy tool for converting decimal to binary or vice versa.

The binary equivalent of 252 (11111100) tells you that 6 bits have been borrowed from the last octet. Don't forget that I am working on a Class B subnet, and I must account for the value 255 in the third octet as well. If you haven't already done so, commit to memory that the value 255 means that all 8 bits are in use. So, if you add up all the bits used to create the subnet mask in the third and fourth octets and insert them into the formulas, you'd get:

Number of Subnets = $2^{14} - 2$

Number of Subnets = $16,384 - 2$

Number of Subnets = $16,382$

Again, 6 bits were used for subnetting, so only 2 bits remain for identifying host IDs.

Number of Hosts = $2^2 - 2$

Number of Hosts = $4 - 2$

Number of Hosts = 2

This tells us that a Class B network with the address 172.16.31.0 and a subnet mask of 255.255.255.252 can address 16,382 subnets of two hosts each. Table 8-7 lists the rest of the Class B possibilities.

Table 8-7		Class B Subnetting	
Subnet Mask	**Subnet Bits**	**Subnets**	**Hosts**
255.255.255.252	14	16,382	2
255.255.255.248	13	8,190	6
255.255.255.240	12	4,094	14
255.255.255.224	11	2,046	30
255.255.255.192	10	1,022	62
255.255.255.128	9	510	126
255.255.255.0	8	254	254
255.255.254.0	7	126	510
255.255.252.0	6	62	1,022
255.255.248.0	5	30	2,046
255.255.240.0	4	14	4,094
255.255.224.0	3	6	8,190

Subnet Mask	Subnet Bits	Subnets	Hosts
255.255.192.0	2	2	16,382
255.255.128.0	1		Not a legal subnet
255.255.0.0	0	1	65,534

Subnetting a Class C network

On the standard Class C address, 24 bits are used to identify the network ID, and 8 bits are used to identify the host ID. To create a subnet, bits are borrowed from the host ID for the network ID. You can borrow up to 6 bits of the fourth octet to create your subnet. The more bits you borrow, the more sub-networks you can create, but at the expense of fewer hosts per subnetwork. You must leave at least 2 bits for the host (no, not a tip; you leave the last two numbers on the right) in the octet; bits are borrowed from left to right. Table 8-8 lists the resulting subnet values created from borrowing bits from the host ID.

Table 8-8	Class C Subnet Mask Values		
Bits Used	Binary Value	Decimal Value	Subnet Mask
6	11111100	252	255.255.255.252
5	11111000	248	255.255.255.248
4	11110000	240	255.255.255.240
3	11100000	224	255.255.255.224
2	11000000	192	255.255.255.192

Table 8-9 summarizes Class C network subnetting. This table can come in handy when you are working on networks, and your computer and subnet calculator aren't available.

Table 8-9	Class C Subnetting		
Subnet Mask	Subnet Bits	Subnets	Hosts
255.255.255.252	6	62	2
255.255.255.248	5	30	6
255.255.255.240	4	14	14

(continued)

Table 8-9 *(continued)*

Subnet Mask	Subnet Bits	Subnets	Hosts
255.255.255.224	3	6	30
255.255.255.192	2	2	62
255.255.255.128	1	Not a legal subnet value (Trust me!)	
255.255.255.0	0	1	254

Examining your subnet options

After you understand where subnet numbers come from (you do, don't you?), then you need to determine how many subnets and hosts per subnet are created for the various available subnets.

Two simple formulas calculate these numbers:

Number of hosts per subnet = $(2^{\text{number of bits used for host}}) - 2$

Number of subnets = $(2^{\text{number of bits used for subnets}}) - 2$

These formulas look somewhat familiar to the one I talk about earlier in this chapter (see the section, "Calculating the number of hosts on a network"); but if you look closely, these formulas are completely different from that one, as well as from each other. These two formulas are used independently to determine the number of hosts available on a subnet and the number of subnets available given the number of bits used in the subnet addressing. Which formula you use depends on what you are using the bits for, the host or the subnet.

Work through this example with me:

A Class C address 192.168.1.1 has a subnet mask of 255.255.255.252. To create this subnet mask, 6 bits have been borrowed (see Table 8-8). So the calculation is this:

Number of subnets = $2^6 - 2$

Number of subnets = $64 - 2$

Number of subnets = 62

If 6 bits were borrowed for subnetting, then 2 bits are available for host IDs. The calculation to determine the number of hosts available on each subnet is as follows:

Number of hosts = $2^2 - 2$

Number of hosts = $4 - 2$

Number of hosts = 2

Applying Your New Knowledge

In this section, I provide you with a bit of practice on developing network subnetting. If you are a genius at subnetting, this may be child's play for you, but if you are learning about subnets, masks, and IP addressing for the first time, the problems in this section should draw on your knowledge of the following:

- ✔ **Binary numbers:** See Chapter 7 for a review.
- ✔ **IP address classes:** See "Separating the IP Classes," earlier in the chapter.
- ✔ **Subnetting a network and developing a subnet mask:** See "Subnetting a Network," earlier in the chapter.

Using what you know, can you determine the subnet address of the Class C address 192.168.1.1 that has a mask of 255.255.255.192? To really show off, go ahead and do it longhand.

In binary, the host address in question is this:

11000000(192)   10101000(168)   00000001(1)   00000001(1)

The subnet mask is this:

11111111(255)   11111111(255)   11111111(255)   11000000(192)

If you "and" these two together by using Boolean algebra, the process is as follows (see "Taking the *boo* out of Boolean algebra," later in the chapter, for information on Boolean algebra and "anding"):

11000000 10101000 00000001 00000001 (Host address)

11111111 11111111 11111111 11000000 (Subnet mask)

11000000 10101000 00000001 00000000 (Network address)

The resulting network address is 192.168.1.0. This is exactly the process used by the host to determine whether or not a packet should be framed and forwarded directly to the host (on the same network) or to a local router interface to be forwarded to a remote network. By stripping away the host portion of the IP address, the network (interface) address is exposed. That, in a nutshell, is how and why subnetting and subnet masks help you to subdivide the network logically into smaller administrative groupings.

Developing valid subnets, hosts, and broadcasts

What are the valid subnets, hosts, and broadcast addresses for the network 192.168.1.0 using a subnet mask of 255.255.255.192?

Piece of cake! You know that the address is a Class C address. (Class C addresses are between 192 and 223 — see "Class C IP addresses," earlier in the chapter.) And with a Class C subnet mask value of 192, two subnets are available with 62 available hosts per network (refer to Table 8-5).

Now for a new piece of information: To calculate the number of valid subnets on a network, subtract the subnet mask (192, in this case) from 256. The equation is: 256 – 192 = 64. Now, beginning at zero, count the number of times you can increment by this number (64, in this case) to reach the mask value, not counting the last increment. In this example, you can increment from 0 to 192 twice:

> 192.168.1.64
>
> 192.168.1.128

These IP addresses are valid subnet addresses, which are also known as the *wire addresses* of the subnets.

The *broadcast address* of a subnet is the highest number available in the subnet (for example, 192.168.1.127), which should be one less than the next subnetwork address. Outside of subnetting, the broadcast address of a network is one in which the host address is all binary 1s, or a value of 255. In subnetting, this is still the case, although it may not appear that way. Subnet broadcast addresses don't always look like broadcast networks when represented in decimal values, but in each case the bits used for the host positions in a subnet broadcast address are all 1s, just like in an octet representing 255.

In this particular example, the broadcast addresses are:

> 192.168.1.127 (in binary   11000000 10101000 00000001 01**111111**)
>
> 192.168.1.191 (in binary 11000000 10101000 00000001 10**111111**)

On each subnetwork, the available range of hosts is all of the IP addresses between the subnet address and the subnet's broadcast address:

> 192.168.1.65 through 192.168.1.126
>
> 192.168.1.129 through 192.168.1.190

Avoiding the subnet mask trap

Try this one to really show-off: What are the subnetwork and broadcast addresses of the address 129.16.1.128 that uses a subnet mask of 255.255.255.0? Don't be misled by the subnet mask in this problem. The default mask (see Table 8-3, earlier in the chapter) for a Class C address is 255.255.255.0, but you were too sharp to fall into that trap. You knew from the host address that this is a Class B address. This also tells you that only 8 bits of the possible 14 are used in the subnet mask. This allows you to calculate that 254 subnets are available ($2^8 - 2 = 254$ subnets). Because only 8 bits are borrowed for the subnet mask, 8 bits must be left for the host ID. As you know, this means that 254 hosts are available per subnet, and that the entire fourth octet is used for each subnet (254 hosts plus 1 broadcast address equals 255 addresses).

To determine the valid subnetworks, you calculate $256 - 255 = 1$, and you find that the valid subnetwork numbers are 129.16.1.0, 129.16.2.0, and on up to 129.16.254.0. So the subnetwork address is 129.16.1.0, and the broadcast address is 129.16.1.255.

Planning a subnet: An exercise

Resolve the addressing problem in this scenario:

Your company has been assigned a Class C address with a network number of 204.200.250.0. Your boss wants you to plan for network expansion but doesn't want to have more than 20 people on any LAN. Come up with a networking scheme.

In this scenario, the driving factor is the number of hosts per subnet. You know that in subnetting a Class C network, you can have a maximum of 62 hosts with two subnets or a minimum of two hosts with 62 subnets, depending on the subnet mask you choose.

To allow for 20 hosts per subnetwork requires a subnet mask of 255.255.255.224. (Remember that to discover the number of host addresses, you take 2 to the power of the number of bits used for the host portion and then subtract 2 from this number: $2^5 - 2 = 30$.)

Using this data, you realize that you have six subnets available. To figure out the subnet numbers, you subtract $256 - 224 = 32$. This would leave you with the values listed in Table 8-10.

Table 8-10	Subnets Available for 204.200.250.0	
Subnet Address	Hosts	Broadcast Address
204.200.250.32	.33 – .62	.63
204.200.250.64	.65 – .94	.95
204.200.250.96	.97 – .126	.127
204.200.250.128	.128 – .158	.159
204.200.250.160	.161 – .190	.191
204.200.250.192	.193 – .222	.223

Who Was That Subnet Masked Man?

In order for a router to know whether a particular host is located on the network attached to it, the router must be able to extract the network ID from a destination address. To do this, a filtering mechanism is applied to the IP address to highlight the address portion needed. This filtering mechanism is the *subnet mask,* which is actually short for *subnetwork address mask.*

The purpose of a subnet mask is to determine whether an IP address exists on the local network or on a remote network. The subnet mask extracts the network ID from a message's destination address, which is then compared to the local network ID. If they match, the host ID is on the local network. Otherwise, the message must be routed beyond the local network.

Taking the boo out of Boolean algebra

The process used to apply the subnet mask uses what is called *Boolean* (boo-lee-uhn) *algebra* to filter out all nonmatching bits and identify the network ID. Not to worry; I'm not making you do algebra, at least not the kind you remember from high school. Boolean algebra applies binary logic to yield binary results. See, nothing to worry about.

Working with subnet masks, you need only four basic principles of Boolean algebra:

- 1 and 1 = 1
- 1 and 0 = 0
- 0 and 1 = 0
- 0 and 0 = 0

Translation: The only way to end up with a 1 is to combine two 1s; everything else yields a 0. This is the fundamental operation in Boolean algebra. Boolean algebra is a crusader — it is always searching for truth, which is represented as a 1 in the world of computers and networks. True and True equals True; a False, or zero, in any pair results in a False.

When the subnet mask is applied to an IP address, a process called *anding* is used to align each of the 32 bits right to left and left to right. Then each pair of bits (one from the IP address and one from the subnet mask) is anded. Any pair that contains two 1s results in a 1; all others result in a 0.

Table 8-11 illustrates how the Boolean algebra anding process works:

Table 8-11	Boolean Algebra Anding	
Element	*Dotted Decimal*	*Binary Equivalent*
Class A address	123.123.123.001	01111011 01111011 01111011 00000001
Default subnet mask	255.000.000.000	11111111 00000000 00000000 00000000
Network ID	123.000.000.000	01111011 00000000 00000000 00000000

Study the Binary Equivalent column of Table 8-11. The result in the Network ID row has only 1s, where 1s were present in both the network address and subnet mask rows.

Similarly, a default Class B subnet mask strips out the 16 bits of the network ID, and a default Class C subnet mask strips out the 24 bits of the network ID. The example in Table 8-11 is fairly easy and straightforward. If you agree, then you have the fundamentals sorted out and will be ready when I start borrowing bits from the host ID to create subnetworks.

Using the magic of the mask to find subnets

IPv4 addresses are a scarce commodity. I want to emphasize this so that you get the idea that when you design a network, you must do so with IP address conservation in mind. Subnetting provides a way to segment a single network IP address into many segments, which creates more networks with fewer hosts each.

A network has its own unique address. In a network address, the host ID portion is all binary 0s. For example, a Class B network address (16 bits in the network ID) such as 129.20.0.0 creates a network with 65,536 individual hosts. Imagine that many workstations are trying to contend for access to the wire! Subnetting allows you to divide this network into a series of subnets with fewer nodes on each subnetwork. Not only does this improve the available bandwidth, but it also cuts down on the amount of broadcast traffic generated. See: Subnetting can be your friend!

In our example network of 172.20.0.0, the network administrator could subnet the network into five smaller networks: 172.20.1.0, 172.20.2.0, 172.20.3.0, 172.20.4.0, and 172.20.5.0. To the outside world, the network is still 172.20.0.0, but internally, routers are able to break the address down into the five smaller subnetworks.

Just in case you are wondering, subnet masks apply only to Class A, B, and C IP addresses.

The subnet mask is the strainer applied to a message's destination IP address to determine whether the destination network is the local network. It works like this:

1. **On a Class C network, if a destination IP address is 206.175.162.18, its binary equivalent is 11001110 10101111 10100010 00010010.**

   Trust me on this.

2. **The default Class C subnet mask is 255.255.255.0, and its binary equivalent is 11111111 11111111 11111111 00000000.**

   Really, that's it!

3. **These two binary numbers (the IP address and the subnet mask) are combined using Boolean algebra, which yields the network ID of the destination:**

   ```
   206.175.162.18   11001110 10101111 10100010 00010010
   AND
   255.255.255.0    11111111 11111111 11111111 00000000
   =
   206.175.162.0    11001110 10101111 10100010 00000000
   ```

4. **The resulting ID (206.175.162.0) is the IP address of the network, which means that the message is addressed to a node on the local network.**

Subnet masks for Class B and Class C networks

The pattern shown in Table 8-11 for Class A subnets continues with Class B and Class C IP addresses and subnet masks. The only differences are that you have fewer options (because of the fewer bits available) and that you are much more likely to work with these networks in real life. Table 8-12 lists a few of the subnet masks available for Class B networks, and Table 8-13 lists all of the subnet masks available for Class C networks.

Table 8-12		Class B Subnet Masks	
Subnet Mask	**Number of One Bits in Mask**	**Number of Subnets**	**Number of Hosts per Subnet**
255.255.0.0	16	0	65,534
255.255.192.0	18	2	16,382
255.255.240.0	20	14	4,094
255.255.255.0	24	254	254
255.255.255.240	28	4,094	14
255.255.255.252	30	16,382	2

Table 8-13		Class C Subnet Masks	
Subnet Mask	**Number of One Bits in Mask**	**Number of Subnets**	**Number of Hosts per Subnet**
255.255.255.0	24	0	254
255.255.255.192	26	2	62
255.255.255.224	27	6	30
255.255.255.240	28	14	14
255.255.255.248	29	30	6
255.255.255.252	30	62	2

Donning the Subnet Mask

When you begin planning a network, one of the first things you do is figure out the number of network IDs and hosts your network requires. To accomplish this, you must account for every WAN connection (connections to outside routers) and every subnet within the network.

Network IDs are assigned by the Internet Corporation for Assigned Numbers and Names (ICANN), but the local network administrator assigns the host IDs. The host ID identifies an addressable device on the local network. This can be almost any addressable device on the network, including computers, routers, bridges, switches, and so forth. You don't have to follow any set-in-concrete rules governing the assignment of host IDs, but some general guidelines are around.

A number for everything, and everything is numbered

A commonly accepted practice is to assign host IDs in groups based on the type of host and to give routers the lowest range of numbers in the host range. For example, if you were to use this scheme to assign host IDs on a network or network segment, your host IDs would be grouped as follows:

> a.b.c.1 through a.b.c.255 — routers
>
> a.b.200.1 through a.b.200.254 — NT servers
>
> a.b.240.1 through a.b.240.254 — UNIX hosts

Configuring the router for IP

After your network is completely worked out, that is, after the network has its subnets and subnet masks, this IP addressing scheme should be configured onto the appropriate interfaces on your local router. Each router interface, like each host computer, must have its own IP address if it is to communicate on an IP network. Each of the interface ports should also be configured with the subnet information for the subnet to which it is attached. Routers can be attached to multiple subnets with each subnet attached to a different router interface. On some routers, it's also possible to connect multiple subnets to a single interface through the use of subinterfaces. See Chapter 11 for more information on routers and their interfaces.

The **ip address** command is used to configure a router interface to its own IP address, subnet, and mask. A router with four interfaces will have four distinct IP addresses, because each address is on a different network or subnetwork. The **ip address** command is entered from the **config-if** (configure-interface) mode of the Cisco IOS (Internetwork Operating System — see Chapter 16) because the command's action affects only a specific interface. In this command, both the IP address and the subnet mask are assigned.

The subnet mask can be entered in dotted decimal notation. However, it can be displayed in dotted decimal notation or in the bit-count format by using the **term ip netmask-format** command. Bit-count format refers to an 8-bit mask (255.0.0.0), 16-bit mask (255.255.0.0), or 24-bit mask (255.255.255.0). An example of what this may look like on a Cisco router is shown in Figure 8-3.

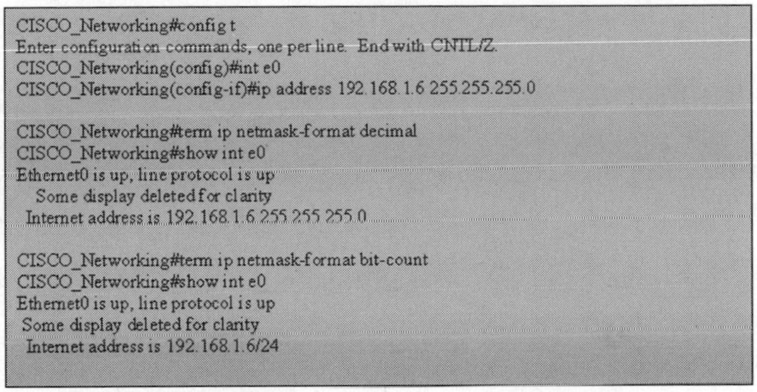

Figure 8-3:
The Cisco
IOS
commands
used to
configure
a router
interface's
IP
assignment.

```
CISCO_Networking#config t
Enter configuration commands, one per line. End with CNTL/Z.
CISCO_Networking(config)#int e0
CISCO_Networking(config-if)#ip address 192.168.1.6 255.255.255.0

CISCO_Networking#term ip netmask-format decimal
CISCO_Networking#show int e0
Ethernet0 is up, line protocol is up
   Some display deleted for clarity
   Internet address is 192.168.1.6 255.255.255.0

CISCO_Networking#term ip netmask-format bit-count
CISCO_Networking#show int e0
Ethernet0 is up, line protocol is up
   Some display deleted for clarity
   Internet address is 192.168.1.6/24
```

Routing IP Addresses

When you build a network, you need to figure out how many network IDs your network requires. To do so, you must account for every WAN connection and subnet on the network. Every node and router interface requires a host address, or ID. No hard and fast rule tells you how you should dole out your allotted IP addresses. Commonly, though, the lowest numbers (1 through 10) are assigned to routers and servers, but how you assign addresses is strictly up to you and your network policies and guidelines.

Configuring an IP address

The proper way to configure an IP address on the router is through the **ip address** command, which assigns each router interface its unique IP address. A router with four interfaces needs four distinct IP addresses because, technically, each interface (and address) is on a different network. The **ip address** command is entered from the **config-if** mode because the action affects only that interface. Both the IP address and the subnet mask are defined in the command. Here is a sample **ip address** command session:

```
Cisco_Networking#config t
Enter configuration commands, one per line. End with
     CNTL/Z.
Cisco_Networking(config)#int e0
Cisco_Networking(config-if)#ip address 192.168.1.6
     255.255.255.0
Cisco_Networking#term ip netmask-format decimal
Cisco_Networking#show int e0
Ethernet0 is up, line protocol is up
.
Some display deleted for clarity
```

(continued)

```
.
Internet address is 192.168.1.6 255.255.255.0

Cisco_Networking#term ip netmask-format bit-count
Cisco_Networking#show int e0
Ethernet0 is up, line protocol is up
.
Some display deleted for clarity
.
Internet address is 192.168.1.6/24
```

The subnet mask is entered in dotted decimal notation as shown in the fourth line of this example. However, it may be displayed in the dotted decimal notation by using the decimal option on the **term ip netmask-format** command. It can also be displayed in the bit-count format by entering the bit-count option of that same command. *Bit-count format* refers to a standard that is commonly used with a notation type called Classless Interdomain Routing (CIDR).

CIDR expresses the subnet network address in the form "/n," where "n" represents the number of bits used to designate the network address. For example, an IP address that uses 8-bits (Class A) to designate its network address (255.0.0.0) is expressed as /8 CIDR block, a 16-bit address (255.255.0.0) is expressed as /16, and a 24-bit address (255.255.255.0) is represented /24, and so forth up to a /30. Classless or bit-count format is not limited to class A, B, and C addresses. In fact, a network address can use any number up to 30 bits on a subnetted network, which would be expressed in bit-count format as /30.

Verifying an IP address

IP addresses can be verified by using ping, trace, and telnet, which are very handy utilities to know. *Ping* is used to verify IP address connections to the Network layer. *Trace* (or *traceroute*) is used to verify the connection between two IP addresses. *Telnet* is used to verify network IP address connections to the Application layer.

Verifying with Telnet

The reason you need to verify IP addresses is to ensure that the various parts of a network can properly communicate with the other parts. For example, if you can Telnet (terminal emulation protocol) into a router from a remote location, you can verify that the interface and route are up and available. Because Telnet operates on the OSI Model's Application layer, when it's functioning, it's safe to assume that all lower layers are also functioning.

Here's a sample Telnet session that is used to verify the connection and route at IP address 205.7.5.1.

```
Cisco_Networking#telnet 205.7.5.1
Trying 205.7.5.1 ... Open
Greetings from a Generic Cisco Lab
User Access Verification
```

Verifying with ping

The ping command verifies OSI Layer 3 (Network layer) connectivity. Ping sends out ICMP (Internet Control Message Protocol) messages to verify both the logical addresses and the physical connection. The ping command issued from a Cisco router responds with a number of single character responses, which are listed in Table 8-14.

Table 8-14	Cisco Ping Response Codes
Response	*Meaning*
! (exclamation mark)	Success
. (period)	Timed out waiting for reply
? (question mark)	Unknown packet type
& (ampersand)	Packet life-time exceeded
M	Could not fragment
Q	Source quench (destination too busy to reply)
U	Destination unreachable

Here are two sample ping sessions on a Cisco router, one successful, the other not so successful:

```
Cisco_Networking#ping 205.7.5.1
Type escape sequence to abort.
Sending 5,100-byte ICMP Echoes to 205.7.5.1, timeout is 2
        seconds:
!!!!!
Success rate is 100 percent (5/5), round-trip min/avg/max
        = 104/110/128 ms

Cisco_Networking#ping 205.7.5.5
Type escape sequence to abort.
Sending 5, 100-byte ICMP Echoes to 205.7.5.5, timeout is
        2 seconds:
.....
Success rate is 0 percent (0/5)
```

For some very good coverage on the ping command in general, visit www.freesoft.org/CIE/Topics/53.htm. I should caution you that the ping command used on a Cisco router is proprietary to Cisco and may not perform exactly like the general TCP/IP ping command. For information specific to the Cisco ping, visit www.cisco.com.

Verifying with traceroute

The traceroute or trace command is used to show the complete route from a source to a destination. Trace sends out probe packets to each router in the path between the source and the destination IP address entered. Traceroute displays the round-trip time for each packet sent to each upstream router. Traceroute has really only two results, time exceeded or destination unreachable. Trace is used to determine where a breakdown in a route may be occurring.

Here's an example of how trace is used: A network has four routers (A, B, C, and D). A trace command is issued on router A to trace the route from itself to router D. A timing response comes back from router B, but the next message indicates that router C is unreachable. You can be fairly certain that the problem lies somewhere on the route between router B and router C. The problem could be with B or C themselves or on the network media connecting them.

Like ping, trace also has its own set of response codes, listed in Table 8-15.

Table 8-15	Trace Command Response Codes
Response	*Meaning*
*	timed out
?	Unknown packet type
nn ms	The roundtrip time in milliseconds (ms)
A	Administratively prohibited (such as with an access list [see Chapter 18])
H	Host unreachable
I	Test interrupted by user
N	network unreachable
P	protocol unreachable
Q	Source quench (destination too busy)
T	Timeout
U	port unreachable

What does ping stand for?

There are those that claim that ping stands for Packet Internet Groper, but I agree with many networkers that this is an obvious case of the acronym preceding the meaning. I believe that the term ping is derived from the sound made by the sonar device on a submarine (like in all of those cool war movies). The action of the ping command simulates the action of the sound wave sent out by the sonar unit. If it finds an object, it "pings" back. The ping command sends out an echo request message to its target. If the target is alive and listening, it sends back the echo response (the "ping").

Here are the results of a sample traceroute session in which all stations were reachable:

```
Cisco_Networking#traceroute 192.5.5.1
Type escape sequence to abort.
Tracing the route to LAB-A (192.5.5.1)
1 LAB-D (210.93.105.1) 4 msec 4 msec 4 msec
2 LAB-C (204.204.7.1) 20 msec 32 msec 28 msec
3 LAB-B (199.6.13.1) 44 msec 48 msec 44 msec
4 LAB-A (201.100.11.1) 64 msec * 60 msec
```

Expanding the IP Horizon

A newer version of the Internet Protocol (IP version 6 or IPv6) that radically adapts the addressing structure of IPv4 is now available for use. I doubt that anything can be done to prevent IPv6 from taking over the Internet addressing realm someday. In a way, IPv6 is good news; the world is running out of IPv4 addresses, and IPv6 certainly solves that problem. But the real problem, as is common when exchanging one system for another, is that in order to change to IPv6, your network operating system, routers, switches, and workstations must all support its use. If they do, great! You have an ample supply of IPv6 addresses available for your network. If your equipment is not compatible and you do not want to throw out your existing network and replace it with nifty new IPv6-compatible gear, then you need to continue finding ways, such as subnetting, to extend IPv4's limitations.

Just in case you're curious, IPv5 (which was also called Internet Stream Protocol or ST2) added ATM (Asynchronous Transfer Mode) support to the Internet Protocol without affecting its addressing structure.

IPv6 uses a 128-bit address structure. This structure is four times longer than the current 32-bit IPv4 address structure and should supply ample addressing, for now, for all networks and hosts. In terms of available addresses, IPv6 provides many trillion more addresses than IPv4. Other advantages of IPv6 over IPv4 include improved security, enhanced support for real-time traffic, and automatic IP configuration from plug-and-play devices. Real-time traffic includes video-conferencing and voice over IP (VoIP). IPv6 includes a flow label that allows routers to identify the end-to-end flow control a packet is using, which allows packets to move from source to destination much faster. Plug-and-play is supported in IPv6, allowing automatic IP address configuration.

The 128-bit address of IPv6 is a hexadecimal format that is broken into eight 16-bit sections delineated by colons. Look at these examples of an IPv6 address:

A733:0000:FEDC:EB62:4532:0000:FA39:4321

or

A733:0:FEDC:EB62:4532:0:FA39:4321

or

A733::FEDC:EB62:4532::FA39:4321

The first example shows the full representation of an IPv6 address, but the second and third examples are alternate representations that reduce and then eliminate the zero octets.

Because an IPv6 implementation worldwide cannot happen overnight, both 32-bit IPv4 addresses and 128-bit IPv6 addresses must be routed at the same time. In order to do this, IPv6 will need to be implemented on one autonomous system at a time with an address translation process in place to convert the 128-bit addresses to 32-bit addresses when sending from IPv6 to IPv4.

Part III
Routing and Switching: Inside and Out

The 5th Wave   By Rich Tennant

"Ahhh - it's a new generation. Snow forts have given way to a field of snowLANs, watched over by a kindly snow nerd."

In this part . . .

Now you get to the good stuff — the first of three parts of the book that relate directly to Cisco networking and Cisco Systems' routers, switches, and other networking and internetworking devices.

I start by looking at the role that a router or switch can play on a local area network (LAN) and then expand into the different configuration specifics. This part also describes how a network can support voice traffic as well as data.

The point of the material in this part of the book is to help you understand how a router works, how it fits into your network, and how it can best serve your needs.

Chapter 9

Installing Routing and Switching

Throughout this book, you find lots of great technical stuff to help you plan, design, and work with your Cisco network. This is fine, but I thought I should devote at least one chapter to the common-sense stuff, such as planning, preparing, and installing your Cisco networking systems. So, to that end, I have included in this chapter a discussion of planning activities, safety considerations, and installation steps that you should use to install your Cisco routers, switches, and hubs.

The following may not be the most exhaustive checklist of what you must do before and during the installation of your Cisco equipment, but I do hit the high points of what you should consider. You'll find that the manuals included with just about every piece of Cisco equipment have a very complete installation guide. If this isn't enough, then by all means visit the Cisco Systems' Web site at www.cisco.com.

Preparing to Install Cisco Equipment

Before you even begin to install your Cisco router, switch, or hub, you need to think about, plan for, and do some specific things. I know that when you see that box with the Golden Gate Bridge logo in blue and red, you're just so excited that all you want to do is get the goodies out of the box and into the network. But for the sake of safety for you and your equipment and to ensure that your equipment is installed so it will operate properly, you should take the time to do a few get-ready steps:

1. **First and foremost, read the safety booklet packed with your equipment.**

   It is titled something like *Regulatory Compliance and Safety Information for Cisco xxxxx*, where "xxxxx" is the name and model number of the switch, router, or hub.

2. **Be absolutely sure that the device you have is exactly the device you ordered, and be sure beyond any doubt whatsoever that it is configured with the power source type that you intended.**

   Many Cisco devices are available in either AC or DC power types.

3. **Always read the installation instructions for your Cisco device completely before connecting it to its power source.**

   The Cisco installation guide tells you that Cisco devices are designed for "TN power system," which means that your electrical system has a direct earth ground.

4. **If the device is a table or desktop type, never place anything on its top that weighs more than 10 pounds.**

   The case or chassis of a desktop device is not designed to support excessive weight, and the device could be damaged. This advice is also good for any networking device, regardless of its size or case design.

5. **Be sure that you are able to properly lift and install your Cisco gear.**

   For devices that must be installed in a rack mounting, such as the larger switches, routers, and firewalls, use the buddy system and get somebody (or two bodies) to help you.

Readying the installation site

Like most computers and networking equipment, Cisco systems are designed to operate in a certain environment. Cisco defines this environment fairly tightly, but most of its parameters are only common sense anyway, so setting up the installation site shouldn't be too tough. The information in this section provides you with some guidelines and advice for choosing an installation site and connection your system to the electrical source.

Snap, crackle, pop

Under the category of "it's only obvious" is the advice to not work on electrical devices, including Cisco equipment, during a lightning storm. If a thunder-and-lightning storm is raging outside, wait until it passes to work on your equipment. This includes actions as simple as plugging them in or unplugging them from the power source. Not even an antistatic wrist strap will protect you if you're holding the power cord when lightning strikes your building.

Choosing an installation site

Where would you put a very expensive key component of your LAN or WAN? Would it be in a site that meets the criteria in this list? I think so.

- Access to the room, desk, cabinet, or rack where the system is installed should be restricted to only those that need access to the area. This is a little overkill for a desktop switch or router; but to protect your rack-mounted systems, you probably want to restrict access by using some form of physical security, such as a special lock or maybe even some form of James Bond–like biological identification system.

- To ensure that the site is safe, install your system in an area that has ample space for people, tools, and documentation around it. Make sure that the area has adequate space for tools, cabling, and other equipment while you are working, and that all tools and spare (leftover?) parts are stowed properly and out of the way.

- In general, the site should be clear of all possible hazards, including such things as wet floors, ungrounded power cables, and any conductive materials, such as metal filings or other manufacturing debris.

- The location of your networking equipment should be clean, well ventilated, dry, and dust free. Like computers, networking equipment pieces have fans and ventilation systems of their own, which can become clogged and stop ventilating.

- You may also want to air-condition the area to prevent high operating temperatures. Consistently high operating temperatures can damage electronic equipment and can cause the equipment to perform erratically (and it's also uncomfortable for you). Cisco recommends that the temperature be maintained between 32°F (brrrrr) to 104°F (whew!). For those of you using the Centigrade scale, this is 0°C to 40°C.

Connecting to the electrical source

Cisco has not quite completed its self-generating power option package for its routers and switches just yet, so you will need to plug your devices into an electrical power source. Follow these tips when plugging in your equipment:

- Never, repeat NEVER, cut the ground conductor off the AC plug on the unit. If you have only an electrical outlet with two holes (which means that it doesn't have the third grounding hole), move to a location that has the proper outlet or get your local electrician in to fix the outlet.

- Make sure that the electrical outlet is connected to an earth ground. If you are unsure of this, call your local electrician to make sure.

- Your Cisco equipment does not include any internal circuitry to protect itself from the local power. If any surge-suppression, power-conditioning, or battery-backup services are needed, you must supply them. Because you are likely to want the network and its components to continue running for some amount of time in the event of a power failure, you should install an uninterruptible power supply (UPS). But don't overlook surge suppression; power spikes can do as much damage as, if not more damage than, a power failure.

Safeguarding your system from ESD and EMI

ESD (electrostatic discharge) results from static electricity building up on you or on your equipment or both. If you do not take safety precautions, even a small amount of ESD can cause major damage to electronic components in your Cisco systems. Even a small ESD — one that you can't see, hear, or feel — can result in complete or intermittent failures of your systems.

I recommend that you observe the following safeguards when installing or servicing any computing or networking equipment:

✔ Wear an ESD wrist or ankle strap anytime you are handling electrical devices or electronic components. Clip the strap to any unpainted metal surface of the device or to an ESD jack, which is a small round connector found on the front or back panels of many Cisco devices, if one is available. The ESD strap protects the system from any static buildup on your body but not that in your clothing, so avoid touching components to your clothes.

✔ After removing an electronic component from a system, lay it on an anti-static surface or place it in a static-shield bag. Never stack electronic cards directly on top of each other.

✔ If you must handle electronic components, such as circuit boards and edge connectors, take care to touch only card edges that do not have connectors — never touch the electronic circuits and components on the faces of the circuit board.

If you need to run the cabling for your system for an extended distance, say from one room to the next, you need to be aware of the potential for EMI (electromagnetic interference), which is generated by just about every type of electrical or electronic equipment at some level. Take care to avoid noisy electrical motors and any existing nondata wiring running near your cabling or power lines.

A strong radio transmitter in the vicinity can, over time, begin to degrade the signal drivers or receivers in your system. Lightning is another system killer. Protect your system from these electrical problems. To safeguard against or to fix these types of problems, I recommend that you consult your electrician or an RFI (radio frequency interference) expert.

Racking it up

Identifying a rack-mountable Cisco device from one that isn't rack mountable is easy. Figure 9-1 illustrates the differences in appearance of desktop and rack-mountable systems.

Figure 9-1:
The difference between a desktop and a rack-mount router is fairly obvious.

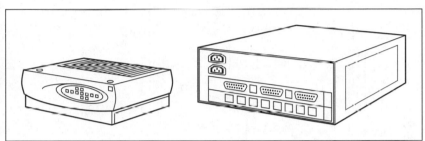

If your router or switch is rack mountable, a rack-mount kit is usually included with the system. The rack-mount kit allows you to mount the device into an upright 19-inch rack system. Before locking down your system in the rack, be sure that no obstructions, such as power strips or support bars, could get in the way later when you need to access the device.

You can install these types of rack systems in your equipment:

- ✔ Two-bar open (Telco) racks
- ✔ Four-bar open racks
- ✔ Cabinets

Many variations and combinations of these exist. The best rack for your installation is the one that works best for your installation; your choice depends on your needs and the amount of room available and the amount of money you want to spend. If aesthetics are important (and remember this is strictly in the eye of the beholder), you may want a cabinet. Otherwise, an open rack may do the job. Figure 9-2 shows a typical rack-mount system.

Cisco recommends that you install your system in an open rack if at all possible. An open rack ensures that the system gets proper airflow. If you have to use a cabinet, be sure that it has proper ventilation, such as fans at the top of each bay.

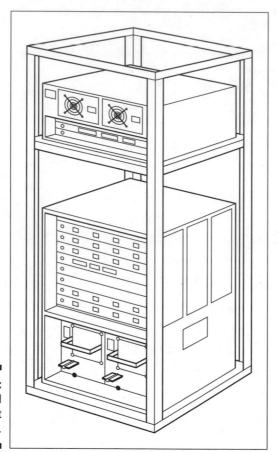

Figure 9-2:
A typical
rack-mount
system.

These tips for installing Cisco equipment into a rack system should be helpful.

- **Let the air flow:** Your systems require an ample, unobstructed flow of cool air to maintain their normal operation. The systems could overheat and perform badly otherwise.

- **Give it space:** You need at least 6 inches of open space around the ventilation openings on the equipment's case or chassis.

- **Blow hot air:** Here's a news flash — heat rises. When laying out a rack, remember that the equipment located at the bottom of the rack puts out heat and that you don't want heavy heat pumpers located at the bottom of a rack. The hot air coming from lower equipment can be drawn into the equipment located higher in the rack and cause the latter to overheat.

- **Start at the bottom:** After installing stabilizers for the rack itself, mount equipment on a rack starting at the bottom. If you place heavy equipment at the top first, the rack may fall over.

✔ **Nail it down (or up):** If you are using a Telco-style rack (the type commonly used by the local telephone company), bolt it to the floor, ceiling, or both, before installing any equipment. Be absolutely sure that the rack is capable of holding the weight that you will be mounting on it.

Connecting to power

Most Cisco systems offer either an AC (alternating current) or a DC (direct current) power supply, or in some cases, both. *AC* power is the type of electricity supplied by the normal, everyday electrical outlets on the wall of your office or home. *DC* power is commonly used in high-volume and high-end networking situations where a cleaner power source is desired.

If your network is designed around high-availability principles, Cisco provides optional redundant power supplies for most of its higher-end routers and switches. The two principles, high availability and redundant power supply, are frequently design elements of systems that must not fail.

Keeping it up

The design and operational concepts of high availability are used to define and build a network infrastructure that does not have a single point of failure. In every place possible, *redundant* (spare) systems are included to provide for a continuity of services if any component of the system fails. High availability often focuses on the power source, but truly reliable systems also include redundant servers, routers, disk drives, and more.

Being redundant isn't a bad thing

A redundant power supply is an optional feature of many Cisco routers and switches (and other Cisco devices as well). The *redundant power supply* automatically kicks in to supply a power source to the device if the primary power-supply module fails. The power supply is the component of electrical computing and networking equipment that fails most often because it must suffer the slings and arrows of electrical spikes, brownouts, and noise. Therefore, if you are designing a system that must not fail, a redundant power supply is a good idea. Check with your Cisco reseller to see if one is available for your particular equipment.

Plugging in to AC power

As I mentioned earlier in this chapter, Cisco systems that operate on AC power are designed to connect to electrical systems that have at least one direct earth ground. This means that, somewhere in the system, a metal rod has been sunk into the ground, and a grounding circuit has been attached to it. This literally grounds your electrical system.

Other than the obvious (I hope) things you should observe when working with AC power, such as don't stand in water when plugging in or unplugging the power cord, the one recommendation that I have is that you allow for access to the AC connections. You should have clear, unobstructed access to both the electrical outlet where the unit is connected and to the back of the device where the power cord attaches to the unit. These power connections are generally the only means available to disconnect the device from the power.

Connecting to DC power

Direct current (DC) power is used in virtually all computing and networking systems. DC power is especially popular in large-scale, high-availability systems that are connected to large battery backup installations. For equipment to be installed in this type of environment, Cisco has a DC power supply that can be used in place of the AC power supply.

If you plan to use DC power for your system installation, I recommend that you consult the manuals that come with your device for installation and safety instructions or visit the Cisco Systems Web site (www.cisco.com) for specific DC power guidelines.

Following the power requirements

Cisco has a long list of power requirements for the location of your systems. If you fail to meet these conditions in your installation, your ability to make a warranty claim due to a power supply failure or the like could be affected. If you are uncertain as to whether your equipment room meets the electrical requirements prescribed by Cisco, I recommend that you hire a certified electrician to install or inspect your facility. This professional help can avoid some very costly potential problems with your Cisco gear down the road.

At minimum, your installation site should meet one of the following electrical codes:

- **United States:** Use the National Fire Protection Association (NFPA) and the United States National Electrical Code (NEC).
- **Canada:** Use the Canadian Electrical Code, Part I, CSA C22.1.
- **Other countries:** Use the local and national electrical codes or refer to IEC 364, Part 1 through Part 7.

Installing the System

Each Cisco system comes with complete installation instructions that are available online from the Cisco Systems Web site as well. If you follow these instructions to the letter, you should have little trouble. Each of the instruction sets includes some generic guidelines on working with electricity, preventing ESD damage, and connecting to a LAN or WAN. The instructions for each specific device focus on installing it in a rack system, if appropriate, connecting up its interfaces, configuring the operating system, and dealing with any cabling and wiring issues unique to the system. The following sections review some of the specific or unique installation requirements for routers, switches, and hubs.

Installing a router by the book

Cisco recommends the use of an installation checklist when installing a router in your network, and I agree. Cisco provides a copy of its recommended checklist format in the installation materials and product documentation. This checklist includes the materials, considerations, and steps that you should have and take to ensure a quality installation.

Our version of the installation checklist that would be used with a router is included in Table 9-1.

Table 9-1	Router Installation Checklist	
Task	*Completed By*	*Date*
Review installation site power for ability to support additional load		
Review backup power source for ability to handle additional load		
Test power source for router		
Unpack router and verify contents against packing slip(s)		
Review "Regulatory Compliance and Safety Information" document		
Review product documentation (printed or CD-ROM)		
Inspect the router for damage and verify installed features and modules		
Power up the router prior to installation in rack system		
Test VTY terminal or modem connection		

(continued)

Table 9-1 *(continued)*

Task	Completed By	Date
Install in rack system or at operating location		
Perform startup and initial configuration setup process		
Test initial operations (login, interface configuration, and so on)		
Back up running configuration		

Keeping an installation log

Cisco also recommends that you keep a record of any action performed on the router (or another Cisco device, for that matter), including any background information on the criteria used to choose the particular router model installed. The installation log should be kept near the router so that anyone needing to perform maintenance or upgrade on the router can refer to the device's history, as well as record their actions, including installation or removal of modules, software upgrades, a record of intermittent problems, and so on. The installation log should also include a copy of the installation checklist and a schedule and record of any regularly scheduled maintenance activities.

Connecting a router to the network

After your router is installed in its operating location and has had its initial operating configuration setup and backup (see Chapters 11 and 13 for information on configuring and backing up the router), the next steps involve connecting its interface ports to the network media. You must deal with a series of considerations for each different cable medium used on the network.

In this section, I discuss how a router is connected to the more common media and connector types: Ethernet, serial, and ISDN BRI connections (see Chapter 14 for information about ISDN). The examples shown in this chapter are of the Cisco 2600 router, but you'll find that most Cisco routers are very similar to this model.

Identifying the ports

Cisco routers generally support up to three types of interface ports: Ethernet, console, and auxiliary (some routers, such as those made specifically for token ring, may not include an Ethernet port). Each of the ports is accessed through an RJ-45 (or an Ethernet AUI [attachment unit interface]) connection on the back of the router. Some router models also allow for the addition of other port/interface types, including fiber-optic, coaxial cable, and serial connections. Figure 9-3 illustrates the port connections on the Cisco 2600 router.

Figure 9-3:
The ports on
a Cisco
router.

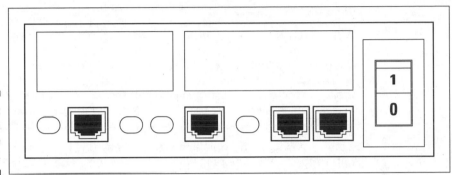

Cisco routers, starting with the 2600 series, have one or more slots into which you can add interface cards or network modules. Check with your Cisco reseller for the following information:

- ✓ Type of interface cards available
- ✓ Number of ports supported on each card
- ✓ Connection restrictions, if any, of each interface

Making the Ethernet connection

Ethernet networking is the most common networking technology in use. Its popularity is based on its relative ease of installation and its established standard IEEE (Institute for Electrical and Electronic Engineering) 802.3. Within Ethernet are a number of implementations, all of which are supported by Cisco routers. Table 9-2 lists the most common of the Ethernet formats.

Table 9-2	Ethernet Implementations		
Type	*Speed*	*Cable Media*	*Connector Used*
10BaseT	10 Mbps	Copper UTP	RJ-45 or AUI
10Base2	10 Mbps	Thin coaxial	BNC
10Base5	10 Mbps	Thick coaxial	BNC/AUI
100BaseT	100 Mbps	Cat5 UTP	RJ-45

Connecting to a serial line

If you want to make a serial connection to your Cisco router, normally you have to add a WAN interface card or a serial network module to your router. To connect a network device to a serial port on your router properly, you need to know a little bit about the connection to be made:

- ✔ **DCE or DTE:** Is the serial device DTE (data terminal equipment) or DCE (data communications equipment)? Devices that communicate over a synchronous serial interface are DCE and DTE devices. DTE devices do not provide a clock signal, but DCE devices do. The clock signal is used to control the communications between the serial device and the router. Routers and PCs are typically DTE devices and modems and CSU/DSUs (Channel Service Unit/Data Service Unit) are normally DCE devices.

- ✔ **Signaling:** What is the signaling standard used by the device? Cisco routers support a wide-range of serial signaling standards: EIA/TIA-232, EIA/TIA-449, V.35, X.21, and EIA-530.

- ✔ **Connector:** What type (standard, number of pins, male or female) of connector is used? Cisco serial interface cards and network modules require a Cisco DB-60 connector at the router, but the other end can be whatever connector your serial device needs. You can order a cable to meet your needs from your Cisco reseller.

One thing to be careful of is the distance limitations of serial interfaces. Distance and data speed are directly related to one another in serial communications. The greater the distance, the slower the speed you can use and *vice versa.* Each Cisco serial interface card and network module lists the recommended distances for each type of signaling standard and connection supported. One rule is that you can generally exceed the standard distances, but by how much depends on how clean your cabling and environment are from electrical interference. Table 9-3 lists some of the distance and speed trade-offs for different serial signaling standards. The speed and distance limitations listed in Table 9-3 affect the connection between a serial interface and the DCE device to which it connects.

Table 9-3	Serial Communications Speeds and Distances	
Rate (Kbps)	*EIA/TIA-232 Distance (Feet)*	*X.21/V.35 Distance (Feet)*
2.4	200	4,100
4.8	100	2,050
9.6	50	1,025
19.2	25	513
38.4	12	256

Rate (Kbps)	EIA/TIA-232 Distance (Feet)	X.21/V.35 Distance (Feet)
56.0	9	102
1544.0 (T1)	Virtually none	50

Making the BRI connection

If you need to connect an ISDN BRI (Integrated Services Digital Network Basic Rate Interface) service to your router and your Cisco device doesn't provide a standard ISDN interface, you will need to order a network module or an interface card. What you will need to know about the connection is the type of interface your ISDN service uses. Most likely it's an ISDN U class interface with a built-in NT1 or an S/T class interface that requires an external NT1 (Network Terminator 1) terminator (at least in North America). See Chapter 14 for more information on ISDN and its interface types.

Installing a router in a WAN

Installing a router in a WAN environment is required in virtually every situation. In fact, the router is what connects a LAN to its WAN. Router installation instructions include some guidelines on installations in a WAN. These types of guidelines are included:

- ✔ Telephone lines do carry electricity, so to avoid a shocking experience, be careful when working with telephone lines.

- ✔ Working with telephone lines during a lightning storm is not a good idea. Actually, my message is "don't do it!" Treat telephone lines the same as you would electrical lines in this situation and stay clear. In fact, don't even use a telephone (except for cordless types) during an electrical storm.

- ✔ A WAN port carries a hazardous level of voltage, even when the power is off. So always detach the cable end that is away from the system first, before working on a port.

Switching Your LAN

If you require a switch in your LAN, the planning and preparation you should do are very much the same as you would do for a router. You must consider all the interfaces to be made to the switch, the distance limitations of each interface and signal type, the specific types of cabling and connectors required, and any special interface equipment (such as modems, network transceivers, or connectors) needed to make the connections.

Figure 9-4 illustrates how switching is applied to a LAN to connect each floor of a building to the backbone and to act as a distribution point for each floor. You must consider the following in such an environment:

- The connection to the backbone
- The different types of connections in use in the distribution field of each switch

Cisco switches use Ethernet connections (10/100BaseT) as their standard, but other types of connections are supported by different Cisco Catalyst switches. If your network requires a connection to the switch other than Ethernet, study the Cisco product guides and consult with your Cisco reseller.

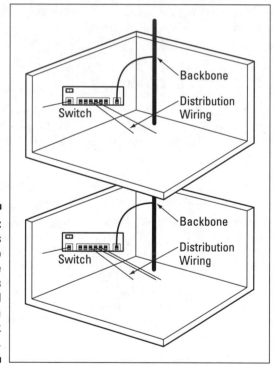

Figure 9-4:
Switches used to distribute LAN signals to individual floors off a network backbone.

Hubbing Your Network

If you have designed one or more hubs into your network, you must make different installation considerations, depending on whether you are using more than one Cisco Micro Hub:

✔ **Stacking multiple hubs:** If you are using only one hub, stacking is not an issue. If you want to stack two or more Cisco Micro Hubs (but not more than four), you can stack one on top of the other and then connect them together through ports located on their rear panels. Cisco Micro Hubs ship with a stacking clip (which looks something like a stick-figure Gumby) and a screw that you can use to anchor them securely together in a stack. If you are using managed hubs (Cisco 1538M hubs), you're limited to two "M" hubs in your stack, and the upper hub must be the primary "M" hub.

✔ **Connecting the stacked hubs:** If you have stacked more than one Cisco Micro Hub, the next step is to connect them together with the connecting cables supplied with the hub. You need to follow one rule for cabling your stacked hubs: The hub on the top of the stack must have its UP connector open, and the bottom hub must have its DOWN connector open. This means that the bottom hub is connected to the next higher hub from its UP connector to the DOWN connector of the next higher hub, and so forth all the way to the top. Don't worry: Although you shouldn't foul it up, if you connect it up or down incorrectly, you won't hurt anything. It may just not work right.

✔ **Connecting network devices to the hub:** You can connect network devices, such as servers and computer workstations and other Ethernet hubs or switches, to your hubs. Each device that you connect to a hub must have an Ethernet 10/100BaseT connection. You'll know the connection is okay if the LED (light emitting diode — the little light above the port) is on and blinking.

✔ **Cabling to the hub:** When you connect a PC or another networked device to a hub, you use a straight cable (one in which the wires are connected to the same pins of the connectors on both ends). However, when you connect two hubs (or switches, etc.), you need a crossover cable, a.k.a. rolled cable (one that crosses two or more wires to a different set of pins on each end of the cable). In a typical crossover cable, at minimum, the wire attached to the Transmit pin of Connector A is connected to the Receive pin on Connector B and Receive pin of Connector A is connected to the Transmitpin on Connector B.

Filling In Those Ugly Gaps

Some Cisco devices have module slots where additional ports or features can be added to a router or switch. When the installation of the system changes and the ports, interfaces, or function are no longer needed, these modules can be removed. When this happens, always remember to put a faceplate over the empty module slot. Faceplates are the covers used to fill empty module bays when they are empty. By replacing the faceplate, you prevent a number of other problems:

✔ Accidentally touching the components inside the chassis and damaging the system or causing other problems for the device

✔ The potential for damage to the system by EMI and RFI

✔ An open slot on the system disrupting the design and efficiency of the airflow through the chassis intended to cool the system's components

Chapter 10

Switching Around the LAN

· ·

· ·

*I*f this book had a subtitle, it would be "Routing and Switching," because that's really what a Cisco network is all about. Routing is the primary focus of a Cisco network administrator's duties, but network switching isn't that far behind. Routing is a very important element of Cisco's overall networking strategy. However, anyone working on a Cisco network should also be well versed in the other major Cisco products, especially switches, and their applications. I won't be surprised if, in the not-too-distant future, separate jobs pop up around the community with titles like "Cisco routing administrator" and "Cisco LAN switching administrator."

In an attempt to provide some fairness and the semblance of equal time, this chapter focuses on Cisco switches, including LAN segmentation with a switch and why you would want to do it. There's more to switching than just segmenting LANs, and I include information on some other important switching areas.

Switching Around the Network

A *switch* is a Data Link layer (Layer 2) connectivity device used in networks to help move data to its destination. A switch's capability ranges from not much more than a smart hub to functions that are virtually the same as a router. But by and large, a switch is used to select the interface that a data packet should use to reach its destination address on a local area network. Switches, which are Layer 2 devices, make forwarding decisions simply on through which of its interfaces a MAC address can be reached.

Compared to a router, a switch is simpler in construction and logic and, as a result, is a much faster device than a router. The main reason a switch is faster than a router is that a router must open a packet to find its destination address and then reframe it before forwarding the packet and a switch doesn't. A router must have knowledge of the network and the routes through the network to be effective. On the other hand, a switch, if it knows on which of its interfaces a MAC address can be found, forwards the message accordingly. However, when it doesn't know on which of its ports an address exists, it simply sends the message to all interfaces as a broadcast.

Talking about switches

You may find that some of the same terms used to describe routers (see Chapter 11) are used for switches as well. For example, when data moves from one switch to another, it takes a *hop*. A switch also has *latency*, which is the short amount of time a switch consumes determining which of its interfaces it should use to forward a packet.

This is as good a place as any to discuss the types of switching:

- Packet switching
- Circuit switching
- Port switching

You need to know how these switching types differ, because you can really have an impact on your network's performance and efficiency if you try to use the wrong ones.

Switching from port to port

A *port-switching* device is an intelligent network device. This means that a port-switching device includes some processing capability.

Perhaps the most common port-switching devices are switching hubs. A *switching hub* forwards packets to the appropriate port by using the packet's destination address. A *nonswitching hub,* you know the everyday, plain old Layer 1 hub, forwards every packet it receives to all of its ports. On the other hand, a switching hub forwards a packet only to the port through which the packet's destination can be reached, which improves the performance of the network.

A common feature of switching hubs, like the Cisco 1538 series hubs, also support *load balancing,* which allows the hub to reallocate its ports to different LAN segments dynamically based on the traffic load and pattern. Therefore, when necessary, a very busy segment can temporarily share an additional port with a not-so-busy segment.

Switches and LANs

A LAN can be segmented for performance purposes with a switch in the same way that it can be segmented with a router or a bridge. (See the next section, "Segmenting a LAN for Fun and Profit.") Because routers are so expensive, and bridges are harder to find and are much more specialized, Cisco networks are most commonly segmented using a switch.

A switch provides the following services to a LAN:

- Full-duplex networking
- Multiple simultaneous connections
- High-speed networking support featuring low latency and high data rates
- Dedicated and adaptable bandwidth per port

The switch's ability to connect to and support virtual LANs (VLANs) using different bandwidths on separate port connections is its most valuable feature, not to mention its value in LAN segmentation.

Segmenting a LAN for Fun and Profit

Dividing a network into smaller addressable parts, known as *segments,* decreases the congestion and chances for message collision on each new segment. Yes, each new segment forms a new collision domain; but if the network is segmented properly, the addition of new segments should not cause problems. Devices on the same segment share the same bandwidth. Data passed outside of a segment may enter another segment, or the backbone, which itself is, on a larger scale, just another collision domain. Dividing a local area network into smaller collision domains, or segments, is called *segmentation.*

The benefits of segmenting a LAN are these:

- Increasing bandwidth per user
- Keeping local traffic local
- Reducing broadcasts
- Creating smaller collision domains
- Avoiding the maximum node and distance limitation problems associated with shared media networks, such as Ethernet and token ring

Probably the first thing I should establish for you is why you would want to segment a LAN in the first place. Your first clue that Cisco believes segmentation is important is the number of white papers on the subject that you can find on the Cisco Web site. However, just because Cisco thinks segmentation is a big thing, you have to make your own decision about segmenting your network.

Not every LAN needs to be segmented, but segmentation is a technique that can be applied to ensure a network's performance as the LAN grows. Think of it this way: When too many cars try to occupy the highways and freeways around cities, the roadways get congested. Networks don't have gawker blocks, thank goodness; but when too many users are demanding too much bandwidth from a network, the network can become congested. On the roads, other factors can contribute to the problem besides too many cars. Perhaps a slow traffic light or a stalled car is the problem, much like a slow server or too little RAM can slow the throughput on a network. However, a network's performance problems can and do start with congestion or the lack of bandwidth or both.

Whatever the cause of the congestion, one of the best and most efficient ways to solve the problem is to break up the network into what amount to smaller networks, called *segments*. Each segment maximizes the network's resources, especially bandwidth, over smaller groups, each of which typically has a common or compatible resource need.

You can segment a network in two ways:

- **Physical segmentation:** A router or bridge is used to create more, but smaller, collision domains. This action minimizes the number of workstations on the same network segment and reduces the demand for bandwidth by simply limiting the nodes on a segment. (See "Segmenting a LAN with a bridge" and "Segmenting the LAN with a router" later in this chapter.)

- **Network switching:** You can use a switch to further divide a physical segment by providing frame switching, which relieves bandwidth congestion on the network segments attached to it.

Segmenting a LAN with a bridge

Using a bridge to segment a network is one of the physical segmentation techniques. You can use a bridge, which operates on the Data Link layer (Layer 2) of the OSI model, to create two or more segments. The network nodes on a bridged network segment are on the same broadcast domain, and messages for a node on a bridged network segment are sent only to the segment on which the node is located, provided the bridge has had a chance to record this information. In this way, a bridge keeps local traffic local and relieves other segments of unnecessary traffic.

However — and this is one of the bad things about using a bridge to segment a LAN — if a destination node is unknown to the bridge, the message is forwarded to all connected segments. A bridge provides only a single path between bridged segments, and usually no provision is made for redundancy, such as multiple connections to a segment. You can bridge a LAN by using two major methods:

- ✓ Transparent
- ✓ Source-route

Crossing the transparent bridge

Transparent bridging occurs primarily on Ethernet networks, where the bridge is responsible for determining the path from the source node to the destination node. A *transparent bridge* examines the incoming frame and reads the destination MAC address. It then looks in its bridging table and, if it finds the address, sends the packet to the appropriate port. Otherwise, the frame is sent to all ports except the one that it came in on.

Bridging from the source

Token ring networks use source-route bridging (SRB). In this bridging method, the responsibility of determining the path to the destination node is placed on the sending node, not on the bridge.

In an SRB environment, the following steps occur:

1. Token ring devices send out a test frame to determine whether the destination node is on the local ring.

2. If no answer is forthcoming (which means that the destination node is not on the local ring), the sending node sends out a broadcast message, which is called an *explorer frame*.

3. The bridge forwards the explorer frame across the network through the network's bridges.

   Each bridge adds its ring number and bridge number to the frame's routing information field (RIF), which is a sort of Hansel and Gretel bread-crumb trail, so it can retrace its route later.

4. The destination device, if it exists, receives and responds to the explorer frame. The sending node gets this response.

5. The sending node initiates communications between the two devices, with each intermediate bridge using the RIF value to determine the path between the two nodes.

Because source-route bridging (SRB) uses RIF information to determine its routes, no bridging table is created.

Segmenting the LAN with a router

Routers, which operate on the Network layer (Layer 3) of the OSI model, allow you to create and connect several logical networks, including those that use different topologies or technologies (such as token ring and Ethernet — see Chapter 3 for information on these networking technologies) into a single internetwork. Inserting a router into a network, which is a physical segmentation, creates separate network segments, which the router treats as independent broadcast domains. Routers provide multiple paths between segments and map the nodes on the segments and the connecting paths with a routing protocol and internal routing tables (see Chapter 11).

Routing over a segmented network is no different than routing over any internetwork.

1. The router receives a frame, strips off the Layer 2 framing, and extracts the destination Layer 3 (IP) network address.

2. One of three things happens:

   • The routing table is searched and if the destination is on a network segment directly connected to the router, the router forwards the frame over the appropriate port interfacing to that segment.

   • If the destination address is on a remote segment or network, the router determines if it has a forwarding address for the packet or if the default route should be used.

   • If multiple segments are attached to the router, chances are that the frame will remain in its collision domains and will not be broadcast throughout the entire network.

Segmenting a LAN with a switch

Using a switch to segment a LAN increases the chances that a message will be forwarded to the right segment and reduces the chances that a collision will occur. Fewer collisions mean better utilization of a segment's bandwidth, which translates to more bandwidth for everyone.

A switch, which operates on the Data Link layer (Layer 2) of the OSI model, typically has a high-capacity back plane (commonly in the gigabit range). The *back plane,* like that in a PC with a backplane motherboard, serves as an interface to the switch's processor and its memory. The speed of a switch's back plane provides an additional pool of bandwidth to its interfaces and the segments attached to them.

When a data frame enters a port, the switch, after reading the destination MAC address, which comes first, reads the source MAC address of the frame and stores it along with the ID of the switch port on which the frame arrived (see Chapter 6) in the *CAM (content-addressable memory) table* — assuming, of course, that this information isn't already in the table. By using the CAM table, a switch can readily look up a node by its MAC address, should anything come into the switch addressed to it. In this way, the switch keeps track of which nodes are on which segments. The CAM table is stored in volatile RAM (you know, the one that loses its memory when the power goes off), which means that the CAM table must be rebuilt if the power is interrupted.

The ports on a switch can be configured to support a virtual LAN (VLAN). A *VLAN* is a logical network segment and broadcast domain with a configuration that is unique to the segments on the other ports of the switch. Simply put, a VLAN is a way to flock birds of a feather together. Each port on the switch can be uniquely configured to provide adjustments for data speed, transmission mode, and any other special LAN characteristics used by the logical network segment represented by the VLAN.

Applying Three Methods to Switching Success

The three most common methods used to forward data packets through a switch are *cut-through* (also known as *real-time*), *store-and-forward,* and *fragment-free.*

- ✔ **Cut-through switching:** This type of switching method has lower *latency* (the additional time required for switching the packet) because it begins to forward a frame as soon as the destination MAC address is read, which is typically within the first 6 bytes of an Ethernet frame.

- ✔ **Store-and-forward switching:** This type of switching has higher latency because it reads the entire frame into its buffer before beginning to forward the frame out to another port. One of the biggest benefits that is realized from the increased latency is error control. By receiving the entire frame, store-and-forward switching is able to recalculate the CRC (Cyclical Redundancy Check) sum and compare it to that included in the frame, which ensures that erroneous frames are not forwarded. In addition, a store-and-forward switch can recognize and discard *runts* (frames less than 64 that may be missing data), *giants* (frames with extra segments), and damaged frames. Discarding these defective frames reduces traffic on the network.

- ✔ **Fragment-free switching:** This switching method is a hybrid of cut-through switching that receives just a little more of the frame before beginning to forward the frame. The amount of the frame received is called the *collision window.* The frame isn't sent out until 64 bytes have been received. All frames shorter than 64 bytes (runts), which may be mistaken for *collision fragments* — the damaged flotsam of frames that have collided on the network — aren't forwarded.

Virtually Segmenting the LAN

A VLAN (virtual LAN) is a logical grouping of networked nodes that communicate directly with each other on Layer 2. VLANs are also called *logical LANs* because they aren't created physically by using Layer 1 media and devices. Instead, VLANs are created logically or virtually through the configuration on a switch. A VLAN is not geographically or functionally fixed in place (such as within a single department of a company or for all account representatives). A VLAN is created and managed on either a router or a switch, which serves as the VLAN controller.

VLANs are usually created in the process of segmenting a network with the objective of load-balancing traffic over the network and managing bandwidth allocations more easily than with the physical management of a LAN. Each station port on a switch can host a separate VLAN with its own data speeds, modes, technologies, and other characteristics.

The primary benefits offered by VLANs are the following:

- Functional workgroups
- Broadcast control
- Enhanced security

Building workgroups

Study Figure 10-1 and follow this scenario to understand VLAN implementation.

- Switch A is located in the MDF (Main Distribution Frame).
- Switches B and C are located in IDFs (Intermediate Distribution Frame) on two different floors, connected by fiber-optic media through a trunking protocol.

In Figure 10-1, each workstation is identified with a code (A1, B2, C3, and so on). The alphabetic character (A, B, or C) represents the switch to which each node is connected, and the number (1, 2, or 3) indicates a workgroup. Because members of workgroups tend to communicate more with other members of the workgroup than with outsiders, grouping them logically into VLANs (VLAN1, VLAN2, and VLAN3) makes sense, despite the fact that they're physically located on different floors.

The point at which the physical wiring from multiple network components is concentrated is called a *distribution frame*. A *main distribution frame* is the central wiring location for a network, such as the telephone closet in a building. An *intermediate distribution frame* is a connecting point located between the main distribution frame and network workstations.

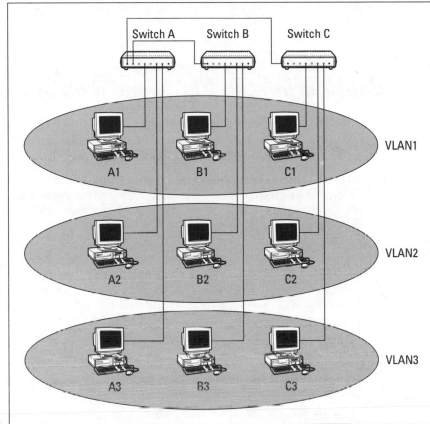

Switch A   Switch B   Switch C

VLAN1

A1   B1   C1

VLAN2

A2   B2   C2

VLAN3

A3   B3   C3

Figure 10-1:
A VLAN
workgroup
created
across three
physical
LAN
segments

Broadcasting to smaller domains

You can think of a VLAN as a logically defined broadcast domain that is unconstrained by the physical location, media, addressing, or transmission rates of its nodes. The virtual broadcast domain created by the VLAN may contain workstations with different characteristics, including location, network medium, and bandwidth. By limiting broadcast messages to smaller and more manageable logical broadcast domains or virtual workgroups (VLANs), the performance of the entire *nonvirtual network* is improved.

Improving security

Implementing a VLAN improves a network's security automatically. Members of one VLAN can't access data being transmitted on other VLANs or on any circuits outside the VLAN. This arrangement means that back in Figure 10-1, the users of the workgroup on VLAN3 are in their own virtual network and are prevented from seeing any of the data being transmitted across either VLAN1 or VLAN2.

Configuring the VLAN one way or another

The assignment of a VLAN can be made in four different ways on the switch:

- **Port address:** Port-assigned VLANs are the most commonly implemented. The ports of a switch can be assigned individually, in groups, in rows, or even across two or more switches, provided the switches are properly connected through a trunking protocol. Port-based VLANs are the simplest to implement and are typically used in situations where DHCP (Dynamic Host Control Protocol) is used to assign IP addresses to network hosts.

- **MAC address:** MAC-based VLANs are rare, primarily due to the increased popularity and use of DHCP on networks. *MAC-based VLANs* enable a user to belong to the same VLAN at all times, even when connecting to the network with a different MAC address or through a different port on the switch. The MAC addresses in a MAC-based VLAN must be entered into the switch and configured as a part of a specific VLAN. Although this setup is great for users who may move about, this type of VLAN can be very complex and difficult for the administrator to manage and troubleshoot. Typically, a MAC-based VLAN is configured and managed through some form of LAN management software, such as Cisco's Virtual Membership Policy Server.

- **User ID:** User-ID-based VLANs are also quite rare because they are complex to set up, administer, and troubleshoot. All VLAN users must be identified and entered into the switch and configured as a part of a specific VLAN. On a user-ID-based VLAN, the user remains a part of the same VLAN regardless of where on the network or on which host they log onto the network.

- **Network address:** Network-address-based VLANs are configured much like MAC-based VLANs, with the exception that nodes are registered by using their logical or IP addresses. Network-address-based VLANs are uncommon primarily because of the use of DHCP to assign workstation IP addresses. Like the MAC-based VLAN, this type of VLAN allows the user to remain part of the same VLAN, even when he relocates to a different physical port connection to the network, provided, of course, that he keeps the same IP address.

Trunking together VLANs

Normally, segmenting a LAN with switches involves the creation of at least two VLANs through a switch. After the VLANs are created, any information about them is shared through the switch using a trunking protocol. Sharing information allows all the switches involved in a VLAN to be fully aware of the VLAN, its hosts, and the locations of the hosts, so that each switch is ready to support it. By default, *trunking protocols,* which are used to pass information between switches, are disabled on all ports.

Before a VLAN can be configured between two switches, trunking be must enabled on the ports to be used to connect the switches together. A *trunk line* carries the combined traffic of one or more VLANs to another switch or router. Trunking services allow VLANs to be extended across the network and over other switches or routers.

The two most commonly used trunking methods are the following:

- **Inter-Switch Link (ISL):** ISL is a proprietary Cisco protocol that's supported only between Cisco devices. ISL supports transportation across Ethernet, FDDI, or token ring environments.
- **IEEE 802.1Q:** The 802.1 subcommittee defines this as an industry standard protocol that allows VLAN information exchange among dissimilar manufacturers' equipment.

Two other trunking methods are used on Cisco networks — IEEE 802.10 and an ATM-based protocol called LANE (LAN Emulation), but they are advanced topics not commonly found on most LANs. I mention them here just so you have heard of them.

Picking the Right Switch for the Job

Cisco has more than ten different series of switches available, one of which will provide an appropriate type of switching to any network. And this number doesn't include the hubs and smart hubs that Cisco lists in the switching products family

These are the most popular switching equipment items offered by Cisco:

- **Catalyst 1900 series:** The switches in this series represent the best combination of value and power in the Cisco Catalyst switch line. These switches provide both 10 Mbps and 100 Mbps, powering both the desktop and workgroup connectivity over UTP wire or fiber-optic cable. (See Chapter 4 for more information on network cabling.)
- **Catalyst 2900 series:** This switch family delivers the same power as larger Cisco switches, but in a smaller package. The Catalyst 2926 is a fixed-configuration 10 Mpbs/100 Mbps auto-sensing switch that uses the same architecture and software as the larger Catalyst 5000. The Cisco

Catalyst 2900 XL switches are 10/100 auto-sensing switches that offer a wide range of different port densities, configuration options, and pricing. The Cisco 2912 and 2924 switches are very common on LANs.

- **Catalyst 3500 series:** The 12-, 24-, and 48-port switches in this series are 10/100 and gigabit Ethernet switches that offer very fast switching. The 3500 series is an excellent choice for high-performance LANs, including such features as Cisco Switch Clustering multidevice management architecture and VoIP (Voice over IP).

- **Catalyst 3900:** This switch offers a stackable, flexible switching solution to token ring networks.

- **Catalyst 5000 series:** This switch series provides large intranets and high-performance switched LANs with media-independent support for all LAN switching technologies over Ethernet, Fast Ethernet, FDDI, ATM, token ring, and gigabit Ethernet. (See Chapter 3 for more information on network technologies.) This switch group is capable of handling more than 10 million packets per second.

Get another book

Cisco does have larger, more sophisticated switching solutions above the Catalyst 5000 series, such as the 6000 and 8500 series, but these switches are normally found only in LAN/WAN integration and CAN (Campus Area Network) situations. If you find yourself in one of these situations, you need much more information than this book can provide.

Chapter 11

Working with Routers

A router is one thing you definitely must be familiar with to implement a Cisco network. This includes being familiar with the way a router "thinks," how it relates to other devices, and its role in the networking world. The challenge to succeeding as a Cisco network administrator is in the router.

However, there are some things you really don't need to know about routers. I realize that if you're starting from scratch, routers (especially Cisco routers) can be intimidating. Just so you don't end up wasting valuable time learning the wrong stuff, don't worry about the following things as you become a Cisco network administrator, even if you want to become certified:

✔ You don't need to be able to field strip and reassemble a router, either blindfolded or not.

✔ You don't need to memorize the processor speeds and specific memory amounts in particular Cisco router models, and normally, determining the proper memory or processor configuration for a router is not a big requirement. This isn't to say that memory, processor, IOS (Internetwork Operating System) version, and configuration aren't important, but typically your Cisco representative or vendor can help you with these things at the start. However, as you go along, you must be able to determine if a router's configuration is remaining adequate for your network's requirements.

✔ About the only components on the router that you really need to care about are the interfaces and memory. You don't need to know the general anatomy of a router.

The Cisco Network Model

Cisco uses a three-tier hierarchical network model, like that illustrated in Figure 11-1. The Cisco network model consists of three layers: the core layer, the distribution layer, and the access layer.

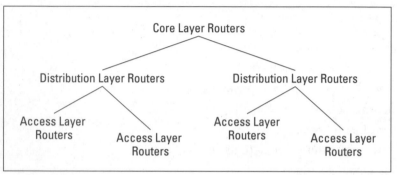

Figure 11-1:
The layers
of the Cisco
network
model
create a
router
hierarchy.

▶ **Core layer:** Also called the *backbone layer,* this layer provides transportation of data between networks. Core layer routers are in the 7200 series or higher.

▶ **Distribution layer:** This layer acts as a demarcation between the core and access layers and provides differentiation between dynamic and static routing and other policy-based functions. (See Chapter 12 for information on dynamic and static routing.) Distribution layer routers are in the 3600 series.

▶ **Access layer:** Users are allowed access to a network or internetwork on this layer of the Cisco network model. Access layer routers are in the 2500/2600 series.

Familiarizing yourself with the model series may be a good idea. You can use a core layer router on the distribution or access layers, but it would be a terrific waste of capability and money. You cannot, repeat cannot, effectively do the reverse. An access layer router is not a good choice for the core layer.

Understanding the primary purpose of each layer of the Cisco network model helps you to understand why a certain router, switch, or module is appropriate for a particular application on a network. In every case, when you install a router on your network, its application is defined on one of the Cisco network model layers, which means you should be aware of which routers are appropriate to that level.

Moving traffic over the core layer

The *core layer* is where the biggest, fastest, and (not surprisingly) most-expensive routers, with the highest model numbers, are found. Core layer routers are used to merge geographically separated networks. The core layer focuses on moving information as fast as possible, most often over dedicated or leased lines. The core layer of any network should be its high-speed switching backbone and, as such, should be designed to switch packets as fast as possible. Therefore, no packet manipulation, such as configuring an access control list or packet filtering, should be done on the core layer because these activities would slow down packet switching.

The primary concern on the core layer is reliability. Usually, when the network backbone fails, the network does also. So the core layer of any network must be designed for *high availability,* which is the design philosophy aimed at eliminating points of network failure. Another concern about reliability is avoiding devices and protocols that have slow convergence. (*Convergence* is the ability of a network's routers and switches to agree to a new network topology after a change has been made to the network.) Switches and routers that have faster convergence and can provide load balancing over multiple links are best suited for use on the core layer.

Core layer routers and switches should provide both routing and Layer 2 switching and bridging over different Layer 3 protocols. (See Chapter 2 for information on the OSI model and its layers.) The overall design goal for a network's core layer should be to eliminate single points of failure.

Distributing data around the network

In the Cisco world, the *campus backbone,* the networking media and devices that interconnect two or more buildings located in close proximity, such as on a business or college campus, exists on the distribution layer. I realize that including the backbone on the distribution layer may contradict the definition that I gave in the preceding section for the core layer, but please understand that I'm actually dealing with different backbones here. The *core layer backbone* is a more universal internetworking backbone than that used within a single LAN or Campus Area Network (CAN).

Routers on the *distribution layer* of the model are used to connect buildings or departments, such as accounting, production, and distribution — each of which is known in Ciscospeak as a *large functional group (LFG).* Distribution routers represent the intermediate level of the Cisco model. On this layer, the packets of the network are filtered and forwarded up and down router layers. Most routing policy decisions that decide the best routing for messages on your network are made on the distribution layer. Mid-level network servers, such as department or network segment servers, can also be found on the distribution level.

The distribution layer serves to separate the access and core layers and acts as a gateway to the core. The boundaries of a network are defined and packet manipulation takes place on the distribution layer of the Cisco network model. Several other activities are performed on the distribution layer:

- Access to LFGs
- Aggregation of addresses or links
- Definition of broadcast and multicast domains
- Routing for virtual LANs (VLANs) (see Chapter 10)
- Router and switch-based security (access lists)

Providing access to the network

The access layer is where the rubber meets the road. The *access layer* is where host computers access a network and where most network traffic finds its destination. Access layer routers and switches are used to segment LANs, which I talk about in a later section (see "Segmenting a LAN with a Router"). They also provide remote access to a network using WAN services.

I don't have much to say about access layer devices, primarily because the access layer operates essentially on the local area network. Devices on the access layer do not make sophisticated decisions or worry about convergence or interconnectivity. The bulk of their responsibility is to provide functionality and access to the local network.

Segmenting a LAN with a Router

Segmenting a LAN with a router may not be the least expensive way to go, but doing so does have benefits. You can find less-expensive ways to segment a network, such as with a bridge, and you can find faster, simpler ways, such as with a switch, but a router can provide benefits that other devices cannot.

This chapter is about routers, so I focus on some facts and characteristics of LANs segmented with routers. In case you're wondering, a WAN (because it is made up of separate networks, each of which has its own intermediary router) and, in general terms, is already segmented.

Most networks began life as fairly simple affairs with small groups of client workstations receiving services from a single server. But like weeds, kudzu, and children, networks always seem to grow and in unexpected ways. A network can grow into a bandwidth-starved monster with the network carrying more broadcast messages than anything else. Sound familiar? No? Then you really must be new to networking. Or you are among those saintly administrators that already know the value of segmenting a network.

Regardless of how you segment a network or which device you use, some general benefits are almost always generated; these benefits are listed in Chapter 10. However, when you segment a network with a router, you can gain specific benefits. One reason to segment a LAN with a router may be as simple as this: You have money to burn, or you have always wanted to get your hands on a Cisco router. However, the real reasons (or at least the ones you should tell your boss) are the following:

- **Reduced size of broadcast domains:** Routers block broadcasts unless specifically instructed to forward them.

- **Smaller networks:** Routers can be used to create smaller networks. When you install a router, the portion of the network behind the router becomes, in effect, a separate and distinct network, as opposed to dividing a LAN into smaller segments with a switch or bridge.

- **Flexible addressing:** Routers segment a network by using logical, rather than physical, addresses. For example, a bridge uses the MAC (Media Access Control) or physical address to make its forwarding decisions, whereas a router uses the logical or IP address.

- **Better administration:** In most cases, a system administrator has more management tools available on a router, such as access control lists, firewall capabilities, its ability to make routing decisions based on a multitude of factors, and more, thanks to the increased memory and IOS capabilities.

Deciding on segmenting your network

You really do need to figure out what you are trying to accomplish by breaking a network into smaller segments. With your goals established, determining whether you need to use a router, switch, or bridge is much easier. Needless to say, if all you need is a bridge, paying for a bridge is much better than paying for a router. Routers are expensive devices with a high degree of sophistication. When you need a router, certainly you should use a router; but when something else will work as well as (or better than) a router, then by all means, use something else.

Consider the following before you segment a LAN with a router:

- A router can segment LANs that include different media types. For example, a LAN may have both Category 5 and Thinnet (coaxial) cable connecting to fiber-optic cabling. But so can a bridge or a switch.

- A router increases *latency,* the amount of delay introduced by networking devices, by adding the delay caused by the router examining each packet entirely and reframing it before sending it on.

✔ A router can also provide more than one active link or route to a destination. On a larger LAN, this ability can provide route diversity and redundancy, which are always good things. Switches can also do this, but if you need routing capabilities in your LAN, your choice is obvious.

From here, you should do the following things as you set up your router:

✔ Choose the best spot for the router.

✔ Understand your router's memory capabilities.

✔ Determine which port(s) you want to install on your router.

✔ Consider the environmental factors.

Picking your router spot

I can't really give you a how-to for segmenting a LAN with a router. Although segmenting a LAN with a router is really more complicated than I may make it sound, you just add a router to the network at some point that makes logical, physical, and routing sense. That's about it. However, doing it right involves some knowledge of the network, its traffic, and its topology. You could just pick a point in the LAN and plug the router in, but most likely, unless you are extremely lucky, you wouldn't see much improvement in the performance of the LAN. Segmenting the LAN with a router really requires that you know where the segmentation would make the most sense for the outcome that you want to obtain.

Routers are generally used to segment fairly large networks, in terms of geography, number of nodes, or volume. What's a good network to segment with a router, you ask? Here are a few criteria that describe a good candidate:

✔ One spread over several floors or buildings.

✔ One that has a high number of nodes in comparison to the bandwidth available, so that the desired average bandwidth goals are not being realized.

✔ One that must provide each workstation or segment with a high amount of bandwidth, regardless of the number of nodes or the size of the segment.

Remembering the router's memory

Just because a Cisco router has four kinds of memory doesn't mean that understanding them is difficult. Cisco routers don't really have any more or fewer types of memory than your personal computer. Thinking of the Cisco router as a special-purpose personal computer may help you to keep the memory types straight. In fact, Cisco claims to be a software company, not a hardware company. Table 11-1 summarizes just about everything you need to know about the memory in a Cisco router.

Table 11-1	Different Memory Types in a Cisco Router
Memory/Type	*Contents*
RAM/DRAM	Active program and operating system instructions, the running configuration file, routing tables
NVRAM	Startup configuration file
ROM	POST, bootstrap, and startup/power-up utilities, usually limited version of Cisco IOS
Flash	Cisco IOS

To simplify your life, don't worry about how much memory is in each router configuration. You should, however, have a very good general understanding of the different types of memory in the router and how and when each is used.

RAM/DRAM a ding dong

The primary working memory in a Cisco router is called *RAM* (random-access memory). Like your PC, the router uses RAM for storing its working files and data. The RAM in the router is specifically DRAM, which stands for dynamic random-access memory and is pronounced "dee-ram" (not to be confused with de Bulls, de Bears, or even de Rams, for that matter), which is the same memory type found in most personal computers. And like the RAM in your PC, if the power is switched off or the power fails, any files and data stored in RAM/DRAM are lost. The *dynamic* part of the DRAM name refers to the fact that DRAM must be refreshed with an electrical charge every few milliseconds to hold its contents, as opposed to static RAM (SRAM), which doesn't need to be recharged to hold its contents (see "NVRAM for static storage" later in the chapter). The dynamic DRAM is volatile RAM, which means that it must have an electrical power source in order to hold data. It's simple: no power = no data.

Just remember that a Cisco router's RAM is volatile DRAM that holds the router's working configuration, data, and files. When the power is turned off, the contents of the RAM simply cease to exist. The contents are lost and cannot be recovered.

In the Cisco router, RAM is used to hold

  ✔ A working copy of the Cisco IOS software (see Chapter 16). This is generally true, but some router models, such as the Cisco 1600 and 2500 router series, run their IOS software from flash memory.

- ✔ The command executive, also known as EXEC, which interprets the commands you enter from the router console (see Chapter 16)
- ✔ Routing tables (see Chapter 12)
- ✔ The active configuration file (see Chapter 17)
- ✔ The ARP cache (see Chapter 8)
- ✔ Packet buffers, which are temporary I/O areas used for processing a packet
- ✔ Packet hold queues, which are used to hold incoming and outbound packets awaiting services by the router

Did I mention that anything stored in RAM is lost when the router is powered off? I hope that you're beginning to see that providing a good power source to your routers, such as an uninterruptible power supply (UPS) with a long standby battery life, is essential. If the power fails or if you turn the router off for some reason (although what the reason could possibly be escapes us), the only real catastrophe will be that you might lose any changes you've made to the active configuration file and haven't copied to NVRAM (nonvolatile RAM). Everything else — the routing tables, the ARP cache, and so on — will be reconstructed by the Cisco IOS as soon as power is restored and the router completes its power-up sequence. But this takes time and can impact the performance of the network until these elements are rebuilt.

NVRAM for static storage

Although DRAM is volatile and must have a power source so that it can hold any data or instructions placed in it, NVRAM — which is nonvolatile RAM — can hold its contents whether the main power source is on or off. This doesn't mean that NVRAM doesn't need power. When the main power source is available, NVRAM can statically store its contents by drawing a very low voltage electrical charge. When the main power source is not available, an onboard battery is used to supply power NVRAM.

What Cisco calls NVRAM, your personal computer calls SRAM (pronounced "ess-ram"), or static RAM. The most important thing stored in NVRAM on a Cisco router is the startup configuration file that is loaded to RAM during the router's boot sequence.

Any changes made to the working (or running) configuration of the router that is held in RAM are not automatically permanent. You should copy a modified running configuration to NVRAM to ensure that the changes become a permanent part of the router's configuration and will be included when the router is next started up. Any changes made to the running configuration not stored in NVRAM would be lost if you ever needed to restart the router.

ROM with a view

Another type of memory, called *ROM* (read-only memory), is even more reliable than NVRAM. Like NVRAM, ROM is nonvolatile and does not lose its contents when the power goes off, even without a battery. Information or programming stored in ROM is put there when the integrated circuit (IC), on which the ROM is based, is manufactured. This manufacturing process burns in the ROM IC's contents and permanently locks in the information or programming instructions on the chip.

The ROM in a router is exactly like the ROM in your personal computer and is used for much the same thing. ROM holds the instructions used to start your system each time you power it up. These instructions are called *firmware*, as opposed to hardware and software, and are literally burned into the *PROM* (programmable read-only memory) chip when it is manufactured. A PROM usually is not upgradeable.

On the Cisco router, ROM holds the instructions used to perform the power-on self-test (POST) diagnostics, the bootstrap program (which is the startup program for the router), and the router's operating system (which will always be the Cisco IOS). Cisco routers contain two copies of IOS, a stripped-down version that is stored in ROM and the fully up-to-date version stored in flash memory (see the next section, "Flashing the EPROM").

Flashing the EPROM

A specific type of PROM can be updated. An *EPROM* (erasable programmable read-only memory) can be updated. An EPROM is erasable and can be written to and updated by using a software-controlled operation called *flashing*. As temporary and volatile as this may sound, it isn't. EPROMs are nonvolatile and retain their contents indefinitely, even without a power source, or at least until the next time they are flashed. And no, the software used to update an EPROM is not called a flasher.

On the Cisco router, the *flash memory* is an EPROM IC chip that holds the image and microcode of the router's operating system, the Cisco IOS. Storing the fully up-to-date IOS version in flash memory enables you to upgrade it without having to remove and replace ROM chips on the router's CPU board, or — worse yet — to continually purchase new routers to get the new and improved features.

Discovering CDP

The Cisco Discovery Protocol (CDP) is a proprietary Cisco protocol that allows you to get (discover) information about directly connected Cisco routers, bridges, and switches. CDP, which is included throughout Cisco's product line, uses a Data Link layer framing type called *SNAP* (Subnetwork Access Protocol) and frames to communicate with routers and other network connectivity devices. Virtually all LAN media and transmission modes support CDP, including Frame Relay and *ATM* (Asynchronous Transfer Mode) (see Chapter 14).

CDP automatically starts when the router is powered on and immediately goes to work by multicasting Data Link layer discovery messages for the purpose of identifying other Cisco devices on the internetwork. Any device wishing to be discovered sends back an SNMP (Simple Network Management Protocol) message containing configuration data on itself. The information in this message allows CDP to display information about the discovered devices, including information about different Network (or higher) layer protocols. CDP caches whatever it discovers in its router's RAM and updates it periodically as the information changes.

CDP does the following things for you and your routers:

- ✔ CDP uses SNAP at the Data Link layer, which makes it protocol independent.
- ✔ CDP detects attached devices regardless of what protocol they're running (for example, TCP/IP, IPX, or AppleTalk).
- ✔ CDP is enabled by default when the router is booted on all interfaces.
- ✔ CDP update requests are multicast by default every 60 seconds by using Layer 2 multicast messages.
- ✔ CDP has a default hold-time. The amount of time that a device holds a CDP update before discarding it is 180 seconds.

Working with All the Best Connections

Cisco routers connect to the world through a wide array of interface ports. Your particular interface needs will determine exactly which ports you configure on your router. But regardless of your need, Cisco has either a router or an add-in module to provide the type of interface you need.

The ports installed on your router should reflect the interface needs of your network. In the myriad router families offered by Cisco Systems, you are bound to find a router to fit your needs and requirements. However, sometimes the router you need operationally just doesn't have the ports you need. This is where the modularity of the Cisco router line can help you. For the Cisco 1600 router series and above, you can add interface modules to the router to configure it to fit your particular needs. If you do customize your router, add only the functions you need in the near future. The interface modules aren't inexpensive and can be added in the future when you actually need them.

Taking command of the console

Every Cisco router comes with one particularly essential interface port. This port, which is either a 9-pin or 25-pin serial or an RJ-45 port, is called the *console port*. It is through the console port that you install and configure the router initially and perhaps in the future.

To install and configure a Cisco router, you connect the console port into a terminal, such as a PC running terminal emulation software. The router and the terminal device can be connected one of two ways. On most newer Cisco router models, an 8-wire Cat 3 or 5 cable (see Chapter 4) with RJ-45 connectors at each end is used. However, on some models, typically older router models, an EIA/TIA-232 cable (also known as a null modem cable) is used. An EIA/TIA-232 cable has an EIA/TIA-232 DTE port on one end (for the PC) and a DCE port (for the router) on the other end. EIA/TIA-232 connectors are either DB-9 or DB-25 plugs. What all of that alphabet soup means is that you can use your portable computer's serial port with either a network cable or a null modem cable and some terminal emulation software, such as Windows HyperTerminal utility.

After you have completed the initial configuration of the router, don't leave your computer connected to the router. You should log off the router and remove the cable. This connection should be used only when it is needed for configuration or administration of the router.

So why am I talking about a protocol?

If this chapter covers the most basic components and activities of a Cisco router, why does it include a section on a specific protocol? CDP is covered here because it is a foundation protocol that performs one of the most basic functions of a router: discovering information about the router's neighbors.

Many of the routing decisions made by the router are based on what the router knows about its neighboring routers. If a neighboring router is up or down or just not responding, this situation has a direct impact on whether or not that router should be included in the routes available for use. So, I thought it would be a good idea to mention how the router learns about the health and well being of its neighbors.

Making the router feel at home

You should consider a number of factors for each interface type in use when preparing to install a router. Chapter 4 provides some detail information on the specific considerations for each type of media in use, but consider these general points:

- ✔ **The type of cabling needed for each port (fiber, thick or thin coaxial, or twisted-pair cabling):** Ensure that you have the appropriate connectors and cable management materials before starting the installation.

- ✔ **The distance limitations for each signal type:** Cisco has a specification on the distance limits that you should use for each of the different signal types it supports.

- ✔ **The cables you need for each specific interface:** Make sure that you have the right kind of cable with exactly the right connectors for each interface port.

- ✔ **The interface equipment needed to support your media type:** Be sure that you have such necessities as transceivers, modems, channel service units (CSUs), and data service units (DSUs).

Before you install your router, make sure that you have everything you need on hand. If you are really brave, you may consider building your own cables, but unless you have had extensive experience building cables, you're better off just buying them. If you insist on building your own cables, refer to the cable pin outs (which wires are connected to which pins in the connector body) in the "Cabling Specifications" appendix of the Cisco "Planning for Installation" white paper.

You can find the Cisco "Planning for Installation" white paper at the following Web site. (A PDF document is available on the site.)

```
www.cisco.com/univercd/cc/td/doc/product/core/cis7010/7010_him/
7010prep.htm.
```

Take my advice: Call your Cisco representative or reseller to order your connecting cables. Yes, you'll pay more, but you'll thank me in the end.

Providing a powerful plethora of ports

A long list of interface modules is available for Cisco routers, should you need to add additional ports to one of the modular routers. This list is representative of the interface modules available from Cisco:

- AnyLAN (voice grade)

- ATM (OC-3 rate) single-mode or multimode

- Channelized DS3 and E3

- DS3 high-speed interface

- E3 medium-speed interface

- Enterprise Systems Connector (ESCON), which is an IBM fiber-optic connector.

- Ethernet 10BaseT and 10BaseFL

- Fast Ethernet 100BaseTX and 100BaseFX

- FDDI single-mode and multimode (half-duplex and full-duplex)

- High-Speed Serial Interface (HSSI — pronounced "hissy")

- ISDN BRI

- Multichannel PA (DSX1, E1, E3, and T3)

- Synchronous serial (V.35, X.21, EIA/TIA-232, E1, EIA/TIA-449, and EIA-530)

- Token ring half-duplex and full-duplex

And a remarkable range of routers

The information in Table 11-2 provides you with an overview of a representative selection of the different Cisco router series. Please understand that Cisco, like all high-technology companies, is constantly updating and upgrading its lines, with products being added or discontinued (called going *EOL* [end-of-product-life] or *EOS* [end-of-service/support]) all the time. What I really mean is that the list in Table 11-2 could very well be obsolete the second this book is printed, but it's my educated guess that the majority of it will be valid for at least a couple of years. Your best bet for an up-to-date list of Cisco routers is to visit Cisco's router products Web site at www.cisco.com/warp/public/44/jump/routers.shtml.

Table 11-2	Cisco Router Series	
Product Series	*Description*	*Applications*
Cisco 12000	Gigabit switch routers	Accepts data from PSTN, ATM, Frame Relay, DSL, and PBX for high-speed transmission over the IP backbone

(continued)

Table 11-2 *(continued)*

Product Series	Description	Applications
Cisco 10000	Edge services routers	High-density T1-aggregation IP edge routers
Cisco 7500	Data, voice, and video routers	Supports multiprotocol, multimedia routing and bridging with a wide variety of protocols and LAN and WAN options
Cisco 7200	High-performance multifunction routers	Chassis-based, modular central site router that provides high-performance and availability with serviceability and manageability features
Cisco 7100	VPN routers	Integrated VPN solution that combines high-speed routing with VPN services
Cisco 6400	Universal access concentrator	Delivers premium router services appropriate for ISPs and CLECs providing DSL services
Cisco 3600	Modular, high-density access routers	Multiservice access routers for medium-size and large-size offices and smaller ISPs
Cisco 2600	Modular access routers	Cost-effective, modular access router for branch offices that supports voice, data, and dial-up access
Cisco 2500	Fixed and modular access routers	Flexible branch office choice that features integrated hubs and access servers for either Ethernet or token ring
Cisco 1700	Modular access router	For secure Internet, intranet, and extranet access with optional VPN and firewall service designed for small branch offices or small and medium businesses
Cisco 1600	Modular desktop access routers	Small footprint routers that are excellent choices for small business or branch offices to connect an Ethernet LAN to the Internet or a corporate WAN
Cisco 1400	xDSL routers	Secure router that features both Ethernet and ATM interfaces that include VPN and firewall support

Product Series	Description	Applications
Cisco 1000	Fixed-configuration desktop access routers	For connecting small offices to ISDN or serial WAN connections
Cisco 900	Cable access routers	Provides telecommuters and small offices with high-speed secure connection and access
Cisco 800	ISDN, serial, and IDSL routers	Inexpensive router series that connects up to 20 users to the Internet or intranet over ISDN, IDSL, or a serial connection; small office router for offices of up to 20 users and corporate telecommuters
Cisco 600	SDSL access routers	A series of affordable, fast routers that connect small office and home office workers to the Internet via SDSL (Symmetrical DSL) service

Protecting the Router from the Environment

You should consider a number of environmental factors before slapping that router into place. Cisco routers have built-in environmental monitoring. They won't give you an air quality report or test your local drinking water, but they will protect the router from potential damage from electrical spikes and high-temperature operating conditions.

Some of the recommended environmental considerations are obvious, or at least they should be, but others are more subtle. To protect the investment you've made in a Cisco router, you should definitely include these considerations in your site preparations:

- ✔ **Airflow:** You must maintain two inches or more clearance between the sides of the chassis and the enclosure walls to allow air to flow properly through cooling ports on the router.

- ✔ **Cooling:** Just because a room has air conditioning doesn't mean that it can stay properly cooled after you install a router and any associated networking equipment. Electrical equipment puts out heat, and you may need to add additional cooling capacity to keep the room at acceptable operating temperatures.

✔ **Equipment rack:** Unless it is absolutely a desktop model, such as any router with a model number of 1000 or below, a Cisco router comes with rack-mounting hardware compatible with most 19-inch rack systems and Telco-style racks. When mounting the router, be sure that you have free access to both the interface processor and the chassis cover panel. You can also set the router on a rack shelf as long as the router can be secured to the shelf. This may be a no-brainer, but don't set the router directly on the floor or in any other area that may collect dust.

✔ **ESD (electrostatic discharge):** When working on, in, or near the router, follow standard ESD-avoidance procedures to protect the router and its modules from damage. A good reference site for ESD information is Indiana University's Knowledge Base at `kb.indiana.edu/data/aeoh.html`.

✔ **Power:** The router needs voltages between 100 and 240V AC and 50 through 60 Hz. Some routers also have options for DC power. Be sure to read the product specifications carefully for the power requirements of your specific router.

✔ **Temperature:** Maintain an ambient temperature of 32°F through 104°F (0°C through 40°C) and keep the area as dust-free as possible. A good rule is if you can stand the temperature, so can the router. If you turn either blue or red, something is wrong!

✔ **Wiring:** When setting up the router site, consider distance limitations, EMI, and connector compatibilities.

After your Cisco router is installed and configured, you can use the **show environment** command to monitor the internal system environmental conditions. The router's environmental monitor continuously checks the interior chassis environment, looking for marginal or alarm-level conditions, such as high temperatures and maximum and minimum voltages. Any out-of-range conditions are recorded and reported.

If your router ever displays warning messages like this

```
WARNING: Fan has reached CRITICAL level
```

or this

```
%ENVM-2-FAN: Fan array has failed, shutdown in 2 minutes
```

be sure that you take immediate action to identify and isolate the problem and then correct it. Of course, you will only see these messages if you maintain a console on the router. Otherwise, you should check the router's log file frequently.

Chapter 12

Going the Full Route

*T*he world of Cisco networking is a world built around routing. In a nutshell, routing is deciding the best path that a message should take to its destination and then sending the message on that path. Some subtle distinctions exist between the different variations of the word route, including routes, routing, and routed, and you should understand these distinctions.

Getting There Is All the Fun!

The most basic of all routing concepts is that of a route. Routes on a network, such as the Internet, are similar to the interstate and local highway system around the United States. Just as you can choose any one of several routes to get from your house to Aunt Sally's on Sunday, a network can also provide several routes to a destination. And just like road construction and other obstacles can change the desirability of one route over another, the path from one computer to another over the network can change. The core purpose of routing is deciding which of the available routes is the best route for each message. The key words to the preceding statement are *available* and *each*. Each message (or message segment) can be sent out over a different route. Because networks are dynamic environments, routes can change, and come and go.

Keeping it static and simple

Suppose that you have a favorite route that you use when you drive to Aunt Sally's. You know, the one where you can really let the old Yugo show its stuff? If you were to invariably use the same route every time you make this trip, you would be, if effect, using a static route. In this context, as well as most others, static means never changing, or fixed in place.

On a network, you (as the administrator) may want packets from one specific router to use a particular route to reach another specific router. Such a route, in the parlance of Cisco networking, is called a *static route*. The network administrator can enter static routes directly into the router (see Chapter 17) to specify that messages being sent to a particular destination address must use a single route.

A static route is a very simple instruction to the router. It essentially consists of only the address (usually the IP address) of the router that should be used to send messages to a certain network. In very simple terms, to send a message from a workstation on one network to a workstation on another network, the router on network A routes the message to the router on network B. (You can find more detail on IP addressing in Chapter 8.) The destination router (Router B) takes care of getting the message to the destination workstation. A static route is used when you want to limit the path to a particular routing destination to a single choice.

Dynamically speaking

Suppose that, during the summer, your favorite route to Aunt Sally's is under construction and as such loses its road-race appeal; you may need to look for other available routes. Your choice will likely be based on the distance, the sights along the way, the lack of hills (no reason to overheat old Yuggie), and the time it takes to get to your destination. When you use this type of analysis to determine the most desirable route to take, you are essentially performing dynamic routing.

An administrator can configure a network router to use *dynamic routes*. The router can use information it receives from other routers on the network to learn about and make judgments on the possible routes it can use to reach destinations on the network.

Choosing the best routing

One of the primary functions, and the one from which they derive their name, of a router is to determine the best route a packet should use to reach its destination. For some destinations, there is only one way and one way only; other destinations have myriad routes that could be used to reach them. Because of these two situations, the network administrator must choose between using static or a dynamic routing as the means of choosing the best route.

Static routing

When a router is configured for static routing only, the administrator must manually update the router whenever a topology change occurs on the network. The change may be a new network segment, a new router added to a nearby network, or even a new neighboring network. These types of changes are topology changes. Using static routing on a network of any significant size may not be the best choice. If the network topology changes, the administrator may need to do a tremendous amount of maintenance to reestablish the network's routes, which can be a pain in several parts of the body.

Static routing is preferable in situations when you need to keep routing information private. Dynamic routing passes information about your network between routers, which are used to determine available routes. If you don't want to share routing information with other networks, use a static route. But, don't be paranoid either. The information being shared typically doesn't include your social security number, bank account, credit card number, or the router's passwords (see "Dynamic routing" later in this section). So, the risk is not high to begin with.

Static routing is useful for certain networking situations. If only one route is available between networks A and B, a static route works nicely. Other examples are a *stub network,* a network with only one possible path, or a dial-on-demand network. In each of these cases, static routes provide the single route required and eliminate the operating overhead of dynamic routing. Default routes are also configured as static routes. When a router can't determine the route to use for a particular packet destination, unless a static default route is defined, the router will drop the packet.

Later in this chapter, I discuss routing algorithms (see "Routing to the Algorithm") and how they determine the best route for a packet to take. However, static routing algorithms aren't really algorithms at all. They're tables of route mappings that have been established manually by the network administrator. These tables do not change (meaning that they are static) until the administrator changes them.

Static routing systems are unable to react to topology changes in the network. As a result, they are generally not suited for use on a large, dynamic network. Static routes work best for network environments where the traffic is predictable and the network design is relatively simple.

Dynamic routing

In a dynamic routing environment, routers make decisions based on information they acquire from other routers about the status of the internetwork. Dynamic information in a router is updated automatically whenever it receives information from other routers about changes in the topology. This information is also passed on to other routers on the network in the form of routing updates.

Because of the rapid growth of networks, especially those connected to the Internet, most of the more commonly used routing algorithms are dynamic routing algorithms. Dynamic routing algorithms adjust to changes in the network by analyzing incoming routing update messages sent by other routers.

If the routing update indicates that a topology change has occurred, the routing algorithm recalculates its routes and passes along this new routing information. As the routing update messages are passed around the network, each router dynamically recalculates its routing tables accordingly and the routing environment of the whole network may change. That's why you should use dynamic routing on networks connected to other networks. However, most small and large companies use static routing to connect to the Internet, even though, it's safe to say, it is definitely a dynamic network.

Although dynamic routing works in virtually all routing situations, it is especially useful in certain environments. For example, in situations where links go up and down frequently, no matter the reason, or where a destination has a number of possible paths, dynamic routing is a better choice over static routing because it eliminates the need for the constant reconfiguration that static routes would require.

Dynamically static routing

Even the most sophisticated dynamic routing algorithms can, on occasion, fail to determine a path for a packet. When that happens, unless one or more static routes are defined, the packet will be dropped (meaning not forwarded). An example of this is a router of last resort (a router to which all unroutable packets are sent), which is used when no other route can be determined for a packet's destination address so that all messages are at least handled in some way.

When a router doesn't know how to reach a destination network addressed by a message, it must somehow decide where to send the message. In cases such as this, the router uses its *default route.* By definition, a default route is the route used for a message when no specific information is available about the destination network. There isn't a great deal of difference between the router of last resort and the default route.

Another usage for a static route in a dynamic environment is for routing paths that you wish to keep private. Static routes are not included in the dynamic routing updates sent out to other routes. By using a static route, a routing path that rarely changes or is secure remains virtually unknown to the internetwork.

Are You Routing or Merely Routed?

Before I get too far into the discussion on dynamic routing, it can't hurt to review the differences between *routed* protocols and *routing* protocols.

- ✔ **Routed protocol:** Using a *routed protocol,* a router examines the addressing of any incoming messages, makes a determination on how best to forward it to its destination, and then forwards the message to that destination.

   ✔ **Routing protocol:** Routers use *routing protocols* to send and receive
     information about the status of the internetwork. Routing protocols
     allow routers to keep their routing table information up to date so that
     when the time comes to decide a path for a packet, the decision is based
     on up-to-date data.

Using a routed protocol, such as IP and IPX (see Chapter 2), the router examines the data packet looking for the destination address and then cross-
checks the destination address with its internal routing table to determine
the path it should use to forward the data packet.

However, when multiple paths can be used to reach a destination network,
the router must decide which of these paths is the best route to use. The
details of how this happens depend on the routing protocol being used.
Examples of routing protocols include Routing Information Protocol (RIP),
Interior Gateway Routing Protocol (IGRP), Open Shortest Path First (OSPF),
NetWare Link Services Protocol (NLSP), Intermediate System to Intermediate
System (IS-IS), and Enhanced Interior Gateway Routing Protocol (EIGRP).
I cover these protocols later in this chapter.

Keeping tabs on routing

A router keeps its static routes and information about dynamic routes in its
routing table. The routing table, which is stored in the router's RAM, is both
maintained by the network administrator (for static routes) and dynamically
updated by routing information updates sent by routing protocols. This
ensures the best and latest information regarding possible routes that are or
aren't available to the router.

Unless the routing table is completely full of static routes and no routing protocol is in use, which could be a true waste of a good router, the routing table
is constantly being updated. As networks appear and disappear, the routing
information for each of the router's ports is upgraded to reflect the true status
of the network. If a router fails or someone trips over its power cord, its neighboring routers are updated to show it as unavailable until the problem is fixed.

The *routing table* contains entries that match up destination addresses or
address ranges to specific information about the route used to reach them.
This information, called *metric,* helps the router determine the best available
(or only) route to a destination address. The metric data that a router holds
typically includes data on the number of hops, bandwidth, cost, and status of
a remote router (network) that is used to determine the best route. In addition, the routing table information includes the IP address of the destination
host or network, the address of the gateway or next upstream router (hop)
used to reach a destination, and the router interface used to reach the gateway or destination. The routing protocol in use determines a routing table's
contents. Most Cisco routers by default use RIP (although it must be configured to be made active), but other routing protocols are commonly used as
well. See "Routing to the Algorithm," later in this chapter, for more information on routing protocols.

Here is an example of the information found in the routing table of a classful (as opposed to classless) routing protocol (see Chapter 8 for information on classful and classless IP addressing):

Destination	Next Hop	Metric	Interface	Protocol
63.23.104.232	63.23.104.2	1	e1	static
192.63.0.0	192.63.145.11	3	e0	rip
202.11.0.0	202.11.124.2	1	e0	rip
203.98.123.0	192.87.34.2	2	s1	local

And a brief description of what each is:

- ✔ **Destination:** The IP address of a remote host or a router to which packets are to be sent. On the third line of this example, notice that any packet addressed to any node on the network under 202.0.0.0 is forwarded using that router table entry.

- ✔ **Next Hop:** This is the address of the next router (gateway) to which the packet is sent as the packet wends its way to the destination address.

- ✔ **Metric:** This is how many hops (routers) the packet traverses to reach its destination's network.

- ✔ **Interface:** The port on the router that the packet should use to reach its destination.

- ✔ **Protocol:** The routing protocol that's used to maintain the information on this route.

Balancing the load

With this information in its routing table, some routers include the ability to perform *load-balancing*. This means that, when one route begins to degrade because of the amount of traffic being sent over it, the router can use the information in the routing table to determine a second (or more) route over which it can send a portion of the traffic to balance the load between the two (or more) routes to the same destination.

Worldly routers are multiprotocol

In general, Cisco routers offer *multiprotocol routing,* the ability to support more than one routing protocol at a time. A router that supports multiprotocol routing maintains separate routing tables for each routing protocol. Depending on the routed protocol in use, the router looks at the associated table and makes its routing decisions accordingly.

The Dynamics of Routing

One thing about networks, especially those that are connected to other networks, is that keeping up with the neighbors can be a very dynamic exercise. As other networks come and go, the number and permutations of available routes from one network to another is very dynamic. This is why dynamic routing should be used on networks connected to other networks, including the Internet. In fact, networks that are interconnected to form a larger network create what is called the internetwork.

An *internetwork* is a network of networks interconnected by routers so that it operates as one large dynamic network. The Internet is an example of a very large (the largest) internetwork. In fact, the Internet gets its name from the word *internetwork*. A local network may not be a part of an internetwork if it has no connection to an outside network or if its routers are used only for internal purposes. But, if that local network were to connect to the Internet or to any other WAN through a router, it would then become a part of an internetwork.

Using multiprotocol routing with dynamically assigned routes is an effective solution when a router must forward different routed protocols to different destination networks based on the protocol being routed. Figures 12-1 and 12-2 illustrate how dynamic routing increases the deliverability of data packets across an internetwork. When Host A sends a packet destined for Host B with a static route from Router 1 to Router 2 to Router 3, the packet arrives if both links, Router 1 to Router 2 and Router 2 to Router 3, are up (Figure 12-1). But if the link between either is down, the packet can't be delivered (Figure 12-2). This would require that the administrator reconfigure the router with a new static route through Router 1 to Router 4 to Router 3.

When Host A sends a packet destined for Host B, assuming that dynamic routing is in use from Host A to Host B, the packet arrives if either route is available — Router 1 to Router 2 and Router 2 to Router 3, or Router 1 to Router 4 to Router 3 (Figure 12-3). If any one link in either route is down, the packet is delivered (Figure 12-4) through the alternative route without intervention by the administrator.

I'm sorry to scare you by invoking the word *mathematics,* but dynamic routing involves the use of a number of calculations and algorithms to determine the best available route for a packet. Don't worry; the router does all the calculating and such.

Two functions are necessary for dynamic routing to be successful:

  ✔ **Well-maintained routing tables:** How well-maintained the routing tables are is determined by a combination of the efforts of the network administrator staying on top of things within his or her own network and the quality of the information provided to the router through dynamic routing updates.

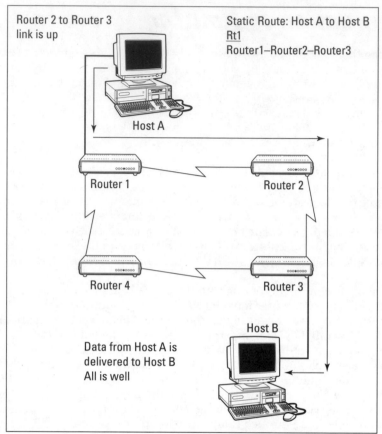

Router 2 to Router 3
link is up

Static Route: Host A to Host B
<u>Rt1</u>
Router1–Router2–Router3

Host A

Router 1

Router 2

Router 4

Router 3

Host B

Figure 12-1:
Static
routes over
a network
with all links
intact.

Data from Host A is
delivered to Host B
All is well

✔ **Timely delivery of network topology changes between routers:**
Routing protocols carry out the delivery of network topology information between routers. The maintenance of the routing tables is the primary mission of a group of algorithms, which determine the best
available routes and update the routing table.

Routing to the Algorithm

You'll find three basic types of routing algorithms:

✔ **Distance vector:** RIP and IGRP are distance vector routing protocols
commonly used on a Cisco network. See "Hopping to the RIP" for more
information on the RIP.

✔ **Link-state:** As a group, link-state protocols, which pass information
about neighbors and path costs, are called shortest path first (SPF)

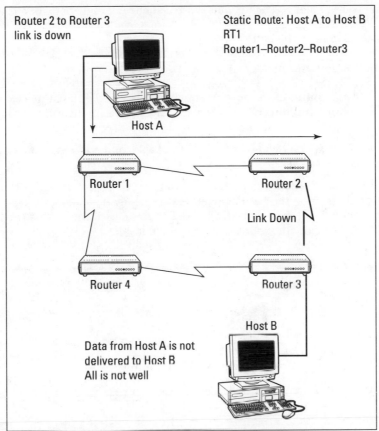

Router 2 to Router 3
link is down

Static Route: Host A to Host B
RT1
Router1–Router2–Router3

Host A

Router 1   Router 2

Link Down

Router 4   Router 3

Host B

Figure 12-2:
Static
routes over
a network
with broken
links.

Data from Host A is not
delivered to Host B
All is not well

protocols. OSPF is the link-state protocol most commonly used on a Cisco network. See "Putting the Router into a Link-State" for more information on link-state routing protocols.

✔ **Balanced hybrid:** This type of routing protocol uses a combination of link-state and distance vector protocols to learn the network topology and to resolve issues associated with convergence. An example of a balanced hybrid protocol is EIGRP. See "Striking a Balance with Hybrid Protocols" for more information on balanced hybrid protocols.

Adding up the metrics

Each algorithm defines just what is a best route in its own way, but it does produce a number, called a *metric,* that is used to evaluate the routes. The metrics produced by the routing algorithms measure some time element in the route. Each metric may measure a single characteristic of a route, or it may be a combination of weighted characteristics. Typically, the lower a route's metric, the better the route.

Some standard routing metrics are used in Cisco routers:

- **Hop count:** Each router through which a packet must pass is considered a hop. Counting the hops on a route gives an indication of the path's length. The lower the path length, the better the route.

- **Ticks:** Each tick represents ¹⁄₁₈th of a second and represents a delay across a route.

- **Cost:** The cost of a path is an arbitrary value associated with each link crossed on the path. Slower links typically have a higher cost associated with them than do faster links. The route with the lowest total path cost is typically the route selected as the fastest.

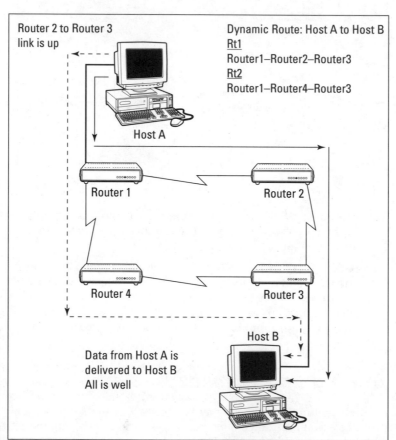

Figure 12-3:
Dynamic
routing on
a network
with all
links up.

Router 2 to Router 3
link is up

Dynamic Route: Host A to Host B
Rt1
Router1–Router2–Router3
Rt2
Router1–Router4–Router3

Host A

Router 1   Router 2

Router 4   Router 3

Host B

Data from Host A is
delivered to Host B
All is well

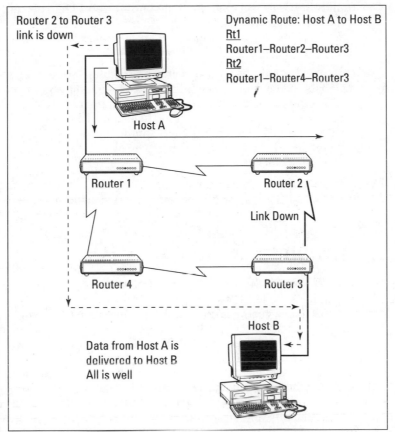

Router 2 to Router 3
link is down

Dynamic Route: Host A to Host B
<u>Rt1</u>
Router1–Router2–Router3
<u>Rt2</u>
Router1–Router4–Router3

Host A

Router 1

Router 2

Link Down

Router 4

Router 3

Host B

Data from Host A is
delivered to Host B
All is well

Figure 12-4:
Dynamic
routing on a
network
with broken
links.

✔ **Bandwidth:** The maximum throughput of a link, in terms of bits per second, is considered its bandwidth. The route with the highest bandwidth is considered the fastest route possible. This is not always the case, because a high-bandwidth link may already have too many users sending data across the link, effectively slowing the link. A link with a lower bandwidth may not have as many users and be able to send the data instantly.

✔ **Delay:** The summation of many factors results in a delay rating, a commonly used metric. These factors include link bandwidth, router queue length, network congestion, and physical distance.

✔ **Load:** This is a dynamic factor that is based on such items as router processor utilization and packets processed per second. Although it's an effective metric, the monitoring of these items may require high resource demand.

✔ **Reliability:** This is a combination of how often a link fails and how long it takes to bring the link back up. Other measures may be included in the overall reliability rating. Typically, the administrator assigns this rating, although some protocols can dynamically calculate the rating for you.

✔ **Expense:** For some operations, it is more important to consider operating costs than performance for a network. Including an expense metric enables the administrator to factor in the monetary cost of a route so that it will be considered in routing decisions. Don't confuse this with the cost metric (which refers to the number of hops and the cost to transfer speed of each hop). The expense metric refers to the actually dollar value of a link.

✔ **MTU (maximum transmission unit):** This metric relates to the maximum length of a message across the entire path measured in bytes.

Determining the distance vector

You know how you have to decide which store to go to for chips and drinks so that you miss the least amount of the game or the ballet? In much the same way, distance vector protocols determine the distance and direction to an address on an internetwork. It isn't important how the streets are laid out, only that one store is six blocks and the other is clear across town.

A router that uses a distance vector protocol periodically passes a copy of its entire routing table to its neighboring routers. A distance vector routing protocol only knows how far it is from or to an individual destination; it doesn't know the actual topology of the internetwork. When the topology of an internetwork changes, all the routers affected pass copies of their routing tables to the all adjoining routers.

Figure 12-5 graphically depicts how these routing table updates occur. Router 1 is directly connected to both Router 2 and Router 6; Router 2 is connected to Routers 1 and 3; Router 3 is connected to Routers 2 and 4; Router 4 is connected to Routers 3 and 5; and Router 5 is connected to Routers 4 and 6. Router 1 sends a periodic update of its routing table to Routers 2 and 6, the routers to which it is directly connected. Likewise, Router 2 sends its updates to Routers 1 and 3; Router 5 sends its updates to Routers 6 and 4, and so on. As you look at Figure 12-5, also remember that routers know each other only by their IP addresses and not the names that administrators give them.

Using hop count as the distance metric, the routing tables of each router would resemble those depicted in Figure 12-6. As illustrated in Figure 12-5, quite a bit of information is being passed back and forth between routers in order to maintain their routing tables.

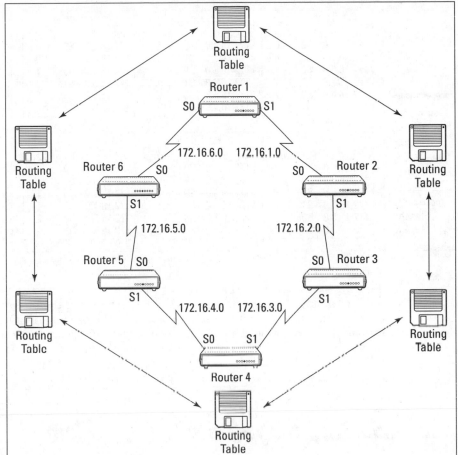

Figure 12-5:
An inter-
network.

Never-ending Hops on Distance Vector Protocols

When all the routers on an internetwork are up-to-date on the current topology of the internetwork, a state of *convergence* exists.

Convergence is good. You may ask yourself, and you should, "What happens if the routers don't contain current information about the internetwork?" Good question, self. The answer is simple: *routing loops*.

Router 1		
Network	Port	Metric
172.16.6.0	S0	0
172.16.1.0	S1	0
172.16.5.0	S0	1
172.16.2.0	S1	1
172.16.4.0	S0	2
172.16.3.0	S1	2

Router 2		
Network	Port	Metric
172.16.1.0	S0	0
172.16.2.0	S1	0
172.16.6.0	S0	1
172.16.3.0	S1	1
172.16.5.0	S0	2
172.16.4.0	S1	2

Router 3		
Network	Port	Metric
172.16.2.0	S0	0
172.16.3.0	S1	0
172.16.1.0	S0	1
172.16.4.0	S1	1
172.16.6.0	S0	2
172.16.5.0	S1	2

Router 4		
Network	Port	Metric
172.16.4.0	S0	0
172.16.3.0	S1	0
172.16.5.0	S0	1
172.16.2.0	S1	1
172.16.6.0	S0	2
172.16.1.0	S1	2

Router 5		
Network	Port	Metric
172.16.5.0	S0	0
172.16.4.0	S1	0
172.16.6.0	S0	1
172.16.3.0	S1	1
172.16.1.0	S0	2
172.16.2.0	S1	2

Router 6		
Network	Port	Metric
172.16.6.0	S0	0
172.16.5.0	S1	0
172.16.1.0	S0	1
172.16.4.0	S1	1
172.16.2.0	S0	2
172.16.3 .0	S1	2

Figure 12-6: Sample routing tables using a distance vector metric and classful addressing.

Routing loops, which are bad, exist when a packet is allowed an unlimited number of hops to reach its destination. For example, if the packet is trying to reach an unknown and nonexistent address, the packet could hop around forever. This condition is known as a *counting-to-infinity* loop. These loops happen because no limits are set for the number of hops that a packet can take. The solutions, and there must be some, involve setting a hop limit on a packet. You know, I think you're really picking this stuff up.

Solving the infinite loop problem

Several solutions are available to solve counting-to-infinity loop problems for distance vector routing protocols:

- **Maximum hops:** Only in routing can infinity actually be less than 16. One solution for counting-to-infinity loops is to set a maximum number of hops as being equal to infinity. Routing protocols have maximum loop counts. For example, RIP (Routing Information Protocol) has a default maximum hop count of 16. If the hop count is greater than 15, the router assumes that the destination network is unreachable.

- **Time To Live (TTL):** This parameter is contained in some routing protocol packets. A TTL factor is a countdown parameter that is reduced by one each time a router examines a packet. If the resulting TTL is equal to 0, meaning it has no time to live, the router discards the packet without forwarding it.

✓ **Split horizon:** In addition to eliminating routing loops, the split horizon technique also helps speed up an internetwork's time to convergence. Essentially, the split horizon technique prevents information about a route from being sent back to the source of the information. For example, say Router A sends a routing update to Router B about a certain routing destination (say, Router C). When Router B sends this update out to its neighboring routers, it doesn't include Router A, because it already knows about the update.

✓ **Poison reverse:** A derivative of the split horizon technique, poison reverse helps solve routing loops by simply making an entry in its routing table that a given route is unreachable. When a router receives an update from a neighboring router indicating that the poisoned route is reachable through it, the router simply ignores the update for that route until a certain amount of time has passed. The poison reverse technique is implemented in conjunction with hold-down timers.

✓ **Hold-down timers:** This routing mechanism is used to block regular update messages that incorrectly indicate that a link is available when, in fact, it isn't. Hold-down timers instruct a router not to accept regular updates on a particular route until a specified time has expired. The specific time is calculated to be just a bit more than the time needed for the internetwork to reach convergence.

Removing the restraint

Three situations can remove a hold-down timer on a router. First, I create a situation in which a hold-down timer would be implemented, and then I list the situations in which the hold-down timer would be removed. Refer to Figure 12-7 when reading the hold-down timer scenario and the removal situations.

Figure 12-7:
An inter-
network.

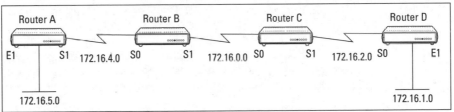

A state of convergence exists on the internetwork depicted in Figure 12-7, and the world is at peace. Suddenly, a series of events turns the peace into chaos (not really, but I'm trying to be dramatic here). Network 172.16.1.0 goes down. The hop count in Router C's routing table indicates that Network 172.16.1.0 is only one hop away. Router D notifies Router C through a triggered update that network 172.16.1.0 is now unreachable. Router C poisons the route and starts a hold-down timer on updates about Network 172.16.1.0. Regular updates are sent from Router A to Router B indicating that it has access to network 172.16.1.0 with a hop count of 3, and Router B forwards a regular update to Router C indicating that it has access to network 172.16.1.0 with a hop count of 4 via Router A. Of course, because it has a hold-down time on a poisoned route, Router C ignores the information from Router B.

In the following situations, the hold-down timer would be removed prior to its expiration, allowing the internetwork to reach convergence:

- ✔ If Router D, the original messenger, sends a new update indicating that Network 172.16.1.0 is once again available, the hold-down timer is removed from Router C.

- ✔ If Router C receives an update from an adjoining router (say, Router B) that indicates that it (Router B) has access to Network 172.16.1.0 and that its (Router B's) hop count is less than the hop count Router C has in its router table, the hold-down timer is removed from Router C. This system ignores any updates received while a hold-down timer is active that contain a poorer (meaning higher) metric than exists for the poisoned route, which allows additional time for convergence to occur.

- ✔ When the hold-down timer expires, the route to Network 172.16.1.0 remains poisoned in Router C's routing table, but Router C will now at least accept any updates regarding routes to Network 172.16.1.0.

Be careful with that trigger, please

Triggered updates are critical to resolving routing loops. A *triggered update* results when a router senses that a link to which it is directly connected has changed from available to unavailable or the reverse. (In the situation described in the preceding section, Router 4 sent a triggered update to Router 3 to notify it that Network 172.16.1.0 was no longer available.) This discovery triggers an update event in which the router immediately notifies its neighbors. Unfortunately, some time passes before a chain reaction of triggered updates can be spread across an internetwork, and during the propagation time, regular updates can be sent across the network with erroneous information.

Hopping to the RIP

RIP (Routing Information Protocol) is a distance vector protocol that uses hop count as its metric for selecting the best path to a destination address. RIP has a usable hop count of 15. A maximum of 16 hops, RIP's version of infinity, indicates that a destination address is unreachable. RIP routing updates are broadcast every 30 seconds by default.

One of the benefits of RIP is its ability to perform load balancing when multiple paths exist. *Load balancing* is the ability to use multiple equal distance paths to deliver data to a destination. By default, load balancing with RIP is enabled with four parallel paths.

RIP is the most basic routing protocol and is best applied to a small internetwork. Virtually every router supports a common implementation of RIP, which allows routers and some servers from different manufacturers to coexist on an internetwork.

RIPing up the router

RIP is configured with the command **router rip** in the global configuration mode (see Chapter 16), which is indicated by the prompt

```
Cisco_Networking(config)#
```

In this example, Cisco_Networking is the host name that has been assigned to the router (see Chapter 16).

After entering the **router rip** command, the attached network must be defined with the **network network-number** command.

```
Cisco_Networking(config)#router rip
```

Given a network number (in other words, an IP address) of 10.1.0.0, the command to define the attached network is

```
Cisco_Networking(config-router)#network 10.1.0.0
```

If the router is connected to more than one network, the additional networks also need to be entered. Each network is entered in the same format as the first network. After all networks have been configured, the router is configured and has permission to send routing updates (called *advertisements*) to other RIP routers associated with each attached network.

Showing off your RIP

To view a router's RIP information, you can use any of the following commands:

✔ **show ip protocol:** This command displays information about routing timers and the network information associated with the entire router. This is a valuable command when attempting to identify a router sending faulty routing information.

✔ **show ip route:** This command displays the entire contents of the IP routing table in the RIP router, including codes that indicate how the router learned about each path.

✔ **debug ip rip:** This command displays RIP routing updates as they come into and are sent out of the router, including information about the interface through which an update arrives. You must be in Privileged Exec mode to use the debug command.

Before you issue a **debug** command, you may want to enter a **term mon** command, which allows you to watch the interactions of the router and the devices connected to its interfaces.

Each of these commands is entered from user or privileged mode on a router. User mode is indicated by the *router_name>* prompt, such as

```
Cisco_Networking>
```

Privileged mode (also known as Enable EXEC mode) is indicated by the *router_name#* prompt, such as

```
Cisco_Networking#
```

I discuss these commands (and the mode in which they must be entered) more fully in Chapters 16 and 17.

Using IGRP for Advanced Routing

IGRP (Interior Gateway Routing Protocol) is a more advanced distance vector routing protocol originally developed by Cisco Systems in the mid-1980s. Because of its advanced features, which include scalability, rapid response to topology changes, sophisticated metrics, and multi-path support, nearly all router manufacturers now support it.

In contrast to RIP's default update time of 30 seconds, IGRP broadcasts periodic updates every 90 seconds, whether it needs to or not. Flash updates (IGRP's version of triggered updates) are also sent out when an IGRP router detects a network topology change, such as a route becoming inactive or a new route being added to the internetwork.

IGRP is a distance vector protocol that doesn't use up lots of system resources and, as a result, can operate on large internetworks on less expensive routers than other protocols. For example, where RIP uses a maximum hop count of 15, IGRP uses 255 (although Cisco routers are configured for a IGRP maximum hop count of 100 by default), which means that IGRP must use other means to limit routing loops, which are discussed in the next section. IGRP also uses flash updates, and this really speeds up the time to convergence. By default, IGRP considers only a network's bandwidth and the amount of network delay in its metric. However, the network administrator can configure other options to create a composite metric that can include other metrics, such as reliability and network load. This provides the administrator with greater flexibility in setting up a router's path determination scheme. IGRP by default supports four paths but can be configured for up to six paths to a destination network, providing for both increased bandwidth and route diversity. In simpler terms, IGRP supports load-balancing and alternative paths techniques.

When the timer goes off, take the poison and split

IGRP uses the same routing loop control techniques found in RIP (see "Hopping to the RIP," earlier in this chapter), including poison reverse, hold-down timers, and split horizon. However, IGRP has slightly different rules for the use of each technique. This section provides a brief description of how IGRP uses each technique:

- ✔ **Poison reverse:** IGRP sends out poison reverse updates when a route metric increases (gets worse) by a factor of 1.1.

- ✔ **Hold-down timer:** The IGRP hold-down timer is set to three times the periodic update interval, plus 10 seconds. This means that because the default update interval is 90 seconds, the hold-down timer setting is 280 seconds.

- ✔ **Split horizon:** Using the split horizon technique increases the speed of convergence on an IGRP internetwork because route updates are not sent back across the same route. If a router doesn't receive an update about a route for three consecutive update periods, that route is marked as unreachable. If seven update periods pass without a route update, that route is removed from the routing table, which helps to reduce the size of routing tables stored in the router's memory.

Setting up IGRP

To configure IGRP on a router, you must be in the global configuration mode, the one with a prompt like the following:

```
Cisco_Networking(config)#
```

To configure the router, enter the command **router igrp autonomous-system-number**, where the *autonomous system number* (ASN) is a globally unique number used to identify your internetwork:

```
Cisco_Networking(config)#router igrp 232
```

After entering this command, you must associate the network number (IP address) of all connected networks to the router using the **network network-number** command:

```
Cisco_Networking(config-router)#network 10.1.0.0
```

This command must be repeated for each network connected to the router for which you want to establish an IGRP link.

Checking out the IGRP status

After your router is configured for IGRP, you can view the information associated with IGRP functions, through the following commands:

- **show ip protocols:** The show ip protocols command displays parameters, filters, and network information for all networks configured on the router.

- **show ip interfaces:** The show ip interfaces command displays the status and global parameters associated with available interfaces.

- **show ip route:** The show ip route command displays the entire contents of the IP routing table contained in the IGRP or RIP router, including codes that indicate how the router learned about each path.

- **debug ip igrp transaction** and **debug ip igrp events:** The debug commands display similar information about transactions and events occurring on the specified networks.

The **show** commands can be entered from the user Exec mode, but the **debug** commands must be entered from the Privileged Exec mode. See Chapters 16 and 17 for more information on the User Exec and Privileged Exec modes of the Cisco Internetwork Operating System (IOS).

Putting the Router into a Link-State

Link-state protocols (LSP), also known as *shortest path first (SPF)* algorithms, maintain a complex database about an internetwork's topology. This database, which is stored inside each router, includes information about other routers and how those routers interconnect. The topology database provides a link-state router with a common view of the entire internetwork. The link-state routing protocols commonly used on Cisco networks include IS-IS (Intermediate System to Intermediate System), NLSP (NetWare Link Services Protocol), and OSPF (Open Shortest Path First), each of which is described later in this section.

A link-state router uses more processing power and memory than a distance-vector router because it is storing more information in memory and executing algorithms to calculate the SPF trees. Initially, link-state routers flood the network with what are called "Hello" messages or link-state packets (LSPs) to learn who their neighbors are. After the initial flooding, link-state routers use relatively little bandwidth for their periodic or topology-change triggered LSP updates.

Getting to know the internetwork

Link-state protocols use a complex five-step process to learn about their internetwork (see Figure 12-8):

1. A link-state router learns from all the other routers in the autonomous system the status of any adjoining routers and keeps track of those routers in its routing table.

2. A router transmits a link-state packet (LSP), also known as a "Hello" packet, to all other routers in the same autonomous system (AS).

   Each of these very friendly LSPs contains all the information the router knows about the networks to which it is directly connected. How very neighborly of it.

3. Using the information provided by LSPs from the other routers in the AS, the router builds its topological database.

4. The router processes this information through the SPF algorithm to determine the lowest cost possible path to every reachable network on the internetwork.

   This results in the creation of an SPF tree with the router at its root.

5. The router then uses the SPF tree to enter the best path to each network into its routing table.

As changes occur in a link-state internetwork, the routers that initially become aware of the change send out notifications to other routers or to a designated master update router that makes sure that all other routers become aware of the changes. Each router then proceeds through the five-step process to recalculate its individual routing tables with the new shortest routes to each network.

Living in the link-state world

It is essential that all routers on a link-state internetwork view the internetwork topology with a common point-of-view, which is no easy task, to say the least. Because each router calculates its routing table entries from the LSP information that it receives, some routers on the internetwork can do so using different LSP information. This can result in the internetwork being split into two or more routing segments, which can result in slower connections between some routers, LSP updates being improperly synchronized, and insufficient processing power to keep up with all the tasks being performed.

To solve the various faulty LSP transmission problems, the well-read administrator implements one or a combination of the following solutions:

- **Configure the router to send LSPs at larger intervals.** This increases the time for convergence to occur and doesn't interfere with triggered updates caused by a change in the internetwork topology.

- **Configure the router to use a multicast approach to sending LSPs, instead of the flood approach typically used.** This allows a small group of routers to act as masters of the internetwork's topology data.

- **Segment the internetwork into LSP domains with a master topology router for each domain.** This effectively reduces the size of the internetwork, reducing the chance of inconsistent LSP information because of synchronization or transmission speed issues.

- **Tag the LSPs with link-state enabled internetworks.** Tagging allows the LSPs to be flagged with time stamps, sequence numbers, aging schemes, and other mechanisms that help to verify that routers use the most current topology data. Be careful of the term "tag" though; it is also used as the parameter to assign a name to NLSP processes.

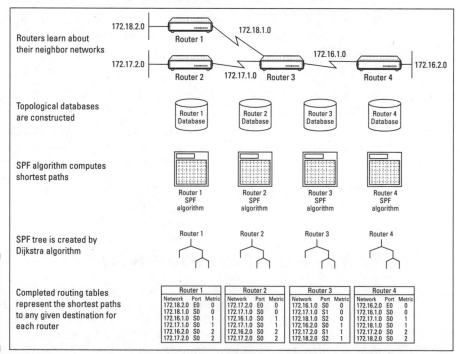

Figure 12-8:
The five steps in link-state routing.

From the OSI world comes IS-IS

Included in the standards of the OSI (Open Systems Interconnect) are the specifications of the IS-IS (Intermediate System to Intermediate System) link-state protocol. This specification defines an end system (ES), which is any nonrouter network node, and an intermediate system (IS), which is either a router or a server or other device that performs routing. The OSI standards define ES-IS (End System to Intermediate System) and IS-IS protocols. IS-IS defines the routing processes between ISs.

A few other important OSI networking terms are

- **Area:** An area is a group of bordering networks and their attached hosts as defined by a network administrator.

- **Domain:** A group of connected areas forms a domain, which provide connectivity to all the end systems in the domain.

- **Level 1 routing:** Routing performed within the defined perimeters of a Level 1 area. A Level 1 area is defined by the relationship between ES nodes and an IS node or nodes. See Figure 12-9.

- **Level 2 routing:** Level 2 routing is performed between the IS nodes of Level 1 areas. See Figure 12-9.

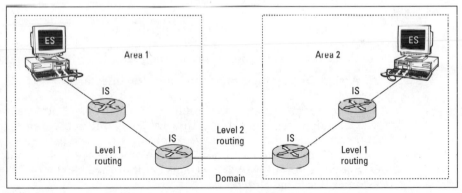

Figure 12-9: The relationships of Level 1 and Level 2 areas in the IS-IS protocol.

Moving up to the middle

The ES-IS (End System-to-Intermediate System) protocol defines the processes used by hosts and routers to create what OSI calls the network configuration, which is very much akin to the topology view used by other routing protocols. Until the router knows about the end systems attached to it, it can't begin its routing processes, which makes sense if you think about it.

IS-IS routing was originally developed by Digital Equipment Corporation (DEC) for use in its DECNet applications, but now the American National

Standards Association (ANSI) has adopted it as a standard for a shortest path first routing algorithm. It is much like other common link-state routing protocols, such as OSPF, but adds support for pure OSI packets as well, which many other link-state protocols do not.

IS-IS you is or IS-IS you ain't my protocol?

IS-IS routing decisions are based on a two-level scheme. Level 1 routers know only the topology of their local area network. Level 2 (intermediate) routers know of other Level 2 routers on the internetwork and the addresses that are reachable. If a Level 1 router has no knowledge of a specific destination address, it passes the traffic up to a Level 2 router for a broader view of the internetwork.

The best place to use the IS-IS protocol is on an internetwork router that must transport both IP packets and pure OSI packets. You should make sure that all IS-IS routers are interoperable. Some manufacturers have proprietary implementations of IS-IS that won't communicate with other manufacturers' equipment.

Configuring IS-IS

To configure IS-IS on a Cisco router, you must enable IS-IS on the router and assign it to the area(s) you want it to monitor. Beyond that, you can take additional steps to enable IP routing for an area on a particular interface and to set certain configuration parameters.

To enable IS-IS on a router is a two-step process:

1. **Create an IS-IS routing process using the** router isis **command.**
2. **Assign the routing process to a specific interface.**

A Cisco router can support IS-IS routing in as many as 29 areas as well as Level 2 routing on the backbone. However, only one of the routing processes can be configured to perform Level 2 routing. After one of the area routing processes is configured for Level 2, all the other processes are automatically designated as Level 1, which is like many other things in life — Miss America, the Super Bowl, and *Survivor*.

To configure a Cisco router for IS-IS, the command *router isis* is (pardon the repetition) entered from global configuration mode:

```
Cisco_Networking(config)#router isis
```

Monitoring IS-IS routing

The commands you can use to monitor the IS-IS processes on a Cisco router are listed in Table 12-1.

Table 12-1	Cisco IOS Commands for Monitoring IS-IS
Command	*Purpose*
show isis database	Displays the entries in the IS-IS link-state database.
show isis routes	Displays the contents of the IS-IS Level 1 routing table.
show isis spf-log	Displays when and why a router has performed a full SPF calculation.
show isis topology	Displays a list of all connected routers from all known areas.

Finding the shortest path, first

The OSPF (Open Shortest Path First) routing protocol is the creation of the IETF (Internet Engineering Task Force), and like IS-IS, it is a derivative of the OSI routing standards. OSPF is an *open standard,* which means that it is available to all manufacturers of routing equipment, which is intended to help to ensure interoperability between their equipment and protocol implementations.

OSPF utilizes three separate databases to make its routing decisions:

- **Adjacency:** The adjacency table contains information about OSPF neighbors.
- **Topology:** The topology database is based on the adjacency database and maintains information about all available routes.
- **Route:** The route table stores the best route to each known destination.

An OSPF router uses Hello packets to announce its existence to any other OSPF routers in its local area. After neighboring routers have sent back hello responses and adjacency database entries are created, a router and a backup router are designated to control communications with other autonomous systems. The primary routing metric used with OSPF is bandwidth.

OSPF is best applied to growing networks consisting of routers from multiple manufacturers or in medium-to-large networks consisting of routers from multiple manufacturers.

Configuring OSPF

The world of OSPF is populated with and requires the coordination of essentially two kinds of routers:

- **Area border router (ABR):** An ABR is a router that is connected to multiple areas.

✔ **Autonomous system boundary router (ASBR):** An ASBR is a router on the edge of an AS.

All the routers in an OSPF network or internetwork must be configured with a coordinated configuration to ensure the proper operation and rapid convergence of the network.

To configure OSPF on a Cisco router, you enter something like the following IOS commands:

```
Cisco_Networking#interface serial 1
Cisco_Networking(config-if)#ip address 10.0.0.2 255.0.0.0
Cisco_Networking(config-if)#ip ospf network point-to-
        multipoint
Cisco_Networking(config-if)#router ospf 1
Cisco_Networking(config-if)#network 10.0.0.0 0.0.0.255 area 0
```

OSPF has several optional interface parameters that can be assigned to customize its application. Remember that the OSPF configuration must be the same on all ABRs and ASBRs. Table 12-2 lists the more commonly used OSPF interface parameters.

Table 12-2	IP OSPF Command Interface Parameters
Parameter	*Purpose*
Authentication	Sets the authentication type to be used by an OSPF interface
Cost	The explicit cost of forwarding a packet on a specific OSPF interface
dead-interval	The time in seconds that can pass without a response to a hello packet before a neighboring router is declared as unavailable
hello-interval	Sets the interval in seconds for the Cisco IOS to send OSPF hello packets
Priority	Is used to establish the OSPF designated router on a network
retransmit-interval	Specifies the number of seconds between link-state advertisement (LSA) retransmissions
transmit-delay	Sets the number of seconds between link-state update packets

Setting the network type

By default, OSPF categorizes networks into two types:

✓ **Broadcast networks:** This OSPF group includes the Ethernet, Token Ring, and FDDI network technologies.

✓ **Non-broadcast multi-access (NBMA) networks:** This OSPF group includes the SMDS (Switched Multibit Data Service), Frame Relay, and X.25 transmission services.

This doesn't mean that an Ethernet network can only be an OSPF broadcast network; you could just as easily configure it to be an NBMA network. For example, if an Ethernet network happens to have a router that doesn't support multicast addressing, it may be a better idea to configure it as non-broadcast (NBMA). And should you wish to avoid configuring neighboring routers on a Frame Relay network, you can configure an OSPF interface as a part of a broadcast network. There's a bit more to it than that, and if you find yourself in the dilemma of choosing which type of OSPF network to use, visit Cisco's Web site at www.cisco.com/warp/public/104/1.html for OSPF configuration information.

The command you'd use to set the network type of an OSPF interface as broadcast is

```
Cisco_Networking(config-if)#ip ospf broadcast
```

The same command, with broadcast replaced with non-broadcast, is used to set the network type to non-broadcast.

Monitoring OSPF

Again, the Cisco IOS show command is the network administrator's best friend when it comes to verifying the configuration and checking up on how things are going with your OSPF network. Table 12-3 lists a few of the show command variations you can use for these purposes.

Table 12-3	OSPF Interface Show Commands
Command	*Purpose*
show ip ospf	Displays the general information of the OSPF routing processes defined on a router.
show ip ospf border-routers	Displays the routing table entries that point to ABR and ASBR routers.
show ip ospf database	Displays the information in the OSPF database. Additional parameters can be used to display only specific information from the database, such as router, network, or database-summary.

(continued)

Table 12-3 (continued)

Command	Purpose
show ip ospf interface	Display OSPF interface-related information.
show ip ospf neighbor detail	Display OSPF-related information on neighboring routers by interface.

For more information on OSPF straight from the Cisco experts, visit Cisco's OSPF Web page at www.cisco.com/warp/public/104/1.html.

Routing in the NetWare world with NLSP

NLSP (NetWare Link Services Protocol) is the Novell derivative of the IS-IS link-state protocol standard that was developed as a replacement for Novell's IPX RIP and SAP (Service Advertising Protocol). IPX RIP and SAP were designed to handle primarily smaller local networks and are not well-suited to larger global networks. NLSP is backward-compatible with both IPX RIP and SAP, so migrating a Novell network to a link-state routing protocol is easy. Not as easy as falling off a log, perhaps, but not too bad, all things considered.

NLSP routers use three databases to make routing decisions:

- ✔ **Adjacency database:** This database contains information taken from responses to hello (LSA) broadcasts sent out by each NLSP router, which could actually be a NetWare server with NLSP enabled.

- ✔ **Link-state database:** This is the common database on all routers in the area. It is also built using the information in the Hello responses.

- ✔ **Forwarding database:** This database contains the best path from a specific router to each possible destination. Each router has different paths to each destination, and thus the forwarding databases on each router are different.

After all the routers have learned about each other, they hold an election to designate one router per LAN segment as the designated router responsible for communicating the topological information about its segment to all other areas of the internetwork.

NLSP also uses a three-level hierarchy for communications:

- ✔ **Level 1** consists of communications between routers within a single area.

- ✔ **Level 2** consists of communications between routers across two areas.

- ✔ **Level 3** consists of communications between routing domains (groups of areas).

NLSP should be enabled only on a Novell NetWare network running IPX. Remember that starting with Novell Netware 5.0, IPX is just one of the options because Novell has finally embraced TCP/IP as its standard protocol for network communications.

To configure NLSP as the routing protocol on an interface, the **ipx nlsp enable** command is entered. And as is the case with other IOS commands, entering **no ipx nlsp enable** turns it back off.

Here are a few of the show commands that can be used to display information about an NLSP configuration:

```
show ipx nlsp database
show ipx nlsp neighbors
show ipx nlsp spf-log
```

Striking a Balance with EIGRP

Balanced hybrid protocols use a combination of features from both link-state and distance vector protocols to learn the network topology and resolve any issues associated with convergence.

Balanced hybrid protocols use distance vectors to determine the best paths to destination networks, but they use more sophisticated metrics in their calculations than a typical distance vector protocol. Convergence occurs quickly with the balanced hybrid approach from its link-state influences. However, balanced hybrid protocols focus on the economy of resource utilization, including bandwidth, memory, and processor.

The best example of a balanced hybrid protocol on a Cisco network is EIGRP (Enhanced Interior Gateway Routing Protocol). EIGRP, which is a proprietary protocol developed by Cisco, is a very stable and scalable protocol. However, if you mix router manufacturers on your internetwork, you must also enable a secondary routing protocol, because EIGRP will typically function only between Cisco routers.

EIGRP utilizes three databases to determine the best path selection for reaching a destination:

- ✔ **Route:** The route table contains information about the best routes to destinations.
- ✔ **Topology:** The topology table contains information about all routes to destinations.
- ✔ **Neighbor:** The neighbor table contains information about other neighboring EIGRP.

EIGRP is capable of routing three different protocols: IP, IPX, and AppleTalk, and when a router is enabled for all three protocols, EIGRP creates nine databases, three for each protocol.

EIGRP uses a process called *route tagging,* which identifies the source (internal or external) of a new route during a session. The Hello protocol is used to establish formal neighbor relationships, which is called *peering.* EIGRP sends routing updates only for the changes and not for the entire routing table. EIGRP also supports IP subnets, variable length subnet masking, and equal path load balancing, and it allows the administrator to select the metric used to calculate the best path.

The workhorse show command can be used to verify and monitor the configuration and status of an EIGRP routing process. The primary six show command variations that can be used for this purpose are listed in Table 12-4.

Table 12-4	EIGRP Show Commands
Command	*Purpose*
show ip route eigrp	Displays the routing table's EIGRP entries
show ip eigrp neighbors	Displays all the neighboring EIGRP routers
show ip eigrp topology	Displays all the topology table's EIGRP entries
show ip eigrp traffic	Displays a count for both sent and received EIGRP packets
show ip protocols	Displays active protocols session information
show ip eigrp events	Displays log entries of EIGRP events such as route additions

EIGRP is an excellent choice for a network of any size that will be growing with Cisco equipment. When non-Cisco routers are included with Cisco routers, a second routing protocol is necessary, because EIGRP communicates only between Cisco equipment.

Running for the Border Gateway Protocol

The BGP (Border Gateway Protocol) is used by all network entities that make up the Internet. Unless you are the system administrator at a regional ISP or the Layer 3 engineer in a large corporation with a large private WAN, you may never need to use BGP.

BGP is primarily used in two situations. One: connecting to two or more ISPs and attempting to balance the load over multiple connections. Two: connecting an enterprise network to multiple ISPs and attempting to load balance over multiple links.

BGP comes in two flavors:

- **Internal BGP (iBGP):** Used between routers within an autonomous system. Route information from one iBGP router is not shared with other iBGP peer routers.

- **External BGP (eBGP):** Used between routers located in different autonomous systems to inject routes owned by one autonomous system into another autonomous system.

BGP utilizes several metrics in determining the best route to a destination, including the following:

- **Weight:** This metric allows a system administrator to manually assign values to learned paths.

- **Local preference:** This metric is used by system administrators to assign values to routes when multiple paths exist.

- **MED (Multi-Exit Discriminator):** This metric identifies which path to use when separate autonomous systems are connected with multiple paths.

Chapter 13

Giving Voice to Your Network

• •

In This Chapter

▶ Defining VoIP networking

▶ Dealing with QoS issues

▶ Explaining the Cisco AVVID architecture

• •

An area that Cisco is rapidly developing is the ability to carry voice traffic over a network. Generically, this is called Voice over IP (Internet Protocol), or VoIP (which is pronounced as Voice over IP — go figure!). It's common for network administrators to have responsibility for a company's phone system as well, because practically nobody else wants that responsibility; and network administrators, in an attempt to build their empires, take on anything even remotely related to networking. It's great for the resume, and it gives them ultimate control over everyone. What power!

Actually, this arrangement makes good sense. Most newer in-building phone systems operate over cabling (typically Cat 3 — see Chapter 4) installed alongside the cabling for the data network. Typically, the cabling for both systems is terminated in the same rooms or closets, so it does make sense to have a single authority overseeing both.

This chapter provides a fairly high-level overview of voice networks and how they can be combined onto a data network with generally good results. To fully explain this topic requires much more than the few pages I am devoting to it. In fact, this topic would take (and it has taken) an entire book to do it justice. Unfortunately, I may only give you enough information to make you truly dangerous, but you should be able to decide if this is something you should look into further.

Understanding Voice Networking

Transmitting voice signals over a network is not something new. The telephone companies have been doing it since not too long after Alexander Graham Bell first invented the telephone, which some still believe to be a tool of the Devil. The telephone and the switched network that carries its signals from you and the person on the other end of your call is called the *Public Switched Telephone Network* or *PSTN*, and it has been in place for more than 100 years. For the first 75 years or so, this network was analog, converting audio waves into electrical impulses for transmission over the mostly copper-wired cables strung just about everywhere. Each signal was carried in an individual 4 Kilohertz (KHz) voice channel (frequency), with multiple channels, in 4 KHz increments, stacked onto the cable. Each channel also supported a range of signal amplitude (signal strength), so that the volume of your voice is moderately carried over the channel as well.

Going digital

In the late 1940s, the PSTN began to be converted slowly into a digital network. This conversion was done for many of the same reasons people use digital signaling for data networks today: greater bandwidth, improved error correction, and better management and control. In today's world, except for the line that connects your home or office to the telephone company's switching equipment, the PSTN is largely digital. Your phone — well, actually the line (called a *local loop*) that connects your building to the PSTN — provides you with what is called Plain Old Telephone Service (POTS) over an analog copper wire that is connected either in your neighborhood or at the telephone company (Telco) switching center or central office (CO). This is why when you want to connect your computer to the telephone system, you need a modem (*mo*dulator/*dem*odulator), which converts your computer's digital signals into analog signals for the POTS line. If the Telco wishes to place your call on its digital system, it takes care of the conversions required.

Today, virtually all the Telco switches are digital. This is good news for WANs; but because of the copper local loops, homes and small offices are limited to digital services that can be partially carried over analog lines, such as ISDN (Integrated Service Digital Network) or DSL (Digital Subscriber Line). Voice sent over the PSTN must be converted from its analog waveform into a digital signal before entering a WAN and being converted back (decoded) to analog so the other person can hear it and make sense of it. Just how this happens is kind of technical and is not really germane to the discussion here, but it involves a process called Pulse Code Modulation (PCM) that samples the amplitude of the analog wave at two times the highest frequency in use. See, I told you it was technical.

Switching the circuit

Another important aspect of the PSTN is that voice signals travel over a circuit that is created in virtual form for each call. The numbers in the telephone number you dial are used to create a virtual path across the PSTN by aligning a series of switches to open a circuit for the call session. This circuit exists only for the duration of the call, after which it is torn down. All voice traffic (and data traffic on the voice system, for that matter) is circuit-switched. Voice signals are channelized and modulated into a particular 4 KHz channel as a series of sound and silence bytes. Voice networks require committed bandwidth on a dedicated, though virtual, circuit for the duration of a session (call).

On the other hand, data signals, in the form of variable length packets or frames (except ATM [Asynchronous Transmission Mode], of course — see Chapter 14), require a routed, unchannelized, packet-switched network to move from source to destination. However, if you are transmitting over some form of leased line, such as ISDN or Frame Relay, your data travel, at least part of the way, over a dedicated circuit. A data network depends on having bandwidth available whenever data needs to be transmitted. Where a voice network expects perfection in its transmissions, data networks have built-in mechanisms to deal with its imperfect nature.

Sending voice over the data network

So, given their differences, how in the heck can data signals be transmitted over the voice network? It can and does work, but everything must work just right with a few voice transmission elements properly controlled. Sending voice over a data network requires the following to be managed:

- **Jitter:** Unexpected and abrupt variations in a signal's characteristics, such as pulse intervals, amplitude, and frequency. The impact of jitter is that short-term deviations in the characteristics of a signal can result in a signal value not being decoded properly. The process used to remove or control jitter on the network involves the use of a buffer, which can be reduced or increased in size proportionate to the severity of delay caused by jitter.

- **Latency:** This common networking term can be used interchangeably with *delay*. Too much latency on a circuit can disrupt the interval timing of signal units causing intermittent signal recognition problems.

- **Loss:** Another common networking characteristic that results in a signal unit not arriving at a destination point. The loss of a single unit may not cause too much impact. However, more than a few signal units lost or continuous signal loss can seriously impact the quality of a transmission.

- **Wander:** In effect, *wander* is long-term jitter and occurs when the clocking of a signal varies for more than one or two cycles. Wander has the same impact as jitter but for a longer time and to more data signals.

Voice networks are able to tolerate all four of these transmission characteristics, but these conditions can wreak havoc on a data network.

Compressing for success

One way that voice attempts to avoid problems on a data network is through compression. Compression has many advantages, but the primary advantage is to reduce the amount of bandwidth required. Compression of the signal also conforms the raw nature of the voice stream into a format that is compatible on the data network.

When a voice signal is transmitted over a digital network, it begins as an analog signal (representing the sound waves of your voice). It is then converted into a PCM (Pulse Code Modulation) format, which involves some compression, using ADPCM (Adaptive Differential PCM), CS-ACELP (Conjugate Structure – Algebraic Code Excited Linear Prediction), or LD-CELP (Low Delay CELP). You've got to love those engineering types for their acronyms and names. These compression techniques reduce the size of the signal from 2:1 (ADPCM) to 8:1 (CS-ACELP) for a faster and more error-free transmission.

When voice is sent over an IP network, it uses essentially the same compression techniques and processes as on a digital network, with some minor variations. Here is what happens:

1. On the transmitting source, 80 PCM voice units are combined to create a 640-bit block.

2. Using CS-ACELP, a codec (*coder*/*deco*der) compresses the block to 160 bits.

3. The compressed block is then placed inside an IP packet, and a UDP (User Datagram Protocol) header is added for identification, addressing, and error control.

4. The Real-Time Transport Protocol (RTP), a little-known TCP/IP protocol, is then used. RTP provides end-to-end delivery services, which include payload identification, packet sequencing, time stamping, and delivery monitoring. RTP also adds its own header to the bundle, resulting in the 512-bit packet shown in Figure 13-1.

Figure 13-1:
The 512-bit voice packet used on IP networks.

IP Header 160 bits	UDP Header 64 bits	RTP Header 128 bits	Compressed Payload 160 bits

When the packet is received at the receiving end, as is the case with all IP (OSI) packets, the process is reversed and the sound is delivered in its original quality to the listener. Of course, this assumes that all went well with the transmission: All the packets arrived at the same rate, and none were lost in transit.

Running through the DSP

Most computers use a device called a Digital Signal Process (DSP) as its codec. DSPs, such as the Cisco C542 and C549 digital signal processors, are special-purpose processors that are used in a variety of computing devices, such as sound cards, fax machines, modems, cell phones, and digital televisions. The original DSP was developed by Texas Instruments for use in its Speak & Spell children's toy.

A DSP receives analog signals and converts them into a digital form by analyzing them and arranging them in a format more easily reproducible than an analog signal. Of course, when a DSP is used as a codec, it also performs the decode action on the receiving end.

VoIP to the rescue

VoIP technology uses a variety of algorithms to reduce the characteristics that could impact the quality of the voice transmission: jitter, loss, and latency. Latency is guaranteed on an IP network; a variability in delay times (jitter) is also likely; and loss, like another undesirable, happens. The primary technique used to mitigate these problems is this: Transmission voids are filled by stretching voice packets that arrive early and blending them with those that arrive later. VoIP also applies echo cancellation technology, which is used when latency grows beyond 15 to 20 milliseconds (msec), compared to the normal inter-packet time of 10 msec.

Talking on the VoIP

Using an enterprise-level example, if a caller in a branch office in Seattle wishes to contact somebody at the company headquarters in Indianapolis, he or she picks up the phone and dials an extension number, usually 3 to 5 digits. In most cases, the phones on a VoIP system are attached or routed through a PBX (Public Branch Exchange) or CPBX (Computerized PBX). The PBX applies its Least Cost Routing (LCR) software for its options for routing the call. Finding that the call is within the VoIP network, the PBX sends the call to a VoIP gateway, which can be a dedicated device, a special server, or a Cisco router.

The gateway then performs its compression activities and forwards packets every 10 msec to its counterpart VoIP gateway at the remote location. If all goes well, that is if the quality of the call, in terms of PSTN standards, can be maintained, the call should go through without a hitch. If either gateway determines that, for some reason, a determined quality of service (QoS) of the call cannot be realized or maintained, the call can be routed back through the PBX to the PSTN, provided this option is available on the VoIP system.

When all is well, the callers shouldn't notice which service the call is being carried on. However, when things aren't right (after all, it *is* an IP network), the callers are apt to complain and find ways around the VoIP network. Unfortunately, VoIP is a sitting duck to users that have access to the PSTN on a regular basis for comparison.

Why use VoIP?

The primary reason VoIP is installed is cost. Compared to the long-distance bills of some companies, VoIP, even after the cost of installation, can result in a significant cost savings. The cost saving numbers for some companies are enough for many companies to ignore the potential quality issues and proceed with the installation of a VoIP system. Of course, the larger or more geographically dispersed a company is has a direct bearing on the size of the savings.

In a smaller company, the savings of a WAN VoIP may not be much at all when compared to the rates being offered by the long-distance carriers. VoIP, when everything is considered, provides a per-call cost that ranges from 4 to 8 cents per minute. Some long distance carriers are offering rates as low as 2 to 4 cents per minute, when purchased in time blocks. However, for a company that makes a high percentage of very long or international calls (around 50 to 70 cents a minute), VoIP begins to compare much more favorably. The bad news here is that VoIP is illegal (can you believe it?) in some countries.

VoIP has a few advantages and disadvantages, as listed in Table 13-1.

Table 13-1	Advantages and Disadvantages of VoIP	
Factor	*Advantage*	*Disadvantage*
Cost	Inexpensive long distance	Initial cost; competitive rates of carriers
Quality	Equal to PSTN in good situations	Latency, jitter, loss, and wander
Convergence	Integration on single network	Cost and technology slow to develop

Considering a few VoIP applications

It may help you to visualize VoIP in action with a few examples. In the following sections, two common application examples are provided, one of which is bound to be something to which you can relate.

VoIP in the enterprise

An enterprise with many branch offices, such as a bank, wishes to reduce its costs and take advantage of its IP network to combine voice and data traffic to and from the main office. By enhancing its data network to handle voice transmissions, the two networks can be combined to realize the goals (see Figure 13-2). The functions of the main office are similar to those described earlier in "Talking on VoIP." However, the VoIP gateways in the branch offices must perform the functions of both an internetwork router and a PBX.

Redundant trunks

Another application for VoIP is to provide either a primary or a redundant (backup) phone system trunk between two locations over an IP network. A company with two locations on the same campus or in the same city needs to provide a *tie line* (trunk) between the PBXs in each location. They have an existing T-1 line connecting the two locations for data networking purposes. By installing a VoIP gateway or adding VoIP services to their routers, the data line can either act as a primary link between the PBXs, should they want to remove an existing tie line leased from their local Telco, or as a backup line that can be used should the primary trunk fail.

Figure 13-2: An enterprise-level implementation of VoIP.

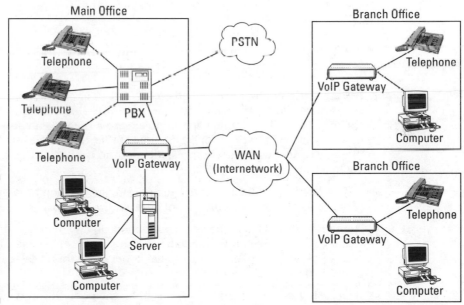

Maintaining the Quality of Service

The advantages of VoIP in cost and bandwidth savings (see "Why use VoIP?" earlier in the chapter) are subject to a few quality of service (QoS) issues that are inherent to IP networks. I briefly mentioned the primary issues of a data network earlier in the section entitled "Sending voice over the data network." However, I need to discuss them further in the context of QoS.

Causing an echo with delay

Delay or latency can cause two problems for voice transmitted over a data network: echo and overlap. *Echo* is caused when the receiving end equipment reflects signals back to the sender. When the delay in the signal circuit gets to be more than 50 msec, echo can become a significant quality problem, and the VoIP system must include some method of echo cancellation.

Overlap, also called *talker overlap,* is when one of the voice streams (from one of the two people in the conversation) begins overlapping the other person's voice. This can happen when the one-way delay grows to more than 250 msec. The VoIP system must include a method to constrain packet delay on the network.

Some of the major causes of delay on VoIP (and data) networks are the following:

- **Accumulation delay:** Also called *algorithmic delay.* Depending on the type and speed of the voice coder and compression algorithm in use, the process of combining voice samples into a bundle can add up to several milliseconds to the processing time. Table 13-2 lists a few examples of voice coders with the compression method each uses and the time each uses to assemble a voice packet.

- **Jitter:** A delay can be added to the packet transmission time by the process used to remove or control jitter on the network.

- **Network delay:** This is the latency inherent on any network. It is the result of the type of physical media and the protocols in use to send and receive network packets. On a typical IP network, this delay can run as high as 70 to 100 msec.

- **Processing delay:** This delay is caused by the encoding and accumulation of voice packets into an IP packet for transmission and is a function of the type of codec and algorithm in use.

Table 13-2	Common Voice Coder Characteristics	
Voice Coder Standard	*Compression Algorithm*	*Frame Assembly Time*
G.726	ADPCM	0.125 microseconds
G.728	CELP	2.5 milliseconds
G.729	ACELP	10 milliseconds
G.723.1	Multi-rate	30 milliseconds

The *G.xxx* numbers used in Table 13-2 represent voice coder standards defined by the International Telecommunications Union (ITU), the global standards body for voice processing.

Dealing with lost packets

IP networks don't guarantee the delivery of a packet, which can be a real problem when dealing with voice packets. (Not that it isn't a real problem for data packets, mind you.) An IP network, partly because of its packet-switching nature, has a high incidence of lost packets when compared to ATM, which is the high-speed network technology the phone company uses to transmit voice frames across their network. IP networks treat voice frames just like they do data frames, and during peak loading or congestion, voice frames are lost just like data frames. It just comes with the territory. Because data frames are not time sensitive, losing one or two is typically not that big of a problem. However, hearing only every other syllable of somebody's speech can be downright disconcerting.

Not to worry. Rather than just complain about this situation, VoIP systems have taken the high road and use several methods to deal with this problem on their own. Here are a few:

- **Instant replay:** When a lost packet is detected, the last packet received is replayed in the slot where the lost packet should have been. However, this only is effective when the incidence of lost packets is low. It obviously would not work well should a number of packets in a row be lost.

- **Send ahead:** This scheme sends the next packet to be sent along with the packet preceding it. This provides a means to replace the missing packet should it not arrive. However, this method requires more bandwidth and can add additional delay.

- **Send more, but a slower speed:** This is a hybrid scheme that uses a lower bandwidth voice coder and sends along the redundant packet for use should the n+1 packet (the packet following any particular packet) not arrive. This scheme takes care of the lost packet problem but not the delay.

Compensating for echo

When the circuit is converted from a four-wire circuit (IP networks) to a two-wire circuit (Telco networks), signal reflections can occur and create the effect of echo on the line. Four-wire circuits have separate send and receive pairs, but the two-wire circuit has only a single wire for each direction. Visualize a freeway that narrows down all of a sudden from four lanes to two — somebody is bound to just give up and return home. Likewise, the telephone network is not able to handle the sudden rush of traffic, and some packets may be reflected back to the IP network.

Echo is a common occurrence even on the PSTN, but the phone system includes a method to deal with it. IP networks are not so equipped. Therefore, VoIP systems must include an echo cancellation technique and include a digital filter on the transmit path to deal with echoing IP packets.

Applying the Cisco Solution

If you haven't read the first part of this chapter, you should do so. That way, you can fully appreciate the majesty of Cisco Systems' Architecture for Voice, Video, and Integrated Data (AVVID — pronounced just like the word *avid*). Just its name should fill you with awe, but the AVVID methodology really is something special.

Becoming an AVVID believer

So what is AVVID all about? *AVVID* is a Cisco proprietary standard for a methodology for effectively and efficiently supporting voice, video, and data on an enterprise network. Actually, AVVID is not a single product that you can just order and install on your network. Rather, it is a set of guidelines for building what is called a converged, highly available, distributed, standards-based network. AVVID provides a framework that allows a growing enterprise to easily implement emerging networking technologies and Internet standards and to provide enhanced customer, e-business, and quality of service solutions. Who could ask for anything more?

The AVVID infrastructure

The Cisco AVVID infrastructure includes five levels, or what Cisco calls "building blocks." To implement an AVVID infrastructure, you are not required to implement all five levels, but they are there should you need them. They are:

✔ **Network infrastructure:** By definition, the infrastructure of any network includes:

- **Clients** — This includes such devices as IP phones, PCs, portable computers, and wireless devices.

- **Networking devices** — Cisco calls these devices "platforms." Networking devices includes such things as routers, servers, switches, and firewalls.

- **Intelligent services** — These are the platforms, network services, and management tools that implement the enterprise's business rules and network policies.

✔ **Control services:** The networking component on this level is the software that controls access and provides the point at which the Internet is tied to the enterprise's e-business elements. The services found on this level include VPN services, voice call controls, QoS policies, video media controls, content distribution controls, wireless access, and directory access controls.

✔ **Communication services:** This level of its infrastructure is where AVVID takes advantage of voice, video, and data convergence by incorporating such technologies as unified communication services, intelligent contact management (you know, contacts such as sales leads and the like), transnetwork collaboration services (multiple network users working on a single document or project), and multimedia viewing applications.

✔ **E-business integration services:** Typically third-party solutions, these tools provide an improved application of voice and data networks to business communications. An example would be call center systems that integrate voice and data services on an agent's workstation.

✔ **Enterprise e-business services:** The services on this level are provided by the enterprise itself across the AVVID network infrastructure to implement the enterprise's strategic, tactical, and operational policies. You know, the proprietary software used by the enterprise that manages its business operations and allows it to compete.

So, which type of convergence do you mean?

Convergence is one of those information technology (IT) terms that have a variety of meanings. It is used for the state of network routers and switches that are completely up-to-date with the internetwork's topology. It is also used to describe the visual combination of the red, green, and blue pixels on a monitor.

When voice and video networking are combined with data networking, the result is called voice and data convergence or voice and data integration. Whether or not, depending on who you believe, voice and data convergence is a real thing, it is certainly something every network administrator should be at least considering for his or her network, assuming a network of some size.

So, be careful how you use *convergence*. The safe bet is always to put "voice and data" in front of it.

Cisco's AVVID provides a framework to integrate data, voice, and video services (which have been typically implemented on completely separate networks) in an enterprise. AVVID aims to eliminate the redundant network management functions and place these services on a single network by using a single set of IP-based networking hardware and software. The desired result is to improve bandwidth utilization, reduce the overall bandwidth requirements, improve the efficiency of network administration activities, and allow new business applications to be deployed more rapidly. These improvements should result in lower facility, network, staffing, and training costs, which are all good unless you are the staff that yielded the cost savings, right?

AVVID and QoS

The primary concern on any converged network is the performance of all types of traffic on a single transmission infrastructure. Data is bursty, tolerant to lost packets, and completely insensitive to delay. On the other hand, voice is a continuous stream with a low tolerance for lost packets and is very sensitive to delay.

A data-only AVVID network running over ATM or Frame Relay (see Chapter 14) uses a technique called traffic shaping. *Traffic shaping* allows a central high-speed site to feed a number of lower-speed remote locations by preventing too much traffic from being sent to any of the remote sites. However, an AVVID voice network must also include additional QoS services to handle the special needs of voice traffic. These include:

- **Compressed Real-Time Transfer Protocol (CRTP):** CRTP compresses IP headers, which reduce the size of any voice packets by as much as 50 percent. This is especially required on low-speed links.

- **Link fragmentation:** Large data packets can cause delay problems on slower speed circuits of less than 768 Kbps, such as Frame Relay (see Chapter 14). To avoid these problems, link fragmentation breaks large data packets into smaller packets the size of a voice packet. The effect is to reduce the delay for any voice traffic running on a converged network.

- **Low Latency Queuing (LLQ):** LLQ is a WAN service that classifies outbound traffic and then places it in a particular queue that has the ability to provide the appropriate handling services. Voice traffic is placed in a high-priority queue, and data is placed in a lower-priority queue.

Implementing an AVVID network

In most cases, any enterprise looking to move to an AVVID network infrastructure likely has many of the components needed already in place. A number of currently available and installed Cisco networking devices are AVVID-ready. Here is a short list of some of the AVVID-ready devices available:

✔ Cisco AVVID-ready switches:

- Catalyst 3500

- Catalyst 4000 series

- Catalyst 6500

✔ Cisco AVVID-ready routers:

- Cisco 2600 series

- Cisco 3600 series

- Cisco 7200

- Cisco 7500

Designing a converged network

Actually, explaining the process of designing a converged network with an AVVID network infrastructure would require a completely separate book to do it justice. (Editor, please note!) Your best bet is to download the Cisco white paper "Designing Your Converged Network" from this link:

```
www.cisco.com/warp/public/779/largeent/avvid/datacom/best_
practices.html.
```

Chapter 14

Working with WAN Technologies

*W*elcome to acronym land! The wacky world of WAN, itself a TLA, is chock-full of abbreviations and acronyms. You may find more TLAs (three-letter acronyms) and FLAs (four-letter acronyms) in this chapter than perhaps any other in this book. Acronyms just come with the territory. I'm not sure I believe it, but I've heard that after Alexander Graham Bell made his first voice connection with Mr. Watson (and no, this is not the same guy who founded IBM), he wrote in his notes, "poor QoS; investigate ISDN or ATM."

Data communications, and especially WAN services, are the domain of protocols, and protocols are the domain of funny-sounding acronyms. In this chapter, I discuss the protocols and services used to connect a network to the outside world, whether it is only to another segment of the same network or to the global network.

Differentiating WAN Services

WAN services are the various protocols and technologies that you can use to connect your LAN to the Internet or to interconnect LAN networks within a single enterprise. Nearly all LANs use at least one WAN service, which is why you don't need to be an expert on every WAN service to manage your network or to manage the people who manage your network. However, you should have a good understanding of the various WAN services available in order to make the best choices for your network and to know the right way to configure your routers.

Deciphering WAN services

To really be prepared to make the best choices for your network and to impress your friends and associates with the girth of your knowledge, I believe that you should know about the following WAN services:

- **ATM (Asynchronous Transfer Mode):** ATM is a connection-oriented, packet-switched network architecture, loosely based on ISDN, that delivers very high bandwidth, up to 38.813 gigabits per second (OC-768 — see Table 14-1).

- **Frame-Relay:** This WAN service creates permanent virtual circuits (PVCs) between points on the network to provide fast packet switching and very fast throughput.

- **HDLC (High-Level Data-Link Control):** This bit-oriented, synchronous protocol is used for high-level connections to X.25and other types of packet-switching networks. HDLC uses variable-length packets to gain throughput efficiency.

- **ISDN (Integrated Services Digital Network):** Some people say that ISDN stands for "It still doesn't network." Actually, ISDN has been around for a while and is still somewhat popular for both home and office use. ISDN sends digital signals over the PSTN (public switched telephone network — you know, the regular telephone system) to carry as much as 1.536 Mbps.

- **PPP (Point-to-Point Protocol):** This is the industry standard, the veritable workhorse, of WAN communications. It should be no surprise that PPP is designed to carry data from router to router, from host to host, or from one network workstation to another; in other words, from point to point.

- **X.25:** Despite the fact that it sounds like a secret government project (which the government denies, of course), X.25 is one of a series of *X* communications standards. The X.25 standard covers how a message is formatted for transmission over a common carrier between networks of dissimilar hardware and software.

Table 14-1	OC (Optical Carrier) Services
Service	*Speed (Mbps)*
OC-1	51.84
OC-3	155.52
OC-12	622.08
OC-48	2488.32
OC-192	9953.28
OC-768	38813.12

The numeric part of the OC service designator, such as the 1 in OC-1, indicates the number of OC-1 (51.84 Mbps) equivalents represented by an OC service. For example, OC-192, a very-high-speed interregional backbone service, has the bandwidth equivalent of 192 OC-1 lines.

Learning the lingo

Okay, so I threw around a few phrases like ". . .high-level connections to X.25 packet-switching networks," and I will again in the remainder of this chapter. I try to be as gentle as I can, but WAN services have their very own language, and you just can't get around it.

So, in the interest of your continued reading and understanding pleasure, I present these definitions of the more important WAN terms that you should know:

- **Bit-oriented:** Services oriented to transferring data in bit streams without regard to packets or cells are called bit-oriented.

- **Cell-switching:** Services that move data in fixed-length packets over pathways between end nodes called virtual circuits are referred to as cell-switching services. ATM (Asynchronous Transfer Mode) is a cell-switching service.

- **Circuit-switching:** Networks, including the PSTN (public switched telephone network), that create (or "nail up") a circuit that exists only to handle a single communications session, such as a telephone conversation, are circuit-switched networks.

- **DCE (Data Communication Equipment):** In data communications, this is the device that physically exchanges the data with a computer or a router (the DTE) and transmits the data over the communications media.

- **DTE (Data Terminal Equipment):** In data communications, this is the device or interface used by a computer or a router to exchange data with a modem or other serial device (the DCE).

- **Data Link Control Identifier (DLCI):** Pronounced as "delcie," this is the identity number assigned to the virtual connection between the DTE and the switch. Every VC (virtual circuit) multiplexed as a part of a physical channel is represented with a unique DLCI. However, a DLCI value is only significant locally to the end point connected to the physical channel on which it resides. What this means is that the equipment at each end of a Frame-Relay connection may use different DLCIs to refer to the same VC.

- **Encapsulation:** The inclusion of one data structure in another data structure that results in the first data structure being hidden or masked during data transmission is called *encapsulation*.

- **Local exchange carrier (LEC):** The company that provides telephone services to your home or business (including dial tone) is your local exchange carrier. The company occupying the central office (CO) where your telephone circuits terminate is the incumbent LEC (ILEC). Any competing company that arranges with the ILEC to provide services from the CO (such as most DSL providers) is a competing LEC (CLEC).

✔ **Packet switching:** Small units of data, called packets, are transferred over the network based on the destination address of the packet. Routed networks are packet-switched networks.

✔ **PVC (permanent virtual circuit):** A software-defined logical connection in a Frame-Relay network that defines the connections and bandwidth between two end points is called a PVC. A PVC is permanently defined and remains defined between the two end points before and after communications sessions.

✔ **SVC (switched virtual circuit):** A virtual circuit that exists only for the duration of a communications session is called an SVC.

✔ **VC (virtual circuit):** A circuit or path between two points on a network that is allocated as needed to meet traffic requirements is called a VC. Two types of VCs exist: PVCs and SVCs.

Connecting with the Mysterious X.25

Way back in the 1970s, many so-called public data networks were actually owned by private companies and government agencies. In most cases, the wide area network of one company or agency was unique and often incompatible with the network of another company or agency. Naturally, when it became necessary for these networks to interconnect, some form of common network interface protocol became necessary.

In 1976, the International Consultative Committee for Telegraphy and Telephony (CCITT), which, by the way, is now called the ITU (International Telecommunication Union), thank goodness, recommended a protocol it called X.25. This protocol defined a packet-switched networking protocol for exchanging data over a connection-oriented service.

X.25 also defines the control information that is passed between these two types of equipment:

✔ **Data Terminal Equipment (DTE):** A user device. DTE equipment typically consists of terminals, PCs, routers, and bridges that are owned by the customer.

✔ **Data Circuit-Terminating Equipment (DCE):** DCE equipment items are typically carrier-owned internetworking devices.

In the following sections, I cover a range of X.25 topics that are definitely of interest to you if you plan to incorporate X.25 services into your network, including:

✔ X.25 addressing schemes

✔ Virtual circuits

✔ X.25 router interfaces

✔ The layers of X.25 communications.

Addressing the X.25 world

On both the X.25 and LAPB layers (see "The layers of the X.25 cake," later in this section), an emphasis is placed on flow control and error checking (see Chapter 6 for more information on these two concepts), which reduce the need for these services to be performed by protocols or services outside of X.25, such as TCP. These services are very important over connections using an unreliable service, such as analog (cell-switching) dialup access to a modem (see "Getting from Point-to-Point," later in this chapter). However, when X.25 is used over more-reliable digital connections, such as Frame-Relay or dedicated digital telephone lines, X.25's insistence on performing flow control and error checking can be a drawback, because these actions aren't really necessary and add additional overhead.

Each X.25 link consists of a DTE at one end and a DCE at the other. The DTE is typically a router or a computer, while the DCE is a switch or concentrator on the public data network. In some services, such as Frame Relay, an intermediary device between the DTE and DCE, called a PAD (Packet Assembler/Disassembler), may also be used.

The X.25 addressing scheme consists of a four-decimal-digit DNIC (Data Network Identification Code) and a NTN (Network Terminal Number) that consists of up to 11 decimal digits. The DNIC ("dee-nick") includes the country code and a provider number that is assigned by the ITU. But wait! There's more! The combination of the last digit of the DNIC and the first eight digits of the NTN make up the unique address that is allocated to a specific X.25 network.

Now for the bad news: X.25 does not include a protocol like TCP/IP's Address Resolution Protocol (ARP) (see Chapter 6 for information on TCP/IP protocols), which means that if you want to connect a router to an X.25 service, you must manually map all X.25 addresses to their associated IP addresses in the router. I don't need to tell you how much fun that can be!

Routers and X.25

A single X.25 interface on a router can be configured to support up to 4,095 (your lucky number) SVCs. By combining multiple SVCs for a single specific protocol, the throughput can be increased if the protocol provides its own packet resequencing. A maximum of eight SVCs may be combined into one path for a protocol.

When implementing X.25 on a Cisco router, you must configure three interface items. You use these commands to do that:

```
encapsulation x25 dte or dce (dte is the default)
x25 address x.121-address
x25 map protocol address x.121-address [options]
```

Using a tunneling process, almost any Network layer protocol (see the next section) can be transmitted across X.25 virtual circuits. *Tunneling* is a process in which packets are encapsulated within an X.25 packet for transmission over a virtual circuit.

The following data communications protocols and services support X.25 WAN services:

- Apollo
- AppleTalk
- Banyan Vines
- Bridging
- Compressed TCP (Transmission Control Protocol)
- DECnet
- IP (Internet Protocol)
- ISO-CLNS (Connectionless Mode Network Service)
- Novell IPX
- XNS (Xerox Network Systems)

The layers of the X.25 cake

X.25 has three layers that track to the lower three layers of the OSI model (Network, Data Link, and Physical). See Chapter 5 for information on the OSI model and its layers. The three layers of X.25 services are

- **X.25** (Layer 3), which is also called the Packet Level, describes the data transfer protocol in the packet switched network. It is similar to the OSI Network layer (Layer 3) model and similarly creates network data units called packets, which contain both control information and user data. The packet level also includes procedures for establishing virtual circuits (temporary associations) and permanent virtual circuits (PVC) which is a permanent association between two DTEs, and defines datagrams — self-contained data units that include the information needed to route the unit to its destination.

✓ **LAPB** (Layer 2), which is also called the Link level, ensures the reliable transfer of data between the DTE and the DCE using a sequence of frames that contain address, control, and data fields. The functions performed by the Link level also include link synchronization, error detection, and recovery. These protocols used on this level of X.25 protocols:

• **LAPB (Link Access Protocol, Balanced)** is a derivative of HDLC (High-Level Data Link Control) that is the most commonly used X.25 Link level protocol.

• **LAPD (Link Access Procedure, D Channel)** is an ISDN protocol (not to be confused with the Los Angeles Police Department).

• **LLC (Logical Link Control)** is an IEEE 802 protocol used to transmit X.25 packets over a LAN.

• **LAP (Link Access Protocol)** is the precursor to LAPB and is no longer commonly used.

✓ **Physical level** (Layer 1) describes interfaces with the physical environment much like the OSI model's Physical layer. An example of an X.25 Physical layer interface is the X.21 *bis* (bis is a techie term taken from the French word for second).

Connecting Up with Frame-Relay

Compared to X.25 (see the previous section "Connecting with the Mysterious X.25"), Frame-Relay is a next-generation protocol that is optimized for better performance and more efficient frame transmission. You should know these key characteristics of Frame-Relay:

✓ **Encapsulation:** Rather than a specific interface type, Frame-Relay is an encapsulation method that operates over virtually all serial interfaces.

✓ **Error-checking and flow control:** Frame-Relay depends on upper-layer protocols to provide flow control and error correction.

✓ **Media:** Frame-Relay was designed specifically for use on fiber-optic cables and digital networks.

Frame-Relay operates on Layers 1 and 2 (the Physical and Data Link layers) of the OSI reference model (see Chapter 2). Although originally designed to operate on ISDN networks, it is frequently implemented on numerous other network interfaces. The Cisco implementation of Frame-Relay supports the following protocols:

✓ AppleTalk

✓ Banyan Vines

✓ CLNS (Connectionless Network Service)

- DECnet
- IP
- ISO (International Standards Organization)
- Novell IPX
- Transparent Bridging (Ethernet)
- XNS (Xerox Network Services)

Framing the frame

Like most WAN services, Frame-Relay provides a communications interface between the DTE and DCE devices. And like X.25, Frame-Relay provides connection-oriented Layer 2 communications over a packet-switched network, although Frame-Relay is faster and more efficient than X.25.

Discussing encapsulation

This is an excellent opportunity to discuss encapsulation. Although briefly mentioned in Chapter 2, *encapsulation* is the process that allows a data packet to move through the various protocols and services to reach its destination.

At various stages on its way out of the source network, the original data bundle has additional information added to it (in the form of headers and trailers) that is used at the destination network to ensure that it gets to its destination with its contents intact. Before all of this information is sent out over a WAN service, it is placed in what amounts to a Physical layer shipping container, a process called encapsulation.

Encapsulating the frame

The encapsulation container for Frame-Relay is a frame, shown in Figure 14-1. Data transmitted over a Frame-Relay line is encapsulated in one of these frames by using this format. The information field segment of the frame is where the original data bundle, along with any added headers or trailers, is placed. You don't really need to know the format of a Frame-Relay frame; you should at least be aware of parts of the Frame-Relay header, because they can impact the performance of the system, as I discuss in the next few sections.

The fields included in the standard Frame-Relay frame, shown in Figure 14-1, are:

- **Flags:** At the beginning and end of each frame is a binary value (01111110) that represents the hexadecimal number 7E (which both represent the decimal number 126 — don't ask).
- **Frame address:** The address field in a frame is comprised of the following elements:

- **Data Link Control Identifier (DLCI):** This 10-bit value represents the VC between the DTE device and the switch.

- **Extended Address (EA):** If DLCI longer than the standard two octets is in use, the EA is set "on" (a 1 value). This is a function reserved for future uses, if needed.

- **C/R bit:** This bit is not currently defined, beyond a name, that is.

- **Forward-explicit congestion notification (FECN):** This bit is used to indicate forward-looking congestion problems on the circuit. See "Handling Frame-Relay traffic jams," later in this chapter.

- **Backward-explicit congestion notification (BECN):** This bit is used to indicate backward-looking congestion problems on a circuit. See "Handling Frame-Relay traffic jams," later in this chapter.

- **Discard Eligibility (DE):** This bit is used to mark a frame that can be discarded should transmissions exceed the CIR. See "Handling Frame-Relay traffic jams," later in this chapter.

✔ **Frame Check Sequence (FCS):** A checksum calculated at the sending end and recalculated at the receiving end as a part of the error-checking procedures.

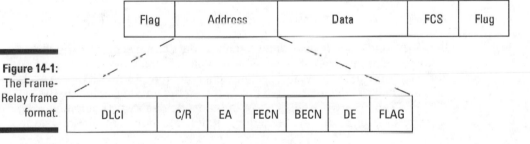

Figure 14-1:
The Frame-Relay frame format.

Committing the DLCI

Frame-Relay has two key players:

✔ **The DTE** (also called *customer premises equipment* or *CPE*), which is typically a router.

✔ **The PSE** (packet-switching equipment), which is located at the network service provider (commonly the phone company or a CLEC), that takes the form of the DCE.

Frame-Relay also has the following characteristics:

✔ Frame-Relay uses statistical multiplexing to combine multiple virtual circuits and transmit them over a single transmission circuit. *Statistical multiplexing* involves interleaving the data from two or more devices onto a single line (DLCI or data-link connection identifier) for transmission over a Frame-Relay network.

✔ Each set of DTEs, which is one or more sending and receiving CPEs, is assigned a DLCI (pronounced as "delcie"). The DLCI identifies the link that carries the combined (multiplexed) data from all of the linked DTEs.

✔ The DLCI is mapped to a specific permanent virtual circuit (PVC) path through the DCE/PSE equipment. With the DLCI in place, the entire path from source to destination is known even before the first frame is sent.

Because not all the VCs (virtual circuits) on a circuit may belong to the same customer, such as on a shared media circuit, the customer is assigned a committed information rate (CIR) for her circuit. The *CIR* is the minimum bandwidth the customer will receive, although additional bandwidth is available to handle periodic bursts of data above the CIR, if necessary. In most instances, the CIR is about one-half of the nominal data rate of a line. In other words, if the circuit is a T-1 line (1.54 Mbps), then the CIR is likely to be 768 Kbps. Frame-Relay can be subscribed at less than a T-1 line in increments of 64 Kbps. So, if a Frame-Relay line is subscribed for 256 Kbps, then the CIR is likely to be 128 Kbps.

Handling Frame-Relay traffic jams

Network congestion is caused by too much data being sent over too little bandwidth. In the Frame-Relay world, this means that when users on a Frame-Relay circuit with a total CIR of 64K send a combined 96K of data, the aggregate bandwidth demand of all of the traffic on the circuit (including the extra 32K) can cause network congestion and must be dealt with somehow. See "Committing the DLCI," the preceding section, for more information on CIR.

A Frame-Relay circuit has two options when a jam occurs. Each has its own funky side effects:

✔ The data creating the congestion must be delayed (retransmitted), but retransmitted data can cause even more congestion.

✔ The data creating the congestion must be discarded (not forwarded). Discarding packets can create data reliability problems between the sender and receiver.

Frame-Relay operates on a kind of honor system that depends on the constraint of its users to avoid problems. But when the honor code breaks down and users send more data than they have bandwidth commitments for, which they do on occasion, Frame-Relay is ready for them with some built-in mechanisms it uses to remedy this situation.

As Figure 14-1 shows, the Frame-Relay frame includes two mechanisms that are used to reduce network congestion:

- ✓ The Explicit Congestion Notification (ECN) fields:
    - • The Forward Explicit Congestion Notification (FECN)
    - • The Backward Explicit Congestion Notification (BECN)
- ✓ The Discard Eligibility (DE) field

Here is how Frame-Relay attempts to reduce network congestion. For this next trick, I need you to divert your full and undivided attention to Figure 14-2 (ignore the man behind the curtain), which depicts a Frame-Relay network with three nodes: A, B, and C. You can see two things:

- ✓ Node B is located between Nodes A and C.
- ✓ Network congestion is occurring in the direction of Node A to Node C.

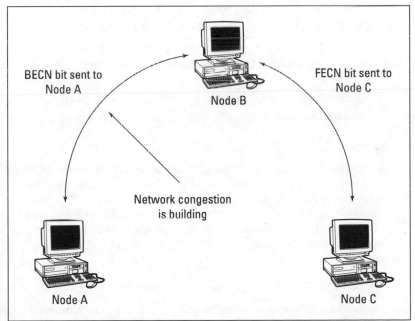

BECN bit sent to Node A

FECN bit sent to Node C

Node B

Network congestion is building

Node A

Node C

Figure 14-2: A Frame-Relay network developing a congestion problem.

FECN

FECN and BECN are used to alert Frame-Relay nodes to problems with transmission over the network usually caused by network congestion. In the ECN method of congestion notification, the key point to remember is that if the FECN or BECN bit is set to 1, congestion exists on the network.

The Forward Explicit Congestion Notification (FECN) is an Explicit Congestion Notification (ECN) field used when frames are sent by Node A to Node C. FECN, as its name implies, is a bit set by a Frame-Relay network in a message frame intended to notify a receiving DTE that it should take steps to avoid an apparent congestion on the network. Node A notifies the stations to which it forwards messages.

- Frames are sent from Node A and pass over the PVC that connects Node A to Node B.

- Node B examines the frames and determines that they need to be passed along to Node C over the PVC connecting it to Node C.

- However, should Node B detect a problem, such as network congestion, the ECNs are put into play, as follows:

  - Node B detects that congestion is beginning and signals Node C by changing the FECN (Forward Explicit Congestion Notification) bit from 0 to 1 on those frames addressed for Node C.

  - Node C and any other nodes between B and C learn from the FECN bit (set to 1) that congestion exists on the affected DLCIs.

- In this way, Node B sends notice to all upstream DLCIs that there is congestion on the network and an alternate route should be found until the congestion is eased.

BECN

What if network congestion is detected between Nodes B and A? Node B can't use the FECN to notify A because A is behind B; but by using the BECN, Node B can notify Node A (and any nodes between B and A) that there is a problem. The *Backward Explicit Congestion Notification (BECN)* is a bit set by a Frame-Relay network in a message frame intended to notify a receiving DTE that it (the sending device) will be taking steps to avoid some apparent network congestion.

- Node B also detects congestion on the circuit between C and A.

- Node B begins watching for frames coming from C toward Node A.

- Node B signals Node A of the congestion by setting the BECN (Backward Explicit Congestion Notification) bit in those frames from 0 to 1.

- Node A, and any other devices between A and Node B, know from the BECN bit (set to 1) that congestion is building on the affected DLCIs.

Throwing out everything over the limit

When a Frame-Relay circuit becomes congested and frames must be discarded as a way to solve the congestion, it is better to have the sending device decide which frames can be discarded instead of having a router pick frames at random to throw out. The idea is that the sending device probably knows which frames are critical and which aren't.

The mechanism used to control which frames are discarded is the *Discard Eligibility (DE) bit*. When the sending device is aware that congestion may exist in the direction in which it is sending frames, it uses the DE bit to designate the expendable frames. The DE bit is set to 1 (or "turned on") in those frames that are knowingly being sent in excess of the CIR (Committed Information Rate) and can be discarded.

If the network is congested, those frames that have their DE bit turned on are discarded until the congestion is relieved. However, if discarding DE frames does not clear up the congestion, then all bets are off, and frames are discarded regardless of their DE bit setting. When no congestion exists, the DE bits of all frames are ignored.

Switching Frame-Relay around on a router

Remember that Cisco routers can be configured to perform Frame-Relay switching and that doing so involves a series of things in pairs. There are two parts to Frame-Relay switching:

- The Frame-Relay DTE (router)
- The Frame-Relay DCE (switch)

A Cisco router can be configured for two types of switching:

- **Local Frame-Relay switching:** Enables the router to forward frames based on the DLCI number found in the frames header. See "Committing the DLCI," earlier in this chapter, for information on the DLCI.
- **Remote Frame-Relay switching:** Enables the router to encapsulate frames into an IP packet and tunnel them across an IP backbone.

Routing Frame-Relay

Configuring a Frame-Relay connection on a Cisco router is done through a simple six-step process. Here are the steps used to configure a Frame-Relay interface on a Cisco router:

1. **Select the interface to be configured.**

   ```
   Cisco_Networking(config)#int s0
   ```

   This command selects serial interface 0 and selects configuration interface mode on the Cisco_Networking router.

2. **Configure a DLCI number to the interface.**

   ```
   Cisco_Networking(config-if)#frame-relay interface-dlci 13
   ```

3. **Select the encapsulation type — cisco or ietf (cisco is the default).**

   ```
   Cisco_Networking(config-if)#encapsulation frame-relay
           ietf
   ```

   Cisco encapsulation is the default type; *ietf* encapsulation is used only when creating an interface that will be used to connect two routers from different manufacturers.

4. **Specify the LMI type (Cisco IOS 11.1 and earlier).**

   ```
   Cisco_Networking(config-if)#frame-relay lmi-type cisco
   ```

   In Cisco IOS Versions 11.2 and later, the LMI type is auto-detected by the router. Otherwise, LMI type "cisco" is the default value.

5. **Map the Frame-Relay interface through Inverse ARP.**

   ```
   Cisco_Networking(config-if)#ip address 192.168.1.1
           255.255.255.0
   ```

   Using Inverse ARP (also known as Reverse ARP — see Chapter 2), which is enabled by default, allows you to avoid entering mapping commands for each virtual circuit and to use the dynamic mapping functions of the **inverse-arp** function. Inverse ARP automatically enables dynamic mapping, which continuously updates the mapping of IP addresses to a DLCI. You can choose not to enable Inverse ARP, in which case you must manually manage the ARP with static mapping entries, which is not something you want to do on a large network with several Frame-Relay connections.

6. **Configure a subinterface.**

   ```
   Cisco_Networking(config)#int s0.13 point-to-point
   ```

   Create a subinterface number 13 that is a point-to-point link. Remember that subinterfaces are specified as s0.n or e0.n, where *n* is the subinterface number.

Mapping IPs to DLCIs

In order for IP devices to communicate with each other over a Frame-Relay network, their IP addresses must be mapped to their DLCIs. Two methods ensure that this mapping occurs: manual and automatic.

The manual method, also known as *static mapping,* uses the **frame-relay map** command to enter the static IP mappings one by one. Static mapping is required when OSPF is used over Frame-Relay, when Inverse ARP is not supported on the remote router, or when you want to control broadcast traffic.

The command used to manually map the IP addresses to the DLCI is

```
Router(config-if)#frame-relay map protocol protocol-address
        dlci [broadcast][ietf|cisco]
```

Here is an example of what might be entered to map a DLCI manually:

```
Cisco_Networking(config-if)#frame-relay map ip 192.168.1.1
        200 cisco
```

The way to automatically map IP addresses to their DLCIs is by using the inverse ARP (IARP) function. IARP is enabled by default on an interface, but it's disabled automatically on a DLCI when the **frame-relay map** command is used. The IARP approach is much easier to configure than the static map approach. However, because configuration errors can occur when a virtual circuit is mapped to an unknown device, the static approach is more stable and less prone to configuration errors.

The steps in "Routing Frame-Relay," earlier in this section, include an example of the command used to automatically map an IP address to a DLCI.

So what's the LMI?

LMI (Local Management Interface) is an interface type that was created in 1990 by a consortium of four internetworking companies (Cisco, StrataCom, Northern Telecom, and Digital Equipment Corp). This group (called the "Gang of Four") enhanced the existing Frame-Relay protocol by allowing routers to communicate with a Frame-Relay network. LMI messages include information about the network's current DLCI values, whether the DLCIs are local or global, and the status of virtual circuits.

To configure the LMI interface type, you need to set two values. You also have an option to set the LMI polling and timer intervals.

✔ **LMI type** — defines the standard to be used to configure the Frame-Relay interface.

✔ **LMI "keepalive" interval** — defines the interval between packets sent over the circuit to keep the circuit open.

In Cisco IOS Versions 11.2 or later, the LMI interface is detected automatically. If you choose not to use the auto-sensing feature, you must configure the interface manually. The LMI interface type you use depends on the type in use at the remote device. The default LMI type is Cisco, which is the Gang of Four LMI, and the default keepalive period is 10 seconds. Use one of these three types:

- ✔ Cisco
- ✔ ANSI
- ✔ Q933A

Connecting to subinterfaces

When multiple virtual circuits are created on a single Frame-Relay or serial interface, each of the VCs is considered a *subinterface*. Using subinterfaces has several advantages, most important of which is the ability to implement different network layer characteristics on each virtual circuit. For example, one subinterface could be running IP routing, while another (on the same Frame-Relay interface) could be running IPX.

Subinterfaces are defined with the command

```
int s0.subinterface number
```

where the subinterface number can be any number in the range from 0 to 4,294,967,295. Typically, the DLCI number is assigned to an interface as the subinterface number. There are two types of subinterfaces:

- ✔ **Point-to-point** is used when connecting two routers over a single virtual circuit.
- ✔ **Multipoint** is specified on the center router in a star topology of virtual circuits.

Keeping watch on the Frame-Relay

You can use several commands to monitor the various activities of a Frame-Relay network, including dynamic mappings, LMI statistics, ECN statistics, and more (see "Handling Frame-Relay traffic jams," earlier in this chapter). The commands used to monitor Frame-Relay activities are

- ✔ **clear frame-relay-inarp:** Dynamically clears any IP-to-DLCI mappings created through the inverse ARP function.
- ✔ **sh int type [number]:** Displays DLCI and LMI information.
- ✔ **sh frame-relay lmi [type number]:** Displays LMI statistics.
- ✔ **sh frame-relay map:** Displays the current map entries.

✔ **sh frame-relay pvc [type number [dlci]]:** Displays the current PVC statistics.

✔ **sh frame-relay traffic:** Display statistics about the Frame-Relay traffic.

✔ **sh frame-relay route:** Displays the configure Frame Relay routes configured in a Cisco router.

✔ **sh frame-relay svc maplist:** Displays all the SVCs under a specific map list.

Communicating on a High-Level

HDLC is the default serial encapsulation method on Cisco routers. HDLC (High-Level Data Link Control) is an ISO (International Standards Organization, you know — the OSI folks) standard. A problem with HDLC is that it may not be totally compatible between devices from different manufacturers, depending on the way each vendor chose to implement it. HDLC provides support for both point-to-point and multipoint services over synchronous serial data links and ISDN interfaces.

HDLC supports four different transfer modes:

✔ **NRM (Normal Response Mode)** allows a secondary device to communicate with a primary device, but only when the primary device initiates the request.

✔ **ARM (Asynchronous Response Mode)** allows either the primary or the secondary device to initiate communications.

✔ **ABM (Asynchronous Balance Mode)** allows a device to work in what is called *combined* mode, which means that it can work as either a primary or secondary device.

✔ **LAPB (Link Access Protocol, Balanced)** is an extension of the ABM transfer mode, but this one allows circuit establishment with both DTE (data terminal equipment) and DCE (data communications equipment).

Getting from Point-to-Point

On a Cisco network, PPP (Point-to-Point Protocol) is used for router-to-router and host-to-network communications over synchronous and asynchronous circuits, including HSSI (High-Speed Serial Interface, pronounced "hissy") and ISDN interfaces. PPP is an industry standard protocol that enables point-to-point data transmissions of routed data. It is largely protocol-independent and allows you to connect a network over data lines. PPP works with several network protocols, including IP, IPX, and ARA (AppleTalk Remote Access).

PPP uses two internal protocols to perform its functions:

- **LCP (Link Control Protocol)** includes the procedures for creating, configuring, testing, and terminating data-link connections, as well as managing serial links for bridges and routers over a WAN.

- **NCP (Network Control Protocol)** allows connections to be established for different network layer protocols. It is often used to provide routing, error control, testing, and addressing services for SNA (Systems Network Architecture) devices.

Meeting PAP and CHAP

You are most likely familiar with PPP from using it on a dialup connection to your ISP (Internet Service Provider). One of the features of PPP is security, including

- PAP (Password Authentication Protocol)
- CHAP (Challenge Handshake Authentication Protocol)

Although authentication is optional on a PPP connection, when it is required it can be performed using either PAP or CHAP. When it is required, the first step in establishing a PPP connection is *authentication* and when PAP is used, this is what happens:

1. The device requesting the connection sends an authentication request that includes the username and password of the requesting party to the processing router.

2. If the router recognizes the username and password as a valid combination, it returns an authentication acknowledgment.

Although PAP offers very basic authentication security, CHAP offers a more robust authentication process. *CHAP* is a procedure used to authenticate requests by users to connect to the network. CHAP, operating as the receiving device, initiates a challenge sequence that the user must verify before the connection can be established.

Here's how CHAP works:

1. A connection is made, and the receiving device transmits a challenge message to the requesting device. The requesting device responds with an encrypted value calculated by using a one-way math function.

2. The receiving device checks the response by comparing the response to its calculation of what should be the same calculated value.

3. If the two values match, authentication is acknowledged. If the values do not match, the connection is usually broken.

Connecting to the WAN with PPP

A router's serial port can be configured to support a PPP interface. This configuration enables the port to emulate PPP data encapsulation, which allows Cisco devices to communicate with non-Cisco devices across a WAN link. PPP is probably the best tool to use when you need to connect devices from different manufacturers over a WAN. This is in spite of the fact that PPP can be more complex to use than the default protocol, HDLC. Of course, Cisco's solution to this problem is to have all Cisco gear.

A serial port must be configured to use PPP before it supports PPP encapsulation over a serial connection. After the port is enabled for PPP, the interface subcommand **encapsulation ppp** is used to complete the configuration, where s0 is the subinterface number being configured:

```
CISCO_Networking(config)# interface s0
CISCO_Networking (config-if)# encapsulation ppp
```

Presenting the ISDN Twins

ISDN service operates over multiple 64 Kbps B channels, which carry payload (voice and data), and either a 16 Kbps or 64 Kbps D channel that carries command signals. It may sound like the names assigned to the channels were accidentally switched somewhere along the way, but they weren't.

- ✔ The bearer channel (B) bears the payload.
- ✔ The data channel (D) carries the data about the payload.

The number and combination of B and D channels differentiate the two available types of ISDN services.

There are two ISDN twins, and they are definitely fraternal twins.

- ✔ Primary Rate Interface (PRI)
- ✔ Basic Rate Interface (BRI)

Both use B and D channels in the same way, but beyond that, these "twins" are very different. Primarily the differences lie in their construction, but the way in which they are used is also a major difference. Which service you choose, providing either is available to you, depends on the access level that your network needs.

Parading along with PRI

One of the best uses for ISDN PRI services on a WAN is providing RAS (Remote Access Service) access to your network. ISDN PRI provides 23 dialup access lines that can be used by remote workers, customers, or whoever to gain dialup access to your network.

How does one ISDN PRI service line provide 23 dialup lines? PRI service consists of 23 B channels (30 in Europe) and one D channel, each of which carries 64 Kbps (the same bandwidth for a telephone system's DS0 line). Okay, with some simple arithmetic, this adds up to 24 channels, the same number of channels available on a T-1 or DS1 circuit, and 24 times 64 Kbps equals 1.536 Mbps. Where did the missing 8 Kbps go? When a T-1 line is channelized (in order for it to serve as a PRI service), 8 Kbps are lost to the channelization process and cannot be used for either data or control signaling. Also, in some implementations, the D channel may only use 16 Kbps of its available 64 Kbps.

Here is a summary of PRI service:

24 (23 B & 1 D Channels) × 64 Kbps (DS1) + 8 Kbps = 1.54 Mbps (T-1 or DS1)

Each of the PRI service's 23 B channels can have a separate telephone number assigned to it. This allows you to terminate 23 different dialup access connections at your network's router. An ISDN PRI line can be terminated in an RJ-45 connector and directly connected to an ISDN PRI interface on several Cisco router models. This simplifies the deployment of dialup RAS connections by reducing what would normally require multiple phone lines, modems, and connecting cables to a single interface point. ISDN PRI interfaces are typically added to a Cisco router as an optional module.

Unfortunately, ISDN PRI is not available everywhere, so if it is something you want to incorporate into your network, check with your Local Exchange Carriers (Incumbent [ILEC] or Competitive [CLEC]).

Bringing on the BRI

ISDN BRI service, which is intended for smaller applications, consists of two B channels of 64 Kbps each and one D channel with 16 Kbps. The arithmetic is much simpler for BRI than that of PRI. A BRI line has a combined bandwidth of 144 Kbps, consisting of the two B channels and one D channel (128 Kbps for the actual data and 16 Kbps used for control signaling). Here is an arithmetic look at the BRI service:

$$(2 \text{ B Channels} \times 64 \text{ Kbps [DS1]}) + (1 \text{ D Channel} \times 16 \text{ Kbps}) = 144 \text{ Kbps}$$

Connecting ISDN BRI to your network requires some special setup and configuration; it's a true case of less requiring more. BRI is usually configured on a Cisco router as a dial-on-demand routing (DDR) link. DDR is a Cisco IOS interface configuration type that provides several functions, including creating the illusion that the router has full-time connectivity over dial-up interface.

In order for calls to be made or received on an ISDN network through the router, specific network-wide configuration information is needed:

✔ **Directory numbers (one for each B channel):** Each channel must have a regular telephone number assigned.

✔ **Encapsulation type:** Typically, PPP encapsulation is used, which also sets the authentication type, preferably CHAP.

✔ **SPIDs (one for each B channel):** Service profile identifiers (SPIDs, pronounced "spids," of course) are assigned by the ISDN service provider to each B channel. However, not all switches absolutely require the use of SPIDs.

✔ **Switch type:** Table 14-2 lists the common switch types used on Cisco routers and their configuration keywords. This information should come from your service provider or LEC. Understand that the list in Table 14-2 is only a sampling of the switch types available.

There is no such thing as a standard SPID

A SPID is derived from the telephone number assigned to an ISDN BRI line. The telephone company can't identify anything without assigning it a telephone number. A SPID may or may not include an area code, and it could have a prefix (the first three digits of the phone number, also know as the local exchange) or suffix (the last four digits of the phone number). The common SPID formats, each unique to a particular switch type, are:

✔ **National ISDN-1 (NI-1/NI-2)** — includes a 3-digit area code, a 7-digit phone number, a 2-digit Sharing Terminal Identifier (from 01 to 32 — typically 01), and a 2-digit Terminal ID code (from 01 to 08 — also typically 01). Examples of this type SPID are

50955512120101 and 50955512130101 for the two lines of the BRI service.

✔ **AT&T 5ESS** — includes the identifier 01, the phone number of the BRI line, and a two-digit Terminal ID code (from 00 to 62 — typically 00) that is subscriber-defined. A BRI line from an AT&T 5ESS switch would have a SPID like 01555121200.

✔ **Northern Telecom (Nortel) DMS-100** — includes a 3-digit area code, the 7-digit phone number of the BRI line, a 1- or 2-digit SPID suffix (either 1 and 2 or 01 and 02), and a 2-digit Terminal ID code (from 00 to 62 — usually 00) that is subscriber-assigned. Examples of DMS-100 SPIDs are 50955512120100 and 50955512130200.

Table 14-2	ISDN Switch Types
Switch Type	Configuration Keyword
AT&T 5ess	primary-5ess
AT&T 4ess	primary-4ess
AT&T basic rate	basic-5ess
ISDN PRI	primary-dms100
National ISDN-1	basic-ni1
Nortel DMS-100 basic rate	basic-dms100

Defining some ISDN basics

Several characteristics are used to define and describe ISDN services, including the terminal type, reference points, protocols, channelization, and the type of service (BRI versus PRI; see the preceding section).

Are you my terminal type?

Two types of terminals or CPEs can connect to an ISDN network:

- ✔ **TE1:** Terminal equipment type 1 complies with the ISDN standards. TE1 devices are designated as ISDN-compatible devices. This includes such things as an ISDN telephone or fax machine.

- ✔ **TE2:** Terminal equipment type 2 can only be used when a terminal adapter is applied because TE2s were around before the ISDN standards were developed. This is stuff like an analog telephone or any interfacing device used to connect to an analog line.

If you are looking to connect your network to an ISDN service, you must know the ISDN terminal type of your terminating devices (usually a router or multiplexer). In most instances, this is a no-brainer, because any Cisco equipment with an ISDN interface is a TE1 type terminal. However, if you have equipment from other manufacturers or equipment a few years old, check with the manufacturer's Web site or your reseller for the ISDN terminal type.

Be sure that you ask your service provider for the "ISDN terminal type," which is information you will need for your router interface.

In order to connect your TE1 or TE2 equipment to an ISDN service, you must also use the correct network termination. Network terminating devices connect four-wire network cabling to two-wire service provided by the ISDN provider (usually a LEC). You can use two types of network termination:

- **Network termination type 1 (NT1):** In North America, NT1 equipment is the customer's CPE device. In most other parts of the world, NT1 devices are included in the network services provided by the ISDN carrier.

- **Network termination type 2 (NT2):** This type of network termination is used for digital private branch exchanges (PBXs).

In most cases, if you are connecting your LAN to an ISDN service, you will be using a NT1 network termination type to connect your TE1 or TE2 to the ISDN service.

A *terminal adapter* (TA) is a device that connects a computer to an ISDN line or any other type of digital communications line. A terminal adapter is like a digital modem that only passes digital signals between the computer and the ISDN service. Basically, a TA connects your TE2 equipment (described a little earlier in this section) to your ISDN service. Terminal adapters are available as either internal expansion cards or as external devices that connect to a serial port.

Knowing your points of ISDN reference

Another defining characteristic of ISDN interfaces (and yes, there are more) are four reference points or interfaces. A *reference point* designates the logical interface type and configuration of an ISDN connection. Five reference points are used to define ISDN logical interfaces:

- **R** — The interface type between a non-ISDN device and a terminal adapter (TA).

- **S** — The interface between a user terminal and an NT2 device.

- **T** — The interface between an NT1 device and an NT2 device.

- **S/T** — A common hybrid interface type used to connect terminal equipment to the NT1.

- **U** — The interface between NT1 or NT2 devices and the line-termination equipment on the carrier's network. The connection between the two-wire service provided by the LEC and your NT1 device is the U interface.

Just a little more about the S/T interface: It's the ISDN network inside your building. It begins at the NT1 device and ends with a bus termination, which is a terminating device placed at the end of your internal ISDN network. You can run ISDN throughout your network providing that the network's total length is 200 meters or less and that you connect eight or fewer devices. The cable connecting each network node can be up to 10 meters in length.

ISDN protocols

One last bit of ISDN definition — one that you may run into in your reading or troubleshooting. There are three basic types of ISDN protocols, which are designated with the letters E, I, or Q in their first letter:

- ✔ **E protocols** support ISDN on the PSTN (Public Switched Telephone Network).
- ✔ **I protocols** define ISDN concepts, terminology, and services.
- ✔ **Q protocols** define signaling and switching.

Figure 14-3 illustrates how all of the termination types, interfaces, and protocols are used together to create an ISDN network.

If you are planning to install an ISDN network, you will need more information than I have provided here. Usually, the interfaces shown between the network terminations in Figure 14-3 are provided by the connecting devices. What you need to provide is caution and interoperable devices.

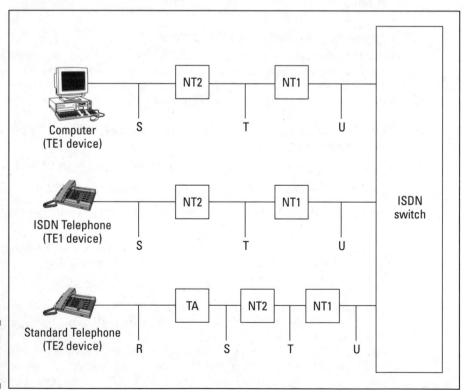

Figure 14-3:
An ISDN
network.

Taking the High-Speed ATM Highway

Most higher-end Cisco routers, switches, and access concentrators provide ATM (Asynchronous Transfer Mode) connections in either T-1 (DS1) or T-3 (DS3) transmission rates in support of both Frame-Relay and clear-channel (dedicated digital) services. As the Internet backbone grows and broadband wireless services, such as IMS (Industrial, Scientific, and Medical), LMDS (local multipoint distribution service) and switched wire-based services, become more available to end-users for WAN connections, public carriers (Telcos) will see increased demand for ATM services.

Differentiating synchronous and asynchronous

Unfortunately, understanding asynchronous without understanding synchronous is difficult. These are types of digital data transmissions that control, frame, or block data bits on transmission medium. At the heart of their difference is a clock or the lack of the same.

Staying in synch

Synchronous transmissions are closely timed to some form of a clock. Each transmitted block is sent in accordance with a set time interval. For example, block 1 is sent exactly at 0.0 msec (milliseconds), block 2 at 7.5 msec, block 3 at 15.0 msec, block 4 at 22.5 msec, and so forth. Synchronous modes are more efficient in situations where a more-or-less constant bit stream is flowing.

Synchronous signals are used to transfer data in and out of a CPU, around the computer's bus, and in and out of its parallel port. On a LAN or WAN, examples of synchronous data protocols are HDLC and SDLC (Synchronous Data Link Control).

Sending everything including the async

Asynchronous signals are not related to a clock. However, this doesn't mean that asynchronous signals are just transmitted willy-nilly either. Asynchronous transmission blocks have start and stop bits to mark the beginning and end of each character or block of data. Asynchronous transfers are more efficient when data is bursty and transmitted irregularly. Nearly all serial communications, except SDLC and HDLC, and virtually all LAN and WAN communications are asynchronous. As is usually the case, there are exceptions and, for example, the DB-60 serial ports on Cisco routers support synchronous devices.

Data transmissions from user workstations and LANs in general are bursty in nature. *Bursty* means that data isn't constantly being transmitted, and data tends to be sent in short flurries of activity. Because the computer is so much faster than the human using it, the computer spends most of its time waiting. When the user downloads something from the Internet, there is a burst of network transmissions made to access and download the requested information. However, while the user reads the data just downloaded, the transmission lines are idle and are awaiting another burst of data.

Looking at the infrastructure

The transmission lines originally installed throughout the United States and the rest of the world to carry wide area and high-speed communications were designed to carry voice traffic. All of the copper lines and, later, fiber-optic cables and the protocols and services that control the movement of signals over these lines were designed with one thing in mind — to get thousands and millions of simultaneous voice sessions to their destinations effectively.

The telephone companies developed time division multiplexing (TDM), which allows them to combine a number of voice circuits into a single physical medium. TDM ties each 64 Kbps circuit to a specific time slot and synchronizing interval. Should TDM, which is a synchronous mode, malfunction, you hear echoes or delays.

Video and multimedia transmissions must be treated like voice communications to avoid separating the sound and sight elements of the transmission. Like voice, video and multimedia are good matches for the use of synchronous transfer modes. However, synchronous transfer facilities can be very expensive.

ATM provides a compromise mode that can serve the needs of streaming data as well as bursty data. ATM breaks the data stream into fixed-length (53-byte) cells (as opposed to TCP/IP variable length frames) that are small enough to be carried across the medium very fast and, if lost, make a minimal impact on the transmission's quality. The combination of the small cell and high-speed communication carrier allows time-critical data, such as your online fashion show, to be transmitted right along with bursty data, such as your online search for information on ATM.

ATM effectively expands and contracts to supply the amount of bandwidth required for a particular communication task. ATM is scalable to a desktop, a departmental or campus backbone, a high-volume WAN, and the globally linked backbone of the Internet.

Digging deeper into ATM

ATM is a virtual circuit -based connection-oriented technology that transmits fixed-length cells over either copper or fiber-optic physical media. ATM is a hardware technology that performs its switching at the Data Link layer (Layer 2) of the OSI model. Because it is a hardware technology, very little in the way of delay is added to the switching process, as opposed to software switching, which adds significantly more latency to forwarding a frame.

ATM protocols are defined in, what else?, a layered model. However, the ATM model has only three layers, which are

- **ATM Adaptation Layer (AAL):** The top layer of the ATM protocol stack is the AAL, which includes different AAL standards to handle different types of data. AAL1 handles constant bit-rate traffic, such as voice traffic; AAL 3 / 4 and AAL 5 are used to handle different types of variable bit-rate data. The AAL procedures are used to interconnect the connection-oriented ATM with connectionless data sources.

- **ATM layer (ATM):** There is only one ATM layer, and it is the common core layer for all modes of ATM technology. The ATM layer handles routing and muxing and demuxing messages. *Muxing (multiplexing)* and *demuxing (demultiplexing)* are shorthand terms used for the process of combining multiple channels into a single channel and splitting a single channel into multiple channels, respectively. The ATM layer also creates the virtual paths (VP) that align the circuits in the path into a virtual circuit. A virtual path consists of semipermanent connections that are stored in the routing tables of routers and switches to map their incoming and outgoing interfaces into the VC to be used in the communication session. The ATM layer also has the responsibility of identifying and managing congestion, faults, and traffic flow.

- **Physical layer (PHY):** On its physical layer, ATM supports multimode and single mode fiber optic, STP (shielded twisted-pair), UTP (unshielded twisted-pair), coaxial cable, and throughputs to OC-192 (38 Gbps). ATM is very scalable and can be implemented as low as 9.6 Kbps, where needed. At 155 Mbps, ATM uses the standards for SONET (Synchronous Optical Networks) or SDH (Synchronous Digital Hierarchy), the latter being the international version of SONET. At 45 Mbps, ATM uses the DS3 standard over coaxial cable, and at 100 Mbps, ATM uses the physical standards for FDDI (Fiber Distributed Data Interchange).

Chapter 15

Designing Your Network

. . . .

. . . .

*Y*ou really shouldn't put the process of designing your network toward the end of your to-do list, which I have done in this book. However, it's something that you can't do, or at least you can't do well, without some knowledge of networking and internetworking fundamentals, media, software, and hardware. For that reason, I have held off on this chapter until after discussing some of the basics. I wanted to give you a chance to gain some understanding of Cisco networking before I addressed the considerations and process steps of network design.

Designing a Cisco network really involves matching the physical and logical components available to the needs of the organization. The easiest way by far to fit the best Cisco tools to your network needs is to work directly with your Cisco reseller or the fine folks at your local Cisco office.

Cisco also provides its version of the design processes and considerations I've described in this chapter. You can find all the internetworking design tips you'd ever want at www.cisco.com/univercd/cc/td/doc/cisintwk/idq4/.

Regardless of the specific design steps I recommend in this chapter, you must remember that every network is unique in some way. Gilster's Law of Network Design says that "You never can tell; and it all depends," which means that you won't find one surefire or pat network design, and the best design for your network really depends on the needs of your organization, its existing hardware and software, and you.

Gathering the Tools

Before you can begin doing the work of network design, you need to measure and collect some technical performance data about your existing network, assuming that you have one. You need to measure the planned network path, collecting the data that will help you to determine the distances over which your network will be stretched. This data must be analyzed to ensure that you aren't exceeding the limitations or capabilities of your physical media or planned networking devices.

If you are designing a new network, then read this section with an eye to the near future when you will need to upgrade your new network. No network configuration lasts forever.

Analyzing the analysis tools

You'll need some application software to generate performance data on your network. These tools can help (you can find the Cisco tools by searching the Cisco Web site at www.cisco.com):

- **CiscoWorks Windows:** This is a very handy tool for displaying in GUI form the status and configuration of Cisco internetworking devices on a network, as well as performing some troubleshooting and diagnostics and configuration activities. Versions of this product are available for the different versions of Windows NT and Windows 2000.

- **CiscoWorks Blue:** This version of CiscoWorks is an IBM mainframe application that provides SNA (Systems Network Architecture) resource information to the two CW client-side workstation applications: CW Blue Maps and SNA View. CW Blue itself doesn't have any end-user interface or functions.

- **CiscoWorks2000:** This product is actually a suite of network solution tools designed for use with virtually all types of networks. Its major components are the LAN Management Solution, the Routed WAN Management, the Service Management Solution, and the VPN/Security Solution.

- **Cisco Routed WAN Management Solution:** This is actually a group of WAN management tools that extends the capabilities of CiscoWorks2000, a bundle of network management software tools that includes Cisco WAN Manager, Equipment Manager, and CiscoView, among other tools. These tools allow you to view, monitor, and analyze the functions of a network, end to end. This bundle includes applications that can be used for configuring, administering, monitoring, and troubleshooting the routers on a WAN.

- **Cisco NetFlow:** This product, which is officially named the Cisco NetFlow FlowCollector with Network Data Analyzer (NDA), works with the IOS of most Cisco switches and routers to analyze network traffic. Data from the NetFlow NDA tools are collected and filtered and then passed back to the NetFlow-enabled devices on the network. This data provides information used for traffic analysis, network planning, and network monitoring. The Network Data Analyzer application can also be used to display the NetFlow data graphically.

- **Cisco Netsys Service-Level Management Suite (Cisco NSM):** This application suite provides tools to help you manage, monitor, and maintain a Cisco *internetwork* (a network that interconnects through a router or switch to other networks). The two primary modules of the NSM are the Connectivity Service Manager and the Performance Service Manager.

- **Cisco Netsys Baseliner:** Although it sounds like the economy version of the Cisco NSM, the Netsys Baseliner is a distinct and separate application that displays, debugs, and validates a network's configuration by creating a working and offline model of your network. This allows you to test and debug over 100 common network problems and simulate any configuration or topology changes before they are implemented. The Baseliner also provides you with a graphical view of your network's configuration. It checks for many common network configuration problems.

- **CiscoView:** This is also included in the CiscoWorks2000suite. CiscoView is a GUI-based management tool that can be used to view the status, activities, and configuration of either local or remote Cisco routers and switches.

- **Network Associate's Sniffer:** Several different Sniffer products exist, ranging from the Basic Analyzer model to the Sniffer Pro Packet over SONET. Sniffer applications perform fault and performance management for networks, capturing data, monitoring network traffic, and collecting network statistics. Visit `www.sniffer.com` for more information on Sniffer products.

- **NetSCARF (Network Statistics Collection And Reporting Facility):** NetSCARF is a set of standalone utility programs that collects and reports statistics on TCP/IP networks. NetSCARF is available free and can be downloaded from `ccuftp.ccu.edu.tw/pub2/packages/ net-research/netscarf/`.

You may want to take the time to evaluate each of these tools, especially the ones that you have to buy, in order to determine which of the tools is best suited for gathering network data on your network. These applications should provide you with two things:

- A graphic of a network's existing components
- The identification of any existing network bottlenecks or performance problems

Checking out the drawing tools

After you have some information on a network, you will probably want to depict your solution to its problems; or if you don't have an existing network, you may want to graphically represent what your networking masterpiece will look like. Despite the fact that your picture is worth at least a thousand words, you will still need to write out the justification and application of the network design for your boss, yourself, or posterity. Everyone will need to know — next week, next month, or next year — just what you were thinking when you designed the network.

You may want to consider these tools for use in documenting the network and your new design:

- ✔ **Microsoft Visio 2002:** This is perhaps the most popular diagramming tool among network administrators. It has a wide assortment of stencils, including network elements, connectors, and other drawing and charting objects that you can apply to create professional looking diagrams. Information on this product is available at `www.microsoft.com/office/visio/`.

- ✔ **Cisco ConfigMaker:** This is a free (downloadable from Cisco Systems' Web site) and easy-to-use Windows-based software tool that allows you to configure a network of Cisco networking devices (routers, switches, hub, and so on) and generate the bill of materials of the network components. To find more information and to download a copy of this tool, visit `www.cisco.com/warp/public/cc/pd/nemnsw/cm/`.

- ✔ **Word processing and other personal productivity software:** You will definitely need a word processor and maybe even an electronic spreadsheet or another application software package for use in documenting your network completely. You probably already have the software found in the Microsoft, IBM (Lotus), or Corel suites.

I can't overemphasize the importance of documenting the design of any new network or changes to an existing network. Trust me: A few months from now, you won't remember why you needed to make any changes that you're making or why you laid out the network the way you did.

Gathering the Facts

Any network that you design must meet one primary objective in order to be considered an effective network: It must support the objectives of the organization. Beyond that, its speed, its size, its complexity, its efficiency, and so on are all meaningless if the network just doesn't work in its environment.

In order to design a network that can fulfill this lofty goal now (and especially into the future), you need to understand where the company or organization is at present as well as where it plans to be (sales, employees, locations, and the like) in three to five years. How far into the future your network plan may extend will vary depending on your situation or the company's goals and objectives. Some network plans require little or no change for even the next ten years; others will be hard pressed to predict next quarter.

Understanding a little about the organization and its environmental influences may also be helpful. This includes such things as products, services, competitors, staffing, and technical infrastructure. At minimum, you need to know the organization's business goals for the near and long-term future.

The organization chart is a good place to begin your topology analysis. The network must support the implied requirements of the organization structure. The organization chart can be the key to such network characteristics and services as security, segmentation, WAN issues, and remote access. A study of the organization structure should reveal any geographical considerations of the network.

Profiling the Network

You should gather a good amount of technical information before beginning the design of a new network or before making major modifications to an existing network. Using a structured approach to gather the information needed is your best bet in order to accomplish two goals:

- No data is missed — all the information that you need is collected and available for analysis.
- The data is automatically documented to show just what it was you had in mind when you designed the network.

I recommend an eight-step process. I also recommend that you not skip a step, even if you are redesigning an existing network that you know quite well. You'd be surprised how unfamiliar you can be with your own network.

The tools you need to gather the information, at the level required, are described earlier in this chapter in the section titled "Gathering the Tools." You should also have a good understanding of the goals and objectives of the company, some information on the history and evolution of the network, and a very good idea of the requirements of the network's users. This information provides a context for the data you will gather as you work through our eight-step information-gathering process.

Taking inventory of the network applications

Figure 15-1 shows a sample form that can be used to document the applications supported on the network. This doesn't mean that you should document all the applications on each network workstation. This step focuses on just the major applications that have a specific impact on the performance and perhaps the structure of the network.

The inventory of the applications should also attempt to document any new applications that are likely to be added to the network in the near future. Again, you are looking only for the major applications that may have an impact on the network's performance.

	Application Name	Application Type	Number of User	Number of Hosts/Servers	Comments
1					
2					
3					
4					
5					
6					

Customer Name: _____   Date of Inventory: _____
Site Address: _____   Sheet number _____ of _____
City, State, ZIP: _____
Contact Person: _____   Phone #: _____

Figure 15-1: A sample form used to inventory the applications supported on a network.

Dear Diary: Keeping a network journal

Every network has a past. Regardless of how good, bad, or indifferent that past may be, it should be documented in a written history. Far too many networks have only an oral history that has been passed on from administrator to administrator, and as you might guess, the story gets more vague each time it is told. The answer to this problem is to steadfastly maintain a written network log and a network journal.

A *network log* contains dated entries that detail each maintenance, upgrade, or configuration change made to the network. It can exist in electronic form, in a text document, a worksheet, or a database, or it can be on a clipboard or in a binder. Its form really doesn't matter. Because nearly all networks will have multiple administrators over their lives, the value of this information store to each new succeeding administrator is immense. It should be kept where anyone working on the network can access it for information or to add an entry.

A *network journal* provides some of the philosophy and reasoning behind the network and its evolution. It is like the ship's log maintained by a sea captain. It addresses the who, what, when, why, and how of toplogy, configuration, and design issues of the network. Each change, modification, or upgrade to the network should be documented with a signed and dated entry that explains just what you were thinking, so that those who follow you don't have to wonder.

Making a list of the network protocols

Document the protocols operating on the network by using a form similar to that shown in Figure 15-2. The list of protocols should include all the protocols being supported on the network, including those of the workstations, peripherals, and WAN interfaces. This list should be inclusive, so that you don't overlook any network activity that is dependent on a particular protocol.

Figure 15-2:
A sample form for documenting the protocols used on a network.

	Protocol Name	Protocol Type	Number of User	Number of Hosts/Servers	Comments
1					
2					
3					
4					
5					
6					

Network Protocol Inventory

Customer Name: _____   Date of Inventory: _____
Site Address: _____   Sheet number _____ of _____
City, State, ZIP: _____
Contact Person: _____   Phone #: _____

Recording the network design

If you have an existing network to document, this step of the design process creates a comprehensive documentation of the network's topology, structure, and naming, among other characteristics. If you have been doing your job all along and maintaining the network log and journal, this step of the process shouldn't be too strenuous. If you have an up-to-date record of the network and its maintenance activity, verify the documentation, correcting it where necessary.

However, if the network has never been documented or if you have been shirking your administrative duties, you need to compile a complete documentation of the network as it exists today. In fact, that wouldn't be such a bad title for the data compilation you'll end up with: "The Network Today."

Whether you collect your data into a single document or into separate documents for each step of the process, you will want to organize it for easy access and analysis. Follow these steps to create the documentation of the network's design:

1. **Diagram the network topology.**

2. **On the topology diagram created in the previous step, document the data transfer speed rating of the hubs, switches, routers, and workstation NICs of each network segment.**

3. **Identify each of the major networking devices (servers, routers, switches, and so on) by name and address. Each device has a network name, ID, and IP address assigned to it. Add this information to the topology diagram for each node.**

4. **Write down the network media used throughout the network. Identify the type of cable used for each network segment, such as UTP, Thinnet, fiber optic, and so on.**

5. **Document all the network's addressing schemes, including the subnet masks (see Chapter 8) in use and the source of and to whom routable IP addresses are assigned and by whom.**

Record any ongoing network problems or concerns expressed by network users regarding the topology, security, performance, and so on, and any design issues to be addressed in the new design. This could involve the use of the network analysis software, such as the tools listed in "Analyzing the analysis tools," earlier in this chapter, or a *protocol analyzer* — a piece of equipment used to analyze the bits sent over the networking cable.

Accounting for network availability

You should focus on two indicators to determine how available the network has been to its users:

✓ **The network's average MTBF (mean time between failures):** You may need to determine this value as an average of the MTBF of each of the network's segments. The MTBF is calculated as the amount of time between *failures,* meaning the network or a segment is not available to users. Use a form similar to that shown in Figure 15-3 to determine the MTBF.

✓ **The financial impact of a network or segment failure:** It is not unusual for financial data to be unavailable, but in some instances, such as in a call center or inside sales department, the downtime of the network can translate directly into money. This is typically expressed as a per-hour amount.

	Segment Identity	MTBF	Date of Incident	Durabin	Cause
1					
2					
3					
4					
5					

Network Ability

Customer Name: _____   Date of Inventory: _____
Site Address: _____   Sheet number _____ of _____
City, State, ZIP: _____
Contact Person: _____   Phone #: _____

Figure 15-3:
A sample
form used
to record
information
on a
network's
availability.

Auditing the network's reliability

Not to be confused with availability, the network's *reliability* is determined by using the tools discussed earlier in this chapter (see "Gathering the Tools"). You can use a network monitor or network management tool on each segment to gather the data needed to make a determination about its reliability. A form like that of the sample shown in Figure 15-4 can be used to gather

- ✔ Total megabytes
- ✔ Total number of frames
- ✔ Total number of CRC errors
- ✔ Total number of MAC errors
- ✔ Total number of broadcast/multicast frames

Noting the network's utilization

About the best way to gather statistics on a network's utilization is to apply the network-monitoring tool you have selected and configure it to collect network utilization stats about once every hour. If the network is *saturated* (carrying data traffic equal to or greater than its bandwidth) or heavily used, you may want to gather data as often as every minute. Remember that *usage peaks* — which are spikes of bandwidth demand — of 40 percent or more above normal traffic levels that last more than one minute indicate high utilization and potential performance problems.

Raw Network Reliability

Customer Name: _____ Date of Inventory: _____
Site Address: _____ Sheet number _____ of _____
City, State, ZIP: _____
Contact Person: _____ Phone #: _____

	Segment Identity	Total Megabytes	Total Number of Frames	Total Number of CRC Errors	Total Number of MAC Errors	Total Number of Broadcast/ Multicast Frames
1						
2						
3						
4						
5						

Figure 15-4: A sample form used to gather raw data about a network.

Evaluating the router

The real story of a network, especially one with a connection to a WAN or with more than one router, is gained by evaluating the status of the existing routers. The configuration of a router that is working well has a wealth of information about the network to which the router is connected, including

- ✔ **The number and type of interfaces on the router:** The interface types installed and configured on the router indicate the transport or network technologies included in the network, such as Frame Relay, Ethernet, token ring, ISDN, and more. Use the **show interfaces** command to list the interfaces on the router.

- ✔ **The processes running on the router:** The **show processes** command displays the active processes running on the router and its resource utilization over the past five seconds, one minute, or five minutes. This command displays a matrix that includes the process ID, name, status, runtime, and other information. The types of processes and their recurrence let you categorize the actions of the router and its network.

- ✔ **The number of available buffers:** Included in the display produced by the **show buffers** command is an analysis of the buffers assigned to specific interfaces. *Buffers* are blocks of memory used to hold network packets during I/O operations. Five buffer types exist: small, middle, big, large, and huge. Buffers are either temporary, created and destroyed as needed, or permanently allocated. One of the key indicators that the router may be experiencing high traffic on a certain interface is the number of times the interface's buffer pool was depleted.

You can choose from virtually dozens of different versions of the **show** command for use in analyzing the actions, configurations, and connections of a Cisco router or switch. The documentation or CD-ROM that came with your Cisco equipment contains a "Command Reference" section that lists the **show** commands available on your particular device.

Use a form similar to the one shown in Figure 15-5 to document the information you learn about each router.

Figure 15-5:
A sample form for documenting a network's routers.

Router Status

Customer Name: _____   Date of Inventory: _____
Site Address: _____   Sheet number _____ of _____
City, State, ZIP: _____
Contact Person: _____   Phone #: _____

	Router Name	5 Minute CPU Utilization	Output Queue Drops/Hr	Input Queue Drops/Hr	Missed Packets per Hr	Ignored Packets per Hr	Comments
1							
2							
3							
4							
5							

Creating a scorecard

After completing the preceding steps, you should have a fairly good understanding of your network, new or old. With your newfound network knowledge, you should be able to grade the network by using a scorecard like that shown in Figure 15-6. Clearly mark those areas in which the network passes or fails.

Network Report Card

Grade	Criteria	Exceptions
☐	All Ethernet segments are at 40% or less utilization	_____
☐	All Toke Rings are at 70% or less utilization	_____
☐	All WAN links are at 70% or less utilization	_____
☐	The average and mean response times are less than 100 milliseconds.	_____
☐	All segments have less than 20% broadcasts/ multicasts.	_____
☐	All segments have less than one CRC error per million bytes of data.	_____
☐	Ethernet, less than 0.1% of the packets result in a collision.	_____
☐	Token Ring, less than 0.1% of the packets result in a collision.	_____
☐	FDDI, one or fewer operations per hour are not related to ring insertion.	_____
☐	All Cisco routers have a 75% or lower "5–minute CPU utilization rate.	_____
☐	All Cisco routers have less than 100 output queue drops per hour.	_____
☐	All Cisco routers have less than 50 input queue drops per hour.	_____
☐	All Cisco routers have less than 25 buffer misses per hour.	_____
☐	All Cisco routers have less than 10 ignored packets in an hour on any interface.	_____

Additional comments: _____

_____

_____

_____

_____

Figure 15-6:
A network
report card.

Classifying the Network

Networks can be classified into one of three general types of networks:

> ✔ **Hierarchical networks:** Cisco uses a three-tier network model that creates a hierarchy of network layers:
>
> • **Core layer:** The Core layer is where the biggest, fastest, and not surprisingly, most expensive routers (the ones with the highest model numbers) are found. Core layer routers merge geographically separated networks and move data as fast as possible, commonly over dedicated, leased lines. Dedicated lines are usually a part of a private network and aren't shared with other users. You won't find anything but switches and routers on this layer. The Cisco 7000 router series is typical of the routers found on this layer.

- **Distribution layer:** Routers on the Distribution layer connect what Cisco calls "large functional groups," such as the accounting department or sales department, or buildings. Distribution routers filter network packets and forward them either up or down to routers on the Core or Access layers. The Distribution layer also handles the routing between VLANs (virtual LANs). The bulk of your routing policy decisions are made on this layer. Distribution layer routers are in the Cisco 3600 series.

- **Access layer:** It is on this layer that host computers access a network and most network traffic finds its destination. Access layer routers and switches are used to create collision domains, segment LANs, and to define VLANs. Access layer routers are in the Cisco 2500/2600 series.

✔ **Redundant networks:** These robust, high-availability networks have *secondary pathing* (redundant routing), as well as redundant routers, switches, or servers, and even cable media. See "Building a redundant, redundant network," later in this section.

✔ **Secure networks:** A secure internetworking design contains hardware, software, or both to implement security services. An example would be a network with a firewall included. See "Securing the secure internetwork," later in this section.

Building a redundant, redundant network

A redundant network is usually designed to provide support for mission-critical systems, services, applications, or network paths. The ultimate in redundancy is that every possible single point of failure is eliminated. Depending on the reliability and availability needs of the network, you may want to adjust the design-level of the network from one that is fully redundant to one where you back up only those individual network components that must not fail. For example, if only the server and router on a network are deemed critical, then they may be the only devices with redundancy. Typically, the redundancy in a network is handled by the addition of a redundant (secondary) routing path between two points.

Four types of redundancy can be designed into a network:

✔ **Node-to-router redundancy:** If a particular network node must always be able to reach a router, it may be a good idea to provide redundant links to a single router or, even better, to two routers. This can be done by configuring the node with two (or more) network adapters connected to a single or multiple routers on separate cables.

✔ **Server redundancy:** If a server must be available at all times, the best solution is to include a mirrored server on the network. The mirrored server should be located on separate network segments and be powered from completely separate power sources. If this is overkill for your needs, then consider using some form of fault-tolerant hard disk system, such as a RAID (Redundant Array of Independent Disks) solution. Probably the least expensive and most easily implemented data redundancy technique is to simply use a tape backup to protect the data.

✔ **Route redundancy:** Providing redundancy over a WAN can be challenging, but when two critical networks are geographically separated, having redundant routes between them is important. A technique called *load balancing* can be applied to provide consistent loading that should translate into reduced network downtime. Load balancing is supported by most IP routing protocols for up to six paths over which network traffic can be balanced. Load balancing also helps smooth over the loss of any one of the servers by switching traffic to one or more other servers.

✔ **Media redundancy:** Designing two (or more) completely different media types into a network, especially a WAN, provides the assurance that should one type of media fail, the other, which should not be affected, can continue to carry the network's traffic. For example, if a WAN is linked by a fiber-optic landline and a wireless LMDS link and the fiber-optic line suffers *backhoe fade* (see the sidebar "Backhoe fade: Can you dig it?") the wireless link can keep the network alive. Of course, this works only if the two media types are not routed back to the same source, which means that true media redundancy requires the addition of route redundancy as well. On a LAN, multiple connections can be used between switches to provide for redundant links.

Securing the secure internetwork

A secure internetworking design is commonly implemented with a firewall, such as the Cisco Secure PIX Firewall. However, a firewall can be any device or software that has the responsibility to protect a network from any outside untrusted network, such as the Internet and its gangs of nasties.

Creating a design for a secure network involves the inclusion of a security device, not only to keep bad things out, but also to keep the bad things inside from doing any harm as well. You can secure a network in several ways. Here are some things you can include in your design to make your network more secure:

✔ **Packet filtering on a router:** You should place packet-filtering services used as a part of a security scheme on the routers before or after bastion hosts on the network, as depicted in Figure 15-7. A *bastion host* is a secure host, in this case buffered by the packet filtering routers, supporting limited applications that can be accessed by outsiders.

✔ **Firewall appliances:** Some network hardware appliances, such as the Cisco Secure PIX Firewall, are specifically designed to operate as firewalls. When these are included in a network, bastion host servers, to which you want to provide access to outside users, are placed in a DMZ (demilitarized zone). The DMZ both physically and logically separates these devices from all other parts of the network, so that access to this part of the network does not provide access to any other network resources. Figure 15-8 illustrates this setup. See Chapter 19 for more information of firewalls in general and the Cisco Secure PIX in particular.

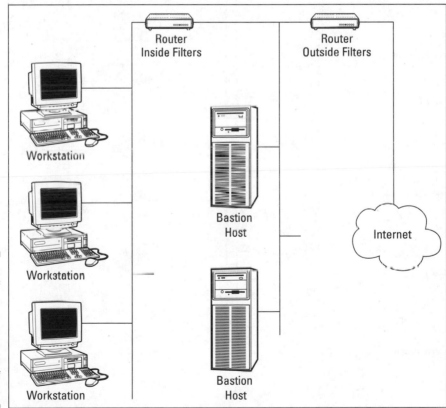

Figure 15-7:
The use of bastion hosts on a network can add to the network's security design.

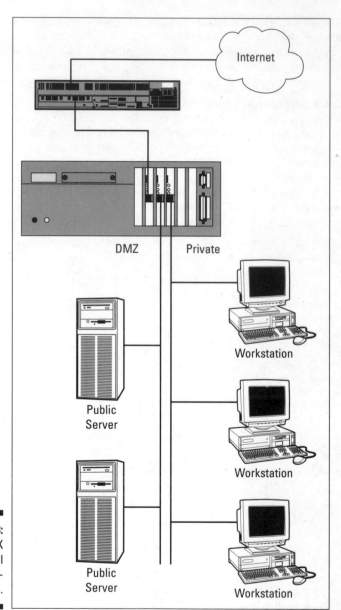

Figure 15-8:
A PIX
firewall
implemen-
tation.

Backhoe fade: Can you dig it?

Fade, in the telecommunications world, is a loss of service quality or connectivity. A connection may fade for several reasons. If you've ever had a cell phone, you understand the concept of fade.

A very common cause of service interruptions is referred to, with tongue-in-cheek, as *backhoe fade*. This phenomenon is the result of somebody digging in the area of a buried cable, which never fails to be the main service fiber bundle. Backhoe fade is usually the cause when your entire town suddenly loses its Internet backbone connection. Backhoe fade is why you see those signs posted that say "Call before you dig!"

Part IV
The Softer Side of Cisco

The 5th Wave   By Rich Tennant

"I guess you could say this is the hub of our network."

In this part . . .

This part could just as easily have been titled "Working with the Cisco IOS" or "Configuring a Cisco Network," but the title I chose better reflects the nature of the administrator's job. Cisco networks must be managed, which includes administration, configuration, monitoring, and in most situations, swearing, stomping, praying, pouting, and sacrificing network segments to the gods.

This part of the book provides an overview of how a network administrator works with a Cisco router, including working with the command line interface and muddling through the configuration processes.

Chapter 16

Working with the IOS

This chapter covers only the most basic router commands and operations, so nothing in it is especially mentally taxing. However, you should have a steel-trap grasp on these commands, concepts, and operations because this is the stuff you work with day in and day out. I guide you through the processes used to log into a router from a variety of different sources. Although you can use more than 17 different operating modes after you have logged in, you should only use about 6 of them in real day-to-day life.

This may not be the most important chapter in the book, but it's certainly among the top 24. If you've had some good hands-on experience with Cisco routers, chances are good that you already know this stuff. However, if you're just getting started, this is very important foundation knowledge.

Operating the IOS

First of all, the Cisco IOS is not a variation of the ISO OSI, although it does share the same three letters of the organization and its network model. The Cisco IOS (Internetwork Operating System) can be likened to the Windows or Linux or UNIX operating system running on your personal computer. IOS is the operating system in many of Cisco's middle- to high-end routers, switches, access controllers, and other devices. And like the other operating systems mentioned, it has most of the standard elements you associate with an operating system: a user interface, a command interface, help, and error messages (an all-too-necessary part, unfortunately).

Believing that the IOS performs all of the functions in a Cisco router or switch is very easy. In reality, *IOS* is a true operating system that supports the functions of other routines and features of its device and those added on optional modules, both hardware and software.

The version of the IOS in a device is a critical factor that determines which functions, features, and capabilities a router or switch may have or support. Table 16-1 lists the major releases of the Cisco IOS and what was notable about each one.

Table 16-1		Cisco IOS Releases
Version Number	Release Date	Features
8.3	10/91	Added HSSI port and improved the setup function
9.0	4/92	Support for token ring and flash memory cards and dial-on-demand (DoD) functions
10.0	5/96	Supported router series 2500, 3000, 4000, and 7000
11.0	2/97	Organized IOS in groups of feature sets that could be used in combination to configure features on various models
12.0	11/98	Added additional feature sets and support for new features, such as VoIP

The current version of the Cisco IOS is release 12.2, released in March 2002. However, as far as what the administrator sees, the IOS has had the same look and feel since its beginning. It isn't the most friendly user interface around, especially to those of you who grew up in the Windows generation, but it is a powerful configuration and control tool. The remainder of this chapter provides a look into its interfaces and functions.

Oh Phooey; There's No GUI

The user interface presented by the Cisco IOS is its Command Line Interpreter (CLI). If you've seen the interface, you know that it is not the most friendly, as in pretty, full-of-graphics, and easy to use. However, the fact of the matter is that if you wish to have success in operating a Cisco router, the path lies through the CLI.

If you remember the DOS command line, that paragon of user-friendliness, you should have little or no problem with the CLI. However, if your technical life has been spent in the warm and safe cocoon of GUI (graphical user interface) screens and mouse clicks, the CLI may present a challenge.

Depending on your background, the CLI can be like an old friend you use every day, or it can be a cursed multiheaded monster that's constantly attempting to turn your life into sheer terror. If the latter is the case, remember that practice and perseverance are the virtues to conquer the monster and win the day. Feel better now? You will.

Meeting the CLI

As an introduction to the command line interpreter, you need to have an overview of the various rules, procedures, and actions you must, may, and can take to set up, configure, and work with your router from the start. Here are the things that we think you need:

- ✔ **Syntax:** You must have a basic understanding of the structure of the various commands and what the most common abbreviations mean.

- ✔ **Access:** You can access the router in only a handful of ways, and you should know the procedure used to enter the router through each.

- ✔ **Logging in:** The router should be secured through a series of passwords, and you must know which of the five passwords you use to gain the level of access you need.

- ✔ **Mode:** You use different command-line modes to enter the various commands of the Cisco IOS (the router's operating system — see Appendix A for a list of the more common IOS router commands), and you do need to know which mode you need to be in to take certain actions.

Spelling and syntax: getting it right

Without sounding too much like your high school English teacher, spelling and syntax are crucial elements of the CLI and its successful use. You want a command to be successfully executed? Make sure that you do at least these two things:

- ✔ Spell the command and its parameters and components correctly.

- ✔ Get all of the command's parameters and components in their right places.

The world of Cisco internetworking is rampant with abbreviations. Fortunately, most of the abbreviations are what I call TLAs (three- [or two-] letter acronyms), such as RIP, OSI, ARP, TCP, IP, and the like; but you will also encounter FLAs (yes, four-letter acronyms) and the dreaded EFLAs (the extended four-letter acronyms). TLAs and FLAs are commonly used as abbreviations for names and descriptors of networking protocols and technologies.

Speaking of abbreviations, you should know that Cisco IOS commands and parameters can be abbreviated to any length that still uniquely identifies the command or parameter. For example, the command **configure terminal** can be abbreviated to **conf t,** which contains enough of the original command to avoid being ambiguous. The shortest unique abbreviation for configure is **conf.** The abbreviation "con" wouldn't work because of the **connect** command. How would your router know which command you actually wanted? On the other hand, **terminal** is the only parameter of the **configure** command that starts with the letter *t,* so you only need that much to have it recognized. You can find other examples of abbreviated commands and parameters throughout this chapter.

At any time, you can enter as much of a command as you remember followed by a space and a ? (question mark), and the IOS will display the syntax and command structure of the command you've entered. This is one way to verify that you're using the correct command before you use it for real. See "Getting By with a Little Help," later in this chapter, for information on getting help on the command line.

Accessing the router

You can access the router for configuration via one of several routes:

- ✔ Asynchronous serial port
- ✔ Auxiliary port
- ✔ Virtual terminal connection with the TCP/IP Telnet protocol
- ✔ TFTP (Trivial File Transfer Protocol) server
- ✔ SNMP (Simple Network Management Protocol) network management station
- ✔ HTTP (HyperText Transfer Protocol) server

All Cisco routers have a console port — an asynchronous serial port — located on the back of the router and aptly labeled CONSOLE. The *console port* is used to connect a computer to the router and, through a *terminal emulator* (such as Windows HyperTerminal, SecureCRT from Van Dyke Technologies, or the like), to create an interactive control console on the router.

Most Cisco routers also have an auxiliary port, labeled cleverly as AUX, located just to the right of the console port. The *auxiliary port* allows a dial-up modem to be attached, and asynchronous remote dialup access can be used along with a terminal emulator to configure or control the router.

In addition to using the console and auxiliary ports, you can also access the router via a virtual terminal connection with the TCP/IP Telnet protocol. *Telnet* is used to connect to remote devices, including routers, over a network.

TFTP differs from FTP (File Transfer Protocol) in that TFTP does not verify each packet of data transferred, which makes it very fast but sometimes unreliable. TFTP is commonly used as a means to store and restore a router's IOS configuration files (see Chapter 17) on a remote host. Because the size of these files is not all that large and because you are generally connecting over a local network, any risk is virtually removed. Any host running the TFTP software is a TFTP server. You can also access a router from a *network management station,* which is any workstation running network management system that supports SNMP, such as HP OpenView or What's Up Gold or the like. Cisco routers (and most of their other networking devices for that matter) are SNMP-compatible, which means that they can be accessed and managed remotely.

If you insist on having a GUI display, then I suggest that you interface to the Cisco IOS through a browser.

Logging into the router

To gain access to a Cisco router, you must know the password for the type of access you want to gain. A single router can have up to five different passwords, one for each type of access, but having only one password set for all login types is not uncommon. It should be noted that none of the five passwords available for use on a Cisco router are preset with a default value. You have to configure and enable any of the passwords you want to use.

However, Cisco warns that the encrypted password created with the **enable secret** command should never be the same as any of the other passwords. The secret password is the system administrator's edge in router security. It is encrypted when created and stored in the configuration files, so it cannot be discovered. All other passwords are stored in clear text in the configuration data.

Figure 16-1 illustrates the action of logging into a router. In general, whether you log in from the console port or the auxiliary port, or over one of the other access methods, you must know a password to gain access to the Exec command interpreter. Using the command line interpreter (CLI), you may access User and Enable (also called Privileged) mode commands and actions, some of which may require an additional password. See "Oh Phooey; There's No GUI," earlier in this chapter, for information on the CLI.

However, your Cisco IOS passwords do not have to be stored as clear text. The Cisco IOS uses the service command to apply a group of IOS services, including one to encrypt passwords. If you do not encrypt a router's passwords, they are easily obtained by anyone who can gain a copy of your configuration. To encrypt your passwords, all except the enable secret that is already encrypted, use the following command:

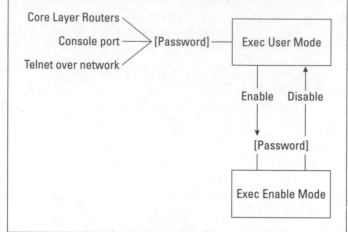

Figure 16-1:
The levels of
passwords
used to log
into the
router.

```
Cisco_Networking(config)#service password-encryption
```

After you have turned on the encryption service, you must next change the passwords you want to have encrypted. To turn off encryption for any future password configurations (already encrypted passwords will remain encrypted), enter the reversing command:

```
Cisco_Networking(config)#no service password-encryption
```

Working with the Exec command interpreter

The working name for the CLI is the Exec command interpreter. The Exec command interpreter has two Exec modes, or command groups, that can be used to perform a variety of functions:

✔ **User Exec:** After you successfully log into the router, meaning that you entered the appropriate password correctly, you automatically enter User Exec mode. In this mode, you can connect to other devices (such as other routers) to perform simple tests and display system information. You'll know that you're in User Exec mode if the prompt displayed on your screen looks like this:

```
Router>
```

In this example, "Router" represents the assigned name of the router. This is the default name. Later in this chapter, I show you how to assign the router a new, better, and funkier name (see "Giving the Router an Identity"). However, it's the greater than sign (>) that's significant here.

When this symbol appears in the prompt, it means you're in User Exec mode.

✔ **Enable Exec:** Also known as Privileged or Privileged Exec, this mode is accessed from User Exec mode through the **enable** command and a password. If an Enable Exec mode password has not been set, this mode can be accessed only from the router console port. You can perform all User Exec mode functions from within Enable Exec mode. Plus, you have access to higher-level testing and debugging and detailed probing of the router functions, plus the ability to update or change configuration files. The prompt that indicates this mode is

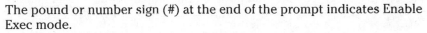
```
Router#
```

The pound or number sign (#) at the end of the prompt indicates Enable Exec mode.

Running in other command modes

Most of the time, your work on the Cisco router is through either the User Exec mode or the Enable Exec mode, but you may have occasion to use a few other command line modes. A few of the command modes you can use on your Cisco router are:

✔ Configuration mode

✔ ROM Monitor mode

✔ Setup mode

ROM Monitor mode

The ROM Monitor mode is displayed during the boot process if no operating system is loaded in the flash memory (see Chapter 17). From this mode, the router's configuration can be completed. After configuring the router so that it may complete the startup process, the **continue** command moves you into User Exec mode. The prompt that indicates this mode is either just a greater than sign or the prompt

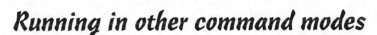
```
rommon>
```

However, the ROM Monitor mode can be avoided by booting the system from an alternative source, such as a TFTP server.

Setup mode

When a router is first configured from the console port, Setup mode is invoked. Setup mode can also be invoked from the Enable Exec mode prompt with the **setup** command, or by rebooting the router after deleting its startup-config file through the **erase startup-config** command.

The **setup** command is a prompted dialog that guides you through the setup process to configure the router. This action has no special prompt. You should know that after you erase the startup-config file, which is stored in the flash memory, the router will be in Setup mode when it is restarted.

Another way to restart the router is to issue the **reload** command.

Configuration mode

Like the Setup mode, you enter the Configuration mode through a command, in this case, the **configure** (or its short version, **config**) command.

To move into what is called the Global Configuration mode, enter the following **config** command at the Enable Exec prompt (the one with the # symbol):

```
Cisco_Networking#config terminal
```

The parameter **terminal** or its abbreviation **t** is absolutely necessary. There are other **config** command variations. For example, the **config net** command can be used to configure a router from the network, and the **config mem** command is used to configure a router from memory. Configuring a router from the network involves loading a configuration file from a TFTP server into the router's RAM before making configuration changes. Configuring a router from memory involves loading the startup-configuration file into RAM and editing it.

Configuration mode (also known as *Global Configuration mode*) allows you to configure the router manually or make changes to the router's status. You may also move to another mode within Configuration mode — the Configuration Interface mode — to make changes to individual interfaces. It is easy to distinguish the configuration mode from the configuration interface mode by their mode prompts. The configuration mode looks like this:

```
Router(config)#
```

And the configuration interface mode looks like this:

```
Router(config-if)#
```

This should be fairly easy to remember. The word *config* without any other additions indicates plain ol' Configuration mode. The word *config-if* indicates that you are in Configuration Interface mode. The suffix *-if* means Interface.

Getting By with a Little Help

Getting help on a Cisco router is actually fairly easy. Two levels of context-sensitive help are available to assist you with IOS commands. In fact, Cisco IOS tries to guess what you are trying to do and provides you with help in both the User Exec and Enable Exec modes.

The two levels of context-sensitive help available on the command line from the IOS are:

- ✔ **Word help:** The IOS tries to recognize the command you are entering from as few keystrokes as possible — sometimes even from a single keystroke.

- ✔ **Command syntax help:** If you are unsure of a command's syntax or required or optional parameters, the IOS will provide you with the command structure and parameter list if you forget.

What's a four-letter word beginning with an h?

Suppose, for example, that you know Cisco has a specific command to perform a task, but you can't remember its command word. By typing its first letter (or as many letters as you feel are needed) and a question mark without a space in between, the router displays a list of the available commands that begin with that letter. If multiple commands meet your criteria, they are all displayed. For example, entering *cl?* on the command line interface produces the following results:

```
Router#cl?
clear clock
```

The display indicates that two commands begin with *cl:* the **clear** command and the **clock** command.

In this example, the # is indicating the Enable Exec mode.

The location of the question mark in the command line entry is very important. If you include no space before the question mark, as in *cl?,* the command line interface lists all the commands that begin with *cl.* If you include a space before the question mark, as in *cl ?,* the command line interpreter attempts to display the next element of syntax for the command.

However, entering the letter *c* followed by a space and then a question mark *(c ?)* will not get you a list of all the commands that begin with *c.* Instead, you will get the response Ambiguous Command. Remember that the space in the command line indicates you wish the CLI to complete the command line for you, if it can. Because it can't, it tells you that it doesn't have a clue as to what command you want.

Choosing from a list

To see all the commands available for a command mode, simply enter a question mark at the command prompt. If the list being displayed requires more than one screen, only the first screen of information is displayed followed by the - - more - - prompt.

For you UNIX, Linux, and DOS buffs, you probably know the **more** command very well. For those of you not of those persuasions, you can advance the display by either pressing the spacebar to advance to the next screen of information or by pressing the Enter key to move the display up one line at a time.

Another trick available to you when you have **more** enabled is that you can use the slash character ("/") to search for a string of text in the displayed output.

Helping the terminally lazy

Another gee-whiz feature built into the user interface of the Cisco router is really great for people who don't like to type. For example, suppose that late at night you've just finished configuring a distant router through a Telnet session. You're so tired that you can barely keep your eyes open, much less type. So, to end the Telnet session, you type **disc** and then press the Tab key. Lo and behold, the word *disconnect* is magically completed for you.

Try this quick quiz: Which key do you press to complete a word or a shortcut command? If you said the Tab key, good going. If you said anything else, take this quiz again and keep taking it until you get the answer right.

Okay, now show me the rest

Another level of context-sensitive help available from the Cisco IOS is *command syntax help* that displays the remaining command elements for a partially entered command string. If you enter the command, or at least enough of the command so that it can be recognized, followed by a space and a question mark, the command line interpreter displays the next parameter of the command. For example, Figure 16-2 illustrates a portion of what is displayed when the command string *show ?* is entered in Enable Exec mode.

```
Cisco Networking_For_Dummies#show?
WORD                Flash device information-format<dev:>[partition]
access-expression       List access expression
access-lists            List access lists
accounting              Accounting data for active sessions
aliases             Display alias commands
arp                     Arp Table
async                   Information on terminal lines used as router interfaces
.
.
.
```

Figure 16-2:
The results
of the
show ?
command
on a Cisco
router.

Controlling the Present through the Past

The user interface of the Cisco IOS includes some features to allow you to review and reuse commands you've entered in the past, to move the cursor around the command line or its history, or both. In this section, we will provide you with an overview of

- **Working with the command history:** The Cisco IOS allows you to scroll back through all previously entered commands to review what you've already entered.

- **Command line shortcuts:** The Cisco IOS includes a variety of keyboard commands, called *enhanced editing,* that allows you to control the cursor position and move it directly to certain points on the command line or its history.

- **Combining the editing features:** When used together, the ability to access the command history and the enhanced editing features, you can move back into the command history to edit and reuse long or complicated commands instead of re-entering them again.

Editing history

Another feature of the Cisco router IOS user interface is access to the command history. If you are of the UNIX/Linux persuasion, this kind of feature is old hat to you; but if you are a DOS/Windows person, this feature will seem like a gift from the gods. Although, for those of you that have moved on to Windows, almost all of the later versions of Windows include a command buffer history.

The command history is a chronological listing of the commands that have been entered or displayed on the router in the current session. Depending on the Cisco device, you may have by default 10 to 20 of the previous commands available for review or reuse. On most Cisco devices, you have the ability to set the size of the command history buffer through the terminal history command.

The command history is a very handy feature because during a logged-in session, you can recall previously entered commands — especially those long or complex commands — and access lists you sweated bullets over and finally got right. Any of the entries in the command history buffer can be edited, copied, or removed. This gives you flexibility and saves you time because you don't have to re-enter a long command string that really only needs some minor editing or a new IP address to be used again. The ability to edit the IOS command history allows you to copy these long sequences for reuse or to check back on an earlier action that may need correcting. Remember that the history is only the short-term past — actually, only the history from the current session is available and then only to the limit of the buffer size set for your device. After you save the running-configuration and log off, poof — it's all gone.

The Cisco IOS uses a special set of keyboard commands, which are included in the enhanced editing commands (see "Using enhanced editing," later in this section) to recall the command history. Some devices, such as the Catalyst switches and high-end routers, have their own set of commands, called the *history substitution* commands, that can be used to access, retrieve, and replace entries in the command history. Table 16-2 lists a few of the history substitution commands available to some Cisco internetworking devices.

Table 16-2	History Substitution Commands
Keyboard Entries	*Action*
Repeating recent commands:	
!!	Repeat the most recent command
!-nn	Repeat the nnth most recent command (where nn is the number of commands prior to the current command)
!n	Repeat command number n
!aaa	Repeat the command beginning with the string aaa (where aaa is a text string)
!?aaa	Repeat the command containing the string aaa anywhere in the command
To modify and then repeat the most recent command:	
^aaa^bbb	Replace the string aaa with the string bbb in the most recent (immediately preceding) command

Keyboard Entries	*Action*
To add a string at the end of a previous command and repeat it:	
!!aaa	Add string aaa to the end of the most recent command
!n aaa	Add string aaa to the end of command n
!aaa bbb	Add string bbb to the end of the command beginning with string aaa
!?aaa bbb	Add string bbb to the end of the command containing the string aaa

Using enhanced editing

Enhanced editing mode is designed to make your life with routers easier. It provides you with such timesavers as the ability to enter one or more commands quickly by repeating one or more entries. Enhanced editing is actually a series of keystroke combinations that move the command line cursor about, recall recent commands, or complete entries for you automatically.

To use enhanced editing commands, you press the key combinations together to cause the associated action. For example, to move to the end of the current command line, press Ctrl+E (uppercase or lowercase; it doesn't matter). The cursor moves to the end of the current command line.

To show how truly enhanced it is, enhanced editing is automatically enabled in either User Exec mode or Enable Exec mode. (See "Working with the Exec command interpreter," earlier in this chapter, for more information.) To disable it, enter the command line **terminal no editing.** To turn it back on, enter **terminal editing.** Some of the other important enhanced editing keyboard commands that you will find handy are listed in Table 16-3.

Table 16-3	**Enhanced Editing Keyboard Commands**
Key(s)	*Action*
Ctrl+A	Move to the beginning of the current line
Ctrl+E	Move to the end of the current line
Ctrl+B (or ←)	Move back one character
Ctrl+F (or →)	Move forward one character
Ctrl+N (or ↓)	Recall most recent command

(continued)

Table 16-3 *(continued)*

Key(s)	Action
Ctrl+P (or ↑)	Recall previous command
Esc+B	Move back to beginning of previous word (or beginning of current word)
Esc+F	Move forward one word
Tab	Complete the current word

Changing history

By combining the Cisco IOS's ability to edit the command history with the enhanced editing feature, you have the complete toolset to really do some serious editing.

Remember, the ↑ or the key combination Ctrl+P can be used to scroll back up through the recent history of commands and actions on the router. These two interchangeable commands, along with the Ctrl+A (move to the beginning of the current line) command, are the most commonly used editing commands.

You can use these configuration commands in editing the command history:

- **show history:** This command displays the contents of the command history.

- **terminal history size:** This command is used to change the default value of how many lines of the command history are to be displayed by a **show history** command. The default is set to show the last ten commands.

- **terminal no editing:** This command turns off the enhanced editing feature and is used to exit enhanced editing.

- **terminal editing:** This command turns the enhanced editing feature on. Enhanced editing is on by default and must be turned off with the **terminal no editing** command.

Let's Play Password

Passwords play an important role in the security of your router, protecting its configuration and access lists from evildoers. In the same way that passwords are used to protect data networking elements by verifying that someone logging in has authorization to do so, passwords protect your network's routers as well. Earlier in this chapter, we discussed when you need a password to log into the router (see "Logging into the router"). A Cisco router can have up to five different passwords, each on a different level. You will find that knowing the processes used to manage and modify router passwords is very helpful.

Don't be so sensitive

Cisco router passwords are case sensitive, which means that it really does matter whether an alphabetic character is uppercase or lowercase in a password. In the ASCII (American Standard Code for Information Interchange) character set, every displayable character has a different hexadecimal and binary value. An uppercase *A* has a different numerical value than a lowercase *a*. So when you create a password, remember that it will be stored exactly how you enter it — in other words, case SenSiTiVe. Also remember that when you use it to access the router, you must enter it exactly as it was stored — again, case SenSiTiVe.

Getting into Configuration mode

The first step in the procedure used to change (which includes setting it for the first time) a password on a Cisco router is to be in Terminal Configuration mode, (also known as Global Configuration mode). To get to Terminal Configuration mode, use the following series of prompts and commands:

```
Router#config t
Enter configuration commands, one per line. End with CNTL/Z.
```

After you're in Terminal Configuration mode, the router name will be followed by the word *config* in parentheses — *(config)* — indicating that you are in Terminal Configuration mode.

Changing the locks

You can set and use five different passwords in a Cisco router:

- Enable Secret
- Enable
- Virtual Terminal
- Console
- Auxiliary

The passwords are in this sequence to indicate their importance to gaining access to the router and having the most access to critical configuration settings. If you are concerned with the security of your router, pay attention to the passwords in this order. The following sections show the commands used to set each password.

Cisco router passwords are divided into two groups with different security policies applied to the groups. The first group, Enable Secret and Enable passwords, is much more secure than the other group — the User passwords — which includes the Virtual Terminal, Console, and Auxiliary passwords.

Setting the Enable Secret password

The Enable Secret password adds a level of security over and above the Enable password. When set, this password, which is one-way encrypted, has precedence over the Enable password.

Without sounding like the CIA, one-way encryption is a hashing algorithm that converts the password into a 128-bit or 160-bit value, depending on the device. This encryption scheme is based on a security process called the *Secure Hash Algorithm*. Cisco claims that it is impossible to decode an Enable Secret password by using the contents of a router's configuration file.

The following statements show the commands used to set the Enable Secret password:

```
Router(config)#enable secret gilster
Router(config)#^Z
```

The ^Z entry is what's displayed when you press Ctrl+Z, which is the enhanced editing command for ending configuration mode and returning to the Exec mode. (See "Using enhanced editing," earlier in this chapter.) If you enter a carat (^) followed by a Z, as is displayed in the preceding example, the command line interpreter won't have a clue what you're trying to do.

Setting the Enable password

Your best bet is to set the Enable Secret password and not use the Enable password. The only difference between these two passwords is the level of encryption (see "Setting the Enable Secret password," earlier in this chapter). The Enable password is not encrypted, which is the best reason to not use it. No claims of invulnerability are made for the Enable password.

The Enable password is also used for older router software versions. The router uses the Enable password only when no Enable Secret password has been created.

The following statements are used to set the Enable password:

```
Router(config)#enable password gilster
The enable password that you have chosen is the same as your
          enable secret.
This is not recommended. Re-enter the enable password.
Router(config)#enable password h3110
Cisco_Networking(config)#^Z
```

Cisco recommends that the **enable password** command no longer be used in favor of the **enable secret** command. The folks at Cisco feel that this provides for better router security.

Setting the Virtual Terminal password

The Virtual Terminal password is used to gain access to a router through a Telnet session. Unless this password, also known as the *vty password,* is set, you cannot Telnet into the router.

The following statements show the commands used to set the Virtual Terminal password:

```
Router(config)#line vty 0 4
Router(config-line)#login
Router(config-line)#password kevin
Router(config-line)#^Z
```

The **line** command enters Line Configuration mode, which is used to configure physical access points, such as Telnet, and the console and aux ports. The **vty 0 4** part of the command line specifies that the password entered will apply to vty (virtual terminal) lines 0 through 4. Setting a different password for each different vty line is possible.

In order to set a password on the vty lines, you must first indicate the lines to be affected. In this case, the command **line vty 0 4** is the first line of the commands and indicates that the actions that follow it should affect the login password for all five virtual terminal lines.

Setting the Console password

The Console password is used to gain access to the router through the console port. To set the console password, use the following commands (changing the password, of course):

```
Router(config)#line con 0
Router(config-line)#login
Router(config-line)#password tur71e
Router(config-line)#^Z
```

Setting the Auxiliary password

The Auxiliary password controls access to any auxiliary ports on the router. To set the password for this interface, use the following commands:

```
Router(config)#line aux 0
Router(config-line)#login
Router(config-line)#password pi22a
Router(config-line)#^Z
```

Giving the Router an Identity

Do nothing. That is, do nothing if you want the generic name "Router" to display on every prompt line, and you don't plan to update or access your router from another router or other SNMP device. Your router is perfectly happy and functional with the router name "Router." But if you have more than one router in your network or you do plan to interact with other nearby routers on the WAN, then it may be a good idea to give your router an identifying name, even if it is only "RouterA."

Not naming your router would be like not giving a baby a name when it is born. This poor child would have to go through life as "Child," "Kid," "Boy," "Girl," or some other unidentifying nondescript name. To avoid an identity crisis for your router, we believe that you will want to give your router its own unique name, or its own *hostname*. If fact, we highly recommend that you assign a hostname for the router.

Follow just two simple rules to assign a hostname to your router:

✔ The router must be in global configuration mode. (See "Configuration mode," earlier in the chapter.) When you're trying to remember all the details of configuring a router, it can seem that all configuration actions are carried out under Configuration mode. That's why I'm making such a big deal out of this.

✔ The command used to assign the hostname is **hostname.** What did you expect? The command you'd use to assign a hostname to your router would be much like this sample:

```
Router(config)#hostname Cisco_Networking
```

To avoid confusion, especially when administering multiple routers on a network from a central location, hostnames shouldn't be duplicated within a LAN. If you have more than one router on a LAN, do yourself a favor and assign each a unique hostname.

Throughout this chapter and the rest of the book, you will see the hostname "Cisco_Networking" assigned to our router. You may not want to use a name quite this clever, ingenious, or descriptive; but whatever naming scheme you choose, the hostnames that you assign should be somewhat meaningful. Hostnames, which are strictly a local issue and if used, should identify each router uniquely. If your network has only one router, then the name is less important, of course. In which case, have some fun and use something like "Cisco Networking For Dummies." Shameless? Me?

Remember these two key things when assigning a hostname to a router:

- ✔ The router must be in Enable Exec (Privileged) configuration mode (see "Working with the Exec command interpreter," earlier in this chapter).

- ✔ The command **hostname** is one word with no space between *host* and *name*.

Set a hostname this way:

```
Router#config t
Enter configuration commands, one per line. End with CNIL/Z.
Router(config)#hostname Cisco_Networking
Cisco_Networking(config)#
```

Waving the Banners

Each router can be configured with a variety of banner messages, messages that are displayed when someone logs into the router. *Banner messages* are text that is displayed at different times in the logging-in process. Four types of banner messages can be used:

- ✔ **Message of the day (MOTD) banner:** This banner is the first text display when a connection is made to the router or a login attempt is being made.

- ✔ **Login banner:** This message, if used, appears after the MOTD and before the login prompt.

- ✔ **Exec banner:** This is the line activation banner displayed after an Exec mode process is created.

- ✔ **Incoming banner:** This banner is displayed only when a reverse Telnet session (meaning you are Telneting to another node from a router) is initiated. The incoming banner, if enabled, appears on the remote router after the login is successful.

Banners are a good way to get the word out about scheduled network downtime or any other endearments that the administrator wants to share with his or her loyal users. Banners are also commonly used to display legal notices or warning messages. Banners can display virtually anything an administrator wants. The message part of the main banner is called the *message of the day* (MOTD), a term borrowed from our UNIX/Linux friends.

Follow these steps to create a MOTD banner:

1. **Put yourself in Global Configuration mode (see "Getting into Configuration mode," earlier in this chapter).**

2. **Follow the** banner motd **command with a delimiting character.**

   Entering the delimiting character at this point declares to the IOS which character you will be using to delimit your message. The choice of the delimiting character that you will use to indicate the end of your message is totally up to you. The delimiting character is entered as a part of the **banner motd #** command string, where # represents the character you've chosen.

3. **Enter the message.**

   Your message cannot contain the delimiting character you've chosen. The command line interpreter knows that the message is ended when you enter your delimiting character. For this reason, this character should normally be a special character not likely to be used in the MOTD message.

Use commands, such as the following, to create or modify the MOTD banner:

```
Cisco_Networking(config)#banner motd $
Enter TEXT message. End with the character '$'.
IOS upgrade scheduled for next Thursday.
$
Cisco_Networking(config)#
```

In this example, you need to press the Enter key after entering the delimiting character *($)* to end the message. Actually, any character not included in the message can be used as a delimiter.

Many administrators routinely use the pound sign character *(#)* as the delimiter.

The result of this would be that the next time anyone logs into the router, the following would be displayed:

```
IOS upgrade scheduled for next Thursday.

User Access Verification

Password:
```

The MOTD banner message is the first line displayed in the login display.

The process used to create the MOTD banner is the same for each of the other banners, with the exception that the keyword identifying each type of banner is used immediately after the command banner, such as banner exec, banner incoming, and banner login.

Assigning Helpful Hints

You may also add descriptions to lines, interfaces, and other configured elements of your router. To do so, the command **description** is used to apply a name, circuit number, or other nomenclature to whatever element is being edited. The **description** command is very simple in that it contains only two elements, the command and the description. Look at this example:

```
Cisco_Networking(config)#int e0
Cisco_Networking(config-if)#description Ethernet link to Web
          Host
Cisco_Networking(config-if)#^Z
```

These statements apply the description "Ethernet link to Web Host" to the Ethernet 0 interface. (See Chapter 17 for information on router Ethernet ports.)

Chapter 17

Configuring a Router

. . . .

. . . .

*R*outers are great networking tools. They connect network segments together, they connect you to other networks, which extend the value of the networks involved, and they connect you to the wide world of the Internet (the big internetwork). They have more benefits for sure, but you can't realize any of them if your router's interfaces aren't configured to support these connections.

Included in this chapter are the router commands, configurations, and setup topics that any self-respecting Cisco network administrator should know (or at least know about). Pay attention to the command syntax and the mode in which each command is executed. Someone in the past said that the devil is in the details. It's my guess that whoever said this did so immediately after configuring a Cisco router for the first time.

Beyond setting a router's basic operating configuration, most of an administrator's work on a router is in configuring the router's interfaces. Exactly which interfaces must be configured depends on your network and to whom it connects. Even routers on simple networks, which are used only for interconnecting to the Internet or a lesser WAN, have at least standard ports (for example, serial, virtual terminal, or console) and very likely an Ethernet interface or two.

To this end, this chapter provides you with a look at what's involved with setting the initial configuration of a router, configuring its interfaces, saving the configuration, and using SNMP (Simple Network Management Protocol) to manage interfaces, routers, and other remote devices.

Setting Up the Router

Arguably, the thrill of being the first person to open the box and unpack a new router is one of the top three thrills a person can experience in life. (I'll leave it to you to supply your version of what the other two might be.) Nothing else is quite like that new-router smell to get your heart pumping. However, as joyful as this experience may be, it soon fades when you plug the router in, fire it up for the first time, and realize that you're in setup mode. If you hear the *Twilight Zone* theme about now, then you've been there and done that.

Watch out! It's a setup!

The first time a router is powered up, it automatically enters setup mode, and the router display should look something like this:

```
Router#setup
--- System Configuration Dialog ---
At any point you may enter a question mark '?' for help.
Use ctrl-c to abort configuration dialog at any prompt.
Default settings are in square brackets '[]'.
Continue with configuration dialog? [yes]:
```

If you want to continue with the setup dialog — and you do! — setup displays its default answer in square brackets ([...]). You need only press the Enter key to accept the default value or response. Beyond the first time you power on the router, you can access setup mode in two other ways, and both are entered in the Enable Exec (Privileged) mode:

- Enter the **setup** command at the # prompt to display the command sequence shown earlier in this section.

- Enter the **erase startup-config** or **erase start** command (with the network administrator's permission, of course) and then power the router off and back on to begin again just like when the router was brand new.

Setup shows an initial interface summary that shows the default values assigned to the router interfaces and then prompts you to accept the current values, if any, for the hostname, Enable Secret, Enable, and Virtual Terminal passwords. Alternatively, you can change them. This sequence looks like this:

```
The enable secret is a one-way cryptographic secret used
        instead of the enable password when it exists.

Enter enable secret [<Use current secret>]:
```

```
    The enable password is used when there is no enable
            secret and when using older software and some
            boot images.

    Enter enable password [gilster]:
    Enter virtual terminal password [ron]: berman
```

As the first line indicates, when the Enable Secret password is used, you
don't need to set an Enable password for most of the newer Cisco routers.
When in doubt, set it to a value that you can remember, just in case. The virtual terminal password is used to gain access to the router through a telnet
session from a remote host.

Setting up the interface

After you finish setting the passwords, the setup process continues by configuring the router's interfaces. Here's a sample of what should be displayed by
setup at this point:

```
Configure IP? [yes]:
    Configure IGRP routing? [no]:
        Your IGRP autonomous system number [1]:

Configuring interface parameters:

Configuring interface Ethernet0:
    Is this interface in use? [yes]:
    Configure IP on this interface? [yes]:
        IP address for this interface [192.168.1.6]:
```

Notice that the setup process first asks you if you want to configure and
enable the IP routing, and then this question repeats for each of the individual interfaces.

The word or value contained in the brackets following the command interpreter's prompt is the default value. If you press the Enter key, the default
value is what is assigned to that particular parameter. Generally, at this level,
you are merely indicating whether or not an interface is in use and whether or
not the interface is a local interface or an internetworking interface connected
to other routers or the outside world (or both). The information entered here
should come from your network planning diagrams that should include the
information needed to configure each of the interfaces installed on the router.
See Chapter 15 for information on how to plan and configure a network.

Understand that if you respond no (with the word *no* or the letter *N*) to any
of the higher level questions, none of its configuration questions will appear.

Here is what the display shown earlier in this section would look like, had a *no* response been entered:

```
Configure IP? [yes]: n

Configuring interface parameters:

Configuring interface Ethernet0: n
```

If you do wish to configure an interface for IP routing, you enter the correct IP address information for each interface. See Chapter 8 for information on IP addressing.

IP routing is enabled as the default. If you wish to turn off IP routing for all interfaces, then you must enter the command **no ip routing.** To turn it back on again at some future point, enter the command **ip routing.** The *yes* is implied.

Summarizing configuration

After you respond to all of setup's enable and configuration requests, the **setup** command displays a summary of the router's configuration as you just defined it and asks whether you want to accept the configuration shown. As a safety against a default value being accidentally entered, no default value appears, and you must enter either *Yes* or *No.* If you answer *yes,* the router's configuration, as defined, is then built and stored in NVRAM, and the router is ready to be put into service.

If you answer *no,* the configuration you have just defined is discarded, the default configuration continues as the active configuration, and you will be returned to the router's default prompt. If you wish to rerun the configuration program, enter the **setup** command.

The configuration running in the router's RAM is the *running-configuration,* and the configuration saved in the router's NVRAM is the *startup-configuration.* Restarting the router loads the startup-configuration into RAM, where it becomes the running-configuration. Copying the running-configuration to NVRAM overwrites the startup-configuration previously stored there.

Showing off your configurations

You have need to review, or show off, your configurations from time to time, perhaps only to see if a modification is needed or has been applied. But you do need to display the contents of a configuration on occasion.

Use the commands listed in Table 17-1 to display the configuration of your choice.

Enable versus enable secret passwords

Cisco routers and switches are administered through the command interpreter of the Cisco IOS. In order to perform administrator functions on the router, you must log into the Exec mode. The Exec mode has two levels: the user Exec mode and the Privileged Exec mode. The Exec mode provides access to commands to set and modify the general configuration of the router. However, the Privileged Exec mode provides access to commands that are used to configure the operating parameters of the router. Because of its sensitive nature, a second and protected password is used to prevent unauthorized access to this level of authority.

Since Cisco IOS release 10.3, the **enable secret** command has been available to set a password

for access to the Privileged Exec mode. The **enable password** command is still available for protecting access to the user Exec mode. The enable secret password is a secure password that is stored in an encrypted form. The enable password is much less secure and is stored in clear text form. If an enable secret password is configured, an enable password is not required, but if the enable password is configured, it must be used. However, if an enable secret password is enabled, the enable password is ignored and not used. These passwords should be different. The IOS will accept them as the same, but it will warn you about using the same password for both.

Table 17-1	Configuration Commands
Configuration	*Command*
Startup	**show startup-config** or **sh star**
Running	**show running-config** or **sh run**

I want to be sure that you understand the shortcut commands used in this example. The unique abbreviation for **show** is *sh*, and in either form, this command can be used to display the contents of a configuration file. The abbreviations *star* and *run* indicate the **startup-configuration** and the **running-configuration** commands, respectively. The Tab key is used to complete a shortcut command line.

To exit Configuration mode, you press Ctrl+Z, or enter "end" or "exit" as many times as required.

If You Start It Up, It Never Stops

After the router receives its initial configuration, the next time you power it on, the router goes through a five-step startup process:

1. A hardware check is performed by running the POST (Power On Self Test), and the bootstrap program is loaded to RAM from ROM.

2. The router uses the configuration register to locate the IOS software.

3. After the IOS is located, it is started from flash memory.

4. The source of the startup configuration file is located.

5. The startup configuration file is copied into RAM from NVRAM or another source.

I discuss each of these steps in more detail in the following sections.

POST it up

The POST (Power On Self Test) on a Cisco router is similar to the POST that runs at startup on a personal computer. The router's POST checks its CPU, memory, and all interface ports to make sure that they're present and operational, just as the PC's POST checks its CPU, memory, and peripheral devices.

If all is well, the *bootstrap* (also called the *boot*) program is read from ROM and begins the process of locating and loading the IOS operating system.

Is your IOS registered?

The primary purpose of the bootstrap program is to find a valid Cisco IOS configuration image from a location specified by the router's configuration-register. The *configuration-register* contains the location from which the IOS software is to be loaded. The value representing the location of the IOS software can be changed by using the **config-register** command from the global Configuration mode. The hyphen between *config* and *register* should be there.

Typically, the Cisco IOS is loaded from flash memory, and that's the default value found in the configuration-register. The router looks for the IOS software to be in one of three places:

- Flash memory
- ROM
- TFTP server

The router knows where to look based on the value in the configuration-register. The configuration-register holds a hexadecimal value that designates the location of the IOS software. The value in the configuration-register actually supplies a bit pattern in the same pattern that can be configured with a hardware jumper block, as was used on very old routers.

Three configuration-register settings determine where the router should look for the boot system:

- **0x02 through 0x0F:** When the configuration-register has the hexadecimal value 0x02 through 0x0F (which represents 0010 and 1111 in binary), the router will look for boot system commands in startup-configuration to tell it where to find IOS. If no boot system commands are in the startup-configuration, the router searches in the default places: flash, then ROM, then a TFTP server.
- **0x00:** If the configuration-register value ends in 0x00 (binary 0000), the router will enter ROM Monitor mode.
- **0x01:** If the configuration register value ends in 0x01, the router boots from ROM.

Changing your boots

If you want to change the source location from which you want the router to load the IOS system files, you can use these two things together:

- The **boot system** command
- The hexadecimal parameter that directs the router to the IOS source that you wish to use

It is the **boot system** command that the router looks for when the configuration-register tells it that the **boot system** commands are included in the startup-configuration.

If no **boot system** commands are in the startup-config, the router will search in the default places (flash, then ROM, and then a TFTP server). If the configuration-register value ends in 0x00, the router enters ROM Monitor mode. If the configuration-register value ends in 0x01, the router boots from ROM.

The following **help** (?) command display shows the various parameters that can be used to tell the router where to look for the IOS.

```
Cisco_Network(config)#boot system ?
  WORD    System image filename
  flash   Boot from flash memory
  mop     Boot from a Decnet MOP server
  rcp     Boot from a server via rcp
  rom     Boot from rom
  tftp    Boot from a tftp server
```

The current setting of the configuration-register is displayed by using the **show version** command.

Finding and loading the configuration

The startup-configuration file, like the IOS, can be loaded from other sources besides the NVRAM, such as a host or server on the network; or in cases where the configuration files are not where the IOS expected to find them, the configuration file can be loaded manually from a range of sources.

For example, to set the IOS to load the configuration file from a host on the network named "ws1," the following commands are used:

```
Cisco_Networking#configure terminal
Cisco_Networking(config)# boot host ws1
Cisco_Networking(config)# service config
Cisco_Networking(config)# ^Z
Cisco_Networking# write memory
```

Otherwise, the startup-configuration file is located in NVRAM and loaded to RAM as the running-configuration file. Any changes made to the configuration after the router has booted are made to the running-configuration and must be saved to the startup-configuration to become permanent, if that is the desire.

It's not a trivial matter

Configuration files can also be stored outside the router itself. Using the Trivial File Transfer Protocol (TFTP), configuration files can be copied and stored on a *TFTP server* (any computer running the TFTP server software). In fact, after you've backed up a copy of the configuration files to the TFTP server, the configuration copy on the TFTP server can be used as the configuration source during the boot sequence.

Backing up to a TFTP host

The primary reason that you would back up the configuration to an outside server is to ensure that the router has a source for its configuration even in the event that the configuration file on the router gets corrupted or accidentally (or possibly, quite intentionally) erased. If the router's configuration is corrupted or removed, the router's boot system can be directed via the configuration-register to look for a TFTP server. And yes, you may actually have reasons to erase the startup-configuration on purpose, should you have saved a bad, corrupted, or erroneous configuration by mistake.

Hosting a TFTP party

A TFTP host can be any computer on a TCP/IP network that has the TFTP server software installed and is able to store files. Almost any computer on a Cisco network can be the TFTP host. Cisco has a shareware version of TFTP that can be downloaded from its Web site (www.cisco.com).

You should check for a few conditions before setting up a TFTP host:

✔ The IP (Internet Protocol) must be enabled, loaded, and running.

✔ You must be able to PING the router from the TFTP host.

✔ The TFTP host must have room for the downloaded configuration file.

Checking ahead for room

The **show flash** command can be used to determine the size of the startup-configuration file stored in flash. It looks like this:

```
Cisco_Networking>sh flash

System flash directory:
File     Length      Name/status
  1       6844384         c3200-d-7_122-15.bin
[6844448 bytes used, 1544160 available, 8388608 total]
8192K bytes of processor board System flash (Read ONLY)
```

If you have more than one IOS version in flash, then you should use the **show version** command to display all the IOS files in flash. But beware: This command will not indicate which of the files is the running IOS image.

Backing up the flash

You should have a backup copy of the router's IOS configuration on a TFTP server just in case the configuration file on the router gets corrupted or erased. Read over this sample of the code used and the results displayed by the router:

```
Cisco_Network(boot)#copy flash tftp
PCMCIA flash directory:
File  Length    Name/status
  1   3070408   c1600-y-1.111-12.AA
[3070472 bytes used, 1123832 available, 4194304 total]
Address or name of remote host [255.255.255.255]?
       192.168.1.2
Source file name?  c1600-y-1.111-12.AA
Destination file name [c1600-y-1.111-12.AA]?
Verifying checksum for 'c1600-y-1.111-12.AA' (file #
       1)...  OK
Copy 'c1600 y-1.111-12.AA' from Flash to server
  as 'c1600-y-1.111-12.AA'? [yes/no]yes
!!!!!!!!!!!!!!!!!!!!!!!!!!!!!!!!!!!!!!!!!!!!!!!!!!!!!!!!!!!!
      !!!!!!!!! Upload to server done
Flash device copy took 00:00:52 [hh:mm:ss]
```

You can upgrade flash memory by using the TFTP server. After you obtain an upgraded IOS image from Cisco, store the image on the TFTP server and use the **copy TFTP flash** command to move it to the router's flash memory. The term *IOS image* is used to indicate the IOS and all of its configurations.

Saving your work

Two types of configuration files are stored on a router: startup and running. Both files can be copied to and from each other, as well as to and from the TFTP server. Why, you ask, would you copy these files to one another? Here are the primary reasons why you would do so:

- ✔ **Running-configuration to startup configuration:** If you make changes to the configuration of a running router, those changes are made to the running-configuration. If you wish to save these changes and make them permanent, the running-configuration must be saved to the startup-configuration. Otherwise, the next time the router is booted and the startup-configuration is loaded, all your changes will be lost. Remember that at boot time, the startup configuration is loaded to RAM to become the running-configuration.

- ✔ **Startup-configuration to running-configuration:** You would copy the startup-configuration to the running-configuration to reset any changes you have made and did not save by copying the running-configuration to the startup-configuration. These changes could be configuration tests or mistakes. Rebooting the router causes the stored version of the system's configuration to be loaded to RAM as the running-configuration.

Use these commands to copy the files:

- ✔ **copy start tftp** — copies the startup-configuration to the TFTP server.
- ✔ **copy run tftp** — copies the running-configuration to the TFTP server.
- ✔ **copy tftp run** — copies the configuration stored on the TFTP server to the running-configuration file on the router.
- ✔ **copy tftp start** — copies the configuration stored on the TFTP server to the startup-configuration file on the router.
- ✔ **copy start run** — copies the startup-configuration from NVRAM to the running-configuration in RAM.
- ✔ **copy run start** — saves the running-configuration to NVRAM, over-writing the previous version of the startup-configuration.

To use these commands, you must be in Privileged Exec mode — the one with the # character prompt.

This example code shows these commands as you would enter them on the router:

```
Cisco_Networking#copy start tftp
Cisco_Networking#copy run tftp
Cisco_Networking#copy tftp run
Cisco_Networking#copy tftp start
Cisco_Networking#copy start run
Cisco_Networking#copy run start
```

By using the command-completion help files that are built into the command line interface, you can simply type only the word **start** or **run** to indicate startup-configuration and running-configuration.

This sample code shows the console output that results from the command to copy the startup-configuration to a TFTP server:

```
Cisco_Network#copy star tftp
Remote host []? 192.168.1.5
Name of configuration file to write [Cisco_Network-
        confg]?
Write file Cisco_Network-confg on host 192.168.1.5?
        [confirm]
Writing Cisco_Network-confg !! [OK]
```

If you forget to update the startup-configuration or if you decide not to, the router will revert to its previous configuration the next time you boot, which could be actually what you planned all along.

Approaching Configuration Manually

An alternative approach to setting up the configuration on a router is to do it through a manual configuration, which is what Cisco calls *completing the setup one step at a time,* as opposed to using the **setup** command. While requiring more time and attention to detail, it provides you with greater control over the resulting configuration. By using the **setup** command, as shown earlier in this chapter (see "Watch out! It's a setup!"), only a very basic configuration is enabled. To manually configure a router, follow these steps:

1. **Get in global configuration mode.**

2. **Begin entering each of the specific interfaces that you want to configure.**

Interface means the ports and connection points on the router. Depending on the router model in use, the interfaces available could include an Ethernet port, one or more serial ports, and others. Ethernet ports are designated by either the word *Ethernet* or the letter *e* followed by a sequence number beginning with zero. Serial ports follow a similar pattern but use the word *serial* or the letter *s* and an integer port number. For example, to designate the first Ethernet port, the code e0 can be used; and for two serial ports, s0 and s1 can be used.

3. **Enter the IP address and subnet mask for each interface.**

   Remember that network nodes use router interfaces to address the router over a certain type of interface media and port. Clients (meaning source nodes) use the subnet mask to determine if a destination address is local or remote.

The following is a sample of the commands used to configure an Ethernet port on a router manually:

```
Cisco_Network#config t
Enter configuration commands, one per line.  End with
     CNTL/Z.
Cisco_Network(config)#int e0
Cisco_Network(config-if)#
Cisco_Network(config-if)#IP address ?
  A.B.C.D  IP address
Cisco_Network(config-if)#IP address 192.168.1.6
% Incomplete command.
Cisco_Network(config-if)#IP address 192.168.1.6
     255.255.255.0
```

To properly configure an Ethernet port, you must enter *both* the IP address and its subnet mask. For more information on IP addressing and subnet masks, see Chapter 8.

Configuring the Router and Its Protocols

Assuming that the router has been set up with its running configuration, you next want to configure the routing protocols, which really means that you need to configure its interfaces. Basically, a router applies its form of intelligence to the question of where a network data packet should be forwarded so that it most efficiently reaches its destination. The "where" in this case refers to which of its interfaces should be used. The decision as to which interface to use is really the hardest part of this process, but it is all for nothing if the port (interface) that the router wants to use is not properly configured.

If a router's interfaces aren't properly configured, including the protocols supported by each, it can't include them in the routing decision. So, obviously, the router needs to know just how you intend to use each of its interfaces, if at all, and some specific things about each port, such as the addresses that can be reached, any security considerations, data speeds, and so on.

Setting up the routing protocol

The first task in configuring the router-to-router traffic is to assign a routing protocol. A *routed protocol* moves data traffic over the network from router to router. Don't confuse this with a *routing protocol,* which is the protocol used by routers to communicate information about the network to other routers. Cisco routers support a wide variety of routing protocols. Table 17-2 lists the routing protocols that you can set up on your router. Each of the routing protocols in Table 17-2 requires additional information to complete its setup on the router.

Table 17-2	Routing Protocols Supported on Cisco Routers
Protocol	*Configuration Keyword*
Border Gateway Protocol (BGP)	bgp
Exterior Gateway Protocol (EGP)	egp
Enhanced Interior Gateway Routing Protocol (EIGRP)	eigrp
Interior Gateway Routing Protocol (IGRP)	igrp
ISO IS-IS	isis
IGRP for OSI Networks	iso-igrp
Mobile routes	mobile
On demand stub routes	odr
Open Shortest Path First (OSPF)	ospf
Routing Information Protocol (RIP)	rip
Static routes	static
Traffic-engineered routes	traffic-engineering

The most common protocol you will use is RIP. However, in some specific situations, you may need to use static routes.

Building the router's configuration

To begin the process of building the router's configuration, you must first be in the global configuration mode. With that out of the way, you can begin entering each of the specific interfaces that you want to configure. Remember that *interface* means the ports and connection points on the router. Depending on the router model in use, this could include an Ethernet port, one or more serial ports, and more. Ethernet ports are designated by either the word *Ethernet* or the letter *e,* followed by its sequence number, beginning with zero. Serial ports follow a similar pattern: the word *serial* or the letter *s* and an integer port number. For example, to designate the first Ethernet port, the code e0 can be used, and for two serial ports, s1 and s2 can be used. Look at this sample of the commands used to configure an Ethernet port manually on a router:

```
CISCO_Networking#config t
Enter configuration commands, one per line. End with CNTL/Z.
CISCO_Networking(config)#int e0
CISCO_Networking(config-if)#
CISCO_Networking(config-if)#IP address ?
  A.B.C.D  IP address
CISCO_Networking(config-if)#IP address 192.168.1.6
% Incomplete command.
CISCO_Networking(config-if)#IP address 192.168.1.6
          255.255.255.0
```

Remember that to configure an Ethernet port properly, you must enter both — that's right, *both* — the IP address and its subnet mask.

Configuring Interface Parameters

If you have additional interface modules or WAN interface cards installed on your router, you'll likely need to configure additional parameters. You need to be in the global configuration mode to configure an interface. The most common interfaces found on Cisco routers are:

- Ethernet interface
- Fast Ethernet interface
- Token ring interface
- Serial interface
- Asynchronous/synchronous serial interface
- ISDN BRI interface
- E1/T1/ISDN PRI interface
- 1-port, 4-wire 56kbps DSU/CSU interface

Moving to the mode

To work on the configuration of an individual router interface, you must first get to the right mode level of the command line interpreter (CLI). Table 17-3 lists the **command line interpreter** commands used to move down to the interface configuration mode.

Table 17-3	Commands Used to Configure an Interface	
CLI Prompt	*Command*	*Purpose*
Router>	**enable**	Moves to privileged Exec mode
Router# mode	**configure terminal**	Moves to global configuration
Router(config)#	**interface ethernet0**	Opens the configuration of the ethernet0 interface port
Router(config-if)#	**exit**	Exits to Global configuration mode
Router#	**copy running-config startup-config**	Saves the modified configuration to NVRAM for IOS Versions 11.0 and after
Router#	**write memory**	Used on IOS versions prior to 11.0
Router#	**disable**	Returns to user Exec mode
Router>		Shows CLI is in user Exec mode

Your best bet for configuring the interfaces on your router is to do it during the initial configuration sequence that runs when you first power up the router for the first time or after you erase the startup configuration.

The **setup** command that runs automatically during the initialization sequence is your first, and perhaps your best, chance to configure each interface. For each interface on the router, a series of prompts is displayed to guide you through its configuration. You only need to enter the specific information needed or accept the default or current value to complete the configuration appropriate for your router and network.

In each of the following sections, I have listed the prompts the **setup** command displays for each of the interfaces possibly included on your router. Depending on the IOS version and router you are using, the configuration message that you see may vary.

Ethernet interface

An Ethernet interface or port connects the router into a network by using Ethernet 10BaseT, 10Base2, or 10Base5 technologies and protocols. This interface assumes a data transfer rate of 10 Mbps on the network. Here is a sample configuration for an Ethernet interface from the **setup** command:

```
Do you want to configure Ethernet0/0 interface [yes]:
 Configure IP on this interface? [yes]:
IP address for this interface: 192.168.1.6
Subnet mask for this interface [255.255.255.0]:
Class C network is 192.168.1.0, 24 subnet bits, mask is /24
 Configure IPX on this interface? [no]: y
IPX network number [1]:
Need to select encapsulation type
[0] sap (IEEE 802.2)
[1] snap (IEEE 802.2 SNAP)
[2] arpa (Ethernet_II)
[3] novell-ether (Novell Ethernet_802.3)
Enter the encapsulation type [2]:
```

Fast Ethernet interface

A Fast Ethernet interface connects the router to a network running Ethernet 100BaseTX technologies and supports data speeds up to 100 Mbps. Here is a sample of the configuration prompts displayed by the **setup** command for a Fast Ethernet interface. You may not see much difference between this configuration and that shown for a not-fast Ethernet port in the preceding section, other than the inclusion of the word *Fast,* that is. But, if you look real close, you will see a couple of additional prompts that deal with duplexing and the connector used.

```
Do you want to configure FastEthernet0/0 interface [yes]:
 Use the 100 Base-TX (RJ-45) connector? [yes]:
 Operate in full-duplex mode? [no]:
 Configure IP on this interface? [no]: yes
 IP address for this interface: 192.168.1.1
 Number of bits in subnet field [24]:
 Class C network is 192.168.1.0, 24 subnet bits, mask is /24
Configure IPX on this interface? [yes]:
IPX network number [1]:
Need to select encapsulation type
[0] sap (IEEE 802.2)
[1] snap (IEEE 802.2 SNAP)
[2] arpa (Ethernet_II)
[3] novell-ether (Novell Ethernet_802.3)
Enter the encapsulation type [2]:
```

Token ring interface

This interface type connects the router into a network running on token ring structures. The network data speeds supported are 4 Mbps or 16 Mbps. Here is a sample of the configuration prompts displayed for a token ring interface by the **setup** command.

```
Do you want to configure TokenRing0/0 interface? [yes]:
 Tokenring ring speed (4 or 16)? [16]:
 Configure IP on this interface? [yes]:
IP address for this interface: 6.0.0.1
Subnet mask for this interface [255.0.0.0]:
Class A network is 6.0.0.0, 8 subnet bits; mask is /8
 Configure IPX on this interface? [no]: y
IPX network number [1]:
Need to select encapsulation type
[0] sap (IEEE 802.2)
[1] snap (IEEE 802.2 SNAP)
Enter the encapsulation type [0]:
```

Serial interface

A serial interface offers more access method options than other interface types on a Cisco router (see the list in "Configuring Interface Parameters" earlier in the chapter). The most common of options supported on a serial port are the following:

- HDLC (High-level Data Link Control)
- HSSI (High-Speed Serial Interface — pronounced "hissy")
- L2F (Level 2 Forwarding)
- PPP (Point-to-Point Protocol)
- PPTP (Point-to-Point Tunneling Protocol)
- SLIP (Serial Line Interface Protocol)
- STUN (serial tunnel)

Choosing between DCE and DTE

Serial interfaces must be designated as either DCE (data circuit-terminating equipment) or DTE (data terminal equipment). The documentation that comes with your interface card or the router includes information on whether it is, by default, a DTE or DCE device or can be configured as either. Table 17-4 lists some examples of DCE and DTE devices.

Table 17-4	DCE/DTE Devices
Type	*Typical Devices*
DTE	Terminal, PC, Router interface
DCE	Modem, CSU/DSU (Channel Service Unit/Data Service Unit), Multiplexer

Here are brief descriptions of the DCE and DTE designations:

- ✔ **DCE (data circuit-terminating equipment):** A DCE device is the network end of a user-to-network connection. The DCE provides a DTE device with a physical connection to the network and a clock signal for timing communications.

- ✔ **DTE (data terminal equipment):** A DTE is typically a router on a network. A DTE connects to the network and receives its clock signal through a DCE device.

Configuring a serial interface

Here is a sample of the prompts displayed by the **setup** command to configure a serial interface.

```
Do you want to configure Serial0/0 interface? [yes]:
Some encapsulations supported are
ppp/hdlc/frame-relay/lapb/atm-dxi/smds/x25
Choose encapsulation type [ppp]:
```

The router will attempt to determine if the serial port is to be DCE or DTE by using the cable attached to the port and the device attached to the other end of the cable. If a serial cable is not attached, which is usually the case during the initial configuration, the router will remind you and ask you to designate the port as either DCE or DTE, with DTE as the default. (See "Choosing between DCE and DTE," earlier in this section.)

```
No serial cable seen
Choose mode from (dce/dte) [dte]:
```

If a cable is attached and the interface is DCE, then you will be asked to set the clock rate for the interface. Otherwise, if the interface is to be DTE, the serial cable and the DCE attached to it will set the clock rate.

You will need to know the clock rate of the DTE equipment you are supporting to set the clock rate for a DCE designation. When in doubt, choose the default rate.

```
Serial interface needs clock rate to be set in dce mode.
The following clock rates are supported on the serial
        interface.
0
1200, 2400, 4800, 9600, 19200, 38400
56000, 64000, 72000, 125000, 148000, 500000
800000, 1000000, 1300000, 2000000, 4000000, 8000000
 Choose clock rate from above: [2000000]:
 Configure IP on this interface? [yes]:
IP address for this interface: 8.0.0.1
Subnet mask for this interface [255.0.0.0]:
Class A network is 8.0.0.0, 8 subnet bits; mask is /8
 Configure IPX on this interface? [no]: yes
IPX network number [6]:
```

If you were to configure a DCE device manually, here is an example of the commands you would enter (in interface configuration mode):

```
interface Serial0/0
encapsulation ppp
clock rate 2000000
ip address 27.0.0.1 255.0.0.0
```

Designating the encapsulation

A serial interface must also be configured for the type of data encapsulation it should expect. The encapsulation types that can be configured to a Cisco router serial interface are listed here along with the **encapsulation** command parameter of each in parentheses:

- Asynchronous Transfer Mode-Data Exchange Interface (**amt-dxi**)
- Frame Relay (**frame-relay**)
- High-level Data Link Control (**hdlc**)
- Point-to-Point Protocol (**ppp**)
- Switched Multimegabit Data Services (**smds**)
- Synchronous Data Link Control (**sdlc-primary/sdlc-secondary**)
- X.25 (**x25**)

Completing a Frame Relay definition

If the interface is being configured for Frame Relay, then some additional configuration information must be entered. Beyond the normal interface configuration data, the LMI (Local Management Interface) and DLCI (data-link connection identifier) information is required. See Chapter 14 for more information on these two Frame Relay technologies.

If you have designated the interface to be **frame-relay**, then the prompts (remember that I am using the configuration prompts from the **setup** command for my examples) request the following information:

```
The following lmi-types are available to be set,
 when connected to a frame relay switch
[0] none
[1] ansi
[2] cisco
[3] q933a
Enter lmi-type [2]:
Enter the DLCI number for this interface [16]:
Do you want to map a remote machine's IP address to dlci?
         [yes]:
IP address for the remote interface: 7.0.0.1
```

(continued)

```
Do you want to map a remote machine's IPX address to dlci?
        [yes]:
IPX address for the remote interface: 00000001:00081A0D01C2
Serial interface needs clock rate to be set in dce mode.
The following clock rates are supported on the serial
        interface.
0
1200, 2400, 4800, 9600, 19200, 38400
56000, 64000, 72000, 125000, 148000, 500000
800000, 1000000, 1300000, 2000000, 4000000, 8000000
Choose speed from above: [2000000]: 1200
Configure IP on this interface? [yes]:
IP address for this interface: 7.0.0.10
Subnet mask for this interface [255.0.0.0]:
Class A network is 7.0.0.0, 8 subnet bits; mask is /8
```

If your are configuring IPX on this Frame-Relay interface, you are prompted as follows:

```
Do you want to map a remote machine's IPX address to dlci?
        [yes]:
IPX address for the remote interface: 00000001:00081A0D01C2
```

Asynchronous/synchronous serial interface

Serial ports can also be configured as asynchronous and synchronous. *Asynchronous,* which is Greek (isn't it all) for "not at the same time," supports those access methods and protocols that operate without regard to the clock rate or a formalized communications structure. In general, asynchronous communications proceed until one of the communicating devices needs to interrupt the process. *Synchronous,* which loosely translates to "at the same time," communications are dependent on a clock rate from a single reference clock and usually require a formalized structure between the two communicating devices.

Chapter 14 can provide you with some information on why you would choose one type of interface configuration over the other. In general, your choice is dictated by the protocol assigned to the port.

Here is a sample of the asynchronous/synchronous configuration prompts you see when configuring a serial interface during the initial configuration of the router. You need to enter the appropriate information for your router and network.

Depending on the IOS version and router you are using, the configuration message that you see may vary.

```
Do you want to configure Serial1/0 interface? [yes]:
Enter mode (async/sync) [sync]:
```

If you choose the default (synchronous), the router responds with the following:

```
Do you want to configure Serial1/0 interface? [yes]:
Enter mode (async/sync) [sync]:
Some supported encapsulations are
ppp/hdlc/frame-relay/lapb/x25/atm-dxi/smds
  Choose encapsulation type [hdlc]:
```

If you choose ppp or hdlc, no additional configuration is necessary. To configure the other encapsulation types, refer to the sections earlier in this chapter pertaining to the configuration of the specific encapsulation type.

If you choose to configure the interface for asynchronous timing, the router responds with the following:

```
Do you want to configure Serial1/1 interface? [yes]:
Enter mode (async/sync) [sync]: async
Configure IP on this interface? [yes]:
Configure IP unnumbered on this interface? [no]:
IP address for this interface: 23.0.0.0
Subnet mask for this interface [255.0.0.0]:
Class A network is 2.0.0.0, 0 subnet bits; mask is /8
Configure LAT on this interface? [no]:
Configure AppleTalk on this interface? [no]:
Configure DECnet on this interface? [no]:
Configure CLNS on this interface? [no]:
Configure IPX on this interface? [no]: yes
  IPX network number [8]:
Configure Vines on this interface? [no]:
Configure XNS on this interface? [no]:
Configure Apollo on this interface? [no]:
```

In this example, notice that, in most cases, the default value was accepted; and only where I chose to designate the interface for async mode, to enter the IP address, and to configure IPX did I enter new data. The information I supplied came from the network planning documents. You don't want to do any guessing at this point in the process.

ISDN BRI interface

To enter configuration data for an ISDN BRI (Integrated Services Digital Network Basic Rate Interface) connection, you need to know the type of ISDN switch to which you are connecting. If you don't have this information, check with the provider of the ISDN service. You can use Table 17-5 to help determine the proper switch type to enter.

Table 17-5	ISDN Switch Type	
Description Type	**Geographic Area**	**IDSN Switch**
Australian TS013 switches	Australia	Basic-ts013
German 1TR6 ISDN switches	Europe	Basic-1tr6
Norwegian NET3 ISDN switches (phase 1)	Europe	Basic-nwnet3
NET3 ISDN switches (UK and others)	Europe	Basic-net3
NET5 switches (UK and others)	Europe	Basic-net5
French VN2 ISDN switches	Europe	Vn2
French VN3 ISDN switches	Europe	Vn3
Japanese NTT ISDN switches	Japan	Ntt
New Zealand NET3 switches	New Zealand	Basic-nznet3
AT&T basic rate switches	North America	Basic-5ess
NT DMS-100 basic rate switches	North America	Basic-dms 100
National ISDN-1 switches	North America	Basic-ni1

Here is a sample configuration for an ISDN BRI interface that is displayed during the initial configuration setup of the router. If you are configuring a BRI port, you must supply the data requested or accept the default value. Depending on the IOS version and the router you are using, the configuration message that you see may vary slightly. During the configuration, if you choose *HDLC*, no additional configuration is necessary. For *PPP*, I show you the additional configuration items. The additional encapsulation options are configured as shown earlier in this chapter (see "Configuring for other encapsulations"). Review Chapter 14 for more information on HDLC and PPP.

```
BRI interface needs isdn switch-type to be configured
Valid switch types are:
[0] none..........Only if you don't want to configure BRI.
[1] basic-1tr6....1TR6 switch type for Germany
[2] basic-5ess....AT&T 5ESS switch type for the US/Canada
[3] basic-dms100..Northern DMS-100 switch type for US/Canada
[4] basic-net3....NET3 switch type for UK and Europe
[5] basic-ni......National ISDN switch type
[6] basic-ts013...TS013 switch type for Australia
[7] ntt...........NTT switch type for Japan
```

```
    [8] vn3...........VN3 and VN4 switch types for France
Choose ISDN BRI Switch Type [2]:
Do you want to configure BRI0/0 interface? [yes]:
Some encapsulations supported are
ppp/hdlc/frame-relay/lapb/x25
Choose encapsulation type [ppp]:

Do you have a service profile identifiers (SPIDs) assigned?
          [no]: y
Enter SPID1: 01555121200
Enter SPID2: 01555121300
Do you want to map the remote machine's IP address in dialer
          map? [yes]:
IP address for the remote interface: 23.0.0.1
Do you want to map the remote machine's IP address in dialer
          map? [yes]:
IPX address of the remote interface: 00000001:00081A0D01C2
To get to 2.0.0.1 we will need to make a phone call.
Please enter the phone number to call: 5095551212
Configure IP on this interface? [yes]:
Configure IP unnumbered on this interface? [no]: y
Assign to which interface [Ethernet0/0]:
IP address for this interface: 23.0.0.10
Enter the subnet mask [255.0.0.0]:
```

Had you accepted the default or responded with *ppp* when prompted with

```
Choose encapsulation type [ppp]:
```

in the above series of prompts, you would also be prompted with the following items:

```
Would you like to enable multilink PPP [yes]:
Enter a remote hostname for PPP authentication [Router]:
Enter a password for PPP authentication:
```

E-1/T-1/ISDN PRI interface

E-1/T-1/ISDN PRI (ISDN Primary Rate Interface) transmission services can be configured (channelized) into separate 64 Kbps channels. These channels can then be used used to carry either voice or data streams. The configuration of the transmission service into channels is done by the service provider, but you must configure the router interface to match the channelization of the line. See Chapter 17 for more information on E-1/T-1/ISDN carrier services.

Here is a sample of the E1/T1/ISDN PRI interface prompts displayed during the initial configuration run of a router. The information you provide to configure the interface is available from the ILEC (incumbent local exchange carrier) or CLEC (competitive local exchange carrier) from whom you are receiving the service. E1, which is a European standard, and T1, the North American standard, are roughly equivalent services.

```
The following ISDN switch types are available:
[0] none............If you do not want to configure ISDN
[1] primary-4ess....AT&T 4ESS switch type for US and Canada
[2] primary-5ess....AT&T 5ESS switch type for US and Canada
[3] primary-dms100..Northern Telecom switch type for US and
         Canada
[4] primary-net5....European switch type for NET5
[5] primary-ni......National ISDN Switch type for the U.S
[6] primary-ntt.....Japan switch type
[7] primary-ts014...Australian switch type
Choose ISDN PRI Switch Type [2]:
Configuring controller T1 1/0 in pri or channelized mode
Do you want to configure this interface controller? [no]:
Will you be using PRI on this controller? [yes]:
```

If the answer to this last prompt is *no,* then you are finished with this configuration step. However, if you are using PRI mode for E1/T1, the following script (or a similar script) appears:

```
The following framing types are available:
esf | sf
Enter the framing type [esf]:
The following line code types are available:
ami | b8zs
Enter the line code type [b8zs]:
Enter number of time slots [24]:
Do you want to configure Serial1/0:23 interface? [yes]:
Configuring the PRI D-channel
Would you like to enable multilink PPP? [yes]:
Configure IP on this interface? [no]: y
Configure IP unnumbered on this interface? [no]: y
Assign to which interface [Ethernet0/0]:
All users dialing in through the PRI will need to be
         authenticated using CHAP. The username and
         password are case sensitive.
Enter more username and passwords for PPP authentication?
         [no]: y
Enter the username used for dial-in CHAP authentication
         [Router]:
Enter the PPP password of the user dialing in on PRI:
Enter more username and passwords for PPP authentication?
         [no]:
```

If you are configuring the interface for a T1 channelized mode, which is the other option to the PRI mode option, the following script or a similar script appears:

```
The following framing types are available:
esf | sf
Enter the framing type [esf]:
The following line code types are available:
ami | b8zs
Enter the line code type [b8zs]:
T1 is capable of being configured for channel 1-24
Enter number of time slots [24]: 3
Configure more channel groups? [no]: y
Enter number of time slots [21]: 3
Configure more channel groups? [no]: y
Enter number of time slots [18]: 3
Configure more channel groups? [no]: y
Enter number of time slots [15]:
Configure more channel groups? [no]:
```

If you are using E1 channelized mode, because you indicated the primary ISDN switch type as [4] primary-net5 - European switch type for NET5 early in this process, the following script or a similar script appears:

```
The following framing types are available:
no-crc4 | crc4
Enter the framing type [crc4]:
The following line code types are available:
ami | hdb3
Enter the line code type [hdb3]:
Do you want to configure Serial1/1:0 interface?: [Yes]:
Configuring the Channelized E1/T1 serial channels
Some encapsulations supported are
ppp/hdlc/frame-relay/lapb/atm-dxi/smds/x25
Choose encapsulation type [ppp]:
Configure IP on this interface? [no]: y
Configure IP unnumbered on this interface? [no]:
IP address for this interface: 129.40.0.1
Subnet mask for this interface [255.255.0.0]:
Class B network is 129.40.0.0, 16 subnet bits; mask is /16
```

1-port, 4-wire, 56Kbps DSU/CSU interface

Some interface connections, such as a ISDN PRI or channelized T-1 (single channel), require a DSU/CSU (data service unit/channel service unit), also called a CSU/DSU. The two halves of this combined service perform the following services:

✔ **Data Service Unit:** A device used in digital data transmissions to adapt a DTE device to a T1 or E1 line. A DSU also provides signal timing.

✔ **Channel Service Unit:** A digital interface device that connects a DTE to the local digital telephone service.

The name (DSU/CSU or CSU/DSU) of this interface type describes exactly what is being connected and supported to the port: a single connection to a 4-wire 56 Kbps, digital telephone carrier.

Here is a sample of the prompts that are displayed during the configuration sequence of the **setup** command for a 1-port, 4-wire, 56Kbps DSU/CSU interface. You need to enter the appropriate information for your router and network. Depending on the IOS version and router you are using, the configuration message that you see may vary. This WAN card can be configured to be used on either a circuit-switched or a dedicated-line service, and examples of both configurations are provided.

Which type of connection you have depends on the service provided to you by your provider. *Circuit-switched* refers to the good old everyday telephone system and would be used primarily for voice traffic. *Dedicated-line* service (also called DDS — dedicated digital service) covers data lines provisioned by the telephone company to carry digital data.

Circuit-switched service

```
Do you want to configure Serial0/0 interface? [yes]:
Some encapsulations supported are
ppp/hdlc/frame-relay/lapb/atm-dxi/smds/x25
Choose encapsulation type [ppp]:
Switched 56k interface may either be in switched/Dedicated
          mode
Choose from either (switched/dedicated) [switched]:
The following switched carrier types are to be set when in
          switched mode
(at&t, sprint or other)
Choose carrier (at&t/sprint/other) [other]:
Do you want to map the remote machine's ip address in dialer
          map? [yes]:
IP address for the remote interface : 117.0.0.2
Do you want to map the remote machine's ipx address in dialer
          map?
[yes]:
IPX address for the remote interface : 2e.45.3bce.df2
Please enter the phone number to call : 55555555555
Configure IP on this interface? [yes]:
IP address for this interface: 117.0.0.1
Subnet mask for this interface [255.0.0.0] :
Class A network is 117.0.0.0, 8 subnet bits; mask is /8
```

Dedicated-line service

```
Do you want to configure Serial0/0 interface? [yes]:
Some encapsulations supported are
ppp/hdlc/frame-relay/lapb/atm-dxi/smds/x25
Choose encapsulation type [ppp]:
Switched 56k interface may either be in switched/Dedicated
          mode
```

```
Choose from either (switched/dedicated) [switched]: dedi
When in dds mode, the clock for sw56 module can be from
         line/internal.
Choose clock from (line/internal) [line]: internal
Warning: internal can be chose only when connected back to
         back.
Serial interface needs clock rate to be set in dce mode.
The following clock rates are supported on the serial
         interface.
auto, 2.4, 4.8, 9.6, 19.2, 38.4 56, 64
choose clock rate from above [56]:
Configure IP on this interface? [yes]:
IP address for this interface: 117.0.0.1
Subnet mask for this interface [255.0.0.0] :
Class A network is 117.0.0.0, 8 subnet bits; mask is /8
```

Setting Up SNMP Network Management

This part of the chapter doesn't directly deal with interface configuration, but after SNMP (Simple Network Management Protocol) services are set up on the router, they are available for use in monitoring and managing the interfaces you configure on the router.

SNMP is a widely-used network monitoring, control, and management protocol that is part of the TCP/IP protocol suite (see Chapter 2). SNMP devices, called *agents* (routers, bridges, switches, hubs, and so on), on a network, report data on their activities to an SNMP server that collects, stores, and analyzes the data. A MIB (Management Information Base) is maintained for each agent and contains data on what information the agent provides and how it is managed. If the router and its interfaces are to be SNMP agents, they must be configured as such.

During the initial configuration process of the **setup** command and right after you set the router's passwords, you will be asked to configure the SNMP network management. The sequence of prompts you see look something like this:

```
Configure SNMP Network Management? [yes]:
    Community string [public]:

Current interface summary

Any interface listed with OK? value "NO" does not have a
         valid configuration

Interface      IP-Address       OK?   Method   Status
               Protocol

Ethernet0      unassigned       NO    unset    up        down
```

(continued)

```
Serial0        unassigned     NO   unset    down     down
Enter interface name used to connect to the management
            network from the above interface summary: Serial0

Configuring interface Serial0:
  Configure IP on this interface? [yes]:
    IP address for this interface: 172.16.10.1
    Subnet mask for this interface [255.255.0.0] :
    Class B network is 172.16.0.0, 16 subnet bits; mask is
        /16

The following configuration command script was created:

hostname CISCO_Networking
enable secret 5 $1$MYXQ$ZgAdF.GO9XME./GGEfbwo/
enable password networking
line vty 0 4
password cisco
snmp-server community public
!
no ip routing

!
interface Ethernet0
shutdown
no ip address
!
interface Serial0
no shutdown
ip address 172.16.10.1 255.255.0.0
!
end

[0] Go to the IOS command prompt without saving this config.
[1] Return back to the setup without saving this config.
[2] Save this configuration to nvram and exit.

Enter your selection [2]:
Building configuration...
Use the enabled mode 'configure' command to modify this
            configuration.
```

A Command Performance

Table 17-6 includes a list of commands that you should know — and you should know when to use them and why.

Table 17-6	Configuration Startup and Save Commands	
Command	*Action*	*When to Use*
show version	Displays the current software version	To verify the current software version and the name of the system image file
show config	Displays the startup-configuration, which includes the current pass-words assigned, and information on the inter-faces and routing protocols configured	To verify the overall configuration
show startup-config	Displays the startup-configuration	To verify the startup-configuration
show running-config	Displays the running-configuration, which is the configuration in use	To verify the running-configuration
setup	Begins the manual configu-ration prompting sequence	To enter or modify all or part of the router's configuration
write mem	Used in IOS Versions 10.3 and earlier to save changes made to the running-configuration	Saves the running-configuration to the startup-configuration; performs the same action as **copy running-config startup-config**
reload	Reboots the router	
erase startup-config	Deletes the startup-configuration in NVRAM	Probably never, unless you want to reset the router back into its initial startup and con-figuration states

You can store multiple IOS versions in flash memory. One way to free up space in flash is to erase unused versions and buffers.

Part V
Privacy, Security, and Other Secrets

The 5th Wave — By Rich Tennant

"A centralized security management system sounds fine, but then what would we do with the dogs?"

In this part . . .

This part of the book is bound to be a favorite for anyone who is into conspiracies and playing bar-the-door with the evildoers lurking on both the local and wide area networks, especially the Internet. In this part of the book, I cover the ways in which a router can be made a part of an overall security plan, including the kinds of things you can do to implement them.

Both an upside and downside of connecting a Cisco router to a WAN is that it can be seen by the world. A world of information and wonder awaits network users out in the wide world of the Internet and the internetwork. However, some people who don't have enough to do can choose to spend their time attempting (and occasionally succeeding) to crack into your network. This part of the book takes a look at the security measures that can be applied to a router, and covers firewalls, proxies, and other barriers to these bad people.

Chapter 18

Securing the Network through the Router

*E*very network administrator has at least one horror story to tell about breaches in security; a hacker, a cracker, or a phreak that got in and got away; or corrupted files and other spine-tingling bits of nastiness. Network security is always a hot topic when administrators of networks of all sizes and levels get together over drinks, typically with lots of caffeine. If network security isn't on your list of important issues, it should be; and if it is, it should be at or very near the top of the list.

Security on routers is something with which all network administrators should be very familiar. When it comes to routers, security means access lists and SAP (Service Advertising Protocol) filters. This can be a very tricky subject, and one you will be challenged with daily.

This chapter is structured much like a Cisco training course, with some lecture and some practice. You can gain the most benefit from this information by working through the examples on a router or a router simulator. Nothing is quite like doing it to learn it. In other words, if you really want to understand access lists, you really should get some practice working with them.

Making Up the Guest List

In the context of a Cisco router, the purpose of an access list is to allow or deny traffic through a router. An *access list* consists of formally structured statements that provide the criteria with which a router can decide what to do with packets entering its interfaces.

Cisco routers support several types of access lists:

- ✔ IP (Internet Protocol) and IP Extended
- ✔ IPX (Internetwork Packet Exchange) and IPX Extended
- ✔ IPX SAP (Service Advertising Protocol)
- ✔ IPX Summary
- ✔ MAC (Media Access Control) Rate Limit
- ✔ Rate Limit Precedence
- ✔ VACL Catalyst 6000

However, the most commonly used types of access lists are the IP and IPX, which work like packet filters, comparing incoming packets to the rules and conditions defined in the access list and taking the appropriate action based on the comparison's results.

Configuring an IP Access List

An access list can be one of two primary types as well as being either numbered (the default type) or named:

- ✔ **Standard IP access lists:** This type of access list analyzes the source IP address in a TCP/IP packet and then takes action to permit or deny the packet to pass through the router based on the outcome of its analysis. Standard IP access lists rely on the source IP address contained in the IP packet.
- ✔ **Extended IP access lists:** This type of access list permits or denies a packet by using a variety of factors, including the following:
  - Source address
  - Destination address
  - IP protocol (TCP, UDP, or ICMP)
  - Specific port (HTTP, FTP, or Telnet)
- ✔ **Named access lists:** Beginning with Cisco IOS Version 11.2, IP access lists can be assigned an alphanumeric name.

Examining the packet and its port

As shown in Figure 18-1, the information contained in an IP packet includes the destination IP address, the higher layer protocol to which the packet is destined (for IP, this is typically either TCP or UDP), and the specific well-known port to be used for the data in the packet.

Extended IP access lists allow the router to filter packets based on the information contained in the Layer 4 header. The content of the protocol field tells the router the type of Layer 4 header to look for. The starting point here is whether the protocol is connection-oriented or connectionless. A *connection-oriented protocol* uses TCP as its Layer 4 protocol. The TCP header is shown in Figure 18-2. A *connectionless protocol* uses UDP for the Layer 4 protocol. The UDP header is shown in Figure 18-3. See Chapter 2 for more information on the OSI Model's Layer 4 and the TCP/IP protocols.

In both connection-oriented (TCP) and connectionless (UDP) transmissions, you are interested in the source and destination port numbers. The port number identifies the server or application software to which the data payload in the packet is to be delivered for processing. Through the port number, the receiving host knows that the incoming data is to be sent to the software that handles HTTP (HyperText Transfer Protocol), FTP (File Transfer Protocol), or SMTP (Simple Mail Transport Protocol), for example. See Chapter 2 for more information these protocols and "Getting around in the better-known ports," later in this chapter, for information on TCP port numbers.

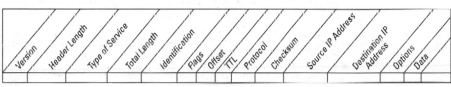

Figure 18-1: The contents of an IP packet.

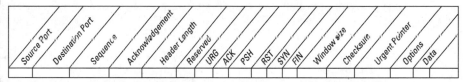

Figure 18-2: The fields of a TCP header.

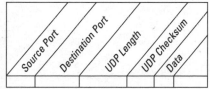

Figure 18-3: The contents of a UDP header.

Extended IP access lists include the information needed to filter traffic based on the higher-layer protocols in use, including TCP, UDP, or the like, along with the corresponding port. As with a standard access list, the TCP/UDP port number determines the application or server software that will process the data.

Standard access lists are fine and work well in situations where only the IP address is enough to determine who can or can't have access through the router to the network.

Extended lists provide the ability to determine access to the network based on the type of activity an IP address is requesting. You may want to allow a particular network segment (IP address range) general access to the network, but disallow all telnet and FTP requests and allow only SMTP e-mail traffic. This level of security is virtually impossible for a standard access list, but it is exactly what the extended access list is meant to do.

Access list rules and conditions

When an access list is created, a unique number is assigned so that the router knows which list to check for a particular protocol and interface. Like everything else in the router, certain rules govern how access list numbers are assigned.

Each type of access list has a block of numbers assigned to it. When an access list is created, the number it is assigned specifies its type to the operating system. Beginning with Cisco IOS release 11.2, standard and extended IP access lists can be given an alphanumeric name. Prior to that, access lists were designated only with a number, and the number had to come from the block of numbers for that type of access list. Table 18-1 lists the access list types you are most likely to encounter and the block of numbers reserved for each in the Cisco IOS.

Table 18-1	Access List Types
Access List Type	*Number Block*
IP Standard	1–99
IP Extended	100–199
Protocol type-code	200–299
48-bit MAC address	700–799
IPX Standard	800–899

Access List Type	Number Block
IPX Extended	900–999
IPX SAP	1000–1099

An implied **deny any** command is at the end of any access list. This command serves the purpose of denying all traffic not specifically meeting the conditions in the filter statements in the access list.

Getting around in the better-known ports

In your role as a Cisco network administrator, you learn quite a few of these port numbers because you work with them frequently, but you don't need to know the complete list by heart. The entire list of designated port numbers, known as the "well-known port numbers," contains a long list of ports representing a wide variety of specific upper-layer protocols.

Another thing you need to remember is that TCP and UDP both use port numbers, and (fortunately) their port numbers are the same for each application.

Table 18-2 contains only a small sample of some of the more commonly used well-known ports for TCP and UDP.

Table 18-2	Well-Known TCP and UDP Port Numbers	
TCP Port Number	UDP Port Number	Application
20	20	FTP - Data
21	21	FTP - CLI
23	23	TELNET
25	25	SMTP
53	53	DNS
69	69	TFTP
80	80	HTTP
161	161	SNMP

Officially, port assignments fall into three categories:

> ✔ **Well-known ports:** Ports 0 to 1023
>
> ✔ **Vendor-specific ports:** Ports 1024 to 2047
>
> ✔ **Client ports:** Ports 2048 and up

For a complete and detailed list, use an Internet search engine to search for RFC 1700 or go to the Internet Corporation for Assigned Names and Numbers (ICANN) Web site at www.icann.org. ICANN is the authority for most of the world for the registration and assignment of certain Internet-related numbers, including TCP and UDP port numbers, Class D (multicast) addresses, SNMP (simple network management protocol) private enterprise numbers, PPP (point-to-point protocol) numbers, and MIME (Multipurpose Internet Mail Extensions) media type numbers.

Applying the Access List

Access lists can contain more than one filtering statement; such statements are evaluated in physical sequence. Creating an effective access list requires that a certain amount of algorithmic logic be applied. If your access list is not carefully constructed, the actual results may be quite different from what you intended.

An access list works like this:

1. An incoming packet is compared to each line of the access list in sequence until a match is found.

2. After a match is made, the action defined in the access list entry is carried out, and any remaining access list lines are ignored. However, if no match is found, the packet is denied because of the implicit deny statement automatically attached to all access lists.

Like a safety net, all access lists end with a statement that denies all access. The catchall statement is called an "implicit deny any," which means that if a packet hasn't matched any lines of the access list to that point, it will be discarded. A two-step process is used to activate both standard and extended access lists (see "Configuring an IP access list," earlier in this chapter).

1. In global configuration mode, you define the access list by entering its lines one at a time, one after the other, in sequence.

2. In interface configuration mode, the access list is applied to a specific interface (e0, s1, and so on). One more thing: You are allowed only one access list per protocol per interface.

If your access list contains multiple lines, maintenance can be a little tricky. With numbered (not named) access lists, you cannot simply add a line in the middle of the list. If you want to change an existing access list through the router's command line interpreter (CLI), you must first remove any and all preceding access list lines, line by line, and then re-enter them with the new line in its proper sequence. More commonly, you can save the configuration file to a PC, use a text editor to make changes to your access lists, and copy the config file back to the router. (See Chapter 17 for information on how to copy and save configuration files).

Standard access lists

The general syntax of a standard IP access list is:

```
Access-list [number][permit or deny][source address]
```

After the access list is built, is it activated by using the **protocol** command. The option at the end of the command is used to indicate whether this access list entry is controlling incoming or outbound traffic in or out). The syntax of this command is

```
protocol access-group access-list number {in|out}
```

A sample session yields this result:

```
Cisco_Networking(config)#access list 1 deny 172.30.16.0
         0.0.0.255 out
Cisco_Networking(config)#int e0
Cisco_Networking(config-if)#IP access-group 1
```

The first command creates access list 1 with an entry to deny access to 172.30.16.0. Next, interface configuration mode is entered, and e0 (Ethernet0) is selected. Finally, the **IP access-group** command is used to assign access list 1 to e0 as an IP outbound access list. Remember to specify either in or out in the entry.

The effect of these commands is to deny any traffic from IP address 172.30.16.0 from going out the Cisco Networking router interface e0. Traffic from that network may come in on interface s0, but it won't be permitted to go out interface e0, even if that was the route it wanted to take.

Extended access lists

Extended access lists filter packets by using data other than just the source address. They also use the following data as filters:

- Destination address
- Source port

✔ Destination port

✔ Specific protocol in use (UDP, ICMP, or TCP)

As with a standard access list, applying an extended access list is a two-step process: Create the list and then apply it to an interface.

The command syntax for the Extended IP access list statement is

```
access-list [number] [permit or deny] [protocol] [source]
            [mask] [destination] [mask]
```

Here is the result from a sample session creating an extended IP access list on interface e0 (Ethernet interface 0) that permits IP traffic from the specific host 172.16.0.1 to any host on 192.168.1.0:

```
Cisco_Networking(config)#access-list 101 permit ip host
            172.16.0.1 192.168.1.0 0.0.0.255
Cisco_Networking(config)#int e0
Cisco_Networking(config-if)#access-group 101 in 172.16.0.1
Cisco_Networking(config-if)#^Z
```

In this example, notice that the next-to-last line uses the **access-group** command to assign access list 101 to the interface. The **access-list** command is used to enter the access list, but the **access-group** command is used to link the access list to the interface.

Extended access lists can also deny (or permit) traffic by port number, higher layer protocol number, or specific Network layer protocols. A common error made, when setting up an access list statement to permit or deny a specific port, is that the port number cannot be denied by IP. It must be done with TCP or UDP.

Well-known ports (port numbers in the range of 1 to 1023) are also called *TCP ports* or *UDP ports,* and that may help you tie the different terms together. When specifying a specific port to deny, remember that the protocol must be either TCP or UDP and that the port must be the correct TCP or UDP port number. (See "Getting around in the better-known ports," earlier in this chapter.)

The command structure used to permit or deny traffic destined for a specific port number adds the port, the operator operand, and the established parameters to the extended access list command:

```
access-list [number][permit or deny] [protocol] [source]
            [mask] [destination] [mask] [port] [operator
                operand] [established]
```

The **port** parameter indicates the port number to be permitted or denied. The **established** option permits TCP traffic to pass only if the packet is using an established connection. The **operator operand** options are

✔ lt = less than

✔ gt = greater than

✔ eq = equals

✔ neq = not equal

Here is a sample command that denies Telnet (port 23) access from IP address 10.1.1.1 into 10.1.1.2:

```
Cisco_Networking(config)#access-list 102 deny tcp host
        10.1.1.1 host 10.1.1.2 eq 23
```

Remember that extended IP access lists must be numbered in the range of 100 to 199. (See Table 18-1, earlier in this chapter.)

Named access lists

Beginning with Cisco IOS Version 11.2, IP access lists can be assigned an alphanumeric name instead of the number required on all previous IOS releases. Using a named access list has two primary advantages over unnamed (numbered) lists:

✔ The limitation of only 99 standard access lists and 100 extended access lists is removed.

✔ Named access lists can be edited.

Two general rules concern using named IP access lists in place of numbered access lists:

✔ A name can only be used once, which means that the same name cannot be used for multiple access lists or even different access list types. (An extended access list and a standard access list can't have the same name.)

✔ Cisco IOS releases before 11.2 cannot use named IP access lists.

The name is entered in place of the number in the **access-list** command syntax:

```
Cisco_Networking(config)#access-list notelnet
Cisco_Networking(config-ext-nacl)#deny tcp host 10.1.1.1 host
        10.1.1.2 eq 23
```

Notice that the command mode in this example changes to *config-ext-nacl*, which represents external network access control list configuration mode.

Verifying the access list

After an access list has been configured and attached to an interface, you should always verify what has actually been put into operation. The **show ip interface** command lists all the active access lists. The following sample router display would be generated by the **show ip interface** command (this display has been modified from its original format; I have edited this display to fit your book):

```
Cisco_Networking#show ip interface
Ethernet0 is up, line protocol is up
...
Outgoing access list is 1
Inbound access list is not set
```

The command **show run,** which displays the running configuration, also displays the interfaces that have access groups assigned to them.

The **show-access list** command, which can be executed from user exec mode, displays all the access lists currently active on a router and how many times (since the last **clear counter** command) the access list has been enforced. You can modify this command by adding the specific access list that you want to see. For example, you could use **show access list 101.** Here's a sample display from this command:

```
Cisco_Networking>show access list
Standard IP access list 1
    deny    172.130.16.0
    (10 matches)
Extended IP access list 101
    permit ip host 172.130.0.1 192.168.1.0 0.0.0.255
    (22 matches)
```

Removing an access list

Removing an access list uses essentially the same procedures that were used to create it, only in reverse.

1. Remove the access list from the interface with the **no ip access-group** command.

2. The access list itself is removed with the **no access list** command.

The following results from a router session that removes the standard access list entered earlier in the chapter. (See "Extended access lists," earlier in this chapter.)

```
Cisco_Networking#config t
Enter configuration commands, one per line. End with CNTL/Z.
Cisco_Networking(config)#int e0
Cisco_Networking(config-if)#no ip access-group 101 in
Cisco_Networking(config)#exitCisco_Networking(config)#no
          access-list 101
Cisco_Networking(config)#^Z
```

In configuration mode, the **no ip access-group 101 in** command removes the assignment of access list 101 from the Ethernet0 interface. Then the **no access-list 101** command removes access list 101 from the running configuration on the router.

One word of caution for removing the access list from an interface: Any packets attempting to cross that interface will be passed along unchallenged. The effect of having no access list is to **permit any.** So, before removing an access list, be very sure that that's what you want to do or that you are going to replace it immediately.

Wildcard Masking

Wildcard masks are used to permit or deny traffic based upon a specific IP address or group of IP addresses. Think of a wildcard mask as the exact opposite of the subnet mask (see Chapter 8). Binary numbers are still used, but now the 0s mean "check the number to see if it is valid," and the 1s mean "ignore the number." It's not true that Cisco did this only to confuse you; it is actually logical if you really think about it.

These examples should help you understand this new twist:

Example 1: You want to deny all outbound traffic coming in from IP address 192.168.1.6. What wildcard mask would you use?

```
              Decimal                    Binary
IP Address 192.168.1.6 11000000 10101000 00000001 00000110
Wildcard Mask  0.0.0.0 00000000 00000000 00000000 00000000
```

A wildcard mask of all zeroes (0.0.0.0) tells the router to check every bit in the incoming IP address to make sure that it is an exact match to the address in the access list statement.

Example 2: What if you want to deny traffic from the specific network of 192.168.1.0?

```
              Decimal                    Binary
IP Address 192.168.1.0 11000000 10101000 00000001 00000000
Wildcard Mask 0.0.0.255 00000000 00000000 00000000 11111111
```

The effect of this wildcard mask (0.0.0.255) is that the router checks each of the first three octets, and if they match the network address, access is denied (in this case) no matter what value the last octet may be.

A secret for figuring out what the wildcard mask should be to determine the subnet mask and then subtract it from 255.255.255.255. This will give you the appropriate wildcard mask. In that preceding example, if you subtract the subnet mask 255.255.255.0 from 255.255.255.255, you get the wildcard mask of 0.0.0.255.

```
  255.255.255.255
 +255.255.255.000      subnet mask
    0.  0.  0.255      wildcard mask
```

Another way to look at this is that the sum of every octet in both the subnet mask and the wildcard mask must total 255.

```
  255.255.224.000      subnet mask
 +  0.  0. 31.255      wildcard mask
  255.255.255.255
```

Moving in a different direction

Wildcard masks are applied in the opposite direction of subnet masks. An IP subnet mask uses the bits covered by the binary 1s as the network ID and those corresponding to the 0s as the host ID. Remember that a subnet mask is trying to extract the network ID.

In wildcard masking, the portion of the IP address covered by the 0 bits is the part extracted to match the IP address in the access list criteria exactly. Any bit in the IP address covered by a 1 bit in the wildcard mask automatically is a match, because they are ignored.

This is an example of an **access list** command, followed by the syntax of the access list entry, and yes, you must enter the hyphen:

```
access-list 2 deny 172.16.10.196 0.0.0.0
access-list number {deny|permit} source [source-wildcard]
```

In this example, the source IP address is 172.16.10.196 and the wildcard mask is 0.0.0.0. The effect of this **access-list** command is that all traffic from the source IP address 172.16.10.196 will be denied. This is the effect of the all zeroes wildcard mask.

Take a look at the following access list. What traffic will this line permit?

```
access-list 3 permit 172.16.0.0 0.0.255.255
```

If your answer is that all traffic from any node on the 172.16 network will be allowed, you are correct! The wildcard mask of 0.0.255.255 instructs the router to match on the first two octets only. So, any source IP address with 172.16 in the first two octets is a match. The 172.16 of the source is covered by the 0.0 of the wildcard, thus these bits must mach exactly in order for this line to permit the traffic. The remaining two octets can have any value at all. Because of the 255.255 in the wildcard mask, the remaining two octets automatically match.

Remember that IP addresses, subnet masks, and wildcard masks have only four octets each. Remembering this will help you separate those 0s that the router displays so closely together. If you think that separating them in our printed examples is hard, it's worse when you are working on an actual router.

Discerning wildcard word meanings

Every time you type in a number, you have a one-in-ten chance of making a mistake. A typo in an access list can cause major problems for your users. The wrong number in either the IP address or the wildcard mask can permit all the wrong people or deny all the right people access to your network. In case you're not sure, both of these conditions are bad.

The developers of the Cisco IOS must be as fumble-fingered as the rest of us because they included a couple of features that help avoid making number entry mistakes when entering an access list entry. The access list wildcard words **any** and **host** can be used when building an access list.

The parameter **any** is the equivalent of the 255.255.255.255 wildcard mask, which says that you aren't concerned about the IP address. A good use for this option is to limit access by port number instead of the IP address (see "Extended access lists," earlier in this chapter). This line

```
access-list 4 permit 0.0.0.0 255.255.255.255
```

has the same effect as this line

```
access-list 4 permit any
```

This command, which you may or not want to use, would permit any traffic that had not been otherwise permitted or denied in an earlier statement. This may be either good or bad, so use it wisely and carefully, if at all.

The wildcard parameter **host** is the equivalent of assigning the wildcard mask 0.0.0.0 to an IP address, which means that the router is to check for a specific address. You would use this parameter like this:

```
access-list 111 permit tcp host 192.240.16.3 in
```

You're in denial, and it isn't a river in Egypt!

A good access list statement to know and use is

```
deny any
```

This command is pretty darn arbitrary. It denies all traffic that was not permitted or denied by a preceding access list criterion. This command is implicitly added to the access list automatically by the router. You may include it if you want, just as a reminder, but you really don't need to.

Remember that an access list is evaluated sequentially from the first line to the last. After the criteria are met, that action is taken on that packet, and any remaining statements are ignored. If a packet does not match any of the criteria in the access list, then the packet is tossed aside by the implicit **deny any** command.

Working with IPX Access Lists

IPX access lists, like IP access lists, can be either standard or extended. However, standard IPX access lists, unlike standard IP access lists, can deny or permit based upon both source and destination addresses. Table 18-3 shows the access list numbers used for IPX access lists.

Table 18-3	IPX Access List Numbers
Access List Type	*Number Range*
Standard IPX access lists	800–899
Extended IPX access lists	900–999
IPX SAP access lists	1000–1099

The named access list option is also available on IPX.

Applying the standard model

The syntax and structure of the IPX standard **access list** command is

```
Access list [number]{permit|deny} source network[network-
          node] destination network [network-node]
```

A couple of shortcuts are available in the IPX **access list** commands. In place of the local network number, you can substitute the number 0 and the number –1 (minus 1) to match all networks. Here are the results of some sample command entries:

```
Cisco_Networking(config)#access-list 801 deny FF 0
Cisco_Networking(config)#access-list 801 permit -1 -1
```

The first entry denies traffic from network FF to the local network; the second entry permits all other traffic.

Using the extended form

In addition to the capabilities of the IPX standard access list, the IPX extended access list can filter traffic based on the IPX protocol (SAP, SPX, and so on) and the source and destination socket (address plus port) numbers.

The command structure and syntax for creating an IPX extended access list is

```
Access list {number} {permit/deny} {protocol} {source}
         {socket} {destination} {socket}
```

The codes that can be used for the common protocols and sockets are listed in Tables 18-4 and 18-5, respectively.

Table 18-4	IPX Protocol Type Numbers
Protocol	*Code*
Any	−1
Undefined	0
RIP	1
SAP	4
SPX	5
NCP	17

Table 18-5	IPX Socket Numbers
Socket	*Code*
All	0
NCP	451
SAP	452
RIP	453

The syntax and structure of the command used to activate an IPX access list is

```
ipx access-group access-list number [in|out]
```

Here are a few sample commands that could be used to create an IPX access list:

```
Cisco_Networking#config t
Enter configuration commands, one per line. End with CNTL/Z.
Cisco_Networking(config)#access-list 801 deny 35 5
Cisco_Networking(config)#access-list 801 permit -1 -1
Cisco_Networking(config)#int e0
Cisco_Networking(config-if)#ipx access-group 801 out
Cisco_Networking(config-if)#^Z
```

The first entry in IPX access list 801 denies access to network 5 from network 35. The second entry permits anything not already denied or permitted and is roughly the equivalent of the **permit any** of the IP access list. The next command assigns the access list to Ethernet0 for outbound traffic.

Using SAP filters

No, this isn't some new device to keep your brother-in-law away! IPX informs clients and neighboring routers of changes in network resources and services availability though SAP (Service Advertising Protocol) advertisements. Routers don't forward these SAP broadcasts (advertisements). Instead, they build SAP tables, which are broadcast every 60 seconds. By setting up an SAP filter, you can limit the amount of information that is sent out in the SAP updates, and you can limit who can access them as well. SAP filters can be either input or output.

✔ **Input SAP filters** reduce the number of services entered into the SAP table, which results in a reduction in the size of the SAP table itself.

✔ **Output SAP filters** reduce the number of services transmitted from the SAP table.

To configure a SAP filter to an interface, the **ipx input-sap-filter** and the **ipx output-sap-filter** commands are entered in interface-configuration mode. Each SAP filter, regardless of input or output, must be assigned an **access list number** command in the range of 1000–1099.

This is a sample of the commands used to configure a SAP filter:

```
Cisco_Networking(config)#access-list 1050 permit
        15.0000.0100.0001 0
Cisco_Networking(config)#int e0
Cisco_Networking(config-if)#ipx input-sap-filter 1050
Cisco_Networking(config-if)#^Z
```

These commands create an access list with the number 1050. This filter is reserved for IPX SAP filters that let the outside world see only the network specified in the command over the Ethernet0 interface. Any packets entering this port will be included in SAP updates.

Working with the ACL Manager

Cisco's handy-dandy family of network and router administration tools, CiscoWorks2000, includes the Access Control List Manager. At the time I wrote this, the current version of the ACL Manager was 1.2, but any version higher than that will only be that much more useful to you.

The ACL Manager provides you with an Internet interface to a group of applications that can be used to manage the access lists on Cisco products installed in an enterprise-level network. By using the Cisco ACL Manager, you can set up and manage IP and IPX access lists and filtering rules through an access list editor, policy template manager, network and service class manager, and other tools that allow you to troubleshoot problem access lists, distribute access lists, and update or correct access list.

Chapter 19

Working with Firewalls, Proxies, and Other Safety Measures

Contrary to common belief, most damage to networks happens from inside rather than from outside. Protecting the network from harm, inside or out, is a major part of any network administrator's job, and it's not always the easy part of the job either.

The primary networking devices used to provide security, beyond that of the router, are firewalls (of the hardware kind) and proxy servers. I don't want to alarm you, but every two or three seconds, a LAN is violated by some evil nasty person lurking on the internetwork. Actually, I made up the two or three seconds part, but I wouldn't be at all surprised to find out that's true. What is true is that mean, evil, and nasty people are waiting to infiltrate your network to do their dirtiest and most heinous work. This stuff would make an excellent horror movie.

Reviewing the Arsenal

You should have a general understanding of what firewalls, proxy servers, and cache servers are and aren't. The latter part is the easiest, so I start there. These devices are not intelligent and cannot, by themselves, tell who is a good guy and who is a bad guy. They have no special analyzing capabilities and do not use artificial intelligence to determine who should or shouldn't have access to a system, a network, or a particular site. No magic is involved, and everything a firewall and a proxy or cache server do is done by definition, configuration, and plan.

Keeping the fire from spreading

A *firewall* is a device that runs software developed specifically to separate the internal network from the external network and to protect the former from the latter. (Sometimes, the reverse is true as well.) This software's job is to inspect each data packet attempting to enter or leave the local network. This examination is made to determine whether the packet will be allowed into or out of the network. This activity is called *packet filtering*. Packet filtering is based on access control lists, very much like those used to permit and deny traffic to a router (see Chapter 18).

A firewall gets its name from the construction technique of building a wall completely to the roofline to prevent fire from jumping from one room to the next through the ceiling or attic. Like a building's firewall, a network firewall prevents bad stuff, the equivalent of a network fire, from spreading from network to network.

A high-end firewall (a fully featured one like the Cisco Secure PIX firewall) typically runs on a specialized operating system and not on a general-purpose operating system like UNIX or Microsoft Windows XP. Having its own unique type of operating system makes the firewall less likely to be accessed through operating system portals and tampered with or defeated. A firewall with a free-access side door would be like a building firewall with a big hole in the center — not much protection there.

Providing a proxy

A *proxy server* is a special-purpose server that acts as a go-between for the internal network and the external network. Unlike a firewall, a proxy server has no real security responsibility, although most proxy servers also provide some level of security. The proxy server acts as an agent on behalf of network nodes to help shield them from the darkness outside the confines of the nice, safe LAN.

Proxy servers are especially helpful when nonpublic, internal IP addressing is used on a LAN. You may recall that blocks of IP addresses (10.xxx.xxx.xxx, 172.16.xxx.xxx to 172.31.xxx.xxx, and 192.168.xxx.xxx) can be used on any internal network and are set aside in the IP addressing schemes for that purpose. Thousands of private networks use at least one of these IP address blocks, which is why these addresses are not used as source IP addresses for traffic sent over the public network. A remote network would have a heck of a time determining which 10.0.0.34 is which. This is where the proxy server comes in.

One of the services provided by a proxy server is *network address translation (NAT)*, which provides a public IP address (an address not in one of the private IP address blocks) for use on the public network (Internet). NAT is also a feature in most routers as well. The NAT service maintains an internal table that associates each internal source address and the destination address in its request with the external public address and a unique port number assigned to it. Typically, the public address provided is the IP address assigned to the proxy server or router itself. The port number assigned to the internal node serves as an identity code so that the requests from multiple internal nodes can be differentiated when the requested data arrives. In this way, the NATing device serves as the internal network node's proxy. For more information on IP addressing, see Chapter 8 and for more information on routers, see Chapter 11.

Figure 19-1 illustrates the basic operation of a proxy server. Here's how it works:

1. Each network node communicates its desire to access a destination on the external network.

   For example, suppose that node 10.0.0.34 wants to access a remote server to retrieve a Web document and communicates this to the proxy server.

2. The proxy server assigns its public IP address and a unique port number to the node.

3. The proxy server then places both the public and the private addresses and the port number assigned in a table, so they can be cross-referenced.

   In Figure 19-1, the proxy server records that the assigned public IP address (200.106.2.25) is temporarily assigned to node 10.0.0.34.

4. When the requested data returns, the proxy server looks up the public address and port number and forwards the incoming data to the internal IP address associated with it.

   In other words, the proxy server acts as the internal node's proxy to the outside network.

By using external network IP addresses, the proxy server hides the internal network from the view of the external network. This provides some security in that the addressing of the internal network is not known beyond the proxy server. Most proxy servers are not separate pieces of hardware, but rather are pieces of application software running on general-purpose operating systems, such as UNIX, Linux, or Windows NT, 2000, or XP on a PC.

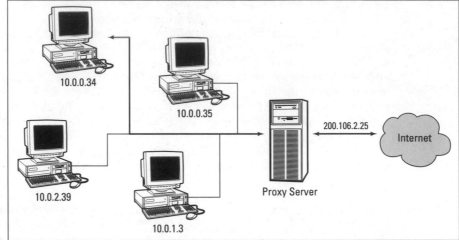

Figure 19-1:
The proxy
server helps
maintain
network
node
aliases.

Caching in on a good thing

In spite of the fact that millions of documents are available on the World Wide Web, about 20 percent of all the Web sites account for the vast majority of the internetwork traffic. What this means to you as a network administrator is that if you or other network users visit a Web site and download it, chances are very good that another user from your network will very soon download the same site. This may be great for the hit count and popularity indices for this site, but it unnecessarily ties up your bandwidth.

Wouldn't it be great if a server on your network could keep copies of the most frequently accessed Web pages or other downloaded files? Well, it is great, and it's called a cache server. A *cache server* is a server that saves frequently accessed Web pages, FTP files, or other files designated by the administrator.

The cache server has two primary benefits:

- ✔ **It reduces network latency.** A cache server creates the convenience of a much faster download to the requesting user because the file is being served from a local server and not the originating server across the internetwork.

- ✔ **It reduces bandwidth utilization.** A cache server reduces the amount of traffic flowing from an internal network out to the external network, which translates into a lower bandwidth utilization and perhaps even fewer bandwidth requirements altogether between the internal and external networks.

Caching the proxy or proxying the cache

Well, here's the twist: A proxy server, which is often set up to provide for firewall service, may also serve as a cache server. Cache servers are often capable of working as proxy servers, too. These double-duty devices are great for companies with limited budgets that want to gain the benefits of both services without spending the money for the dedicated devices.

Remember that the more you have a single computer do, the more powerful (and expensive) that machine must be to prevent its performance from suffering. When caching or proxy server performance suffers, the benefit of these timesavers evaporates, and users spend more time waiting for their data. So, whether combining caching and proxy servers onto a single computer is a good idea for your network depends on your network and the nature of your users.

Cache servers can be software applications running on a standard server or PC hardware platform; but more often, you find that a network cache server is a specialized device performing only caching. Cache servers have complex formulas that they use to determine which sites, pages, or objects should be cached. They also automatically update those pages or parts of pages that are frequently changed.

Looking Over the Cisco Catalog

Because this book is about using Cisco Systems' products in networks, we need to look at Cisco's firewalls, proxy servers, and cache servers. Although we can't state that Cisco makes a product to fit each network and its needs, it does make a great range of products from which you may find one that meets your particular requirements. For information on Cisco Systems' products, look at its online product catalog at www.cisco.com/univercd/cc/td/doc/pcat/.

Firing up the firewall

Cisco's firewall series is called the Cisco Secure PIX (which, as far as I can tell, doesn't stand for anything other than a product name) firewall. Currently, five Cisco PIX firewall models are available:

✔ **PIX 535:** Designed for use in large corporation (enterprise installations) and service provider networks, this model of the PIX provides over 1 Gbps of throughput bandwidth and is able to process as many as 500,000 connections concurrently. The PIX 535 includes 3DES (triple data encryption standard) and 2,000 VPN tunnels. For more information on encryption and VPN, see the sidebar entitled "Security data through encryption: The DES" and the section entitled "Creating a Virtually Private Network" later in the chapter.

✔ **PIX 525:** This firewall device is also best-suited for enterprise and service providers. It can connect to a variety of network technologies, including Ethernet, token ring, and FDDI (see Chapter 3). The PIX 520 can handle up to 360 Mbps of throughput and as many as 280,000 simultaneous connections. Like the PIX 535, the PIX 525 also offers 3DES and 2,000 VPN tunnels.

✔ **PIX 515E:** This Ethernet-only device is designed to support the needs of small and medium businesses. The PIX 515E can handle up to 125,000 simultaneous connections with a maximum of 188 Mbps of throughput.

✔ **PIX 506E:** As more and more small businesses become connected to the outside world via the Internet, and with the emergence of the telecommuter, the COHO (company office/home office), and the SOHO (small office/home office), a need has arisen for increased security services for these smaller entities. The Cisco PIX 506E is a desktop model that provides up to 20 Mbps of firewall throughput and 3DES for VPN use.

✔ **PIX 501:** A SOHO/COHO firewall that offers 10 Mbps of firewall throughput and 3 Mbps of 3DES for VPN connections.

Security data through encryption: The DES

You may have heard network security people speak of DES (Data Encryption Standard), which is pronounced as "dez" or even 3DES (triple DES) in reverent tones. DES is an IBM encryption algorithm that was further improved upon by the U.S. National Security Agency (NSA) for encrypting transmitted data. In technical terms, it breaks data into 64-bit blocks and then encrypts them by using the Boolean exclusive OR with a 56-bit key.

DES decryption is fast, which is why it is widely used. Its key is kept secret and can be used many times. Some applications also generate a key randomly for each session, such as the popular RSA (see "Token and PKI authentication," earlier in this section).

Triple DES extends the key to 168 bits, but because it requires multiple passes to decrypt the data, it requires more time. Other variations of 3DES are EEE2 and EDE2, which use two keys, and EEE3, which uses three keys.

A new method, AES (Advanced Encryption Standard), may be the replacement for DES. AES uses keys of 128, 192, and 256 bits and can be encrypted and decrypted in a single pass.

Just having a Cisco Secure PIX firewall may not be quite enough to completely secure your network. Other tools may be required to complete the job, depending on the situation. Cisco has partnered with several other vendors to provide additional solutions and utilities to extend the capabilities of the Secure PIX firewall series. Here is a brief description, by category, of several of these programs.

Monitoring and reporting

Here are a few software products that will help you verify the configuration of your firewall as well as help you generate a list of who has been trying to access your network:

- **HP OpenView:** This Hewlett-Packard product is probably the most widely used of the network node manager (NNM) utilities. HP OpenView, which is available for a range of operating systems, provides in-depth graphical views of your network. Cisco provides a free software module, PIXView, to enhance HP OpenView software for monitoring the PIX firewall. For more information, visit www.openview.hp.com.

- **Ipswich What's Up Gold:** This is a powerful network-monitoring tool that watches your network; and should configured devices go down, What's Up Gold notifies you by pager, e-mail, or telephone, so you can get the network back up fast. For more information, visit www.whatsupgold.com/downloads/.

- **Private I:** This utility from OpenSystems.com allows you to verify the configuration of your PIX firewall by translating the syslog data of the PIX. Its built-in reporting tool, ReportVU, turns the log data into easily understood information. You can access a demo or beta version of this tool at www.opensystems.com.

- **Telemate:** This utility from Telemate.net is only one of a suite of utilities available to report on how your network is being used and by whom. Another related utility available from this company is Netspective, which categorizes the source IP addresses used by the people who have been accessing your network. For more information, visit www.telemate.net.

Content filtering

This list of products includes applications that allow you to limit by site or content where on the Internet network users can visit:

- **Tumbleweed Integrated Messaging Exchange:** This application is a policy-based e-mail content security system that enables businesses to create a secure, interactive communications channel to their customers and partners. Working with existing security measures, it allows network administrators to configure and enforce Internet mail policies for the entire enterprise. Visit www.tumbleweed.com for more information.

✔ **SurfinGate:** This security utility from Finjan Software performs gateway-level content inspection, including filtering of executable files, Java, ActiveX, JavaScript, VBScript, cookies, and browser plug-ins. SurfinGate allows network managers to selectively block specific files from being downloaded to end-user network computers and to allow access to specific files. For more information and a demo version, visit `www.finjan.com`.

✔ **Websense:** This application is used to restrict access to certain Internet sites and content, with the belief that this will make network users (meaning workers) more productive. It prohibits certain content from downloading to network nodes. Visit Websense, Inc.'s, Web site at `www.websense.com`.

Token and PKI authentication

Sometimes, regular passwords just aren't enough to protect your network security from being penetrated. These software products provide additional public key or token protection:

✔ **CRYPTOAdmin:** This product provides a more secure user authentication process using PKI (Public Key Infrastructure) to keep out unauthorized users. CRYPTOAdmin is from CRYPTOCard Corporation. Visit `www.cryptocard.com` for more information and a downloadable version.

✔ **CRYPTOCard:** This is a token-based product from the same company that produces CRYPTOAdmin. A *token* is a one-time use password or security code that is generated by a token-security device, such as a credit-card-sized or key-chain code calculator. These devices are provided to authorized users who use them to log onto a network. The device is read directly like a credit card, or it displays a changing number that is entered as a one-time password. Visit `www.cryptocard.com` for more information.

✔ **KyberPASS:** This product uses PKI to implement security policies and simplify security administration. This software authenticates users, provides access control to information, and secures applications. For more information visit Kyberpass's Web site at `www.kyberpass.com`.

✔ **RSA SecurID:** This approach to token authentication is based on both a password or PIN and a token generated by what RSA Security calls an *authenticator*. RSA stands for Rivest, Shamir, and Adleman, the developers of the encryption method applied. Visit `www.rsasecurity.com/products/securid` for more information.

A Cisco tool and a great information site

This is the miscellaneous part of the list. Cisco provides a great tool for inventorying and analyzing your network for security holes, and an Australian company provides a great site for security information:

✔ **Cisco Scanner:** This Cisco utility scans your network, looking for any security weak points. It automatically creates an inventory of all the devices and servers on your network, which it then uses to identify any point of vulnerability on the network. Any security weaknesses are then displayed in a grid. For information on this Cisco product, visit `www.cisco.com/univercd/cc/td/doc/pcat/nssq.htm`.

✔ **Computer and Network Security Reference Index:** This index site contains links to information sources on network security provided for education and application of computer security. Visit it at `www.vtcif.telstra.com.au/info/security.html`.

Firing up the caching engine

Cisco makes a series of caching servers that can be used in conjunction with Cisco routers and switches to reduce the amount of traffic and demand placed on the Internet by a network and to provide a small level of increased security.

The Cisco cache engines (and its content engines for that matter) work like this:

1. A user requests a Web document from a remote Web server.

2. The router or switch redirects the user's request to the cache engine.

3. One of two things occurs:

   • Should the cache server have the information, it supplies the requested document, eliminating the need to go on the Internet for it.

   • If the cache server doesn't have the user's document, it accesses the remote server for the information, stores a copy in its cache, and forwards a copy on to the user's workstation.

4. Routers and switches work with the cache server through the WCCP (Web Cache Communications Protocol).

   The WCCP is used to redirect HTTP (HyperText Transfer Protocol) requests coming from the original site into the cache engine's cache.

Cisco offers four models of caching servers in its content engine series, which replaced the cache engine series. Depending on the model of cache server, these caching appliances work in tandem with Cisco routers or switches.

This brief description of the Cisco Content Engine models should help you make a choice for your network:

- **Content Engine 7320:** This is a high-end Internet content delivery device designed for use on the WAN edge by large enterprises and service providers to connect to the Internet over OC-3 transmission services.

- **Content Engine 590:** This is a high-end cache engine best suited to large enterprises and ISPs using DS3 or higher bandwidth.

- **Content Engine 560:** As you might suspect, this model is a mid-range cache engine designed for medium to large enterprises and mid-sized ISPs.

- **Content Engine 507:** This is an entry-level cache engine that is well-suited for smaller offices with bandwidth around the level of a T1 (1.54 Mbps).

Creating a Virtually Private Network

A *virtual private network* (VPN) uses advanced encryption techniques and tunneling protocols to create a secure, end-to-end private network over the Internet. In effect, a VPN turns the public network into a private network. Don't misunderstand; the Internet is still a public nonexclusive network, but the VPN makes one small part of it extremely private.

Tunneling for gold

Using the Internet for a VPN eliminates expensive leased DDS or Frame Relay lines (see Chapter 14) to create a private network between two points. Not only can using a leased service for a VPN be difficult to arrange, some transmission services can have long lead times and may be complicated to setup (if they are even available) for some remote locations. A VPN exists between two connecting points only while it is in use. With the right equipment or software, a traveling user can connect to the corporate offices from anywhere he or she can get Internet access. The VPN provides the user with a secured, private network over the Internet from anywhere he or she may roam. A VPN can also be used to secure access with suppliers and partnering companies to allow them to use applications running on the company servers. But the overriding reason for a VPN is its advanced security features.

Cisco has a wide range of VPN products that range from VPN-enabled routers and firewalls to dedicated VPN routers and access concentrators. Cisco divides its VPN products into two primary groups:

✔ **Site-to-Site VPN:** This group of products extends a company's WAN by creating secured, encrypted links between two or more fixed sites, such as a branch office and the corporate headquarters, over the Internet.

✔ **Remote Access VPN:** This product group supports secured, encrypted remote connections between mobile or remote users and the corporate network using Internet access from an ISP or other third-party network service provider.

Tunneling over the Internet

Although it may sound like it involves digging or boring holes in the Internet, *tunneling* could very well be called *smuggling*. Tunneling protocols, which are the mainstay of VPNs, create packets into which packets from other protocols are placed. This is the way that protocols like IPX or AppleTalk can be connected over the Internet, a process called *IP tunneling*. The tunneling protocol (TP) places the entire packet from the host protocol inside a transport packet before sending it over the network. At the other end, the TP extracts the host protocol packet and sends it on its way. In many respects, TPs are more like transport services than protocols.

Tunneling from point to point

Probably the most common tunneling protocol is Microsoft's *Point-to-Point Tunneling Protocol (PPTP)*. This TP encapsulates the packets from other protocols for transmission over an IP network. Because it supports various encryption techniques, such as RSA (Rivest-Shamir-Adleman) encryption, PPTP is used for VPNs. *RSA encryption* is a very secure encryption technique developed by RSA Data Security, Inc., (www.rsa.com) that uses a two-part key. The originator keeps one part, the private key; and the other part, the public key, is published with the message. Another tunneling protocol gaining popularity is the L2TP (Layer 2 Tunneling Protocol) developed by the IETF (Internet Engineering Task Force) as a combination of Microsoft's PPTP and Cisco's Layer 2 Forwarding (L2F). The L2TP was developed specifically for VPNs created over the Internet. L2TP supports non-IP protocols, such as AppleTalk and IPX, and incorporates the IPSec protocol.

Tunneling with security

The growing use of the Internet for secure transmissions has prompted the IETF to develop and publish a security protocol standard called *IPSec*, or IP Security, to provide authentication and encryption services over the Internet. IPSec works at Layer 3 (see Chapter 2) to secure everything sent over the network. IPSec was designed specifically for use with TCP/IP protocols and is likely to become the standard protocol for VPNs on the Internet.

For more information on VPNs

Here are some Web sites and my favorite VPN book that you can use to find more information on VPNs:

- ✔ Cisco's VPN Web site: `www.cisco.com/warp/public/779/largeent/learn/technologies/VPNs.html`.

- ✔ The Internet Engineering Task Force (IETF) Web site: `www.ietf.org`.

- ✔ Tina Bird and the Shmoo Group's VPN Information on the World Wide Web: `http://vpn.shmoo.com/`.

- ✔ SoftFX's VPN Insider: `www.vpninsider.com`.

- ✔ My favorite VPN book: *Virtual Private Networks For Dummies* by Mark Merkow (Wiley).

Chapter 20

Implementing VPNs

*T*he days when the employees, customers, and vendors of a company had to physically show up at the company's place of business to work, buy, or sell are waning. The Internet is the catalyst that allows employees to work from home or on the road; customers to access product information, check order status, or place orders; and vendors to receive orders, post shipping information, and transmit invoices directly into the company's network.

The Internet, the TCP/IP protocols, and the new wizardry of networking device manufacturers (especially Cisco Systems) have created opportunities for secure internal and external networks over which a company can conduct much of its business.

Don't confuse what I'm describing here with something like Amazon.com or eBay.com, although in many ways their Web sites and services use many of the service types to which I'm referring. The private online services of a company are just a bit more secured than either of these fine online vendors use.

A company has essentially two generic choices for secured networks, each designed for supporting internal, external, or both, users: intranets and extranets, respectively. Companies' choices for secured networks fall into two generic categories: intranets or extranets, which can be set up to support either internal users or external users, respectively. Users on an internal network connect through an intranet and external users can access a local network through an extranet.

This chapter deals primarily with the technology used to implement a secured network available to any external user. This type of network is a virtual private network, or VPN. This chapter covers the what, why, and in general terms, the how of VPNs.

Getting a Virtual Understanding of VPNs

In the not too distant past, a WAN (wide area network) was the only means a company had to connect remote users into its network. In order to secure the network, or at least make an attempt, a company had to depend on the inherent security of leased communications lines, which were not always secure. This included such services as ISDN (Integrated Service Digital Network), Frame Relay, ATM, or other high-speed dedicated services. These services allowed the company to expand its private network beyond its walls and open it to geographically disperse users.

The downside of leased communications services is the cost. At one point, a brilliant deep-thinker came up with the idea that the Internet, which is essentially free, could be used to enable remote employees, customers, and vendors to access the company's private network. Somehow, the fact that free is always a better price had eluded everyone. Fortunately, as it always happens, someone eventually noticed, and the idea for virtual private networks was born.

What's a VPN, and what can it do?

The first thing you need to understand is that a virtual private network is not virtually private. The virtual part refers to a network that is created virtually for each access by a remote user. The goal of a VPN is to be absolutely private or secure. Perhaps VPNs would be better served by a name that would better identify what they are and do, such as Absolutely Private Virtual Networks. Regardless, the powers that be choose to use VPN over the more descriptive APVN — go figure!

A company or organization can use the VPN for virtually any type of data transmission, including file transfers, business transactions, database access, and even dial-up access. In doing so, a number of benefits can be realized. Here are just a few of them:

- ✔ **Extend the geography of the network:** A VPN enables remote users, no matter where they are in the world, to connect and interact with the company's private network as if they were sitting inside the company's walls.

- ✔ **Improved security:** This is typically the primary reason a company installs a VPN. The encryption and compression services of a VPN add a dimension of security that isn't as easy to implement over other WAN services.

✔ **Increased productivity:** A VPN allows remote users to access network resources directly, which enables them to work more efficiently than if the same work had to be done by e-mail, over the phone, or by physically traveling to the company's offices (which in itself could save a considerable amount of money).

✔ **Reduced overall networking costs:** Sure, you have to make an initial investment to install a VPN, but in the long run, by avoiding the use of leased, dedicated communication services (not to mention the long distance bills), the cost of operating the network is reduced. In addition, the company may no longer need to support or purchase equipment such as modem banks or those costly WAN communication services. Isn't everyone's goal to be freed from the bondage of the telephone company?

The essential VPN

In essence, a VPN is a private network that connects remote users who are using public network services, which in most cases is the Internet. A VPN creates a virtual network that is routed through the Internet from the private network to the remote user or users.

A basic VPN consists of:

✔ A main central LAN, typically at a company's headquarters

✔ Individual users, another remote LAN, or both connecting from remote locations

To set up the VPN, some special hardware or software is required to provide the gateway into the private LAN and to encrypt the transmissions between the VPN *end points* (the security part of the VPN that keeps the network private). Figure 20-1 shows the components that make up a basic VPN. VPN gateways, as shown in Figure 20-1, can be used to securely connect remote local area networks or remote dialup users to a central location through the Internet (lovingly called the "cloud").

Tunneling to the definitive VPN

A VPN provides a secured connection between two or more private networks over the public network, which at first brush may seem a bit contradictory. How can privacy be maintained over a public and largely unsecured byway? The answer lies in the tunneling and encryption technologies that are the foundation of a VPN.

Tunneling, when used in the context of a VPN, isn't like the tunneling that soldiers did during the Great War and that prisoners do in escape movies. *VPN tunneling* is more like carving a virtual tunnel with completely impenetrable walls through the Internet. Think of the Lincoln tunnel or the Chunnel between England and France. A VPN is a direct and secure path between two network points that keeps away the water, fish, and evildoers and enables data to pass through dry, safe, and secure.

The concept of VPN tunneling is discussed in more detail later in "Tunneling across the Internet."

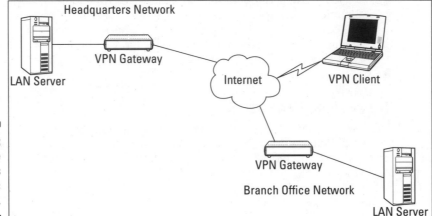

Figure 20-1:
The elements of a basic VPN.

Getting down to cases

You can use a VPN in a number of different variations and in a number of specific networking situations. However, nearly all VPN applications are a variation of one or more of the following three general application types:

- ✔ **Access VPNs:** This type of VPN provides remote access to a company's intranet or extranet using the same security policies applied on the internal network. Access VPNs are the nonspecific type of VPN that users can access from virtually any type of Internet connection, including dial-up, ISDN, DSL (Digital Subscriber Line), wireless, and so on. This enables a variety of users, including mobile users, telecommuters, or branch offices, to have access.

- ✔ **Intranet VPNs:** This type of VPN is used to connect corporate headquarters and remote or branch offices over a shared, dedicated connection. An intranet VPN extends the internal network policies of the intranet, including security and reliability, to the remote site.

- ✔ **Extranet VPNs:** This type of VPN connects customers, suppliers, partners, or other external communities to a company's intranet using the same network policies applied on the private network.

Intranets and extranets

An *intranet* is a private internal network that a company's employees use to access secured data and other network resources. Essentially, an intranet is a secured internal network that looks like a Web site and operates by using the same protocols and services used on the Web that extends the network globally. By definition, only a company's employees can access an intranet. Hence, the use of the prefix *intra*, meaning inside, as opposed to the Internet, where *inter* means between. Comparing an intranet to the Internet, an intranet is secure and has low accessibility, and the Internet has fairly low security and high accessibility.

An extranet, on the other hand, is an intranet that has been opened up to users outside the company, such as customers, vendors, dealers, and such. The primary difference between an extranet and a company's globally accessible Web site is that only those users whom the company has granted access (via a special logon account or password) can gain access to certain extranet resources on the company's network.

Tunneling across the Internet

The primary transport concept of a VPN is its tunneling protocol. Tunneling protocols may conjure in your imagination visions of tunnels being cut through the ether of the Internet, like a white hole through space (as opposed to a black hole). For me, I envision that, when I wish to transmit secured data between two points of the internetwork, the tunneling function begins pushing a hole through the Internet between just those specific points. When I'm finished, I picture the tunnel collapsing and evaporating. Well, it may sound like science fiction, like the sand worms of *Dune*, *Beetlejuice*, or *Tremors*, but a VPN tunnel isn't quite as cool. In fact, its simplicity may be disappointing to some.

When a packet is prepared to be transmitted via a tunnel, three types of protocols are involved:

- **Passenger protocol:** This is the protocol being encapsulated. It can be PPP, IPX, NetBEUI, or another networking protocol.

- **Encapsulating protocol:** This is the protocol used to create and open the encapsulated packet before and after it is transmitted across the VPN.

- **Carrier protocol:** This protocol is the transmitted protocol that carries the encapsulated packet over the network. IP is commonly the carrier protocol used.

Carving the tunnel

A tunneling protocol uses a special type of packet encapsulation to carry data across the internetwork. A tunnel is a virtual connection established between two (or more) end-points via a tunneling protocol. To create a tunnel, a tunneling protocol places the packets from a networking protocol, such as AppleTalk, IPX, NetBEUI, and others, inside a PPP packet and then encapsulates the whole bundle inside an IP packet for transport. Add to this the fact that the encapsulated data may also be encrypted, which makes the contents extremely secure. Of course, the receiving end must be able to disencapsulate the bundle and decode the encrypted packet if needed so that its native protocol can process the packet.

The most commonly used tunneling protocols are:

- **Layer 2 Forwarding (L2F):** L2F is a Cisco protocol used for creating VPNs over dial-up networks. L2F encapsulates non-IP packets for transport. However, it does not include an encryption standard.

- **Point-to-Point Tunneling Protocol (PPTP):** PPTP is generally associated with Microsoft, but Microsoft was only one of several companies involved in PPTP's development. Like L2F, PPTP encapsulates non-IP protocols. However, it doesn't define a single encryption scheme. This means that two end-point VPN devices could be incompatible if they use different encryption schemes.

- **Layer 2 Tunneling Protocol (L2TP):** Cisco endorses and implements L2TP, which was developed by the IETF (Internet Engineering Task Force). L2TP combines the best features of PPTP and L2F. Like L2F, L2TP is a Layer 2 protocol (See Chapter 5) and, as such, is designed to operate on services such as Frame Relay, ATM, or SONET. (See Chapter 14 for more information on these and other transmission services.)

- **Internet Protocol Security (IPSec):** IPSec is a set of related Layer 3 (Network layer) protocols defined by the Internet Engineering Task Force (IETF). The IPSec protocols can be used to create a VPN solution. IPSec encryption is also now used in PPTP and L2TP to provide a standard encryption method. The design goal of IPSec was to protect against middleman attacks, which makes it perfect for VPNs. See Chapter 18 for more information on IPSec and other security protocols.

- **Secure Sockets Network Security Protocol (SOCKS):** SOCKS is a somewhat different VPN protocol in that it is a Layer 5 (Session layer) protocol. SOCKS enables network administrators to limit the access to certain applications over the VPN. However, the downside to SOCKS is that it requires the configuration and use (and expense) of a SOCKS proxy server and SOCKS-enabled software on the client computers.

A variety of proprietary VPN protocols are also in use. However, most VPN device manufacturers are now turning to IPSec as their standard. IPSec includes the capability to encrypt data between a variety of device connections, including router-to-router, firewall-to-router, PC-to-router, and PC-to-server.

The essential VPN protocol services

All VPN protocols share four common functions:

- ✔ **Authentication:** This process makes VPN users prove their identity, either through account names and passwords or through an identity number, before users can gain access to the network.

- ✔ **Authorization:** VPN users have certain access rights assigned to them, which are tied to their authentication identity.

- ✔ **Encapsulation:** This is carried out through the encapsulation processes of the tunneling protocol. Don't confuse encryption with encapsulation. Not all tunneling protocols apply encryption, at least not on every network. However, encapsulation provides mechanisms that allow the receiver to be assured that the data was not tampered with in transit.

- ✔ **Encryption:** This is the process that, in essence, scrambles the contents of either the entire packet or just the packet payload in order to make it unreadable to anyone who might intercept it on its way across the internetwork.

Keeping secrets secret

Limiting access to a network is only half of what is needed to secure data and keep your secrets secret. Encryption is the other half of the solution. Encryption provides a mechanism to keep your data private as it flows across the wide-open spaces of the Internet. If data is sent "in the clear," meaning in text and readable form, a packet sniffer can easily intercept the data somewhere along its journey from source to destination.

Secure VPNs include an encrypting system that encodes data into what is called cipher text. If both the sending end and the receiving end are using the same encryption system, the data can be encoded before it is sent and decoded after it is received. Anyone who intercepts the data in transit will spend considerable time and effort to make sense of its encrypted form.

Although a variety of encryption schemes are available, the following two basic encryption types are the most common:

- ✓ **Asymmetric:** This type of encryption is complex and uses mathematically derived encryption keys, one of which is public and the other private. Because of its complexity, asymmetric encryption is primarily used for smaller, highly secure data or during the authentication process.

- ✓ **Symmetric:** This less complex encryption type is typically used to encode large packets of data being transmitted between related parties. It uses the same private session key to encode and decode the data.

You will see encryption schemes defined with an associated number of bits, such as 8-bit, 16-bit, 32-bit, and on up to 256-bit encryption. The more bits, the longer the encryption key. And the longer the encryption key, the more difficult it is to crack.

Building a VPN

First, you need to understand the building blocks that you can use to construct a VPN. Cisco makes a number of products that can apply increasing levels of the essential VPN services (see "The essential VPN protocol services" earlier in the chapter). However, in most VPN implementations, a variety of hardware and software elements are typically applied to provide the security and access control required.

The VPN building blocks

In general, a VPN requires the following elements:

- ✓ **Authentication, Authorization, and Accounting (AAA) server:** In remote access VPN systems, when a request for access comes in, the request is sent to an AAA server, which is a special-purpose proxy server. The AAA server then verifies who the requester is (authentication), what the requester is allowed to do (authorization), and what the requester actually does (accounting). The accounting information is useful for auditing security issues, utilization tracking, or billing purposes.

- ✓ **Firewall:** The purpose of a firewall is to create an impenetrable barrier between a local network and the Internet. Firewalls can be used to restrict access based on the port number, packet type, or IP addresses included in an incoming packet. Cisco makes a full line of firewalls, the Secure PIX Firewall series, for use in somewhat larger networks. However, many of Cisco's VPN-ready routers, such as the Cisco 1700 series routers, can add a firewall function through the IOS (Internetwork Operating System). In Cisco's opinion, a firewall is an essential element of a VPN.

✔ **Network access server (NAS):** A NAS is used to provide access through the VPN to protected network resources for remote access users.

✔ **VPN client:** If the VPN is a remote access type, then typically users must have VPN client software loaded on their computers. The VPN client serves as a smaller scale VPN gateway for the user and manages transmissions across the VPN.

✔ **VPN gateway:** The encapsulation, encryption, and decryption of data are done on the VPN gateway, which can either be a specific, dedicated device, such as a Cisco VPN Concentrator, or through VPN software running on a server. Many proprietary and turnkey VPN solutions are available, including Cisco's (listed in the following section). Proprietary solutions include what Cisco calls a "VPN network and policy management center," which, because there is no single VPN standard, performs most of the essential VPN services.

Examining the Cisco solutions

Cisco Systems produces a variety of systems that you can use to implement a VPN. Without detailing every single product and model, here are the major device categories you can use to install a VPN in your organization:

✔ **VPN access concentrator:** Cisco VPN Concentrators incorporate the latest and most advanced encryption and authentication methods currently available. These include Scalable Encryption Processing (SEP), which provides the same level of security and VPN services to businesses whether they have less than 100 users or run large enterprise applications with as many as 10,000 simultaneous users.

An example of a Cisco VPN concentrator is the Cisco 3000 Concentrator series. The devices in this series can be used in both single-user-to-LAN (which requires a user-end VPN client) and LAN-to-LAN VPN connections.

✔ **VPN-capable routers:** The Cisco 7100, 7200, and 7400 series routers can be configured to support VPN. Virtually all Cisco routers can also be configured to provide firewall services. Cisco also has a software enhancement for its existing routers and firewalls called Cisco Easy VPN, which has two components: Cisco Easy VPN Remote and Cisco Easy VPN Server. The remote component allows Cisco routers, firewalls and other hardware to act as remote VPN clients. The server component manages the central or host site, processing all incoming requests for VPN services.

✔ **Secure PIX firewalls:** The PIX firewall series performs a wide variety of security and privacy functions, including NAT (network address translation), proxy server, packet filtering, and VPN support.

Over a remote access VPN, Cisco depends on PPP as the carrier for secured IP packets. In a LAN-to-LAN VPN, Generic Routing Encapsulation (GRE) is used to encapsulate packets for transmission on Cisco hardware. Where GRE is not used, IPSec tunnel mode (see Chapter 18) is used as the encapsulating protocol, which can be used in either remote access or LAN-to-LAN applications.

Part VI
The Part of Tens

The 5th Wave

By Rich Tennant

"It's okay. One of the routers must have gone down and we had a brief broadcast storm."

In this part . . .

This part of the book provides you valuable information in bits of ten — ten network design tips that can help you create a better network; ten tips for a safe and trouble-free installation; and ten things you should pay attention to when configuring a Cisco router.

Use them or not, they are here for your information and later reference.

Chapter 21

Ten Great Network Design Tips

· ·

In This Chapter
▶ Tips for designing a Cisco network
▶ Verifying a network design

· ·

Should you ever be so lucky as to have the opportunity to design your very own Cisco network, you have my condolences. Yes, I am ambivalent about this task. Designing your very own network allows you to put into use all your ideas for how a network really should be put together. On the other hand, when you are the designer of the network, you must shoulder the blame (and credit) for how the network performs in real life. Often, the creative and brilliant design that looked so wonderful on paper could use just a little more design work in reality.

In this chapter, I have included ten areas, considerations, or issues that I believe must be a part of a successful network design. If you have never designed (or redesigned) a network, then hopefully the information in this chapter will help you. If you are an old hand at this, your reaction after you've read this chapter may be, "I knew that!" And that's great! I'm glad that I could be of service to remind you.

Ten Steps to Include When Designing a Network

Here are ten steps that you really should include when designing your network:

Determine the users' needs

If you think that you know more about your users' needs than they do, think again! Regardless of how you feel about it or what you believe to be their true requirements, the users definitely know what they need the network to do.

Regardless of whether you are in a new network development where little or no technology already exists, or what the true techies call a "greenfield" situation, or designing an extension, upgrade, or major overhaul of a network, you should ask first, document, and then design.

Document the existing network

If you have an existing network, it likely will be the basis of any future network. So make sure that the existing network is well documented — good and bad. The good is what it does well, and the bad is what it could do better. The bad is often why you are redesigning the network in the first place, but make sure that you include the good stuff in the new, redesigned network, as well.

Determine the appropriate structure

Using what you've read about in the preceding steps, you should now be able to decide the arrangement, topology, and technology that best supports the needs of the users and addresses the best of the existing network. If you can't, then you must repeat these steps until you can. Chances are, if you had an Ethernet network with departmental segmentation before and that wasn't the problem causing a redesign, then that's what you should have moving forward. You likely are not replacing a functioning Fast Ethernet network with a token ring, but it could happen.

If you are designing a new network, the physical arrangement of the organization and the users will be a major consideration in designing the layout of the network as well as its topology. If the organization is all in one building, it may be spread over separate floors. If the organization is in many buildings on a campus, then that will definitely impact your decision on both structure and topology.

Create a network drawing

This is the perfect time to convert your vision to a drawing. This will help you to visualize what you had in mind and perform your first reality check. This drawing will be the visual reference for your network design as you go forward. As you complete each subsequent step, you should update the drawing and include an increasing amount of detail about the elements depicted. Even if you aren't much of an artist or draftsperson, tools like Microsoft's Vision 2002 (or any later edition) are available to bring out the artist in anyone.

Choose the hardware and media

Okay, now that you have laid out the network and have chosen the topology that you're going to use, you must choose the network hardware and data transmission media best suited to the demands of the network. This is actually a fairly big phase of the design process.

- ✔ **First, you must choose the network media best suited to the performance requirements established by the users.**

  For example, if the consensus is that the network must be Fast Ethernet, then you know right away that you can no longer use the Cat 3 wiring in the wall and must replace it with Cat 5. Some things are just obvious. If the network is to be Ethernet with a data speed of 10 Mbps or faster, the wiring is Cat 5 or better.

- ✔ **Set the physical distance limitations of the network.**

  This nails down the switching and routing devices to be used. These devices must also be fitted to the functions, topology, and speeds planned for the network. Cisco includes a number of tools and guides on their Web site (www.cisco.com) to assist you in this activity.

- ✔ **Redraw the network layout, this time to scale.**

  Make sure that all the segments are properly served with adequate bandwidth and that the media runs do not exceed the distance limitations. This is also an excellent time to apply your naming convention and assign network names to the switches and routers on the net.

Select routing and switching protocols

Each of the Cisco routers and switches that you have included in the design of the network most likely has a range of routing, bridging, and switching protocols from which you can choose. Use caution to ensure that the protocols you choose are interoperable with all equipment on the network. Remember that some protocols may be best suited for LANs and others to WANs.

Determining which is best in which situations may require some research. Again, the Cisco Systems' Web site is an excellent source for information. For a list of the protocols available on a particular device, consult the *Cisco Product Catalog*. You can review this document at the following Web site:

```
www.cisco.com/univercd/cc/td/doc/pcat/
```

Choose the operating system

The network operating system (NOS) that will operate the network from the main network server must be chosen or reconfirmed. However, this isn't the only operating system that will operate on the network. In addition to determining the features of the NOS that must be installed, you should also determine the features (and version) of the Cisco IOS that your network will require.

Document the new design

If you have been updating your network design drawing as you went along, you now need only to write a narrative that describes what you have included on the network diagram. If you have been skipping that part of the design process, you will unfortunately now need to create both a detailed network drawing and an explanation of the network details depicted.

It would be valuable at this point if you met again with your users to explain to them, in nontechnical terms, just what the network has been designed to provide to them. A review with the technical or Information Technology (IT) staff of your organization would be an excellent idea at this point as well. Remember that these peer review sessions are also called "turkey shoots" for a reason.

Review the network's design

One good way to conduct a review of your network design is in a peer-review session, which I also refer to as "turkey shoots." Presenting your design concepts and policies to a gathering of your peers is an excellent way to catch the obvious problems, errors, and "gotchas" of your network design. One area of focus in such a review should be any security aspects of the design.

Test the network

Remember that nothing is quite like real life for providing the ultimate test. If at all possible, you need to build up the network design by using the actual routers and switches to test their interoperability and compatibility prior to deploying them around the network. Of course, this is only feasible with completely new networks or in very wealthy companies.

At minimum, test the network under as many peak use conditions as possible. Try to simulate every operating condition you identified way back in the step that identified the users' needs. Don't be too surprised if a user discovers the one weakness that you forgot to test the minute he logs onto the network.

Designing around Network Congestion

In much the same way that highways become congested at rush hour, networks can become congested when too much network traffic tries to move along too little bandwidth. Congestion is a common reason for network redesign, or at least adjustment.

Common causes for network congestion are

- Segments or collision domains with too many users for the available bandwidth

- Too many users vying for the same networked applications, such as bandwidth hogs like desktop publishing or multimedia, or too many large files moving across the network

- A large percentage of workstations accessing the Internet

- Network workstations' processing power that has increased faster than the network's capabilities

Congestion can be avoided or minimized by including some basic design considerations:

- Place network clients on the same network as the servers that the clients will use most. This reduces the amount of traffic moving over the network's backbone from segment to segment.

- Move applications and files from one server to another to help balance traffic and contain it to one segment. If you can't move software and files, then try moving the user workstations to balance the demand. I don't mean *physically* move them, but consider using a VLAN implementation instead.

- Design the network to keep as much traffic as possible on its local segment and free up the network overall for intersegment and Internet-bound traffic.

- Increase the number of servers supporting user client/server activities, so that more servers are providing resources to more local segments.

- When all else fails, you should apply what is perhaps the most commonly used solution to network congestion: Increase the number of network segments by inserting a switch or a router into the network. This step may require a quick design review of the network, though.

A Checklist of Network Must-Haves

The items in the checklists in the following sections may seem like no-brainers, but sometimes the simplest (and most obvious) things can be overlooked in a design.

Don't forget these in a small LAN

These items are essential for a small LAN:

 ✔ You need at least two network workstations (clients).

 ✔ The workstations must each have at least one NIC installed.

 ✔ A client/server network must have at least one server.

 ✔ The workstations must be connected to the network via a hub.

 ✔ Some form of network-compatible cabling must be used to connect the workstation NICs and the server to the hub.

 ✔ The server requires a NOS.

 ✔ If the network is connecting to the outside world, it will need a modem or a small router.

You'll need these to connect offices

In addition to the items required for the small LAN, you'll need to add the following to your network to connect geographically dispersed offices:

 ✔ If the offices are just on different floors of the same building, then one or more switches can be used to connect them.

 ✔ If the offices are in different geographical locations, you may need to use routers to interconnect the LAN of each office to the WAN.

 ✔ Assuming that the WAN is also connected to the Internet, you will need a router for that purpose as well.

 ✔ You can't have a WAN without some form of WAN service. This could be in the form of ISDN, Frame Relay, or a leased-line from the telephone company, an ILEC (Incumbent Local Exchange Carrier — the local phone company), or a CLEC (Competing Local Exchange Carrier — such as a network service provider).

 ✔ If users are allowed to access the network via a dial-up connection, you will need to provide an access server.

Chapter 22

Ten Network Installation Tips

*I*nstalling a network requires the same analysis, planning, and attention to detail, regardless of its size or complexity. Whether you are building a simple network with one segment or a complex network with hundreds of segments on a corporate campus or WAN, you need to know the network's objectives and how it must meet the needs of the organization. For any installation to be successful, the planning is the same. The only question is one of degree.

In this chapter, I list ten steps to take in any network installation project. How much time each takes depends on how much detail is required for your network, but one thing is sure: You must give each step all the time that it requires and not rush the planning to save time. Any shortcuts taken in the preinstallation processes may very well show up later as problems on the network.

Using a Site Preparation Checklist

Cisco includes several preinstallation, site preparation, and safety checklists in the documentation of nearly all of its products and definitely for all of its router and Catalyst switch products. You can also get these checklists online at the Cisco Web site (www.cisco.com). These checklists are general guides that list what you should consider when preparing a site for networking equipment.

You should locate and apply these two specific guides:

- The Preinstallation Checklist
- The Site Preparation and Safety Guide

Checking out the Preinstallation Checklist

With Cisco routers, you should be given a Preinstallation Checklist to complete. This checklist serves two purposes. First, it lets Cisco know who your contact person is to be for the installation, how to contact him or her, and where and when you would like to install the router. It also provides a list of preparation questions that, when answered, will provide you with virtually every consideration for preparing to install the router. These questions are included in the Preinstallation Checklist:

- Will the equipment be installed in a rack or a table?
- Is the appropriate power source available?
- If required, are the WAN circuit components (CSU/DSU, Frame-Relay circuit, and so on) installed and ready to be connected?
- Is the LAN connection installed and ready to be connected?
- Is an RJ-11 connection for an active analog phone line (to be used for dial-up access) available within 50 feet of the installation location?
- Are all required LAN and WAN cables in the appropriate length and with the proper connectors ready and available?
- What is the Cisco IOS version to be installed on the router?
- What tests are to be performed, and who is to perform them, to prove that the installation is successful?

Studying the Site Preparation and Safety Guide

Right off the bat, you will get the feeling that if you don't know what you are doing, you should leave the installation of your router or switch to a trained professional. In fact, the first words in this guide — right after it tells you that you should read the guide before installing or servicing your system — are that only trained and qualified personnel should ever install, replace, or repair your Cisco equipment.

Next, it tells you that the guide is designed to keep you from electrocuting yourself and to prevent other accidents that may cause bodily injury. I'm definitely all for that!

These things are highlighted in the Site Preparation and Safety Guide:

- ✔ Choosing the best possible site for installation
- ✔ Protecting the system from electrical problems
- ✔ Properly grounding the system
- ✔ Keeping the area around the system safe during and after installation
- ✔ Properly installing the system in a rack-mounting
- ✔ Lifting the system without injuring yourself
- ✔ Providing the proper electrical power source
- ✔ Preventing ESD (electrostatic discharge) damage to your system
- ✔ Installing and servicing the system safely to avoid electrical, laser, and EMI (electromagnetic interference) problems

Preparing the Site's Environment

A Site Environmental Guideline is included in the installation materials that come as a part of your Cisco system's documentation. This document contains the minimums and maximum for each of the environmental characteristics that you need to address as a part of your installation preparations.

For example, the environmental characteristics required for the Cisco 6400, listed in its environmental guidelines, are summarized in Table 22-1.

Table 22-1	Environmental Guidelines for the Cisco 6400	
Characteristic	**Minimum**	**Maximum**
Ambient operating temperature	25° Fahrenheit (−4° Celsius)	104° Fahrenheit (40° Celsius)
Relative humidity	5%	95%
Operating altitude	-200 feet (-61 meters)	10,000 ft (3,048 m)
Operating vibration	-5 to 200 Hertz	

Racking It Up

One topic that Cisco installation guides cover in extreme detail is how to properly install your system in a rack-mount. However, the one point I want to make about rack-mount installations is that you must plan this type of installation very carefully, taking into consideration the equipment already installed in the rack or the equipment that you plan to install in the rack at some later time.

You must provide for proper airflow and wire management, as well as common-sense weight distribution, when installing any equipment into an existing or a new rack-mount. Probably the most important of these, not that any are really unimportant, is the weight distribution. Don't forget that two-rail rack systems must be bolted to the floor and that you want to put the really heavy stuff on the bottom and the lightest equipment at the top.

Planning the rack according to its functional mates (switches with punch-down blocks, or routers with firewalls) may not actually provide you with the safest installation when you consider the weight of the devices. And never arrange your rack by color or any other nontechnical or whimsical way. Should a top-heavy rack topple over, not only is it likely to hurt you or a co-worker, but it may well damage your very expensive equipment.

Flooring the Load

Along with the considerations of weight distribution of a rack-mount system (see the preceding section), you should at least consider the weight distribution and floor loading of the entire networking system. Many buildings, especially high-rise buildings and older buildings, have floor loading specifications or codes with which you must comply.

No one piece of networking equipment, including servers, routers, firewalls, switches, racks, and so on, is all that heavy by itself. However, when you add up all the equipment that is stacked in one or two rack-mount bays, then you may have a great deal of weight sitting on a small piece of flooring. You may need to space rack bays apart or locate the rack on a part of the floor supported by a weight-bearing beam or joist.

Table 22-2 contains a sample of the device weight information included in the installation guidelines for the Cisco 6400 switch. Not every component is listed, but you can see how the weight of devices can add up.

Table 22-2	Component Weights for the Cisco 6400	
Component	*Weight/lbs*	*Weight/kg*
Empty chassis	37.80	17.20
AC Power Entry Module	10.90	4.95
DC Power Entry Module	6.20	2.80
Blower/Fan module	10.95	4.97
Totally populated chassis	130.00	59.02

Powering the System

Not all Cisco gear is powered by 110 AC electrical power. In fact, much of the higher-end equipment is available in either AC-powered or DC-powered models. Each piece of Cisco equipment has a very definite power requirement. You can find the power considerations for your system in the Site Preparation and Safety Guide, as well as in the documentation of the system.

The power considerations of a Cisco router include the wattage of the internal power supply (AC or DC), the operating range allowable for the power source, and any wiring recommendations. For example, Cisco 7500 series routers have the following power specifications:

- **600-watt internal power supply:** Either an AC-input power supply or a DC-input supply
- **AC voltage and current range:** 100 to 240 VAC and 50 to 60 Hz
- **DC voltage range:** –40 and –52 VDC (–48 VDC nominal)
- **AC wire specification:** 12 AWG with three leads, an IEC-320 plug (router end), country-dependent plug (power-source end)

In addition to ensuring that you have adequate and appropriate power sources for your system, you also need to make sure that you have protected your system against low-voltage, over-voltage, and surge conditions on the power source. You should also provide an ample UPS (uninterruptible power supply) power backup to power the system until your generator kicks in. You do have a generator, don't you?

Many of these considerations may seem a bit over the top if all you are planning to install is a Cisco 805 router and an 8-port hub. Remember that you still need to address the power requirements of the system, just not as in-depth as you would with the 7505 router.

Clearing the Cable Path

Before you get too carried away with all the nice new green toys from Cisco, you absolutely must do one thing before you can hook it all up. I mentioned in the section "Using a Site Preparation Checklist," earlier in this chapter, that you must have the LAN cabling and connections ready to connect to the router or switch when installing that device. However, you must take care of a few steps involving your cabling before you get to that point.

Critical to installing a network is installing its cable media. In many cases, cabling was installed by the electricians that helped build the building even before you were hired. Or it was installed when the building was remodeled, or you yourself just finished pulling the network cable into place. If the cabling issue has not been resolved, then you need to complete this job before you can complete the installation of your network.

Perhaps the most critical aspect of this part of the installation is making sure that you have a clear path for the cable. The cable needs to run cleanly without bends and kinks from one connector to the next. If you have chosen to install a wireless system, which is becoming more common lately, then make sure that nothing obstructs or interferes with the devices you want to connect. In either case, wire or wireless, your network will perform better with no problems along the media path.

Sweeping the Cable Path

This section may seem like it belongs in the preceding section, but I feel so strongly about it, I've chosen to eat up one of your ten installation tips with it.

Even with the network media placed into the best possible pathways available, the whole network can be brought to its electronic knees by an electrically noisy pop machine or that nearby radio tower or that radioactive waste dump under your building. The cable path may be like a wide-open four-lane highway, but if it must pass through interference for radio frequency (RF), electromagnetic interference (EMI), or other electrical or magnetic noise hazards, it is all for naught.

In short, you really should check the network path for potential EMI, RF, and other hazards to your network cable media as a part of your installation preparations.

Tooling Up for the Job

Unfortunately for you frustrated Tim "the Toolman" Taylor wannabees, few specialized tools are required for the installation of a network. Largely, the tools you need for installing a network are a screwdriver, a pair of wire cutters, and a crimper suited to the connector that you are using. You could use a lifting device to raise a high-end router, firewall, or switch into place so you can attach it to the rack-mount rails. You could also use a digital multimeter, or a fox-and-hound style cable tone tester, to verify electrical and cable connections. But beyond that, you shouldn't need special tools.

Of course, the easiest way to make sure that you have all the right tools needed for the cable and system installation is to hire installers. Cisco will contract for the installation of your system, as will most Cisco value-added resellers (VARs).

Scheduling Downtime to Test

If you are adding or updating equipment in an existing network, you will need to schedule some downtime to fully test the new configuration of the network. If you work in an environment like mine, then this time will come after midnight, when the logged-in subscriber base is smaller. If you work in a small office environment, then you may be able to employ network users in the test.

In most test situations, though, schedule network downtime for a time that is the least disruptive for the users of the network. Keep in mind why and for whom the network exists. Unfortunately, unless you own a large software company in the Seattle area, the network does not exist solely for you.

Training, Training, Training

If you are a network administrator or are working at becoming one, you have my permission to reproduce this section and give it to your supervisor.

Dear Networking Supervisor,

Perhaps the most important, and often most overlooked, part of preparing for a network installation is the training of the key individuals who will be charged with the efficient, reliable, and secure operation of the network. Companies will spend thousands, even hundreds of thousands, of dollars to purchase the routers, switches, cabling, workstations, and software used to build the network but will scrimp on the training of the people who are expected to make it all work. If keeping the network running were all magic, then it would be no problem. If Cisco were able to manufacture a system that fit perfectly in every situation, just by plugging it in, then training wouldn't even be needed. But training is needed. So train the network administrators. The investment in training always pays dividends, if not in operational efficiency, then at least in employee morale.

Best of luck with your new network.

Chapter 23

Ten Things to Check When Configuring a Cisco Router

*T*en things that you should make absolutely sure to include in the procedure you use to control the configuration process of your routers, and a
few helpful hints about some of these actions, are included in this chapter.
Although other considerations may be necessary in setting up your network,
these are the ten that I believe you must include in your router configuration
process.

Your Equipment

You're probably in one of two situations: You have ordered the specific equipment that you need, and you have been working with Cisco routers and
switches for some time now. Or you are brand new to all this, and you really
do want our help in defining the steps that you should take to configure a
router. In either case, these steps provide a good checklist against forgetting
a very valuable step in this critical activity.

Follows these tips to get started:

- Make sure that you have your router's documentation and locate any information about the router on the Cisco Web site (www.cisco.com). You need this information whether or not you have configured a router before.

- Make sure that you have all the appropriate cables, adapters, and connectors. Nothing is more frustrating than stopping work because you don't have a vital piece of equipment.

- Test to be sure that your PC or notebook computer has the applications you'll need, such as HyperTerminal and Notepad, and that you know how to operate them. If you are using a notebook or laptop computer, check that you have a power supply and, if you will be working where no AC power is available, that the battery is adequate for the job.

- Make sure that the IOS version is the one you need for the network project. With some network implementations, you may also need more than the standard memory that was shipped with your router.

The Configuration Methodologies

How you configure your router today will impact how you, or your replacement, will configure it in the future. Documenting exactly how you configure the router is important. Do you run the setup routine when you power the router up for the first time? (Although this is the common practice, you can use other options.) Do you use the automatic setup routine, or do you manually enter the configuration, one line at a time? Do you instead copy the initial configuration into the router in the privileged EXEC mode?

Using a common router configuration from a previously configured router can be quite a timesaver. Remember that the configuration file is a text file and that you can use a text editor to create or modify a configuration, changing those items that are unique to a particular router, such as its hostname, banner, IP address, and any interface information. The file can then be copied to the router.

Not just any text editor should be used to edit the configuration files. For example, the Windows Notepad, a commonly used text editor, can add extra spaces and line feeds, which may really muck up your configuration and cause a headache or two when you copy it back to the router. A better choice is the plain old MS-DOS EDIT command.

Regardless of how you configure the router, the configuration will affect how you modify the configuration in the future. Of course, what you do today does not mean that you can't use a different manner in the future, but it may affect how the configuration process is documented today. And documenting the configuration and the process used are the most important parts of these decisions.

Network Management

How are the network, and especially the routers and switches, to be managed? If the network is a simple affair with a small office router and a small number of nodes, management may be easily performed without the need for sophisticated management tools. However, if the network is very large, you need to decide which SNMP traps you want to see. As a part of the router's configuration, you must decide which traps are to be sent and where this information is to be sent.

LAN Addressing Scheme

Before you place your router into service on the network, you should check, and then check again, the IP addresses used in its configurations. Verify that, if you have decided to use an internal IP addressing scheme, you have consistently done so throughout the configuration. If you have used a specific numbering scheme to designate routers, switches, servers, and even printers and workstations on the network, check to see that your scheme is consistently applied.

Be sure to check the access list wildcard masks and the application of subnet masks in the configuration. In case I haven't mentioned it, you should document the IP addressing scheme used on the network.

LAN Protocols

Be sure that all the LAN protocols required for all network nodes to talk with all other parts of the network are installed and enabled. Also, be sure that any unneeded LAN protocols are removed or disabled, so that your network performance is not affected. Too many LAN protocols can hurt the network's performance just as much as too few can.

WAN Addressing Scheme

Remember that you can't use an internal IP addressing scheme to communicate with the outside world over the Internet. You must be sure that the IP addressing scheme to be applied to WAN interfaces is a public scheme that is routable and built to conserve IP addresses. For example, link interfaces should use a 255.255.255.252 subnet mask, when possible — assuming you are using a classful addressing scheme. This yields a network ID, one IP address for each WAN interface, and a broadcast address, conserving other IP addresses for other uses.

If you are working with Frame-Relay in your WAN configuration, you will also need to know the DLCI for your end of the Frame-Relay connection. For ATM, FDDI, SONET, or SMDS connections, you will need the specific information needed to configure the network beyond its IP addressing.

Be sure to document the structure of the WAN connections and the IP addressing scheme used.

WAN Protocols

You must make several decisions when configuring a router to work in a WAN environment. These include the decision of whether to enable NAT (Network Address Translation), and if so, whether to use a one-to-one or one-to-many IP addressing pool. Another decision is whether the security needs of the network require static IP addressing. And yet another is which routing protocols are to be configured for use.

In the WAN environment, you must look beyond your network in making these choices. Using proprietary Cisco protocols, such as EIGRP, is a bad choice (meaning it won't work) if the next upstream hop is not a Cisco router. In situations where equipment from different vendors must communicate, an open-standard protocol, such as RIP, would be a better choice.

Router Security

Two elements affect the security of the router itself. The first is its physical location and how accessible it is to nonadministrators. You should follow your instincts that tell you to lock the router away, not only from prying eyes but from the fingers and hands associated with them as well.

The second element of router security is the passwords on the router that screen access to the router's configuration. Be sure that every open access interface has a password associated with it. Make sure that each of the passwords you want to use, including the console, the virtual terminal (vty), auxiliary, and enable secret passwords, are properly set and active.

Access List Verification

If you have included access lists as a part of your router's configuration, you absolutely must test them, test them, and test them again. If you have forgotten that an implicit deny is automatically placed at the end of any permit list, your testing should identify this for you when the one entry you forgot to include gains access.

Your testing should also address the fact that the access lists are processed in sequence, and that after a condition is met, the appropriate action is taken, and all other conditions are ignored.

The Configuration Archive

If you do not have a backup copy of the current configuration, you must make one before anyone notices and way before you begin making changes. Never assume that you won't make mistakes.

After you have made all your changes, make another copy (not over the other one, please) to capture the new configuration. Name the files appropriately, use good media (such as Zip disks or CD-ROMs), and store them in a safe and secure place. Remember that TFTP (Trivial File Transfer Protocol) is a good tool for this purpose.

Perhaps the biggest single reason for these backups is that days or weeks may pass before the big error in the configuration shows up, and you may want to restore to the last working configuration quickly and easily.

Don't forget to save your configuration changes to the router as well. If you change the running configuration files and then fail to copy it to the NVRAM, your efforts will be all for naught if the router ever needs or happens to restart

Appendix

Cisco IOS Commands

• •

*H*ere are many of the IOS commands found in Cisco IOS release 12.*x* or later that you may encounter working on a Cisco network.

This Command . . .	Does This
access-list access-list-number {permit | deny} address mask	Establishes MAC address access lists
access-list access-list-number {permit | deny} type-code wild-mask	Builds type-code access lists
no access-list access-list-number	Removes a single access list entry
bandwidth	Sets a bandwidth value for an interface
channel-group channel-number	Assigns a Fast Ethernet interface to a Fast EtherChannel group
clear counters [type number]	Clears the interface counters
clear interface type number	Resets the hardware logic on an interface
clear rif-cache	Clears entries from the Routing Information Field (RIF) cache
clock rate bps	Configures the clock rate for the hardware connections on serial interfaces
cmt connect [interface-name [phy-a | phy-b]]	Starts the processes that perform the CMT function
compress {predictor | stac}	Configures compression for LAPB, PPP, and HDLC encapsulations
copy flash lex number	Downloads an executable image from Flash memory on the core router to the LAN Extender chassis
crc size	Sets the length of the cyclic redundancy check (CRC)

(continued)

This Command . . .	Does This
dce-terminal-timing enable	Prevents phase shifting of the data with respect to the clock
description string	Adds a description to a T1 controller
down-when-looped	Informs the system that it is down when a loopback is detected
duplex {full | half | auto}	Configures the duplex operation on an interface
encapsulation encapsulation-type	Sets the encapsulation method used by the interface
framing {sf | esf}	Selects the frame type for a T1 data line
full-duplex	Specifies full-duplex mode on full-duplex single- and multi-mode port adapters
half-duplex	Specifies half-duplex mode on an interface
hold-queue length {in | out}	Specifies the hold-queue limit of an interface
interface type number	Configures an interface type and enters interface configuration mode
interface dialer interface-number	Designates a dialer rotary group leader
invert txclock	Inverts the transmit clock signal
keepalive [seconds]	Sets the keepalive timer for a specific interface
linecode {ami | b8zs | hdb3}	Selects the line code type for a T1 line
loopback	Diagnoses equipment malfunctions between interface and device
media-type {aui | 10baset | 100baset | mii}	Specifies the physical connection on an interface
mop enabled	Enables an interface to support the Maintenance Operation Protocol (MOP)
mtu bytes	Adjusts the maximum packet size or maximum transmission unit (MTU) size
physical-layer {sync | async}	Specifies the mode of a slow-speed serial interface on a router

This Command . . .	Does This
port	Enables an interface to operate as a concentrator port
show bridge group	Displays all bridge groups in the system
show controllers serial [slot/port]	Displays information specific to serial interfaces
show interfaces [type number] [first] [last] [accounting]	Displays statistics for all interfaces configured on the router
show interfaces ethernet	Displays information about an Ethernet interface
show interfaces ip-brief	Displays a brief summary of an IP interface's information and status
show interfaces serial	Displays information about a serial interface
show ip interface [brief] [type] [number]	Lists a summary of an interface's IP information and status
show rif	Displays the current contents of the RIF cache
shutdown	Disables an interface
speed {10 | 100 | auto}	Configures the speed for a Fast Ethernet interface
squelch {normal | reduced}	Extends the distance limit on a 10BaseT beyond the standard 100 meters

Index

• X •